COMPARATIVE REASONING IN INTERNATIONAL COURTS AND TRIBUNALS

Domestic law has long been recognised as a source of international law, an inspiration for legal developments, or the benchmark against which a legal system is to be assessed. Academic commentary normally re-traces these well-trodden paths, leaving one with the impression that the interaction between domestic and international law is unworthy of further enquiry. However, a different – and surprisingly pervasive – nexus between the two spheres has been largely overlooked: the use of domestic law in the interpretation of international law.

This book examines the practice of five international courts and tribunals to demonstrate that domestic law is invoked to interpret international law, often outside the framework of Articles 31 to 33 of the Vienna Convention on the Law of Treaties. It assesses the appropriateness of such recourse to domestic law as well as situating the practice within broader debates regarding interpretation and the interaction between domestic and international legal systems.

DANIEL PEAT is Assistant Professor of Public International Law at the Grotius Centre for International Legal Studies at Leiden University. Before joining Leiden University, he worked at the International Court of Justice as an Associate Legal Officer for President Abdulqawi A. Yusuf. Daniel was awarded a PhD in Law from the University of Cambridge, where he was a member of Gonville & Caius College and a recipient of the WM Tapp Studentship. He is a graduate of The Graduate Institute, Geneva, and the London School of Economics, where he was awarded the Lauterpacht/Higgins Prize for Public International Law. Daniel co-edited *Interpretation in International Law*, published by Oxford University Press in 2015, and acts as Rapporteur for the International Law Association Study Group on the Content and Evolution of the Rules of Interpretation.

T0381596

CAMBRIDGE STUDIES IN INTERNATIONAL AND COMPARATIVE LAW: 145

Established in 1946, this series produces high quality, reflective and innovative scholarship in the field of public international law. It publishes works on international law that are of a theoretical, historical, cross-disciplinary or doctrinal nature.

The series also welcomes books providing insights from private international law, comparative law and transnational studies which inform international legal thought and practice more generally. The series seeks to publish views from diverse legal traditions and perspectives, and of any geographical origin. In this respect it invites studies offering regional perspectives on core *problématiques* of international law, and in the same vein, it appreciates contrasts and debates between diverging approaches. Accordingly, books offering new or less orthodox perspectives are very much welcome. Works of a generalist character are greatly valued and the series is also open to studies on specific areas, institutions or problems. Translations of the most outstanding works published in other languages are also considered.

After seventy years, Cambridge Studies in International and Comparative Law sets the standard for international legal scholarship and will continue to define the discipline as it evolves in the years to come.

Series Editors
Larissa van den Herik
Professor of Public International Law, Grotius Centre for International Legal Studies, Leiden University
Jean d'Aspremont
Professor of International Law, University of Manchester and Sciences Po Law School

A list of books in the series can be found at the end of this volume.

COMPARATIVE REASONING IN INTERNATIONAL COURTS AND TRIBUNALS

DANIEL PEAT

Leiden University

CAMBRIDGE
UNIVERSITY PRESS

University Printing House, Cambridge CB2 8BS, United Kingdom

One Liberty Plaza, 20th Floor, New York, NY 10006, USA

477 Williamstown Road, Port Melbourne, VIC 3207, Australia

314-321, 3rd Floor, Plot 3, Splendor Forum, Jasola District Centre, New Delhi - 110025, India

79 Anson Road, #06-04/06, Singapore 079906

Cambridge University Press is part of the University of Cambridge.

It furthers the University's mission by disseminating knowledge in the pursuit of education, learning and research at the highest international levels of excellence.

www.cambridge.org
Information on this title: www.cambridge.org/9781108401470
DOI: 10.1017/9781108233828

First published 2019
First paperback edition 2020

A catalogue record for this publication is available from the British Library

Library of Congress Cataloging in Publication data
Names: Peat, Daniel, author.
Title: Comparative reasoning in international courts and tribunals / Daniel Peat, Leiden University.
Description: New York : Cambridge University Press, 2019. | Includes bibliographical references and index.
Identifiers: LCCN 2018060750 | ISBN 9781108415477 (alk. paper)
Subjects: LCSH: International courts – Rules and practice. | International and municipal law. | Comparative law.
Classification: LCC KZ6269 .P43 2019 | DDC 341.5/5–dc23
LC record available at https://lccn.loc.gov/2018060750

ISBN 978-1-108-41547-7 Hardback
ISBN 978-1-108-40147-0 Paperback

CONTENTS

FOREWORD

Daniel Peat's important book throws new light on the practice and theory of treaty interpretation. Although there has long been sustained attention to various aspects of the relationship between international and domestic law on the one hand, and to the rules of treaty interpretation on the other hand, the intersection of both questions, which is the subject of the book, has – surprisingly – not been seriously addressed. The book identifies this serious gap in scholarship and offers a novel and sophisticated approach to fill that gap. The book's contribution to legal scholarship is significant not only for its treatment of this specific question but also for the more general insights it offers to the theory of treaty interpretation and to the theory on the relationships between international and domestic law.

The book's first original and convincing contribution is in addressing the interpretation of international texts. Peat rejects the view that regards the rules on treaty interpretation grounded in the Vienna Convention on the Law of Treaties as the only possible rules. He examines the drafting history of the Vienna Convention, as well as the codification efforts that preceded it, to demonstrate that those rules were never intended to have what he terms an 'evaluative dimension'. This understanding provides the basis for the subsequent analysis of the interpretative practice of international courts and tribunals, much of which falls outside the scope of the Vienna Convention provisions. The book's findings challenge conventional wisdom and question the centrality of Articles 31–33 of the Vienna Convention of the Law of Treaties as constraining treaty interpretation.

Second, and more broadly, the findings of the book introduce a new dimension to the debate about the complex interdependency between international law and domestic law that has captured the attention of many scholars over generations. It does so by elucidating a relationship between domestic and international law that has until now passed relatively unnoticed and is undertheorised. In fact, the debate was grounded on the assumption that these two bodies of law were neatly separated into two layers, inviting scholars to argue which layer was hierarchically superior to the other. The book's findings question this assumption by showing that international rules of interpretation are not insulated from domestic law influences. These findings demonstrate the sterility of the ancient debate about monism vs. dualism, and invite us to reflect upon the appropriateness of referrals by international tribunals to domestic law in interpreting legal texts and about the extent to which domestic courts may, in turn, do the same when they interpret international law.

Eyal Benvenisti
Cambridge, November 2018

PREFACE

This is not the book I intended to write. The book grew out of a doctoral thesis at the University of Cambridge, which I completed in 2016. Initially, that project aimed to look at the role general principles of law might play in the regulation of transboundary damage and, in particular, whether a general principle of strict or absolute liability could be said to exist for extremely hazardous activities. The first stage of the project entailed conducting research into the nature of general principles as a source of law. It soon became clear to me that the very concept of general principles was unsettled: to some, such principles were inherent in the operation of all legal systems; to others, they were to be induced from domestic legal systems. As was pointed out to me during my preliminary defence, this was scarcely the basis on which I could build a convincing normative argument.

Whilst conducting this research, however, I started to find something that looked strange: courts and tribunals often drew on domestic law not as a means to substantiate or evidence a general principle of law but rather as an interpretative tool, frequently without explaining how or why that domestic law was relevant. As I examined this phenomenon more closely, I realised that the practice challenged some widely held preconceptions: namely, the centrality of the Vienna Convention to the interpretation of international law and the relatively strict division between domestic and international legal systems.[1] This sat uneasily with the canonical approach that marked most of my legal education and merited, in my opinion, further study.

But this book has also been marked by another chapter in my life. Three years spent working at the International Court of Justice taught me some valuable lessons. Amongst the most important of those was the realisation that international law is not always neat; it cannot always be rationalised in the manner that academics are trained to do. The use of

---

[1] For non-Kelsenians, at least.

domestic law is, I think, one of those instances. It would be nice to justify tribunals' comparative reasoning within the framework, for example, of a novel theory of interpretation or an evolution of the doctrine of sources. But to do so would be to neglect the nuances in interpretative practice, and the enormously different legal, historical and political contexts in which the courts and tribunals operate. Sometimes it is better just to lay out a hitherto unrecognised practice and tackle the issues – both broad and narrow – it raises. That is what this book tries to do.

Of the myriad people and institutions that have assisted me during the process of this research, a few deserve special mention. First and foremost, I would not be in the position in which I now find myself without the support of my parents, Yvonne and Gerald Peat. Gonville & Caius College generously provided me with a WM Tapp studentship for the duration of my doctoral research, without which this book would not have been possible. My doctoral supervisor, Michael Waibel, provided constant support and advice throughout this process, which I appreciate immensely. Andrea Bianchi and Matthew Windsor have been exemplary friends and collaborators over the course of our *Interpretation in International Law* project, and my thinking has developed greatly as a result of our work together. I have also benefitted immensely from my interaction with colleagues during the work of the International Law Association Study Group on the Content and Evolution of the Rules of Interpretation, and especially with Panos Merkouris, Fay Pazartzis and Geir Ulfstein. Thanks are also due to the many friends and colleagues that have commented on parts of this book, including Julian Arato, Andrea Bianchi, Eirik Bjorge, Daniel Costelloe, Richard Gardiner, Asier Garrido-Muñoz, Nina Grange, Cristina Hoss, Valentin Jeutner, Jessica Joly Hébert, Amelia Keene, Massimo Lando, Odette Murray, Giulia Pinzauti, Joe Sampson, Stephan Schill, Andreas Televantos, Ingo Venzke and Matthew Windsor.

Some elements of Chapters 5 and 7 have been published in revised form in the *Journal of International Dispute Settlement* and the *Canadian Journal of Comparative and Contemporary Law*. I thank the Editors-in-Chief of those journals for granting permission to use that work.

TABLE OF CASES

International Jurisdictions

i. Arbitral Awards

ii.   European Court of Human Rights

iii.   European Union

iv. Permanent Court of International Justice and International Court of Justice

v.   ICTY, ICTR, ICC and SCSL

vi.   WTO

Domestic Jurisdictions

i. Germany

ii. United Kingdom

iii.   United States

TABLE OF TREATIES

ABBREVIATIONS

AB	Appellate Body of the World Trade Organization
AJIL	*American Journal of International Law*
BYIL	*British Yearbook of International Law*
CJICL	*Cambridge Journal of International and Comparative Law*
CLJ	*Cambridge Law Journal*
CoE	Council of Europe
DSM	Dispute Settlement Mechanism
DSU	Dispute Settlement Understanding
ECHR	European Convention on Human Rights (Convention for the Protection of Human Rights and Fundamental Freedoms)
ECtHR	European Court of Human Rights
EJIL	*European Journal of International Law*
GATT	General Agreement on Tariffs and Trade 1994
HRLR	*Human Rights Law Review*
ICC	International Criminal Court
ICJ	International Court of Justice
ICL	International Criminal Law
ICLQ	*International & Comparative Law Quarterly*
ICSID	International Centre for the Settlement of Investment Disputes
ICTR	International Criminal Tribunal for Rwanda
ICTY	International Criminal Tribunal for the former Yugoslavia
IHL	International Humanitarian Law
ILC	International Law Commission
IMT	International Military Tribunal at Nuremberg
IMTFE	International Military Tribunal for the Far East
JICJ	*Journal of International Criminal Justice*
JIDS	*Journal of International Dispute Settlement*
JIEL	*Journal of International Economic Law*
JWIT	*Journal of World Investment & Trade*
LJIL	*Leiden Journal of International Law*
LNTS	League of Nations Treaty Series
NYU JILP	*New York University Journal of International Law and Politics*
OJLS	*Oxford Journal of Legal Studies*

PCIJ	Permanent Court of International Justice
Recueil des cours	Collected Courses of the Hague Academy of International Law
RGDIP	*Revue Générale de Droit International Public*
RIAA	Reports of International Arbitral Awards
RPE	Rules of procedure and evidence
SCSL	Special Court for Sierra Leone
UKSC	Supreme Court of the United Kingdom
UN	United Nations
UNTS	United Nations Treaty Series
VCLT	Vienna Convention on the Law of Treaties 1969
VJIL	*Virginia Journal of International Law*
WTO	World Trade Organization
YBILC	*Yearbook of the International Law Commission*
ZaöRV	*Zeitschrift für ausländisches öffentliches Recht und Völkerrecht*

1

Introduction

The interaction between domestic law and international law is a topic of perennial interest for international lawyers.[1] Domestic law has long been recognised as a source of international law,[2] an inspiration for legal developments[3] or the benchmark against which a legal system is to be

---

[1] In this book, the term 'domestic law' is preferred to 'municipal law' or 'national law'. Municipal law is sometimes used in a narrow sense of the term to refer to law emanating from a local municipality, thus excluding legislation passed by a central legislature. National law, on the other hand, refers only to laws passed by the central legislature, to the exclusion of regulations enacted by the executive or laws passed by regional or municipal authorities. As this study examines principally the use of domestic legislation passed by the central legislature but also touches upon regulations passed by the executive, it will refer to 'domestic law' in the broad sense of the term. See ILC, Draft Articles on Responsibility of States for Internationally Wrongful Acts, with commentaries, (2001) II [2] YBILC 31, 38, para 9; J. Ketcheson, *The Application of Domestic Law by International Tribunals* (PhD University of Cambridge 2013) n 1.

[2] See for example, ILC, Second Report on the Identification of Customary International Law, by Michael Wood, Special Rapporteur, UN Doc. A/CN.4/672, para 34; 2 BvR 1506/03 (German Federal Constitutional Court), para 51; R. Jennings & A. Watts, *Oppenheim's International Law*, vol 1 (9th edn, OUP 2008), § 12; *Procès-Verbaux of the Proceedings of the Committee of Jurists, June 16th–July 24th 1920 with Annexes*, 306, 335. Similarly, 'umbrella clauses' in bilateral investment treaties enable obligations entered into under domestic law between the investor and host state to be enforced before an international investment tribunal; see for example, Article 2(2) of the Agreement between the Government of the United Kingdom of Great Britain and Northern Ireland and the Republic of Argentina for the Promotion and Protection of Investments, signed 11 December 1990, entered into force 19 February 1993.

[3] See for example, ILC, 'Identification of Customary International Law: Text of the draft conclusions', Report of the ILC on the work of its seventieth session, 30 April–1 June and 2 July–10 August 2018, UN Doc. A/73/10, conclusion 5 and conclusion 6 (2); H. Thirlway, *The Sources of International Law* (OUP 2014) 95; P. M. Moremen, 'National Courts Decisions as State Practice: A Transjudicial Dialogue?', (2006) 32 North Carolina JIL 259; W. Friedmann, 'The Use of 'General Principles' in the Development of International Law', (1963) 57 AJIL 279.

assessed.[4] Often, it is simply treated as mere fact, indicative of the legality of a state's actions.[5] Academic commentary normally re-traces these well-trodden paths, leaving one with the impression that the interaction between domestic and international law has been thoroughly mapped, and is unworthy of further enquiry. However, a different – and surprisingly pervasive – nexus between the two spheres has been largely overlooked: the use of domestic law in the interpretation of international law. The present book aims to fill that gap in the literature.

When Hersch Lauterpacht wrote his seminal thesis, *Private Law Analogies in International Law*,[6] in 1926, international law was still a system in which states were the only actors and in which uncodified rules of custom and general principles of law played a pivotal role. Even at that time, positivist doctrine failed to grasp the pervasive influence of domestic law on international rules and principles. In the words of Lauterpacht,

> States and tribunals have recourse to analogy [with domestic law] because international relations give rise to such analogies, and because international law is not developed enough to supply a solution in such cases. But the science of international law gives here no guidance to judges and arbitrators, because it rejects, under the influence of positivist theory, any analogy whatsoever.[7]

Since that time, however, international law has profoundly changed. The international legal system has expanded both horizontally and vertically. The concept of the subjects of international law has broadened to include not only over 100 new states but also international organisations, whilst the scope of international law has expanded to cover matters that were previously considered to be solely in the domestic domain, such as the protection of human health, environmental protection and criminal law. As a result, individuals, corporate entities and non-governmental organisations all unavoidably interact with international law on a daily

---

[4] H. L. A. Hart, *The Concept of Law* (3rd edn, OUP 2012) Chapter X; G. Van Harten, *Investment Treaty Arbitration and Public Law* (CUP 2008).

[5] See for example, *Case Concerning Certain German Interests in Polish Upper Silesia (Merits)*, 1926 PCIJ Series A, No. 7, 19. ('From the standpoint of International Law and of the Court which is its organ, municipal laws are merely facts which express the will and constitute the activities of States, in the same manner as do legal decisions or administrative measures.')

[6] H. Lauterpacht, *Private Law Analogies in International Law with Special Reference to International Arbitration* (LLD London School of Economics 1926). This was subsequently published as H. Lauterpacht, *Private Law Sources and Analogies of International Law (With Special Reference to International Arbitration)* (Longmans, Green & Co. 1927).

[7] Lauterpacht, *Private Law Analogies*, iii.

basis.[8] Put simply, contemporary life is indelibly shaped by international rules.

As a result of these changes, the interactions between domestic law and international law occur more frequently and in more contexts than ever before.[9] It is perhaps unsurprising therefore that the line between domestic and international law is increasingly blurred, with legal concepts, rules and principles crossing freely between the two spheres.[10] However, just as when Lauterpacht wrote *Private Law Analogies*, the mainstream literature fails to appreciate fully the ubiquitous influence of domestic law on international law.

1.1 Conceptual Framework

1.1.1 Traditional and Contemporary Accounts of the Interaction between Domestic and International Law

Mainstream scholarship has often focussed on the more traditional relations between the domestic and international systems,[11] such as whether domestic systems adopt a 'monist' or 'dualist' approach in relation to the incorporation of international law.[12] This approach has

---

[8] See A. Cassese, *International Law* (2nd edn, OUP 2005) Chapter 7; K. Parlett, *The Individual in the International Legal System* (CUP 2011).

[9] See the Foreword by Lord Bingham in S. Fatima, *Using International Law in Domestic Courts* (Hart 2005) xii. ('To an extent almost unimaginable even thirty years ago, national courts in this and other countries are called upon to consider and resolve issues turning on the correct understanding of international law, not on an occasional basis, now and then, but routinely, and often in cases of great importance.')

[10] For a sceptical viewpoint, see M. Shahabuddeen, 'Municipal Law Reasoning in International Law', in V. Lowe & M. Fitzmaurice (eds), *Fifty Years of the International Court of Justice: Essays in Honour of Sir Robert Jennings* (CUP 1996).

[11] This book proceeds on the basis that domestic and international legal systems are, in fact, distinct systems of law. This is the most common characterisation of the two legal systems but one that has been criticised, most notably by Hans Kelsen, who considered international and domestic law to form one system; see H. Kelsen, *Pure Theory of Law* (2nd edn, University of California Press 1967) 328–44.

[12] See for example, D. T. Björgvinsson, *The Intersection of International Law and Domestic Law: A Theoretical and Practical Analysis* (Edward Elgar 2015) 16 ('most authors start their exposition of issues relating to the relationship between international law and national law by referring to those theories'). Cf J. Crawford, *Brownlie's Principles of Public International Law* (8th edn, OUP 2012) 48–9 (recognising that the 'relationship between international and national law is often presented as a clash at a level of high theory, usually between "dualism" and "monism"', but that 'neither offers an adequate account of the *practice* of international and national courts'); B. Conforti, 'Cours général de droit international public' (1988) 212 Recueil des cours 9, 31 (stating that 'nous

long been recognised, however, as an unhelpful and outdated way of characterising the interaction between international and domestic legal systems,[13] and many authors now acknowledge that 'the orthodox international and public law theories about how international and domestic law interact do not recognise the complexity, and sometimes contradictory nature, of the international/national legal interface'.[14] In particular, the vast majority of contemporary scholarship recognises that international law is not just passively received by the domestic legal system as an immutable set of rules.[15] Instead, there is a symbiotic relationship in which domestic legal systems play not only a role in the identification of international rules,[16] but also a more direct role in shaping, enforcing and ensuring the coherence of international law.[17]

Understanding how the domestic and international legal spheres interact in practice is crucial because it often diverges from formal, positivist notions of the relations between the two systems. Within the traditional sources doctrine of international law (as reflected in Article 38 of the Statute of the International Court of Justice), domestic law or the judgments of national courts may constitute state

---

sommes peu intéressé par la manière classique dont ce sujet est habituellement abordé, et qui consiste à reprendre les disputes séculaires entre les monistes et les dualistes').

[13] G. Fitzmaurice, 'The General Principles of International Law Considered from the Standpoint of the Rule of Law', (1957) 92 Recueil des cours 1, 71 (stating that 'the entire monist–dualist controversy is unreal, artificial and strictly beside the point').

[14] H. Charlesworth et al., 'International Law and National Law: Fluid States', in H. Charlesworth et al. (eds), *The Fluid State: International Law and National Legal Systems* (The Federation Press 2005) 2.

[15] See K. Knop, 'Here and There: International Law in Domestic Courts', (2000) 32 NYU JILP 501, 505–6.

[16] See for example, H. Thirlway, *The Sources of International Law* (OUP 2014) 124; A. Roberts, 'Comparative International Law? The Role of National Courts in Creating and Enforcing International Law', (2011) 60 ICLQ 57, 61–3.

[17] See for example, H. Schermers, 'The Role of Domestic Courts in Effectuating International Law', (1990) 3 LJIL 77; A. Nollkaemper, 'Decisions of National Courts as Sources of International Law: An Analysis of the Practice of the ICTY', in G. Boas & W. Schabas (eds), *International Criminal Law Developments in the Case Law of the ICTY* (Martinus Nijhoff 2003); A. Nollkaemper, 'The Role of Domestic Courts in the Case Law of the International Court of Justice', (2006) 5 Chinese JIL 301; A. Nollkaemper, *National Courts and the International Rule of Law* (OUP 2011); Roberts, 'Comparative International Law?'; A. Nollkaemper & O. K. Fauchald (eds), *The Practice of International and National Courts and the (De-)Fragmentation of International Law* (Hart 2012); A. Nollkaemper, 'Conversations Amongst Courts: Domestic and International Adjudicators', in C. P. R. Romano et al. (eds), *The Oxford Handbook of International Adjudication* (OUP 2013). Also in this context see *Oxford Reports on International Law in Domestic Courts*, available at http://opil.ouplaw.com/page/ILDC/oxford-reports-on-international-law-in-domestic-courts.

practice capable of establishing a rule of customary international law, evidence the existence of a general principle of law or act as a subsidiary means of determining the content of international law within the meaning of Article 38(1)(d) of the Statute.[18] The influence of domestic systems on international law, however, extends well beyond the role that it occupies in the traditional sources doctrine. Domestic court judgments, for example, are 'routinely cited as evidence of the meaning of international law, often without States or commentators critically analyzing whether they accurately reflect existing international law'.[19] As such, those judgments obtain an authority that cannot be explained in terms of custom or general principles of law, which far surpasses mere identification of the law.[20]

This insight is particularly important because the manner in which domestic systems interpret and apply international law cannot be understood as the mere transliteration of a rule from one sphere to another. Rather, it is a creative process in which rules and principles take on their own shape.[21] Recent scholarship on comparative international law builds on this by exploring how and why international law 'might take on different qualities as it is domesticated in particular States or regions'.[22] Linguistic, geopolitical, institutional and social factors all play a role in determining how international law is understood within domestic legal orders, creating diversity that challenges our conception of international law as universal.

---

[18] R. Higgins, *Problems and Process: International Law and How We Use It* (Clarendon Press 1994) 218; Thirlway, *Sources*, 124–6; Roberts, 'Comparative International Law', 61–2. As an example, see *Jones* v. *Saudi Arabia* [2006] UKHL 26, paras 59–63.

[19] Roberts, 'Comparative International law?', 63. See also, A. Nollkaemper, 'The Independence of the Domestic Judiciary in International Law', (2006) 17 Finnish YBIL 261, 272.

[20] Nollkaemper, 'The Independence of the Domestic Judiciary', 272–3.

[21] Knop, 'Here and There', 506; Roberts, 'Comparative International law?', 60–1 (stating that the uncritical use of domestic decisions to identify domestic law 'gives great discretion to those engaged in comparative analysis to upgrade foreign decisions they like (characterizing them as impartial law enforcement) and downgrade ones they dislike (dismissing them as partial State practice)').

[22] Roberts, 'Comparative International Law?', 79. See also, A. Roberts et al., 'Conceptualizing Comparative International Law', in A. Roberts et al. (eds), *Comparative International Law* (OUP 2018) 6 (defining comparative international law as follows: 'comparative international law entails identifying, analyzing, and explaining similarities and differences in how actors in different legal systems understand, interpret, apply, and approach international law'); A. Roberts, *Is International Law International?* (OUP 2017).

1.1.2   The Orthodox Approach to Domestic Law and the Interpretation of International Law

Within the field of interpretation, scholarship has often treated domestic law as being of relatively marginal importance. It is widely acknowledged that domestic law may be pertinent if it constitutes subsequent practice in the application of a treaty that is relevant under Article 31(3)(b) of the Vienna Convention on the Law of Treaties, or if it evidences the existence of a customary rule of international law or general principle of law that is a relevant rule of international law within the meaning of Article 31(3)(c) of the Vienna Convention.[23] Beyond these bounds, the study of the interaction between domestic and international spheres is normally limited to describing and evaluating how domestic courts interpret and apply treaties.[24] Such studies are crucial if we are to comprehend how international law is understood and applied 'on the ground'. But they approach the question from a largely unidirectional perspective; that is to say, they examine how domestic legal systems interpret and apply international law, and not how domestic law influences or shapes the interpretation of international rules and principles by international courts and tribunals.

Literature within certain sub-fields, notably European human rights law and the law of the European Union, has recognised that domestic law plays a more influential role with regards to interpretation of international law than might be suggested by the provisions of the Vienna Convention.[25] By focussing on the reasoning of specific courts, however,

---

[23] See R. Gardiner, *Treaty Interpretation* (2nd edn, OUP 2015) 257–9; ILC, 'Identification of Customary International Law: Text of the draft conclusions', Report of the ILC on the work of its seventieth session, 30 April–1 June and 2 July–10 August 2018, UN Doc. A/73/10, conclusion 5 and conclusion 6(2).

[24] See for example, C. McCrudden, 'CEDAW in National Courts: A Case Study in Operationalizing Comparative International Law Analysis in a Human Rights Context', in Roberts et al. (eds), *Comparative International Law*; H. P. Aust & G. Nolte (eds), *The Interpretation of International Law by Domestic Courts: Uniformity, Diversity, Convergence* (OUP 2016); E. Bjorge, *Domestic Application of the ECHR: Courts as Faithful Trustees* (OUP 2015); D. Sloss (ed), *The Role of Domestic Courts in Treaty Enforcement: A Comparative Study* (CUP 2010).

[25] See for example, P. Mahoney & R. Kondak, 'Common Ground: A Starting Point or Destination for Comparative-Law Analysis by the European Court of Human Rights', in M. Andenas & D. Fairgrieve (eds), *Courts and Comparative Law* (OUP 2015); P. Mahoney, 'The Comparative Method in Judgments of the European Court of Human Rights: Reference Back to National Law', in G. Canivet et al. (eds), *Comparative Law Before the Courts* (BIICL 2005); P. G. Carozza, 'Uses and Misuses of Comparative Law in International Human Rights: Some Reflections on the Jurisprudence of the European Court of Human Rights', (1998) 73 Notre Dame Law Review 1217;

the influence of these studies has been insulated from the mainstream general international law literature. The resulting lack of a cross-cutting analysis of comparative reasoning has obscured the pervasiveness of domestic law as an interpretative aid and stymied an explanation of its theoretical underpinnings. Outside of those relatively circumscribed confines, the role that domestic law plays in the interpretation of international law has not been fully examined.

This stands in stark contrast to the proliferation of literature examining the use of comparative law by domestic supreme courts. Spurred by a spate of highly contentious judgments handed down by the US Supreme Court in the early 2000s,[26] comparativists and constitutional lawyers have thoroughly examined the normative arguments for and against the use of comparative law by domestic courts, gathering empirical evidence to corroborate their claims.[27] This rich literature – most of

K. Dzehtsiarou, *European Consensus and the Legitimacy of the European Court of Human Rights* (CUP 2015); K. Lenaerts & K. Gutman, 'The Comparative Law Method and the Court of Justice of the European Union: Interlocking Legal Orders Revisited', in Andenas & Fairgrieve (eds), *Courts and Comparative Law*; K. Lenaerts, 'Interlocking Legal Orders or the European Union Variant of *E Pluribus Unum*' in Canivet et al. (eds), *Comparative Law Before the Courts*; M. Kiikeri, *Comparative Legal Reasoning and European Law* (Springer 2001); C. K. Kakouris, 'Use of the Comparative Method by the Court of Justice of the European Communities', (1994) Pace International Law Review 282; Y. Galmot, 'Réflexions sur le recours au droit comparé par la Cour de justice des Communautés européennes', (1990) 6 Revue française de droit administratif 255.

[26] *Graham* v. *Florida*, 560 US 48 (2010); *Roper* v. *Simmons*, 543 US 551 (2005); *Atkins* v. *Virginia*, 536 US 304 (2002); *Lawrence* v. *Texas*, 529 US 558 (2003).

[27] See for example, J. Bell, 'Researching Globalisation: Lessons from Judicial Citations' (2014) 3 CJICL 961; J. Bell, 'The Argumentative Status of Foreign Legal Arguments' (2012) 8 Utrecht LR 8; G. Sitaraman, 'The Use and Abuse of Foreign Law in Constitutional Interpretation' (2009) 32 Harvard Journal of Law and Public Policy 653; V. Jackson, 'Constitutional Comparisons: Convergence, Resistance, Engagement' (2005) 119 Harvard LR 109; J. Waldron, 'Foreign Law and the Modern *Ius Gentium*' (2005) 119 Harvard LR 129; E. A. Young, 'Foreign Law and the Denominator Problem' (2005) 119 Harvard LR 148; N. Dorsen, 'The Relevance of Foreign Legal Materials in US Constitutional Cases: A Conversation between Justice Antonin Scalia and Justice Stephen Breyer' (2005) 3 International Journal of Constitutional Law 519; S. Calabresi & S. Zimdahl, 'The Supreme Court and Foreign Sources of Law: Two Hundred Years of Practice and The Juvenile Death Penalty Decision' (2005) 47 William & Mary LR 743; M. D. Ramsey, 'International Materials and Domestic Rights' (2004) 98 AJIL 69; A. -M. Slaughter, 'A Global Community of Courts' (2003) 44 Harvard International Law Journal 191. For monograph-length treatments of the topic see for example, E. Mak, *Judicial Decision-Making in a Globalised World* (Hart 2013); M. Bobek, *Comparative Reasoning in European Supreme Courts* (OUP 2013); J. Waldron, '*Partly Laws Common to All Mankind*': Foreign Law in American Courts (Yale UP 2012); B. Markesinis & J. Fedtke, *Judicial Recourse to Foreign Law: A New Source of Inspiration?* (UCL Press 2006).

which dates from the past 15 years – has shone a fresh light on the use of extrinsic materials by courts, allowing commentators to delve into the theoretical questions that the use of foreign law raises. Why, for example, do courts give weight to sources extrinsic to their legal system? What – if anything – constrains a judge's discretion when interpreting a provision, and what provides the benchmark against which to assess the appropriateness of an interpretation? Underpinning these debates are disagreements about the very nature and purpose of interpretation itself.

1.1.3   The Concept of Comparative Reasoning and Scope of This Book

The purpose of this book is to build on the aforementioned bodies of literature by examining how and why domestic law is used by international courts and tribunals to interpret international law.[28] It analyses the practice of five international jurisdictions and explores the issues of methodology and principle raised by their use of domestic law, demonstrating that such law is often invoked outside the context of Articles 31 and 32 of the Vienna Convention and outside the remit of the traditional sources doctrine. In doing so, it shines new light on the interaction between the domestic and international spheres, whilst also showing that interpretation is a more complex and nuanced activity than is commonly supposed.

A few words on the scope of this study are required. 'Comparative reasoning', as reflected in the title of this book, is capable of being understood in a broad or a narrow sense. In the broad sense of the term, it refers to all interpretative material used by a decision-maker, including domestic legislation, judgments of domestic courts, judgments of international courts and tribunals and other international treaties.[29] For example, the International Criminal Tribunal for the former Yugoslavia has referred to the case law of the European Court of Human Rights in the context of examining when a defendant is unfit to stand trial,[30] investment tribunals have drawn on the reports of the

---

[28] In this book, international law refers to not just treaties, but also reservations to multilateral treaties, declarations made under Article 36(2) of the Statute of the ICJ ('Optional Clause declarations'), WTO schedules of commitments, and the Statute and Rules of Procedure and Evidence of the ICTY.

[29] For an example of the broad use of the term, see E. Bjorge, 'Comparative Law and the Method of Law: Ascertainment of the International of Justice', in Andenas & Fairgrieve (eds), *Courts and Comparative Law*.

[30] *Prosecutor* v. *Strugar* (Appeals Chamber Judgement) IT-01-42-A (17 July 2008), para 47.

Appellate Body of the World Trade Organization in order to elaborate what is required by 'necessity',[31] and the European Court of Human Rights has made numerous references to the case-law of the Inter-American Court of Human Rights.[32] The meaning of the term as it is used in this book, however, is narrower: it is used to refer solely to domestic legislation and regulations, and the judgments of domestic courts.

This book focusses on the use of domestic law for two reasons. First, unlike the use of other extraneous interpretative material (such as the case-law of other international courts and tribunals),[33] the use of domestic law has not been the subject of recent academic attention. This practice raises issues not just regarding the age-old question of if and when domestic law should act as a source of or inspiration for international law, but also more general issues regarding the proper role of the interpreter and the interpretative method. Second, as a practical matter, it would be very difficult to address thoroughly in a monograph all the issues raised by comparative reasoning, broadly understood. The choice has thus been made in this book to focus on the use of domestic law by international courts and tribunals.

The scope of the present study is limited to the practice of international adjudicative bodies. It is clear that the bulk of the day-to-day life of international law is constituted by the practice of non-judicial bodies, such as government legal advisors and lawyers in private practice. However, the accessibility of the interpretative practice of these actors is limited, with only a handful of states producing edited collections of materials that could be drawn on. The practice of many international courts and tribunals, on the other hand, is easily accessible as publicly available, electronic versions of judgments and in searchable databases. The focus on judicial practice is

---

[31] *Continental Casualty Company* v. *The Argentine Republic*, ICSID Case No. ARB/03/9, Award (5 September 2008), para 192. On the use of extraneous precedent by international investment tribunals more generally, see A. K. Bjorklund & S. Nappert, 'Beyond Fragmentation', in T. Weiler & F. Baetens (eds), *New Directions in International Economic Law: In Memoriam Thomas Wälde* (Brill 2011).

[32] See for example, *Sergey Zolotukhin* v. *Russia* (10 February 2009), App. No. 14939/03, para 40. See more generally, ECHR, *References to the Inter-American Court of Human Rights in the case-law of the European Court of Human Rights: Research Report* (Council of Europe 2012); G. Ulfstein, 'Interpretation of the ECHR in light of other international instruments', Pluricourts Research Paper No. 15–05.

[33] See in particular, H. G. Cohen, 'Theorizing Precedent in International Law', in A. Bianchi, D. Peat & M. Windsor (eds), *Interpretation in International Law* (OUP 2015); Bjorklund & Nappert, 'Beyond Fragmentation'.

hence a function of practical considerations rather than a reflection of the relative import of judicial institutions in international law.

The courts and tribunals that are the focus of this study – the International Court of Justice (ICJ), the panels and Appellate Body (AB) of the World Trade Organization (WTO), international investment tribunals, the European Court of Human Rights (ECtHR) and the International Criminal Tribunal for the former Yugoslavia (ICTY) – were selected in order to examine the use of domestic law over a wide range of subject-matter and within diverse legal regimes. Three differences between these jurisdictions are particularly noteworthy.

First, the book surveys the practice of courts and tribunals that adjudicate upon inter-state disputes (the ICJ and the panels and AB of the WTO), as well as those that decide cases brought by individuals against states (international investment tribunals and the ECtHR) and those pertaining to individual criminal responsibility (the ICTY). By examining this range of tribunals, we are able to see if differences in their practice with respect to the invocation of domestic law may be influenced by the structure of the dispute settlement body. Second, the courts and tribunals operated, and continue to operate, in different historical and legal contexts. For example, the ECtHR has delivered over 20,600 judgments since its inception,[34] and is able to draw on a large body of jurisprudence to guide its interpretation of the European Convention on Human Rights. In contrast, when the ICTY was created in May 1993, it was faced with a statute that contained 'not much more than the skeletons of crimes'[35] within its jurisdiction and scant international criminal precedent on which to draw.[36] As will be demonstrated, the context in which the court or tribunal operates is of crucial importance in understanding its recourse to domestic law. Third, the character of the applicable law before each court and tribunal is largely distinct, and these differences might lead one to think that domestic law would be more readily invoked in certain legal regimes as opposed to others. For example, domestic law might seem *prima facie* to be more relevant to the interpretation of an international crime as opposed to the interpretation of a multilateral trade treaty, as both domestic and international criminal law address individual criminal responsibility. By examining how domestic law is used over a range of

---

[34] European Court of Human Rights, *ECHR: Overview 1959–2017* (Council of Europe 2017) 3.

[35] G. Mettraux, *International Crimes and the ad hoc Tribunals* (OUP 2005) 5.

[36] See for example, *Prosecutor* v. *Dusko Tadić*, IT-94-1, Decision on the Prosecutor's Motion Requesting Protective Measures for Victims and Witnesses (10 August 1995), para 20.

jurisdictions, we are better able to understand whether comparative reasoning is dependent on the particular historical or legal context of a tribunal, or whether there are certain commonalities that exist between the tribunals' interpretative approaches.

Finally, the understanding of interpretation adopted in this book must be clarified. Interpretation is a term that is employed in a variety of ways to connote a range of different activities.[37] In particular, the dividing lines between law creation and interpretation, on the one hand, and the interpretation and application of the law, on the other hand, are especially unclear and prone to confusion. Moreover, the very process of ascertaining the law has been often understood as an interpretative process.[38]

Without broaching the extremely difficult task of attempting to define interpretation,[39] the focus of this book is best captured by what has been called 'interpretation for content-determination purposes', according to which 'a judge interprets the law which she is empowered to apply, with a view to determining ... the applicable standard of behaviour or the normative guideline for the case of which she is seized'.[40] The distinguishing feature of this definition of interpretation is that it does not involve an enquiry into the legal pedigree of the rule itself, which would normally require an examination of the doctrine of sources (even if such an examination is implicit).[41] The scope of the study is hence limited to instances in which the court or tribunal has not drawn on domestic law as a source of international law, but rather as a way of understanding the meaning of an extant legal instrument.[42]

---

[37] See P. Brunet, 'Aspects théoriques et philosophiques de l'interprétation normative', (2011) 115 RGDIP 311; R. Kolb, *Interprétation et création du droit international* (Bruylant 2007) 11. Cf L. Solum, 'The Unity of Interpretation', (2010) 90 Boston University LR 551, 560–1.

[38] See in particular, J. d'Aspremont, 'The Multidimensional Process of Interpretation: Content-Determination and Law-Ascertainment Distinguished', in Bianchi et al. (eds), *Interpretation in International Law*, 116–18; D. Hollis, 'The Existential Function of Interpretation in International Law', in Bianchi et al. (eds), *Interpretation in International Law*. For the *locus classicus* of this argument, see R. Dworkin, *Law's Empire* (Harvard UP 1986).

[39] Some possible definitions are explored in D. Peat & M. Windsor, 'Playing the Game of Interpretation: On Meaning and Metaphor in International Law', in Bianchi et al. (eds), *Interpretation in International Law*, 9–16.

[40] d'Aspremont, 'The Multidimensional Process of Interpretation', 117.

[41] ibid.

[42] The distinction between interpretation and application is even less clear, with the latter inevitably involving the former to some degree. The focus of the present study is the pronouncements of judicial or arbitral bodies, which take place in a particular context in which the court or tribunal is called upon to apply the law to a specific set of facts. As such,

1.2   The Structure of This Book

The main aim of this book is to demonstrate that domestic law has been used to interpret international law in a variety of different contexts by a range of tribunals, and to explore the issues of principle and methodology that this practice raises. As such, it does not attempt to provide an exhaustive and comprehensive overview of every instance in which domestic law has been invoked by the surveyed jurisdictions; rather, it selects certain illustrative examples which pose questions of particular interest from the perspective of international law.

The second chapter of this book sets the scene for the rest of the study by examining the genesis of Articles 31 and 32 of the Vienna Convention. It demonstrates that despite frequently professing to hold starkly divergent views, the main actors in the codification process leading to the Vienna Convention understood interpretation to be a highly context specific process, the result of which cannot be dictated *a priori* by legal rules. As such, Articles 31 and 32 do not possess – and were not intended to possess – what has been called an 'evaluative dimension'.[43] This justifies the structure and approach taken in the following chapters of this book, which do not rally practice under the rubric of Articles 31 and 32 of the Vienna Convention. Instead, each chapter places particular importance on the specific context in which the use of domestic law occurred, highlighting the significance of context for both the understanding and the evaluation of such interpretation.

Chapters 3 and 4 examine the practice of two inter-state tribunals – the ICJ and the panels and AB of the WTO. Chapter 3 examines cases in which the ICJ has drawn on domestic law to interpret international legal instruments that were unilaterally drafted by a state. The chapter assesses

---

no attempt will be made to distinguish the two processes as a general matter, the analytical utility of which would be questionable in the context of the present study. One exception, which is excluded from this study, is when an international rule contains a *renvoi* to domestic law, such as whether an alien has been expelled pursuant to a decision reached 'in accordance with the [domestic] law', or whether nationality has been properly conferred for the purposes of exercising diplomatic protection. This does not fall within the understanding of interpretation outlined above. For a summary of the main conceptions of the distinction between interpretation and application, see Gardiner, *Treaty Interpretation*, 28–30. See further, G. Hernández, 'Interpretative Authority and the International Judiciary', in Bianchi et al. (eds), *Interpretation in International Law* 175–81.

[43]   G. Postema, 'Positivism and the Separation of Realists from Their Scepticism' in P. Cane (ed), *The Hart–Fuller Debate in the Twenty-First Century* (Hart 2010) 271–2. See also, A. Marmor, *The Philosophy of Law* (Princeton UP 2011) fn 2.

whether the unilateral origins of those legal instruments may justify recourse to the domestic law of the drafting state, examines whether the interpretation of Optional Clause declarations and treaty reservations are analogous, and explores how interpretation of these instruments differs from the Court's approach to treaty interpretation.

Chapter 4 assesses the use of domestic law by the panels and AB of the WTO to interpret members' schedules of commitments. It considers whether the purportedly *sui generis* nature of schedules of commitments leads to the conclusion that greater emphasis should be placed on the intention of the state whose schedule is being interpreted, as potentially evidenced in its domestic law. The chapter also explores the circumstances in which it might be acceptable to presume knowledge of a member state's domestic law on the part of other states, and how the character of schedules of commitments differs from those instruments examined in the preceding chapter.

Chapters 5 and 6 examine the practice of jurisdictions that adjudicate claims brought by individuals against states. Chapter 5 assesses the argument that international investment tribunals should draw on comparative public law in order to interpret bilateral investment treaties, insofar as comparative public law may manifest a general principle of law. The practice of tribunals, however, demonstrates that domestic law has not been used as evidence of a general principle of law but rather has been invoked to interpret treaty standards, such as the obligation to accord fair and equitable treatment to investors, often being used as an auxiliary or subsidiary means of interpretation. The chapter explores why domestic law might be relevant to the interpretation of standards and addresses the attendant methodological considerations that arise.

Chapter 6 studies the use of domestic law by the ECtHR, a technique which is often referred to as the 'consensus doctrine'. It analyses the judgments rendered by the Grand Chamber of the Court over the 10-year period from 2005 to 2015, demonstrating that the majority of judgments in which the Court invoked comparative law related to the interpretation of a standard enshrined in the Convention, such as what is 'necessary in a democratic society'. Principled and methodological criticisms of the consensus doctrine are assessed in light of this survey and possible theoretical underpinnings of the doctrine explored.

Chapter 7 examines the use of domestic law by the ICTY. As the first international criminal tribunal to be established since the Nuremberg and Tokyo international military tribunals in the wake of the Second World War, the ICTY, faced with a laconic statute and scant precedent, drew on domestic law to interpret legal institutions imported from domestic systems and to interpret crimes in the absence of any other relevant interpretative material. This chapter demonstrates that the Tribunal's judgments had an indelible influence on the development of international criminal law, and contrasts the position of the ICTY to that of the present-day International Criminal Court. It explores whether concerns related to the principle of legality and the unique character of the international criminal law regime constitute valid criticisms of the Tribunal's invocation of domestic law.

The Limits of the Vienna Convention

2.1 The Evaluative Dimension of Rules

On 12 January 2016, 10 sailors from the United States Navy accidently navigated into the Iranian territorial sea under the mistaken impression they were in Saudi Arabian waters. Within hours, Iran's Islamic Revolutionary Guards had captured the vessels, seized 13,000 pages of intelligence from computers on board and detained the sailors.[1] Unsurprisingly, Iran's actions drew strong condemnation from US government officials. As in many warps of life, legal rules provided both the language and the standard against which the actions of Iran were assessed. Government and military officials did not criticise Iran's actions as being unfair or unjust; instead, their comments focussed on the *legality* of Iran's actions: some labelled it as an 'outrageous' act that was 'inconsistent with international law',[2] whilst others called it an act in 'apparent violation of international law and centuries of maritime custom and tradition'.[3]

---

[1] 'Iran just made another claim about the Navy sailors it detained. Add it to the list', *The Washington Post*, 15 March 2016, available at www.washingtonpost.com/news/check point/wp/2016/03/15/iran-just-made-another-claim-about-the-navy-sailors-it-detained-add-it-to-the-list/?utm_term=.6f702f348a80.

[2] 'Defence Secretary Carter: Iran's Treatment of Sailors "Inconsistent with International Law"', *The Tower*, 18 March 2016, available at www.thetower.org/3112-defense-secretary-carter-irans-treatment-of-sailors-inconsistent-with-international-law.

[3] Statement of Senator John McCain, Chairman of Senate Armed Services Committee, on Obama Administration's Response to Iran's Detainment of US Sailors, 13 January 2016, available at www.mccain.senate.gov/public/index.cfm/press-releases?ID=6c628211-5f08-4029-9a7e-51454e8cdcd3; see also, US Chief of Naval Operations Admiral John Richardson, 'Riverine Command Boat Investigation Press Remarks', available at www.navy.mil/

One aspect of law's normative character is that it provides standards by which those within the legal system 'evaluate their behaviour and that of others ... [as well as providing] the standards for condemning the actions of others and holding them publicly accountable'.[4] In this respect, it provides the benchmark of what is and what is not permissible in a certain society. Gerald Postema has called this the 'evaluative dimension' of law.[5] But the evaluative dimension of law entails certain presuppositions. It presupposes that we have determined which law is applicable to the case at hand, that we know what the relevant law means, and that we have qualified the particular acts at issue in a certain (legally relevant) way.[6] Criticisms of Iran's conduct in the Arabian Gulf, for example, were based on a certain understanding of the law of the sea, the immunity of state vessels and the circumstances that led to the US Navy ships being located in Iranian territorial waters. But, perhaps more importantly, the evaluative dimension of law presupposes that the legal rule at issue spells out clearly what actions are and are not permissible.

It might be thought that a study into the interpretative practice of courts and tribunals could be approached in a similar fashion, using rules of interpretation as the framework within which to evaluate whether a certain interpretative approach (such as the use of domestic law) is permissible or not. Such rules, termed 'disciplining rules' by Owen Fiss, 'constrain the interpreter, thus transforming the interpretive process from a subjective one into an objective one, and they furnish the standards by which the correctness of the interpretation can be judged'.[7]

In international law, there is certainly a plausible claim that we have such disciplining rules. The application of the rules of interpretation, contained in Articles 31 to 33 of the Vienna Convention on the Law of

---

navydata/people/cno/Richardson/Speech/RiverineCommandBoat_Investigation_
PressConference_CNORemarks.pdf.

[4] G. Postema, 'Conformity, Custom and Congruence: Rethinking the Efficacy of Law' in M. Kramer (ed), *The Legacy of H. L. A. Hart: Legal, Political, and Moral Philosophy* (OUP 2008) 55.

[5] G. Postema, 'Positivism and the Separation of Realists from Their Scepticism' in P. Cane (ed), *The Hart–Fuller Debate in the Twenty-First Century* (Hart 2010) 271–2. See also, A. Marmor, *The Philosophy of Law* (Princeton UP 2011) fn 2.

[6] A. Tutt, 'Interpretation Step Zero: A Limit on Methodology as "Law"', (2013) 122 Yale LJ 2055 (noting the methodological 'step zero' that requires the interpreter to decide whether a prescribed interpretative methodology governs in any given case; a decision that cannot be made in reference to the statute itself).

[7] O. Fiss, 'Objectivity and Interpretation', (1982) 34 Stanford LR 739, 745.

Treaties (VCLT),[8] by international courts and tribunals has been described as 'virtually axiomatic'.[9] This ubiquity has led one author to claim that the VCLT provisions 'are fixed rules [that] do not permit the

---

[8] Articles 31–32 VCLT provide that:

Article 31
General rule of interpretation

1. A treaty shall be interpreted in good faith in accordance with the ordinary meaning to be given to the terms of the treaty in their context and in the light of its object and purpose.
2. The context for the purpose of the interpretation of a treaty shall comprise, in addition to the text, including its preamble and annexes:
   (a) any agreement relating to the treaty which was made between all the parties in connexion with the conclusion of the treaty; (b) any instrument which was made by one or more parties in connexion with the conclusion of the treaty and accepted by the other parties as an instrument related to the treaty.
3. There shall be taken into account, together with the context:
   (a) any subsequent agreement between the parties regarding the interpretation of the treaty or the application of its provisions; (b) any subsequent practice in the application of the treaty which establishes the agreement of the parties regarding its interpretation; (c) any relevant rules of international law applicable in the relations between the parties.
4. A special meaning shall be given to a term if it is established that the parties so intended.

Article 32
Supplementary means of interpretation

Recourse may be had to supplementary means of interpretation, including the preparatory work of the treaty and the circumstances of its conclusion, in order to confirm the meaning resulting from the application of article 31, or to determine the meaning when the interpretation according to article 31:

(a) leaves the meaning ambiguous or obscure; or (b) leads to a result which is manifestly absurd or unreasonable.

Article 33 VCLT deals with the interpretation of plurilingual treaties, and will not be addressed in this chapter.

[9] R. Gardiner, *Treaty Interpretation* (2nd edn, OUP 2015) 16. For recognition that Articles 31 to 33 of the VCLT reflect customary international law, see for example, *Avena and Mexican Nationals (Mexico* v. *USA)* (2004) ICJ Rep 37–8, para 83; WTO Appellate Body Report, *Japan – Taxes on Alcoholic Beverages* WT/DS/8, 10 and 11/AB/R (4 October 1996) 10; ECtHR, *Golder* v. *UK*, 21 February 1975, App. No. 4451/70, para 32; *Arbitration Regarding the Iron Rhine ('IJzeren Rijn') Railway (Belgium/The Netherlands)*, Award of 24 May 2005, XXVII RIAA 35, para 45.

interpreter a free choice amongst interpretative methods',[10] whilst another has argued that the rules lay down 'a description of the way an applier shall ... determine the correct meaning of a treaty provision'.[11]

At first glance, such assertions seem plausible. However, upon further inspection, they are vulnerable to criticism on both theoretical and historical grounds. In relation to the former, some authors have highlighted the theoretical problems encountered when an attempt is made to constrain the act of interpretation by rules, which must themselves be the subject of interpretation.[12] This chapter, however, elaborates the historical critique in order to demonstrate that the VCLT provisions were never intended to lead the interpreter inexorably to the 'correct' interpretation. In this respect, the VCLT articles were not intended to possess an 'evaluative dimension'.

The records of the debates on treaty interpretation that took place within the *Institut de Droit international*, the International Law Commission (ILC) and at the Vienna Conference on the Law of Treaties show that the international lawyers involved in the codification of the rules of interpretation did not have a preconceived notion of what constituted a 'good' interpretation. Instead, despite their differences, they agreed that interpretation was highly context-specific, resulting in a 'recursive and inelegant process that would spiral in toward the meaning of a treaty, rather than as a rigidly linear algorithm tied to a particular hierarchical sequence'.[13] As a result of this surprisingly consistent

---

[10] A. Orakhelashvili, *The Interpretation of Acts and Rules in Public International Law* (OUP 2008) 309 ('the text of the Vienna Convention, the process of its drafting, and the practice of its application are all unanimous in affirming that the rules on treaty interpretation are fixed rules and do not permit the interpreter a free choice among interpretive methods').

[11] U. Linderfalk, *On the Interpretation of Treaties: The Modern International Law as Expressed in the 1969 Vienna Convention on the Law of Treaties* (Springer 2007) 29. Cf G. Hernández, 'Interpretation' in J. Kammerhofer & J. d'Aspremont (eds), *International Legal Positivism in a Post-Modern World* (CUP 2014) 317, 326.

[12] G. Letsas, 'Strasbourg's Interpretive Ethic: Lessons for the International Lawyer', (2010) 21 EJIL 509, 534; J. Klabbers, 'On Rationalism in Politics: Interpretation of Treaties and the World Trade Organization', (2005) 74 Nordic JIL 405, fn 43; J. Klabbers, 'International Legal Histories: The Declining Importance of the *Travaux Préparatoires* in Treaty Interpretation?', (2003) 50 NILR 267, 270; C. Djeffal, *Static and Evolutive Interpretation: A Functional Reconstruction* (CUP 2015) 67–70. In legal theory more generally, see S. Fish, 'Fish v. Fiss', (1984) 36 Stanford LR 1325; A. D'Amato, 'Can Legislatures Constrain Judicial Interpretation of Statutes?', (1989) 75 Virginia L Rev 561, 563; D. Patterson, 'Interpretation in Law', (2005) 42 San Diego LR 685, 690–1; F. E. Guerra-Pujol, 'Probabilistic Reasoning', (2016) 38 University of La Verne LR 102, 103 et seq. Cf R. Dworkin, *Law's Empire* (Hart 1998) 49–52.

[13] J. D. Mortenson, 'The *Travaux* of *Travaux*: Is the Vienna Convention Hostile to Drafting History?', (2013) 107 AJIL 780, 781. Cf *Aguas del Tunari, S.A. v. Republic of Bolivia*, Decision on Respondent's Objections to Jurisdiction, 21 October 2005, ICSID Case No. ARB/02/3,

approach, the Vienna Convention provisions accommodate a variety of textual, subjective and teleological factors, the relative importance of which is to be determined by the interpreter in light of the particular circumstances of the case at hand.[14] In this respect, there is a margin of discretion that is relatively unconstrained by legal norms.[15]

The purpose of this chapter is two-fold. In the first instance, it demonstrates that the VCLT provisions were intended to leave 'substantial

para 91. ('Interpretation under Article 31 of the Vienna Convention is a process of progressive encirclement where the interpreter starts under the general rule with (1) the ordinary meaning of the terms of the treaty, (2) in the context of the entire document as well as closely related documents and (3) in light of the treaty's object and purpose, and by cycling through this three-step enquiry, iteratively closes in upon the proper interpretation.')

[14] M. Koskenniemi, *From Apology to Utopia: The Structure of International Legal Argument* (Reissue with New Epilogue, CUP 2005) 334, n 89 ('Article 31 of the Vienna Convention is of the nature of a compromise: it refers to virtually all thinkable interpretative methods'). See also 870th Meeting of the ILC (1966) I (II) YBILC 186 (Waldock). Cf 769th Meeting of the ILC (1964) I YBILC 312 (Amado) ('interpretation should be left to the good sense of future judges'); H. Kraus, 'Réponse de H. Kraus', (1950) 43[I] Annuaire de l'Institut de Droit international 446. ('L'obtention de résultats justes dépendra du doigté juridique et de l'intuition. A mon avis, il y a là un domaine qui ne pourra être enserré que dans une mesure très limité dans des canones.')

Whether Articles 31–33 should be referred to as 'rules' is highly questionable – the term is used here because it is commonplace in the literature, although as Isabelle Van Damme notes, 'the qualification of Articles 31 to 33 VCLT as binding "rules" does not seem satisfactory for norms that govern interpretation . . . the "rules" of treaty interpretation may better be described as principles'; I. Van Damme, *Treaty Interpretation by the WTO Appellate Body* (OUP 2009) 35. See also J. Klabbers, 'Virtuous Interpretation', in M. Fitzmaurice et al., *Treaty Interpretation and the Vienna Convention on the Law of Treaties: 30 Years On* (Brill 2010) 29–30 (noting that it would be extremely unorthodox to construe a violation of the rules of interpretation as an internationally wrongful act); S. Rosenne, 'Conceptualism as a Guide to Interpretation', in S. Rosenne, *An International Law Miscellany* (Martinus Nijhoff 1993) 444 (noting that Article 31 'deliberately abandons . . . all attempt to set forth "rules" for interpretation').

[15] U. Linderfalk, 'Is Treaty Interpretation an Art or a Science', (2015) 26 [1] EJIL 169, 189. See also Gardiner, *Treaty Interpretation*, 28 ('the Vienna Rules . . . [combine] a clear indication of *what* should be taken into account with some rather less prescriptive pointers as to *how* to use the indicated material, and in the final analysis leaving a margin of appreciation for the interpreter to produce an outcome'); Z. Bankowski et al., 'On Method and Methodology', in R. S. Summers & D. N. MacCormick (eds), *Interpreting Statutes* (Dartmouth Publishing 1991), 21 (stating 'that standards of good interpretation could never be fully reduced to or reconstructed as some sort of posited or positive rules'); H. Lauterpacht, 'Restrictive Interpretation and the Principle of Effectiveness in the Interpretation of Treaties', (1949) 26 BYIL 48, 53–4 ('the selection of any particular rule, out of a number of competing and occasionally mutually inconsistent rules, is necessarily a matter of discretion'); Comments of M. de la Pradelle (1956) 46 Annuaire de l'Institut de Droit international 325. ('L'interprétation est un art que le juge doit exercer en prenant en considération la situation particulière du texte qui lui est soumis.')

leeway for idiosyncratic approaches to interpretation within the bounds staked out by the VCLT's broad interpretive principles'.[16] This point is not novel; however, like many topics related to the more theoretical aspects of interpretation, the implications of this flexibility for the study of interpretation have not been fully explored.[17] In the second instance, this chapter justifies the approach taken in the following chapters of this book, which do not rally practice under the rubric of Articles 31 and 32 of the Vienna Convention. Instead, each chapter places particular importance on the specific context in which the use of domestic law occurred, highlighting the significance of context for both the understanding and the evaluation of such interpretation. This chapter demonstrates that the drafters of the VCLT were acutely aware of the irreducibly context-specific nature of interpretation, even if they did not directly address many of the uses of domestic law examined in this book.

At the outset, it should be emphasised that this chapter does not argue that the VCLT articles play no role in interpretation. Rarely will one find an international court or tribunal that does not justify their interpretation by reference to Articles 31 and 32,[18] even if those articles are treated as nothing more than a '*clause de style*'.[19] It is questionable whether this

---

[16] M. Waibel, 'Demystifying the Art of Interpretation', (2011) 22 EJIL 571, 573. See also, P. Allott, 'Interpretation – An Exact Art', in A. Bianchi et al. (eds), *Interpretation in International Law* (OUP 2015) 377. ('A legal ship containing a bolted-together contradiction is not a seaworthy legal ship. Article 31 is accordingly worthless as a general *rule* of interpretation. It is a poem about interpretation.') See also D. Alland, 'L'Interprétation du droit international public', (2012) 362 RdC 41, 161 ('[l]oin de canaliser l'attribution de sens, la palette des méthodes manifeste son irréductible liberté').

[17] Cf J. Kammerhofer, 'Review of Alexander Orakhelashvili, *The Interpretation of Acts and Rules in Public International Law*', (2009) 20 EJIL 1282, 1283. Some might attribute this to the general aversion to theory that has been shown in the literature on interpretation, which treats interpretation as 'just another doctrinal topic'; see J. Kammerhofer, 'Taking the Rules of Interpretation Seriously, but Not Literally? A Theoretical Reconstruction of Orthodox Dogma', (2017) 86 Nordic JIL 125, 127. ('It seems that talking about (treaty) interpretation in international law begins and ends with an interpretation of the Vienna Convention's rules on interpretation. Theory seems not just superfluous, but it is positively unwelcome: interpretation is just another doctrinal topic.')

[18] See Djeffal, *Static and Evolutive Treaty Interpretation: A Functional Reconstruction* 140. Cf F. Zarbiyev, *Le discours interprétatif en droit international contemporain* (Bruylant 2015) 23 (criticising the literature for treating the VCLT rules as if they were the 'paramètres exclusifs de tout débat sérieux portant sur la thématique').

[19] M. H. Arsanjani & W. M. Reisman, 'Interpreting Treaties for the Benefit of Third Parties: The "Salvors' Doctrine" and the Use of Legislative History in Investment Treaties', (2010) 104 AJIL 597, 598. Although this is not always the case: see *Salini Construttori SpA v. Kingdom of Morocco*, ICSID Case No. ARB/00/4 (Decision on Jurisdiction), Award of 23 July 2001, paras 43–58.

in and of itself provides any benefits: whilst some authors have suggested that the ubiquity of the VCLT provisions may enhance legal discourse, there is little to substantiate their claims.[20] Nevertheless, it is notable that the VCLT articles hold an important place in how we speak about interpretation today.[21] Perhaps more importantly, although the provisions of the VCLT do not guide the interpreter to the 'correct' interpretation in any given case, they do set the outer limits of the interpretative enquiry by prescribing the materials that should be taken into account by the interpreter, where those materials are present. The text of the treaty, for example, cannot be ignored in a free-ranging search for the intentions of the parties, nor can one disregard any relevant subsequent practice of the parties in the application of the treaty. Within these broad limits, one might say that the VCLT articles provide the standard for criticism of a particular interpretation.[22] However, the claim advanced in this chapter is not that the provisions of the VCLT are of no importance, but rather that they were not intended to serve as the framework against which we can judge whether an interpretation is correct in any given situation. In order to do that, we need to understand the context – broadly understood – in which the interpretation took place. In the words of one commentator, the Vienna Convention provisions were never seen as a 'complete formulae in the sense of lists of ingredients to be used every time, still less as algorithms in the sense of sets of sequential instructions'.[23]

This chapter is composed of three sections. The following section (Section 2.2) describes the evolution of the rules of interpretation in the codification projects of the *Institut* and ILC, and the ensuing debates at the Vienna Conference, highlighting the fundamental similarities between the approaches taken by the main protagonists. Section 2.3

---

[20] See Djeffal, *Static and Evolutive Interpretation*, 140. Djeffal himself notes that he does 'not have the means to show that this has a beneficial effect such as enhancing a rational discourse'; *Static and Evolutive Interpretation*, fn 329. Similarly, Klabbers labels any suggestion that the widespread citation of VCLT enhances inter-systemic communication as 'optimistic'; Klabbers, 'Virtuous Interpretation', 33.

[21] Cf G. Hernández, 'Interpretation', 325 ('although [the VCLT provisions] are a useful heuristic device through which to filter the debates within international legal scholarship, they cannot substitute for the reality of interpretation as both a cognitive and law-creative process').

[22] See e.g., *Industria Nacional de Alimentos S.A. and Indalsa Perú S.A. v. The Republic of Peru*, ICSID Case No. ARB/03/4 (Decision on Annulment), Dissenting Opinion of Sir Franklin Berman, paras 5–8. I am indebted to Richard Gardiner for this point.

[23] Gardiner, *Treaty Interpretation*, 452.

examines why the rules of interpretation were codified if they do not prescribe one interpretative approach. Section 2.4 outlines the relevance of the previous sections to the evaluation of interpretation generally and the implications for the specific approach taken in this book.

2.2   The Evolution of the Rules of Interpretation

The debates that took place regarding treaty interpretation throughout the mid-twentieth century are often characterised as a pitched battle between textualists, for whom 'if the text is clear, recourse to extra-textual means of interpretation should not be necessary',[24] and subjectivists, who argue 'that the text of the treaty should be regarded as simply the formal embodiment of the parties' shared intentions and [require] the interpreter to make, as a matter of course, a far ranging enquiry into non-textual matters'.[25] These labels, however, obscure the points of common ground that existed between the different camps.[26] The debates demonstrate that the majority of participants had remarkably similar views of the process of interpretation despite frequently professing to be at odds with each other. Jurists identified with the textualist school of interpretation, such as Sir Gerald Fitzmaurice and Sir Humphrey Waldock, never adopted literal interpretation as their sole interpretative methodology nor did those labelled subjectivists, such as Sir Hersch Lauterpacht, suggest that the text should be ignored in a free-ranging search for the intentions of the parties.[27] Instead, the main actors in the codification process were in agreement that the rules of interpretation should embody a flexible approach, rejecting literal interpretation in favour of a search for the intentions of the parties that commenced with the ordinary meaning of the text. On the rare occasions when a more rigid methodology was proposed, it was given short shrift by the membership. None of the principal actors in the codification efforts contended that there was one set method that led an interpreter to the 'correct' interpretation, nor

---

[24] Hernández, 'Interpretation', 331. Cf G. Letsas, 'Intentionalism and the Interpretation of the ECHR', in M. Fitzmaurice et al., Treaty Interpretation and the Vienna Convention on the Law of Treaties: 30 Years On (Brill 2010) 266.

[25] J. G. Merrills, 'Two Approaches to Treaty Interpretation', (1969) 4 Australian YBIL 55, 55. See also, F. G. Jacobs, 'Varieties of Approach to Treaty Interpretation', (1969) 18 ICLQ 318, 318–19.

[26] Cf Gardiner, Treaty Interpretation, 463.

[27] See G. G. Fitzmaurice & F. A. Vallat, 'Sir (William) Eric Beckett, KCMG, QC (1896–1966): An Appreciation', (1968) 17 ICLQ 267, 302–13. Cf Djeffal, Static and Evolutive Treaty Interpretation, 103–4.

was such a method ever embodied in a codification project. Instead, it was recognised that it was for the interpreter to determine, in light of the circumstances of the case at hand, the appropriate method and materials.

Other works have recounted the treatment of rules of interpretation from the classical period through the Renaissance and into modernity.[28] This chapter will not retrace that history. Instead, it will pick up the story at the codification efforts that took place in the early 1950s in the *Institut de Droit international*, the work of which played an important role in shaping the debates in the ILC and at the Vienna Conference.[29]

2.2.1   L'Institut de Droit International

The early twentieth century saw several codification efforts that addressed treaty interpretation, most notably the Harvard Draft Convention on the Law of Treaties, published in 1935.[30] However, the

---

[28] See in particular, D. Bederman, *Classical Canons: Rhetoric, Classicism, and Treaty Interpretation* (Ashgate 2001). See also Djeffal, *Static and Evolutive Interpretation*, Chapter 4; Gardiner, *Treaty Interpretation*, Chapter 2; Orakhelashvili, *The Interpretation of Acts and Rules*, 301–8. The *dramatis personae* examined in these studies invariably include: Gentili, *De iure bellis libri tres*, Book III, Chapter XIV, Grotius, *De iure Belli ac Pacis Libri Tres* (trans A. C. Campbell, Batoche 2001) Chapter 16; Pufendorf, *Of the Law of Nature and Nations*, Book V (trans B. Kennett, 1719) Chapter XII; Vattel, *The Law of Nations*, Book II, Chapter XVII (trans anon., Liberty Fund 2008); T. C. Yu, *The Interpretation of Treaties* (Columbia UP 1927); L. Ehrlich, 'L'interprétation des traités' (1928) 24 RdC 5; Y. -T. Chang, *The Interpretation of Treaties by Judicial Tribunals* (Columbia UP 1933).

[29] See for example, Third Report of the Special Rapporteur, Sir Humphrey Waldock, (1964) II YBILC 55, para 10 (citing the 1956 *Institut* resolution as inspiration for the draft general rule of interpretation); 766th Meeting of the ILC, (1964) I YBILC 289 (Rosenne) (drawing on the comments of Sir Eric Beckett in the *Institut*); Comments of Sir Ian Sinclair (United Kingdom), United Nations Conference on the Law of Treaties, First Session (26 March–24 May 1968), Official Records, UN Doc. A/CONF.39/C.1/SR.33, p. 177, para 5 (stating the UK upheld the view expressed in the *Institut* resolution); Comments of Mr Ruda (Argentina), ibid., p. 180, para 22 (citing the *Institut* resolution as indicative of contemporary doctrine).

[30] See Harvard Draft Convention on the Law of Treaties, (1935) 29 AJIL Supp 653, 937 (Article 19 (a): 'A treaty is to be interpreted in light of the general purpose which it is intended to serve. The historical background of the treaty, *travaux préparatoires*, the circumstances of the parties at the time the treaty was entered into, the change in these circumstance sought to be effected, the subsequent conduct of the parties in applying the provisions of the treaty, and the conditions prevailing at the time interpretation is being made, are to be considered in connection with the general purpose which the treaty is intended to serve'). See also Seventh International Conference of American States, 'The Interpretation of Treaties', 1933, (1935) 29 AJIL Supp 1225, and the Pan-American Draft

work that most directly influenced the Vienna Convention articles commenced in 1950 when Hersch Lauterpacht, then Whewell Professor of International Law at the University of Cambridge, presented his first report on the interpretation of treaties to the *Institut de Droit international.*[31]

In his private writings, Lauterpacht had expressed scepticism about the value of codifying rules of interpretation.[32] For him, such rules were nothing more than an *ex post facto* justification for a decision made on other grounds:

> they are not the determining cause of a judicial decision, but the form in which the judge cloaks a result arrived at by other means. It is elegant – and it inspires confidence – to give the garb of an established rule of interpretation ... [b]ut it is a fallacy to assume that the existence of these rules is a secure safeguard against arbitrariness or partiality.[33]

These doubts were reflected in Lauterpacht's early work at the *Institut.*[34] In his first report, he issued a staunch warning against the *Institut*'s project of codification and against the utility of rules of interpretation more generally, arguing that the application of rules of interpretation rarely, if ever, directed the interpreter to a particular result. Instead, many of the rules that had commonly been cited by tribunals and doctrine were 'contradictory and mutually cancelled each other out'.[35] Despite this generally

Convention on Treaties, (1935) 29 AJIL Supp 1205 (Article 3: 'The authentic interpretation of treaties, when considered necessary by the contracting parties, shall likewise be in writing').

[31] The *Institut* is a body of eminent jurists whose purpose is to promote the progress of international law by inter alia codification; Article 1(c), Statute of the Institute of International Law.

[32] See in particular, Lauterpacht, 'Restrictive Interpretation', 53–5.

[33] Lauterpacht, 'Restrictive Interpretation', 53. Cf J. Klabbers, *International Law* (CUP 2013) 364 (claiming that the VCLT provisions have 'given some support (often quite illusory support) to the claim of tribunals that their reasoning and the decisions arrived at had an objective validity even before they reached them, and have thus lightened the felt burden of responsibility'); Harvard Draft Convention, 947 (stating the rules of interpretation 'in all probability developed as neat *ex post facto* descriptions or justifications of decisions arrived at by mental processes more complicated than the mere mechanical application of rules to a text').

[34] Introducing his work, Lauterpacht stated that none of the resolutions of the *Institut* had previously addressed the interpretation of treaties, and there was no reason to regret that; H. Lauterpacht, 'De l'interprétation des traités', (1950) 43[I] Annuaire de l'Institut de Droit international 366. ('Aucune des Résolutions adoptées, dans le passé, par l'Institut de Droit international, ne porte sur la question de l'interprétation des traités ... il n'y a sans doute pas lieu de la regretter.')

[35] Lauterpacht, 'De l'interprétation', 372 ('beaucoup d'entre elles soient contradictoires et s'excluent mutuellement').

pessimistic view, Lauterpacht accepted that there might be some value in the *Institut* addressing the topic, even if it was to decide that there were no generally applicable rules of interpretation to speak of – a position that was clearly his preference.[36] Such a negative declaration 'would contribute in a large measure to the elucidation of the legal aspects of the problem, and discourage recourse to time-honoured but fundamentally unhelpful maxims'.[37] If, on the other hand, the *Institut* did insist on codifying some rules, he thought that it would be pointless to do so without establishing some kind of hierarchy between them.[38]

One obvious candidate for codification by the *Institut* was the rule most commonly invoked by states, courts and tribunals, according to which there is no need to interpret that which is clear.[39] Lauterpacht criticised this rule as circuitous, pointing out that it was only possible to say that something had a 'clear' or 'ordinary' meaning after interpreting the term itself.[40] In his view, arriving at such a conclusion was a holistic exercise that entailed examining other evidence that could shed light on the intention of the parties. However, despite voicing a strong aversion to 'clear meaning' theory, Lauterpacht understood the importance of the text in treaty interpretation. He recognised that the interpretative process must start somewhere and that it was 'reasonable and even essential that the process starts with what appears to be the natural, common, or "ordinary" sense of the terms used'.[41] This was merely to be a starting point, a rebuttable presumption that could be overturned by more persuasive evidence of the intentions of the parties.[42]

---

[36] See Lauterpacht, 'De l'interprétation', 376 ('à supposer que, *contrairement à l'opinion qui est à la base du présent rapport*, les Membres de l'Institut estiment qu'il conviendrait de retenir au moins quelques-uns des canons traditionnels d'interprétation', emphasis added).

[37] Lauterpacht, 'De l'interprétation', 373. ('Même si une déclaration de cette nature était énoncée en la forme négative, elle contribuerait dans une large mesure à élucider l'aspect juridique du problème, a décourager le recours à des formules consacrées par le temps mais foncièrement inutiles.')

[38] Lauterpacht, 'De l'interprétation', 376.

[39] Lauterpacht, 'De l'interprétation', 376. This was termed the rule of 'ordinary' or 'clear' meaning by Lauterpacht.

[40] Lauterpacht, 'De l'interprétation', 377.

[41] Lauterpacht, 'De l'interprétation', 387 ('il est raisonnable et même essential que ce processus commence avec ce qui paraît être le sens naturel, commun ou "ordinaire" des termes utilisés').

[42] Lauterpacht, 'De l'interprétation', 389.

Underlying Lauterpacht's approach was the idea that the overarching goal of interpretation was the search for the intention of the parties,[43] for which he considered there to be no better evidence than the preparatory work of a treaty.[44] He was not, however, blind to the problems of using preparatory work, as his critics subsequently suggested. He recognised that the preparatory work is often incomplete, contains contradictory statements, or gives undue importance to the most verbose or eloquent (but not necessarily the most influential) delegates.[45] Crucially, he understood that the preparatory work was only one piece in a puzzle, the importance of which depended on the circumstances of the case at hand:

> We do not suggest that the preparatory work offers, in itself, a method that allows one to find the intention of the parties. Logic, context, grammar, the 'natural meaning', presumptions, the principle of *effet utile*, the historic background and the presumed purpose of the treaty (the discovery of which the preparatory work holds a certain importance), the attitude of the parties subsequent to the adoption of the treaty, – all these elements play a considerable and legitimate role in the search for the intention of the parties.[46]

Whilst it would be wrong to overemphasise the importance of preparatory work by pretending that it had the same authority as a treaty text, it would, in Lauterpacht's view, be equally futile to deny the value of preparatory work entirely.[47] The resolutions that

---

[43] Lauterpacht, 'De l'interprétation', 423 ('l'intention des parties doit être le facteur fondamental en matière d'interprétation des traités').

[44] Lauterpacht, 'De l'interprétation', 392 ('si l'interprète a pour tache de rechercher l'intention des parties, comment pourrait-il mieux arriver au but, en cas de litige, qu'en étudiant les procès-verbaux et les documents relatifs aux négociations, les instructions transmises aux délégués, les comptes rendus des discussions, les états successifs du projets, les déclarations prononcées d'un commun accord, les rapports autorisés, bref tous les documents qui ont précédé la conclusion du traité?').

[45] Lauterpacht, 'De l'interprétation', 392–4. See also H. Lauterpacht, 'Observations complémentaires et projet définitif de Résolutions', (1952) 44[I] Annuaire de l'Institut de Droit international 197, 214–15.

[46] Lauterpacht, 'De l'interprétation', 394. ('On ne soutiendra pas que ces travaux offrent, seuls, une méthode permettant de rechercher l'intention des parties. La logique, le contexte, la grammaire, le "sens naturel", les présomptions, le principe de l'effet utile, les conditions historiques et l'objet présumé du traité (pour la découverte duquel les travaux préparatoires ont une certaine importance), l'attitude des parties postérieurement à l'adoption dudit traité, – tous ces éléments jouent un rôle considérable et légitime dans la recherche de l'intention des parties.')

[47] Lauterpacht, 'De l'interprétation', 396.

Lauterpacht initially proposed to the *Institut* in 1950 embodied this view of interpretation.[48]

Certain members of the *Institut* submitted observations on Lauterpacht's provisional report in writing, and it was Sir Eric Beckett, at the time Legal Adviser at the British Foreign Office, that made the most detailed – and *prima facie* critical – comments.[49] Although Beckett purported to disagree with Lauterpacht on almost all points of his report,[50] his observations show an understanding of the process of interpretation that is remarkably like Lauterpacht's. Indeed, the only point on which the two significantly diverged was the utility of rules of interpretation in international law. Whilst Lauterpacht was generally sceptical, Beckett argued that codification would allow courts to defend themselves against charges of subjectivity or arbitrariness by providing legal principles of general application upon which to base their reasoning.[51]

Beckett is well known for his criticism that Lauterpacht too readily permitted recourse to the preparatory work of a treaty.[52] In Beckett's view, such an approach allowed an interpreter to find support for any argument that they wished to advance – in his words, it provided the interpreter with a '*tabula in naufragio*'.[53] But if one digs a little deeper,

---

[48] Lauterpacht, 'De l'interprétation', 433, resolutions 1–2. Lauterpacht also included more substantive interpretative principles in his proposal; namely, on the limited role of restrictive interpretation (resolution 3); the legitimacy of recourse to *effet utile* (resolution 4); on the absence of the common intention of the parties (resolution 5); and the absence of a distinction between '*traités-lois*' and other types of treaty (resolution 6).

[49] Whether Beckett's tone was due to a misunderstanding of Lauterpacht's report, or wilful misrepresentation due to some personal animosity, is a matter of pure conjecture. It is notable, however, that Lauterpacht was not included in the British team at the merits stage of the *Corfu Channel* case, whilst he had been on the team at the preliminary objections phase. The team was assembled in both phases of the case by Beckett, in his capacity as Legal Adviser. See E. Lauterpacht, *The Life of Hersch Lauterpacht* (CUP 2010) 414.

[50] 'Comments by Sir Eric Beckett', (1950) 43[I] Annuaire de l'Institut de Droit international 435.

[51] Comments of Beckett, 436. Beckett also noted that if any of the arguments against rules of interpretation had any weight, they would be equally applicable to domestic law; Comments of Beckett, 435. For a similar argument, see also G. Gottlieb, 'The Conceptual World of the Yale School of International Law', (1968) 21 World Politics 108, 125.

[52] See E. Bjorge, 'The Vienna Rules, Evolutionary Interpretation, and the Intention of the Parties', in A. Bianchi et al., *Interpretation in International Law* (OUP 2015) 197; Orakhelashvili, *The Interpretation of Acts and Rules*, 306; B. N. Mehrish, 'The Role of *Travaux Préparatoires* as an Element in the Interpretation of Treaties', (1970) 40 Yearbook of the Association of Attenders and Alumni of The Hague Academy of International Law 43, 45–6.

[53] Comments of Beckett, 440 ('plank in a shipwreck').

the similarities between the two approaches are striking. Beckett was not an advocate of literal interpretation nor was he as hostile to the preparatory work as may be expected. Instead, like Lauterpacht, he understood the meaning of a term to be 'clear' only at the end of an interpretative process that encompassed the 'study of the treaty as a whole ... [the] arguments on the circumstances which led up to the conclusion of the treaty, [and] its relationship with other treaties that preceded it'.[54] This statement must be read in connection with his definition of a treaty, which was expansive:

> A treaty will, of course, include everything that was signed at the time even though this consists of the main document, called the treaty, together with a whole lot of letters, protocols, and even (probably) agreed minutes ... there may exist yet further specially initialled minutes which have been deliberately prepared for the purposes of its interpretation. These must for the purposes of interpretation be regarded as part of the treaty itself.[55]

If, after consulting these materials, the meaning was 'clear', Beckett argued that the interpreter could not have recourse to the preparatory work *'for the purpose of arriving at a different view* unless the position is that it can be demonstrated that the meaning so arrived at represented the intention of *neither* party'.[56]

When one considers the practical implications of Beckett's schema, the apparent division between his approach and that of Lauterpacht falls away. Under the former, even if the preparatory work fell outside the broad definition of a treaty quoted above, the interpreter could freely consult such material for two reasons. First, an interpreter could have recourse to the preparatory work to confirm a meaning arrived at through other means, as this would not be using the preparatory work *for the purposes of arriving at a different view* of the meaning. Second, a diligent interpreter would verify the preparatory work to check that the parties did not intend to attribute a special meaning to the term; indeed, studying the preparatory work would seem to be one of the primary means by which an interpreter could ascertain whether the 'clear' meaning of the treaty 'represented the intention of *neither* party'.[57] Despite his anti-*travaux* rhetoric, Beckett was not as hostile to recourse to

---

[54] Comments of Beckett, 441.

[55] Comments of Beckett, 442.

[56] Comments of Beckett, 441 (first emphasis added).

[57] Cf Comments of Sir Humphrey Waldock, UN Conference on the Law of Treaties, First Session (Summary records of plenary meetings and of the meetings of the Committee as a whole), UN Doc. A/CONF.39/C.1/SR.33, 184, para 71 (stating that the cases in which

preparatory work as it at first seems. Seen in this light, Beckett's criticism of Lauterpacht seems less strident. Beckett, like Lauterpacht, accepted that a variety of documents produced during the drafting of a treaty should, if available, be consulted as a matter of course.[58] Indeed, Lauterpacht came to the same conclusion, noting that 'the differences between his [Beckett's] ideas and those proposed in the report are not as profound as they seem at first sight'.[59]

The idea that there were significant differences between those that supported and those that were hostile to recourse to preparatory work was perpetuated by Lauterpacht in his second report, delivered at the Sienna session of the *Institut* in 1952.[60] A significant section of Lauterpacht's 1952 report was dedicated to justifying his views on the use of preparatory work, which was seemingly motivated by the delivery of the International Court of Justice's Advisory Opinion on the *Competence of the General Assembly for the Admission of a State to the United Nations* in 1950. In that Opinion, the Court stated that '[i]f the relevant words in their natural and ordinary meaning make sense in their context, that is an end of the matter'.[61] Whilst still defending preparatory work as the best way of ascertaining the intentions of the parties, the Court's statement led Lauterpacht to concede that there were some circumstances – at least, according to the jurisprudence of the ICJ and its predecessor – in which a term was so clear that recourse to preparatory work was superfluous;[62] a concession that was reflected in his amended project of resolutions.[63]

---

a special meaning could only be arrived at by reference to the preparatory work were 'comparatively rare').

[58] A notably stricter approach than either Lauterpacht or Beckett was taken by Sir Arnold McNair, who argued that a tribunal should give effect to the ordinary meaning of a term taken in its context, without recourse to extraneous material; 'Observations de Sir Arnold D. McNair', (1950) 43[I] Annuaire de l'Institut de Droit international 449.

[59] 'Remarques complémentaires du rapporteur, M. Lauterpacht', (1950) 43[I] Annuaire de l'Institut de Droit international 457.

[60] H. Lauterpacht, 'Observations complémentaires et projet définitif de Résolutions', (1952) 44[I] Annuaire de l'Institut de Droit international 197 (calling 'la principale divergence de vues entre les membres de la Commission … [était] l'usage des travaux préparatoires').

[61] *Competence of the General Assembly for the Admission of a State to the United Nations*, ICJ Reports 1950, pp. 4, 8.

[62] Lauterpacht, 'Observations complémentaires', 211.

[63] Lauterpacht, 'Observations complémentaires', 216, 222, resolution 2. ('Dans chaque cas, le tribunal devrait apprécier si et dans quelle mesure, étant donné l'absence manifeste de toute difficulté qui empêcherait de donner effet au sens ordinaire et naturel des termes du traité, un examen détaillé des travaux préparatoires est nécessaire.') Lauterpacht requested that the *Institut* defer the debate and vote on his resolutions until the following

The topic was finally discussed in plenary at the Grenada session of the *Institut* in 1956. In the intervening period, Hersch Lauterpacht had taken up a seat at the International Court and stepped down from his role as *rapporteur* on the project. Sir Gerald Fitzmaurice, successor to Sir Eric Beckett as Legal Adviser to the British Foreign Office, took over the reins. From the outset, Fitzmaurice tried to distinguish his approach from that of Lauterpacht, noting that the latter's emphasis on the intention of the parties had proved particularly controversial.[64] However, despite these criticisms and the attendant amendments to the project of resolutions, Fitzmaurice did not stray far from Lauterpacht's main ideas. This is evident when one compares the main elements of Fitzmaurice's 1956 final project of resolutions to the draft resolutions that Lauterpacht presented at the 1952 Sienna session. Crucially, both considered that the ordinary meaning of the text should be the starting point of interpretation, a presumption that could be displaced in light of evidence that parties had intended to give that term a different meaning. For Lauterpacht, it was 'legitimate and desirable, in the interests of good faith and stability of international relations, to take the natural meaning of the terms as the point of departure for interpretation',[65] whilst for Fitzmaurice, '[t]he agreement of the parties being realised in the text of the treaty, it is appropriate to take the natural and ordinary meaning of the text as the basis of interpretation'.[66]

Similarly, although Fitzmaurice professed to give a more 'moderate' place to preparatory work as a result of concerns raised by other members in Sienna, the difference between the two projects is slight.[67] Lauterpacht's 1952 draft recognised that:

---

session of the *Institut*, once he had been able to amend the project in light of members' further comments. He presented an amended project of resolutions at the 1954 session in Aix en Provence, although they were not the subject of debate; M. H. Lauterpacht, 'De l'interprétation des traités', (1954) 45[1] Annuaire de l'Institut de Droit international 225.

[64] Sir G. Fitzmaurice, 'De l'interprétation des traités', (1956) 46 Annuaire de l'Institut de Droit international 317, 321.

[65] Lauterpacht, 'Observations complémentaires', 222, resolution 1 ('il est légitime et désirable, dans l'intérêt de la bonne foi et de la stabilité des transactions internationales, de prendre le sens naturel des termes comme point de départ du processus d'interprétation').

[66] Fitzmaurice, 'De l'interprétation des traités', 349, resolution 1. ('L'accord des parties s'étant réalisé due le texte du traité, il y a lieu de prendre le sens naturel et ordinaire des termes de ce texte comme base d'interprétation.')

[67] Fitzmaurice, 'De l'interprétation des traités', 321.

recourse to the preparatory work, when they are accessible, is a legitimate and desirable means of establishing the intentions of the parties ... In each case, the tribunal must assess if and the extent to which, given the manifest absence of any difficulty that would preclude giving effect to the ordinary and natural meanings of the terms of the treaty, a detailed examination of the preparatory work is necessary.[68]

Article 2 of the *Institut's* 1956 resolution, on the other hand, stated that:

> it is incumbent on the tribunal ... to appreciate if, and to what extent, it is necessary to use other means of interpretation.
>   Amongst the legitimate means of interpretation are: *a)* Recourse to the preparatory work ... [69]

Fitzmaurice's 1956 articles were ultimately a slimmed-down version of Lauterpacht's 1952 draft. He deleted the articles that dealt with 'substantive' rules of interpretation, such as restrictive interpretation and *effet utile,* restricting the draft to 'solid principles' to which, in his view, no one could object.[70] By relying 'on two or three basic general principles', Fitzmaurice followed a minimalist approach to the rules of interpretation that he proposed in his academic writings.[71]

2.2.2   The 1964 ILC Debates

In parallel with the work of the *Institut,* the ILC had started work on the law of treaties in 1950, a topic to which it had accorded priority in its First Session in 1949.[72] All four rapporteurs that were charged with leading the

---

[68] Lauterpacht, 'Observations complémentaires', 222. ('Le recours aux travaux préparatoires, lorsqu'ils sont accessibles, est notamment un moyen légitime et désirable aux fins d'établir l'intention des parties ... Dans chaque cas, le tribunal devrait apprécier si et dans quelle mesure, étant donné l'absence manifeste de toute difficulté qui empêcherait de donner effet au sens ordinaire et naturel des termes du traité, un examen détaillé des travaux préparatoires est nécessaire.')

[69] Fitzmaurice, 'De l'interprétation des traités', 349 ('il incombera au tribunal, en tenant compte des dispositions de l'article premier, d'apprécier si, et dans quelle mesure, il y a lieu d'utiliser d'autres moyens d'interprétation ... Parmi ces moyen légitimes d'interpréter se trouvent: a) Le recours aux travaux préparatoires').

[70] Fitzmaurice, 'De l'interprétation des traités', 339. Of course, some members of the *Institut* did take issue with Fitzmaurice's project; see comments of Petros Vallindas, 'De l'interprétation des traités', (1956) 46 Annuaire de l'Institut de Droit international 317, 339.

[71] G. G. Fitzmaurice, 'The Law and Procedure of the International Court of Justice: Treaty Interpretation and Certain Other Treaty Points', (1951) 28 BYIL 1, 2–3.

[72] Report of the International Law Commission on its Work of its First Session, (1949) I YBILC 278, 281, para 20.

Commission's work on the law of treaties were British: James Brierly, Sir Hersch Lauterpacht, Sir Gerald Fitzmaurice and Sir Humphrey Waldock.[73]

Although it was only when the project reached the hands of the final rapporteur that the ILC considered the topic of treaty interpretation, there is good reason to believe that the first three rapporteurs would have been sceptical about the idea of codifying rules of interpretation.[74] James Brierly had voiced caution about the codification process generally, noting that the codification of international law would necessarily involve political choices regarding *what* to codify. In his view, the term 'codification ... disguised the real difficulties and induced men to think of codification as a means of international progress that can be adopted without any important concessions being made by our nations'.[75] For his part, Lauterpacht expressed deep scepticism about the utility of rules of interpretation in both his private writing and in his work as rapporteur for the *Institut,* as noted above.[76] Although guiding the *Institut's* work on treaty interpretation to conclusion, Fitzmaurice was more hesitant about the idea of codifying the law of treaties in conventional form, instead preferring the ILC's work to take the form of a code for two reasons.[77] First, he thought that the rules regulating treaties should have an independent normative basis, such as customary international law.[78] Whilst he did not spell out the reasons for this, it seems clear that Fitzmaurice was aware that the ILC could be charged with circular reasoning if it were to include in a convention any articles that were progressive developments of the law, and not codifications of existing customary international law. Such rules would in effect only have any legal force because they were included in a treaty – the very instrument they were meant to regulate. Second, Fitzmaurice thought that much of the law of treaties was comprised of 'enunciations of principles and abstract rules' that were ill-suited for codification in treaty form.[79] In his view, adopting a code

---

[73] James Brierly was rapporteur from 1950 to 1952; Sir Hersch Lauterpacht from 1952 to 1955; Sir Gerald Fitzmaurice from 1955 to 1961; and Sir Humphrey Waldock from 1961 to 1966.

[74] Cf Klabbers, 'Virtuous Interpretation', 17.

[75] J. L. Brierly, 'The Codification of International Law', (1948) 47 Michigan LR 2, 4.

[76] Lauterpacht, 'De l'interprétation des traités', 366; Lauterpacht, 'Restrictive Interpretation', 53– 5.

[77] 'First Report on the Law of Treaties by G. G. Fitzmaurice', (1956) II YBILC 105, 106–7, para 9 (hereinafter 'Fitzmaurice First Report').

[78] ibid.

[79] Fitzmaurice First Report, p. 107, para 9.

instead of a treaty would render 'permissible the inclusion of a certain amount of declaratory and explanatory material in the body of the code, in a way that would not be possible if this had to be confined to a strict statement of obligation'.[80] Although he did not explicitly state which aspects of the law of treaties he considered to fall in this category, it seems clear that he had interpretation in mind: Fitzmaurice delivered his first report to the ILC in the same year that he delivered his final report to the *Institut,* in which he emphasised the codification of principles over substantive rules.[81]

This uncertainty regarding the value of codifying rules of interpretation was acknowledged at the outset of Waldock's Third Report, the first to address treaty interpretation, which was delivered in 1964.[82] Ultimately, however, he argued that the codification of the rules of interpretation was an important enterprise for several reasons.[83] First and foremost, he considered that the codification of the rules of interpretation would oblige states to abide by the agreements that they had made, giving real force to the principle of *pacta sunt servanda.* Second, Waldock considered that the ongoing controversy in the literature regarding the respective importance of the text versus the intentions of the parties called for a clear position to be taken by the ILC. Third, other draft articles in the ILC's project on the law of treaties presupposed a method for determining the intentions of the parties. One such article would later become Article 28 of the VCLT, which specifies that '*[u]nless a different intention appears from the treaty or is otherwise established*, its provisions do not bind a party in relation to any act or fact which took place or any situation which ceased to exist before the date of the entry into force of the treaty with respect to that party'.[84] In light of these articles, Waldock considered that the ILC was obliged to define how an interpreter might discern such an intention. Finally, he considered that codified rules of interpretation would be of practical use for those drafting treaties.

---

[80] ibid.

[81] Fitzmaurice, 'De l'interprétation des traités', 338–9 ('le préambule va à la rencontre des remarques faites par M. Basdevant, selon lesquelles les principes énoncés ne devraient pas revêtir la forme d'un code mais celle d'un guide').

[82] 'Third Report on the Law of Treaties by Sir Humphrey Waldock', (1964) II YBILC 5 (hereinafter 'Waldock Third Report').

[83] Waldock Third Report, pp. 54–5, para 8.

[84] Emphasis added.

In his Third Report, Waldock made several decisions that indelibly influenced the direction that the ILC took. The first was to define the scope of the rules that the ILC codified. According to Waldock, many of the principles and maxims of interpretation frequently cited by tribunals are:

> for the most part, principles of logic and good sense valuable only as guides to assist in appreciating the meaning which the parties may have intended to attach to the expressions which they employed in a document. Their suitability for use in any given case hinges on a variety of considerations which have first to be appreciated by the interpreter of the document ... [i]n other words, recourse to many of these principles is discretionary rather than obligatory.[85]

Waldock thought it inadvisable to codify such principles and maxims because their application was indelibly context-dependent, and that 'detached from that context they retain a certain fictitious ring of unassailable truth'.[86] In contrast, he thought that 'the comparatively few rules which appear to constitute the strictly legal basis of the interpretation of treaties'[87] could be usefully codified. Although he did not explain what he meant by the 'strictly legal basis of interpretation', Waldock seemed to suggest that there were certain elements that the interpreter should take into account in each and every instance, if present. He recognised, however, that the relevance of even those elements depended very much on the circumstances of the case at hand.[88]

Waldock's Third Report proposed four draft rules of interpretation that were inspired by the 1956 resolution of the *Institut* and Gerald Fitzmaurice's articles in the *British Yearbook* on the practice of the ICJ.[89] The cornerstone of Waldock's approach – and the subsequent *leitmotif* of the VCLT project – was that:

> the basic rule of treaty interpretation [is] the primacy of the text as evidence of the intentions of the parties ... the text must be presumed to be the authentic expression of the intentions of the parties; and that, in consequence, the starting point and purpose of interpretation is to

---

[85] Waldock Third Report, p. 54, para 6.
[86] Harvard Draft Convention, p. 939; quoted at Waldock Third Report, p. 54, para 8.
[87] Waldock Third Report, p. 54, para 8. See also Draft Articles on the Law of Treaties, (1966) II YBILC 218–19, para 5.
[88] 'Sixth Report on the Law of Treaties by Sir Humphrey Waldock', (1966) II YBILC 94 (hereinafter 'Waldock Sixth Report'), p. 94, para 1.
[89] Waldock Third Report, p. 55. para 10.

elucidate the meaning of the text, not to investigate *ab initio* the intentions of the parties.[90]

Waldock expressly contrasted his approach to the position taken by Lauterpacht in the *Institut*, which he understood to 'place the main emphasis on the intentions of the parties and in consequence admit a liberal recourse to the *travaux préparatoires*'.[91] However, Waldock's project of draft articles did not diverge significantly from Lauterpacht's *Institut* draft resolutions. First, it did not adopt literal interpretation as the exclusive, or even preponderant, method of interpretation. Instead, Waldock simply considered that, 'whilst not excluding recourse to other indications of the intentions of the parties in appropriate cases, [the 1964 draft] makes the actual text the dominant factor in the interpretation of the treaty'.[92] Second, Waldock's 1964 draft admitted use of the preparatory work of a treaty in three cases: to *confirm* the ordinary meaning of a term;[93] to *establish* that the parties had intended to use a special meaning of a term;[94] or to *determine* a manifestly absurd or ambiguous term.[95] This presaged the final form of Article 32, which draws a distinction between the use of the preparatory work of a treaty to *confirm* the meaning arrived at by virtue of Article 31 or to *determine* the meaning when interpretation according to Article 31 is ambiguous, obscure, absurd or unreasonable.

In debates, the ILC members largely rallied behind Waldock's 'generally permissive'[96] draft articles, with no member proposing that the provisions on interpretation be deleted.[97] Discussions at the 1964 session centred on the respective roles of the text and the preparatory work in interpretation, and with it the question of whether the ILC should adopt a particular

---

[90] Waldock Third Report, p. 56, para 13. Draft Article 70 provided that: 'The terms of a treaty shall be interpreted in good faith in accordance with the natural and ordinary meaning to be given to each term – (a) in its context in the treaty and in the context of the treaty as a whole; and (b) in the context of the rules of international law in force at the time of the conclusion of the treaty.' Waldock Third Report, p. 52.

[91] Waldock Third Report, p. 53, para 4.

[92] Waldock Third Report, p. 56, para 13. Cf ibid., p. 57, para 16. ('*Paragraph 2* concerns cases where either the natural and ordinary meaning of the terms in their context does not give a viable result or for one reason or another the meaning isn't clear. In these cases, *and in these cases only*, it is permissible to fix the meaning of the terms by reference to evidence of the intentions of the parties outside the ordinary sense of their words.')

[93] Draft Article 71(2)(a), Waldock Third Report, p. 52.

[94] Draft Article 70(3), Waldock Third Report, p. 52.

[95] Draft Article 71(2)(b), Waldock Third Report, p. 52.

[96] 765th Meeting of the ILC, (1964) I YBILC 278, para 39 (Rosenne).

[97] See 765th Meeting of the ILC, (1964) I YBILC 275, para 8 (Briggs); ibid., 276, para 24 (Tabibi); ibid., 278, para 47 (Tunkin); ibid., 280, paras 77–8 (Ago).

methodology of interpretation. The majority of members, including Roberto Ago, Shabtai Rosenne and Mustafa Kamil Yasseen, agreed with the general approach of the draft articles, proposing, if anything, more liberal recourse to the preparatory work.[98] The minority of members, on the other hand, argued that a more literal approach to interpretation should be adopted.[99] For his part, Waldock stood somewhere in the middle, reiterating the importance of the text as a factor of stability and certainty, whilst recognising at the same time that 'it was unrealistic to imagine that the preparatory work was not really consulted by States, organizations and tribunals whenever they saw fit, before or at any stage of proceedings'.[100]

Whilst the records show that the reaction of the members was 'splintered and somewhat uncertain',[101] a twist of fate gave the membership the opportunity to reject literal interpretation almost unanimously. During the latter stages of the 1964 session, Waldock presented revised draft articles that purported to limit the scope of recourse to the preparatory work, seemingly in the mistaken belief that he had been instructed to do so by the members of the Commission.[102] Crucially, his changes eliminated recourse to the *travaux* to confirm a meaning arrived at by application of the general rule. Such an approach would have given significantly more weight to the text of the treaty by curtailing the interpreter's ability to examine wider evidence of the parties' intentions. However, faced with the new draft, the members were nearly unanimous in their desire to reinstate the 'fairly wide use of the *travaux préparatoires*' permitted by Waldock's previous draft,[103] emphatically

---

[98] 766th Meeting of the ILC, (1964) I YBILC 282, para 5 (Ago); ibid., 283, para 17 (Rosenne; 'to state that the *travaux préparatoires* had been used only to confirm an opinion already arrived at on the basis of the text of the treaty was coming close to a legal fiction'); ibid., 286, para 49 (Yasseen; 'thought it was self-evident that interpretation was almost impossible on the basis of the text of the treaty alone'); 769th Meeting of the ILC, (1964) I YBILC 308, 313, para 56 (Yasseen); ibid., 314, para 64 (Rosenne).

[99] 766th Meeting of the ILC, (1964) I YBILC 282, 287, para 57. (Bartos); ibid., 287, para 61 (Verdross) ('The intention alone was not, however, a conclusive guide: it had to be expressed in the text of a treaty, however imperfect.')

[100] 769th Meeting of the ILC, (1964) I YBILC 308, 314, para 65 (Waldock). See also ibid., 314, para 71 (Waldock; 'Throughout, the Commission had shown a strong predilection for textual interpretation in the interests of stability and certainty of treaty relations. All were agreed that text was not everything and that preparatory work had its place').

[101] Mortenson, 'The *Travaux* of *Travaux*', 793.

[102] 769th Meeting of the ILC, (1964) I YBILC 308, 309, para 3; ibid., 314, para 65 (Waldock). See also Mortenson, 'The *Travaux* of *Travaux*', 794.

[103] 770th Meeting of the ILC, (1964) I YBILC 315, 17, para 39 (Waldock). The members voted 13 to none to reinstate the ability to use the *travaux* to confirm a meaning arrived at under the general rule.

rejecting any suggestion that the text was in itself sufficient to discern the intention of the parties.

2.2.3   The 1966 ILC Debates

The draft articles were next debated by the ILC in 1966, a year after states' representatives in the Sixth Committee of the UN submitted comments on the draft articles adopted by the Commission in 1964.[104] Governments were generally positive about the 1964 draft articles, accepting the foundational principles that the text was the presumptive object of interpretation and that other, more persuasive manifestations of the parties' intent could displace the ordinary meaning of a provision.[105] Some governments, however, voiced dissent. Of particular note were the comments of the USA, which foreshadowed the views expressed forcefully by Myres McDougal at the Vienna Conference.[106] The USA questioned the wisdom of codifying principles of interpretation as 'rules' and criticised what it saw as the 'apparent primacy given to the ordinary meaning' and the undue restriction on recourse to the preparatory work that was reflected in the 1964 articles.[107]

Waldock's response to the comments of the USA was unequivocal. In relation to whether principles of interpretation should be codified as 'rules', he understood the comment 'primarily as a *caveat* against formulating the general principles for the interpretation of treaties in such a manner as to give them a rigidity which might deprive the process of interpretation of the degree of flexibility necessary to it'.[108] This was, in his view, a misunderstanding of the approach that the ILC had taken at the 1964 session:

> The Commission was fully conscious in 1964 of the undesirability – if not impossibility – of confining the process of interpretation within rigid rules, and the provisions of [the 1964 draft articles] when read together,

---

[104] See 'Comments of Governments', (1966) II YBILC 91–4.

[105] See for example, 'Comments of Governments', (1966) II YBILC 91 (Czechoslovakia, Hungary), 92 (Netherlands, Turkey, United Kingdom), 93 (Kenya).

[106] The US member of the Commission at the time, Herbert Briggs, seemed to be sympathetic to McDougal's approach; see H. W. Briggs, 'Book Review of "The Interpretation of Agreements and World Public Order – Principles of Content and Procedure"', (1968) 53 [3] Cornell LR 543. Nevertheless, he disagreed with the USA's characterisation of the ILC draft articles as hierarchical; 884th Meeting of the ILC, (1966) I [II] YBILC 269, para 13 (Briggs).

[107] 'Comments of Governments', (1966) II YBILC 93 (the USA).

[108] Waldock Sixth Report, para 1.

as they must be, do not appear to constitute a code of rules incompatible with the required degree of flexibility ... [i]n a sense, all 'rules' of interpretation have the character of 'guidelines' since their application in a particular case depends so much on the appreciation of the context and circumstances of the point to be interpreted.[109]

Elsewhere in his Sixth Report, Waldock reiterated that it was the interpreter's appreciation of the particular circumstances of the case at hand that guided the process of interpretation, and not any preordained method of interpretation that was codified in the draft articles. Most strikingly, he described the elements enumerated in the draft articles as non-hierarchical, stating that they would be, 'so far as they are present in any given case, thrown into the crucible and their interaction would give the legally relevant interpretation'.[110] Waldock was therefore clear that, to his mind, the draft articles adopted in 1964 did not mandate a particular methodology of interpretation, but simply listed the factors that might, depending on the circumstances of the case, be legally relevant.

In the debates, members supported Waldock's statement that the draft articles did not create a hierarchy amongst the various methods of interpretation,[111] a point that Roberto Ago expressed in particularly unequivocal terms: '[t]he separation of [the draft articles] ... did not in any way imply that the Commission was taking a position in favour of one theory rather than another'.[112] Similarly, the Brazilian member, Gilberto Amado, remarked that the Special Rapporteur had convincingly 'shown that the various means of interpretation could be employed simultaneously ... [there] was no hierarchy and no precedence of one means of interpretation over another'.[113] The result of the near unanimity amongst members in the debates was, in the words of Waldock, 'a return to the scheme of the 1964 text',[114] which was adopted without dissent.[115]

---

[109] Waldock Sixth Report, 94, para 1.

[110] Waldock Sixth Report, 95, para 4.

[111] See for example, 871st Meeting of the ILC, (1966) I [II] YBILC 193, para 5 (De Luna) ('the various rules formulated by the Commission were, so to speak, the ingredients of interpretation'); 195, para 27 (El Erian); 197, para 48 (Yasseen). ('The means enumerated were only various aspects of the same operation; they were arranged, not in any order of precedence, but in a practical order which was self-evident in view of the circumstances.')

[112] 873rd Meeting of the ILC, (1966) I [II] YBILC 205, para 23 (Ago).

[113] 873rd Meeting of the ILC, (1966) I [II] YBILC 207, paras 45–6 (Amado).

[114] 883rd Meeting of the ILC, (1966) I [II] YBILC 267, para 95 (Waldock).

[115] The 'General Rule of Interpretation' (then Article 69) was adopted 16 votes to none, and the provisions on the 'Supplementary Means of Interpretation' (then Article 70) was

2.2.4 The Vienna Conference

The final draft articles adopted by the ILC were sent to the General Assembly, which decided to convene an international conference to 'embody the results of [the ILC's] work in an international convention and such other instruments as it may deem appropriate'.[116] In his commentary to the draft articles that was forwarded to the General Assembly, Waldock emphasised the three main ideas that underpinned the ILC's proposed text: first, that 'the starting point of interpretation is the elucidation of the meaning of the text, not an investigation *ab initio* into the intentions of the parties';[117] second, that 'the [general rule of interpretation] cannot properly be regarded as laying down a legal hierarchy of norms for the interpretation of treaties';[118] and, third, that 'it would be unrealistic and inappropriate to lay down in the draft articles that no recourse whatever may be had to extrinsic means of interpretation, such as the *travaux préparatoires,* until after the application [of the general rule]'.[119] The draft articles passed up to the assembled delegates at the Vienna Conference did not dictate a particular methodology but rather recognised the inevitably recursive, non-linear character of interpretation.

The Vienna Conference considered the articles on interpretation in its First Session over a short period of three days,[120] during which the debates were coloured by the very first intervention that took place – that of the delegate of the United States, Yale Professor Myres McDougal. McDougal had vociferously criticised the ILC draft articles in his private writings, arguing that '[t]he great defect, and tragedy, in the International Law Commission's final recommendations about the interpretation of treaties is in their insistent emphasis upon an impossible, conformity-imposing textuality'.[121] According to McDougal, the ILC treated the text as the 'exclusive index of the shared expectations of the parties to an agreement [which] is an exercise in primitive and potentially destructive formalism'.[122]

---

adopted 15 votes to none; 884th Meeting of the ILC, (1966) I [II] YBILC 270, paras 31, 40.

[116] UNGA Res. 2166 (XXI), 5 December 1966, UN Doc. A/6516, para 2.

[117] Draft Articles on the Law of Treaties with commentaries, (1966) II YBILC 220, para 11.

[118] Draft Articles on the Law of Treaties with commentaries, (1966) II YBILC 220, para 9.

[119] Draft Articles on the Law of Treaties with commentaries, (1966) II YBILC 223, para 18.

[120] UN Conference on the Law of Treaties, First Session (Summary records of plenary meetings and of the meetings of the Committee as a whole), UN Doc. A/CONF.39/C.1/SR.31, SR.32, SR.33 (19 April 1968–22 April 1968).

[121] M. McDougal, 'The International Law Commission's Draft Articles upon Interpretation: Textuality *Redividus*', (1967) 61 AJIL 992.

[122] McDougal, 'Textuality *Redividus*', 997.

At the Vienna Conference, he continued on the same line of attack, criticising the draft articles for embodying an 'over-rigid and unnecessarily restrictive' textual approach, which was based on the 'obscurantist tautology' that the text could be interpreted without reference to extraneous evidence of the parties' intentions.[123] In addition to being futile (if not impossible), this approach was, in his eyes, at odds with the overwhelming body of arbitral and state practice, which 'bore out the right of the interpreter to take into account any circumstance affecting the common intent that the parties had sought to express in the text'.[124]

After criticising the ILC's approach, McDougal introduced a US counter-proposal which sought to fundamentally alter the articles on interpretation.[125] According to McDougal, instead of adopting the fundamentally flawed textualism of the ILC, the US proposal made the 'text of the treaty and the common public meaning of words ... the point of departure of interpretation, but not the end of the enquiry', and permitted recourse to whatever extraneous means of interpretation might be relevant to the common intent of the parties.[126] The proposal effectuated this by removing the division between the primary and supplementary means of interpretation, simply providing a list of elements that could be taken into account by the interpreter.[127]

---

[123] UN Conference on the Law of Treaties, First Session (Summary records of plenary meetings and of the meetings of the Committee as a whole), UN Doc. A/CONF.39/C.1/SR.31, 167, para 38 (USA).

[124] UN Conference on the Law of Treaties, First Session (Summary records of plenary meetings and of the meetings of the Committee as a whole), UN Doc. A/CONF.39/C.1/SR.31, 167, para 42 (USA).

[125] A/CONF.39/C.1/L.156.

[126] UN Conference on the Law of Treaties, First Session (Summary records of plenary meetings and of the meetings of the Committee as a whole), UN Doc. A/CONF.39/C.1/SR.31, 168, para 49 (USA).

[127] The US proposal read:

A treaty shall be interpreted in good faith in order to determine the meaning to be given to its terms in the light of all relevant factors, including in particular:

(a) the context of the treaty;
(b) its objects and purposes;
(c) any agreement between the parties regarding the interpretation of the treaty;
(d) any instrument made by one or more parties in connexion with the conclusion of the treaty and accepted by the other parties as an instrument related to the treaty;
(e) any subsequent practice in the application of the treaty which establishes the common understanding of the meaning of the terms as between the parties generally;
(f) the preparatory work of the treaty;

It should be evident from what has been described above that McDougal both exaggerated the emphasis that the draft articles placed on the text of a treaty and downplayed – or outright ignored – the fundamental similarities between the US proposal and the ILC's approach. Whilst the reasons for this mischaracterisation are unclear, McDougal's comments must be read in light of his main work on interpretation, *The Interpretation of Agreements and World Public Order*, which was co-authored with his Yale colleagues, Harold Lasswell and James Miller, and was published just one year before the Vienna Conference.[128] The conception of interpretation that McDougal and his associates (collectively referred to as the 'New Haven School') put forward in their book was in some ways surprisingly similar and in other ways starkly different from the doctrinal debates that had occurred in the *Institut* and the ILC. According to the New Haven School, the goal of interpretation was to give effect to the intentions (or 'shared expectations') of the parties, of which the text was but one indication.[129] However, where the New Haven School really diverged from other schools of interpretation was the normative limits it placed on interpretation. According to their approach, the intentions of the parties were only to be given effect insofar as they coincided with the 'accepted goal values and instrumental specifications of public order', such as respect for territorial boundaries, independence from external control and the prohibition of the use of force.[130] Whilst the authors considered that this did

(g)   the circumstances of its conclusion;
(h)   any relevant rules of international law applicable in the relations between the parties;
(i)   the special meaning to be given to a term if the parties intended such term to have a special meaning.

[128] M. McDougal et al., *The Interpretation of International Agreements and World Public Order: Principles of Content and Procedure* (reissue, Kluwer Academic Publishers 1994). See also, R. Falk, 'On Treaty Interpretation and the New Haven Approach: Achievements and Prospects', (1967–8) 8 Virginia JIL 323; G. Gottlieb, 'The Conceptual World of the Yale School of International Law', (1968) 21 World Politics 108.

[129] McDougal et al., *The Interpretation of International Agreements*, xviii.

[130] McDougal et al., *The Interpretation of International Agreements*, xxxvii. Indeed, whilst McDougal evidently considered the ILC orthodoxy to have adopted one particular interpretative methodology (textualism), exactly the inverse was also true. In an elegant review of McDougal's work, Gerald Fitzmaurice criticised *The Interpretation of Agreements and World Public Order* for, amongst other things, being 'written in a highly esoteric private language'. More substantively, Fitzmaurice argued that McDougal and his colleagues failed to successfully lay down the interpretative methodology that they professed to: 'one of the great paradoxes of this book [is] that, intended to place the "decision-maker" on a sort of conveyor belt which will lead him, as it were

no more than reflect the practice of international courts and tribunals,[131] critics considered that it would open the door to unbridled judicial activism.[132]

Despite the underlying similarities between the US and ILC proposals, McDougal's intervention provoked lively debate amongst the assembled delegations, providing many of them with the opportunity to explicitly assert their support for the ILC's 'crucible' approach. Whilst some were sympathetic to McDougal's reading of the draft articles,[133] the majority recognised that his characterisation of the ILC draft articles bore no resemblance to reality. This view was forcefully expressed by the delegate of the United Kingdom, Ian Sinclair, who argued that McDougal's speech seemed to be directed towards reviving the idea that a treaty could be interpreted independently of the text, a view that he declared was 'often asserted' (although without stating by whom).[134] In response to McDougal's charge of rigid textualism, Sinclair stated that it was inconceivable that the ILC had intended to adopt a literal approach to interpretation which advocated that the 'interpreters of treaties should arbitrarily select dictionary meaning when construing treaty texts'.[135] This understanding was shared by the majority of delegates at the conference, which commended the Commission for preparing articles that were 'flexible enough to become a most useful instrument of treaty interpretation'.[136] Indeed, such overwhelming support for the ILC's draft articles is hardly surprising considering that 14 members of the

---

painlessly, if not always to the right spot precisely, then to some haven very close to it, an exactly contrary impression of near disorientation is left on the mind of the reader'; G. Fitzmaurice, 'Vae Victis or Woe to the Negotiators! Your Treaty or Our "Interpretation" of It?', (1971) 65 AJIL 358, 360, 365.

[131] McDougal et al., *The Interpretation of International Agreements*, liv, fn 50.

[132] G. Fitzmaurice, 'Vae Victis or Woe to the Negotiators!', 372.

[133] See for example, UN Conference on the Law of Treaties, First Session (Summary records of plenary meetings and of the meetings of the Committee as a whole), UN Doc. A/CONF.39/C.1/SR.31, 168, para 54 (Ukrainian SSR); 174, para 32 (Spain); UN Conference on the Law of Treaties, First Session (Summary records of plenary meetings and of the meetings of the Committee as a whole), UN Doc. A/CONF.39/C.1/SR.33, 183, para 57 (Portugal).

[134] UN Conference on the Law of Treaties, First Session (Summary records of plenary meetings and of the meetings of the Committee as a whole), UN Doc. A/CONF.39/C.1/SR.33, 177, para 3 (UK).

[135] ibid., para 7 (UK).

[136] UN Conference on the Law of Treaties, First Session (Summary records of plenary meetings and of the meetings of the Committee as a whole), UN Doc. A/CONF.39/C.1/SR.33, 180, para 23 (Argentina); See also: ibid., 179, paras 19–20 (Sweden); ibid., 182, para 47 (Finland); ibid., 181, paras 35–6 (Nigeria); ibid., 182, para 43 (Cuba).

Commission were present at the Vienna Conference as representatives of their countries.[137]

The discussion of the rules of interpretation at the First Session of the Vienna Conference came to a close with an intervention by Sir Humphrey Waldock in his capacity as Expert Consultant to the Conference, who, like Sinclair, had McDougal's comments firmly in his sights. In his intervention, he aimed to lay to rest any misconception that the draft articles embodied a strict methodology. Along with other members of the ILC that were present at the Vienna Conference,[138] he rejected squarely McDougal's claim that the ILC had advocated a literal approach to interpretation, emphasising that 'nothing could have been further from the Commission's intention than to suggest that words had a "dictionary" or intrinsic meaning in themselves'.[139] He also took aim at the contention that the ILC's draft articles prioritised the text to the detriment of other indications of the parties' intentions, noting that any arrangement was based on matters of practical consideration rather than an hierarchical ordering.[140]

The First Session of the Conference closed with the resounding rejection of the US proposal by 66 votes to eight.[141] The ILC draft articles on

---

[137] Mortenson, 'The *Travaux* of *Travaux*', 809.

[138] See for example, the comments of Eduardo Jiménez de Aréchaga and José María Ruda; UN Conference on the Law of Treaties, First Session (Summary records of plenary meetings and of the meetings of the Committee as a whole), UN Doc. A/CONF.39/C.1/ SR.31, 170, para 66 (Uruguay); UN Conference on the Law of Treaties, First Session (Summary records of plenary meetings and of the meetings of the Committee as a whole), UN Doc. A/CONF.39/C.1/SR.33, 180, para 23 (Argentina).

[139] UN Conference on the Law of Treaties, First Session (Summary records of plenary meetings and of the meetings of the Committee as a whole), UN Doc. A/CONF.39/C.1/ SR.33, 184, para 70 (Waldock).

[140] ibid., 184, paras 72–3. Waldock noted that the only reason the elements enumerated in Articles 31 and 32 were distinct was because 'the two sets of elements were founded on slightly different legal bases'. The 'slightly different legal bases' to which Waldock referred were described in his commentaries to the draft articles: 'The elements of interpretation in article 27 [now Article 31 VCLT] all relate to the agreement between the parties *at the time when or after it received authentic expression in the text* ... the Commission was of the opinion that the distinction made in articles 27 and 28 [now Article 32 VCLT] between authentic and supplementary means of interpretation is both justified and desirable'; Draft Articles on the Law of Treaties with commentaries, (1966) II YBILC 220, para 10.

[141] UN Conference on the Law of Treaties, First Session (Summary records of plenary meetings and of the meetings of the Committee as a whole), UN Doc. A/CONF.39/C.1/ SR.33, 185, para 75.

interpretation were referred to the drafting committee by the Committee of the Whole with only stylistic amendments. The articles were subsequently adopted at the Second Session of the Vienna Conference, held in April and May 1969, with no further substantive discussion.[142]

Although often defining their positions in juxtaposition to those of their colleagues, those involved in the codification efforts took a remarkably similar view of interpretation, which recognised the highly context specific nature of the activity and the impossibility of determining *a priori* what constitutes an appropriate interpretation in any given context. As a result, the rules codified in the VCLT are permissive, non-hierarchical and eminently capable of being invoked in a wide range of different scenarios. What they do not do, however, is dictate to the interpreter how to interpret a text.

2.3   The Purpose of Codification

Given the non-determinative nature of the rules of interpretation, the purpose of codifying such a flexible, generally permissive approach to the interpretation of treaties might be questioned. During the debates that led up to the Vienna Conference, surprisingly few members of the ILC expressly addressed the purpose that they thought codified rules of interpretation would serve. Those that did broach the matter generally considered that codification would serve some practical purpose, such as facilitating the work of international courts and tribunals or foreign ministry officials, or promoting the uniform interpretation of treaties.[143] For his part, Waldock, in his Third Report, stated that the reasons for codification were four-fold: first, to ensure that States were held to their treaty obligations; secondly, to take a clear position in the on-going debate between 'textualists' and 'subjectivists'; thirdly, to elucidate a method of finding the intention of treaty parties, which is necessary for the application of other provisions of the VCLT; and, finally, to act as

---

[142] UN Conference on the Law of Treaties, Second session (Summary records of plenary meetings and of the meetings of the Committee as a whole), UN Doc. A/CONF.39/SR.13, 57–8, paras 66, 74. Article 31 was adopted by 97 votes to none; Article 32 was adopted by 101 votes to none.

[143] 870th Meeting of the ILC, (1966) I YBILC 186, para 17 (Rosenne) (stating that the Commission's purpose in including rules of interpretation in the draft articles was to 'facilitate the transaction of international business and to prevent transient difficulties from developing into international disputes'); 871st Meeting of the ILC, (1966) I YBILC 196, para 36 (Tsuruoka) (stating that the rules 'would certainly be of practical utility . . . [and] would also ensure uniform interpretation and application by the parties, and they might perhaps reduce the risk of disputes over the application and interpretation of treaties').

a practical guide to those drafting international treaties.[144] However, the fact that none of the members of the Commission proposed deletion of the articles on interpretation does seem to suggest that there was an implicit recognition that any comprehensive project on the law of treaties must necessarily include rules on interpretation.[145]

A similar situation obtained at the Vienna Conference. Whilst some delegates questioned the very idea of codifying the rules of interpretation,[146] the few delegations that did state why they thought the articles on interpretation had a place in the Vienna Convention asserted the practical benefits that codification was thought to bring.[147] The vast majority of delegates, however, seemed to simply assume that the rules on interpretation had their rightful place in the treaty.

More recently, it has been suggested that the motivation which lay behind codifying the VCLT rules was a rejection of '*bête noire*' of the ILC: the New Haven School's policy-oriented approach to interpretation.[148] According to this view, the inclusion of the rules of interpretation was intended to conclusively reject the idea that interpreters should be given free rein to effectuate to what they considered to be the treaty's underlying goals.[149]

The suggestion that the rules of interpretation were codified as response to the New Haven School's approach to interpretation is doubtful. As a practical matter, the *magnum opus* of the New Haven School, *The Interpretation of Agreements and World Public Order,* was published just one year before the Vienna Conference – too late to influence the debates in the ILC, where the bulk of the debates that shaped the VCLT provisions took place.[150] Furthermore, it is not clear that the VCLT

---

[144] 'Waldock Third Report', pp. 54–5, para 8.

[145] Cf F. Berman, 'Why do we Need a Law of Treaties?', (2016) 385 *Recueil des cours* 9, 25 (stating that rules on interpretation 'irresistibly claimed their place as necessary, come what may').

[146] UN Conference on the Law of Treaties, First Session (Summary records of plenary meetings and of the meetings of the Committee as a whole), UN Doc. A/CONF.39/C.1/ SR.31, 170, para 68 (Ghana); cf UN Conference on the Law of Treaties, First Session (Summary records of plenary meetings and of the meetings of the Committee as a whole), UN Doc. A/CONF.39/C.1/SR.32, 173, para 16 (Tanzania).

[147] UN Conference on the Law of Treaties, First Session (Summary records of plenary meetings and of the meetings of the Committee as a whole), UN Doc. A/CONF.39/C.1/ SR.33, 179, para 18 (Sweden); ibid., 179, para 21 (Argentina); ibid., 180, para 29 (Kenya).

[148] Mortenson, 'The *Travaux* of *Travaux*', 788.

[149] S. Rosenne, 'Interpretation of Treaties in the Restatement and the International Law Commission's Draft Articles: A Comparison', (1966) 5 Columbia J Transnational L 205, 221. See also Mortenson, 'The *Travaux* of *Travaux*', 790.

[150] Cf Gardiner, *Treaty Interpretation*, 65.

articles were in fact shaped in response to the New Haven School. Those that suggest the existence of a causal link believe that the ILC's treatment of the text as the presumptive object of interpretation signalled the clear rejection of the New Haven School's approach to interpretation.[151] However, the New Haven School did not claim that the text of the treaty could be completely cast aside in an unconstrained search for the intention of the parties. Instead, somewhat like the approach adopted by the ILC, the New Haven School recognised that the text served as the first, provisional indication of the parties' intentions (or, in its terminology, 'shared expectations'):

> The approach which seeks genuine shared expectations does not neglect the words of the purportedly final text, if any exists. It does, however, regard any initial version of their relation to shared expectation as provisional, and requires that the interpreter engage in a course of sustained testing and revision of preliminary inferences about the pertinent subjectivities. And of course this calls for scrutiny of the whole context of communication.[152]

To be sure, there was animosity between the two camps, especially between Myres McDougal and Sir Gerald Fitzmaurice.[153] However, it seems more likely that the ILC members and delegates at the Vienna Conference held their own ideas about why the rules of interpretation had a place in the Convention – whether for aesthetic, practical or principled reasons – if they reflected on the purpose of the articles at all.

2.4 The Thin Evaluative Dimension of the VCLT

This chapter has shown that throughout the codification projects of the *Institut*, the ILC and the Vienna Conference, there has been striking consistency with regard to interpretation. Despite sometimes professing to hold fundamentally different views, those guiding the projects (and, indeed, the majority of those involved) considered that the ordinary meaning of the text should be the starting point for interpretation, which could be displaced by evidence of the parties' intention to adopt a contrary meaning. At every stage of discussions, the successive projects permitted recourse to extraneous indications of the intentions of parties,

---

[151] Mortenson, 'The *Travaux* of *Travaux*', 820.
[152] McDougal et al., *The Interpretation of International Agreements*, xviii. Cf Waldock Third Report, p. 56, para 13.
[153] See the debate between McDougal and the ILC/Fitzmaurice in McDougal, 'Textuality Redividus'; Fitzmaurice, '*Vae Victis* or Woe to the Negotiators!'; and McDougal et al., *The Interpretation of International Agreements*, xl, xlvii–xlviii.

such as the preparatory work, for the purposes of verifying if the parties had in fact intended a provision to have a special meaning or to confirm the ordinary meaning of the text. As a result, throughout the codification process, the rules of interpretation accommodated a variety of textual, subjective and teleological factors, the relative importance of which was to be determined by the interpreter in light of the particular circumstances of the case at hand. To wit, the rules of interpretation in the Vienna Convention accommodate a variety of interpretative approaches, but do not dictate one particular method.

As suggested in Section 2.1, one might say that the Vienna rules possess an evaluative dimension in a broad sense of the term; that is, Articles 31 and 32 prescribe the materials that, if present, should be consulted by an interpreter, and circumscribe the ways in which the preparatory work of a treaty may be used by an interpreter. The ordinary meaning, context and object and purpose of a treaty must all be taken into account, as well as the other elements of the general rule, such as subsequent practice and relevant rules of international law, when present. In that respect, it could be said that the VCLT articles have a 'thin' evaluative dimension. But outside of these relatively broadly staked parameters, the Vienna Convention leaves it to the good judgment of the interpreter to determine which elements to place emphasis on in light of the circumstances of the case at hand and the context in which the interpretation occurs.

This has implications for how we think about interpretation. Considering whether an interpreter has acted in accordance with the VCLT provisions tells us something – but not very much – about the appropriateness of an interpretation. Neither the acceptance of teleological interpretation in the human rights context nor the adherence to a more literal form of interpretation by the WTO Appellate Body can be explained, understood or evaluated by reference to the VCLT. Instead, in order to evaluate whether an interpretation is appropriate in a given instance, we need to enquire further into the context in which the interpretation occurs and the values that underpin the particular legal regime.[154]

The 'thin' evaluative dimension of the VCLT provisions also has implications for the approach taken in the following chapters of this

---

[154] Cf Neil MacCormick, *Rhetoric and the Rule of Law* (OUP 2005) 1 ('the whole enterprise of explicating and expounding criteria and forms of good legal reasoning has to be in the context of the fundamental values that we impute to legal order').

book. As those chapters demonstrate, the use of domestic law is often motivated by – and is only comprehensible in relation to – certain factors that are extrinsic to the VCLT provisions, such as the presence of lacunae in the relevant legal regime or the character of the norm being interpreted. Whether these factors justify the use of domestic law, or impact on the methodology that should be adopted by courts and tribunals, must be examined against the backdrop of the particular legal regime. To simply rally the relevant practice under the rubric of the VCLT articles would only tell half the story.

3

Domestic Law in the Jurisprudence of the International Court of Justice

3.1 Introduction

Of the courts and tribunals surveyed in this book, those that deal with inter-state disputes have been most reticent to invoke domestic law to interpret international law. Some commentators have suggested that this may be due to a concern of bias towards the cited countries,[1] a remark that certainly seems to have weight and perhaps explains why the courts and tribunals examined in this and the following chapter have tightly circumscribed their reference to domestic law, generally limiting the cited law to the parties to the case at hand.

However, other factors would also seem to distinguish inter-state courts and tribunals from those examined in subsequent chapters. The most obvious of these is the weaker analogy between domestic law and international law related to inter-state affairs, insofar as the latter aims to regulate the actions of states, not individuals.[2] Whilst international criminal law, human rights law and international investment law arguably have clear parallels with domestic criminal law, constitutional law and public and administrative law, respectively, the rules regulating inter-state conduct have traditionally been analogised to

---

[1] 'Observations of Judge Philip Jessup', (1985) 61 [I] Annuaire de l'Institut de Droit international 252, 253. ('The Court [ICJ], qua Court, naturally hesitates to cite individuals or national courts lest it appear to have some bias or predilection.')

[2] Of course, that is not to say that inter-state disputes do not have an impact on individuals, or that individuals' rights or actions may constitute the very subject-matter of a dispute between states. See for example, *Ahmadou Sadio Diallo (Republic of Guinea v. DRC), Merits, Judgment,* (2010) ICJ Rep 639; *Avena and Other Mexican Nationals (Mexico v. US), Judgment,* (2004) ICJ Rep 12.

domestic private law, especially to the law of contracts and trusts,[3] and more recently to constitutional and public law.[4] Yet, there are evident limits to how far these analogies are applicable to inter-state relations.[5]

This chapter and the following chapter explore the use of domestic law by two inter-state courts and tribunals. This chapter examines the jurisprudence of the International Court of Justice (ICJ), whilst the following chapter analyses the case law of the panels and Appellate Body of the World Trade Organization (WTO). Although the cases examined vary significantly in terms of subject matter, certain common themes are identifiable. In particular, the relatively rare instances in which domestic law has been used raise questions regarding the circumstances in which domestic law may indicate the intention of a state.

The following section of this chapter examines three cases in which the ICJ drew on domestic law for interpretative purposes: *Anglo-Iranian Oil*,[6] *Aegean Sea Continental Shelf*[7] and *Fisheries Jurisdiction*.[8] The reasoning of the Court in these judgments raises issues regarding the extent to which the rules of interpretation applicable to declarations made under Article 36(2) of the Statute of the Court ('Optional Clause declarations') and reservations to multilateral treaties are akin, how and why such rules differ from the rules of

---

[3] See for example, H. Lauterpacht, *Private Law Sources and Analogies of International Law (With Special Reference to International Arbitration)* (Longmans, Green and Co. 1927), Chapter IV; *International Status of South-West Africa, Advisory Opinion,* Separate Opinion by Sir Arnold McNair, (1950) ICJ Rep 128, 147–50; *Case concerning Right of Passage over Indian Territory, Preliminary Objections,* Dissenting Opinion of Judge Chagla, (1957) ICJ Rep 125, 177–8; *Oil Platforms (Iran v. US), Judgment,* Separate Opinion of Judge Simma, (2003) ICJ Rep 324, paras 65–74. Cf H. Thirlway, 'Concepts, Principles, Rules and Analogies: International and Municipal Legal Reasoning', (2002) 294 Recueil des cours 265.

[4] See for example, A. von Bogdandy et al., 'From Public International to International Public Law: Translating World Public Opinion into International Public Authority', (2017) 28 EJIL 2017; J. Klabbers et al., *The Constitutionalization of International Law* (OUP 2009); T. M. Franck, 'Is the UN Charter a Constitution?' in J. A. Frowein et al., *Verhandeln für den Frienden/Negotiating for Peace* (Springer 2003); P. -M. Dupuy, 'The Constitutional Dimension of the Charter of the United Nations Revisited', (1997) 1 Max Planck YB UN Law 1. Cf N. Krisch, *Beyond Constitutionalism: The Pluralist Structure of Postnational Law* (OUP 2010).

[5] See for example, J. Weiler, 'The Geology of International Law – Governance, Democracy and Legitimacy', (2004) 64 ZaöRV 547, 550; M. Wood, '"Constitutionalization" of International Law: A Sceptical Voice', in K. H. Kaikobad & M. Bohlander (eds), *International Law and Power: Perspectives on Legal Order and Justice* (Martinus Nijhoff 2009).

[6] *Anglo-Iranian Oil Co. Case (UK v. Iran), Preliminary Objection,* (1952) ICJ Rep 93.

[7] *Aegean Sea Continental Shelf (Greece v. Turkey), Judgment,* (1978) ICJ Rep 3.

[8] *Fisheries Jurisdiction (Spain v. Canada), Jurisdiction,* (1998) ICJ Rep 432.

interpretation applicable to treaties, and the circumstances in which extraneous evidence of a state's intention, including domestic law, may be admissible. Although the Court has accepted that reference to domestic law is, in principle, permitted,[9] its invocation of such law is nevertheless open to certain criticism. The concluding section draws together common themes that are raised by the Court's use of domestic law.

3.2 Jurisprudence of the International Court

The World Court has come a long way since the PCIJ's famous pronouncement that '[f]rom the standpoint of International Law and of the Court which is its organ, municipal laws are merely facts which express the will and constitute the activities of States'.[10] Since then the Court has recognised domestic law not just to be relevant to the formation of international law,[11] but has also acknowledged that domestic law is sometimes a necessary component in the functioning of an international rule itself: the determination of nationality for the purposes of diplomatic protection or the definition of the rights of a shareholder are prime examples.[12] Nevertheless, it would be still correct to say that the Court has in general shown, and continues to show, little disposition to refer to the decisions of national courts or domestic legislation in its reasoning, even when cited by parties in pleadings.[13]

---

[9] See for example, *Anglo-Iranian Oil,* 107, and the judgments examined in section 3.3, below.

[10] *Case concerning Certain German Interests in Polish Upper Silesia, PCIJ Ser. A No. 7,* p. 19. Cf G. Gaja, 'Loi (national): un simple fait', in H. Ascencio et al. (eds), *Dictionnaire des idées reçues en droit international* (Pedone 2017) 370.

[11] See *Jurisdictional Immunities of the State (Germany v. Italy) (Merits) Judgment,* (2012) ICJ Rep 99, paras 70–7, 85, 96, 118; *Arrest Warrant of 11 April 2000 (DRC v. Belgium), Judgment,* (2002) ICJ Rep 3, para 58. For an earlier example, see *The Case of the SS 'Lotus',* PCIJ Ser. A No. 10, pp. 28–30. More generally, see I. B. Wuerth, 'Sources of International Law in Domestic Law', in J. d'Aspremont & S. Besson (eds), *The Oxford Handbook of the Sources of International Law* (OUP 2017) 1127–9; A. Roberts, 'Comparative International Law? The Role of National Courts in Creating and Enforcing International Law', (2011) 60 ICLQ 57, 62; P. Moremen, 'National Court Decisions as State Practice: A Transjudicial Dialogue?', (2006) 32 North Carolina JIL & Commercial Regulation 259.

[12] *Ahmadou Sadio Diallo (Republic of Guinea v. DRC), Judgment,* (2010) ICJ Rep 639, para 104; *Barcelona Traction, Light and Power Company, Limited, Judgment,* (1970) ICJ Rep 3, para 38. See also, *Pulp Mills on the River Uruguay (Argentina v. Uruguay), Judgment,* (2010) ICJ Rep 14, para 205 (stating that 'it is for each State to determine in its domestic legislation . . . the specific content of the environmental impact assessment required in each case').

[13] Cf M. O. Hudson, *The Permanent Court of International Justice, 1920–1942* (Macmillan 1943) 614.

This section examines three instances in which the Court has employed domestic law in its interpretative reasoning, each separated by an interval of about 20 years. Two other cases that are not examined in depth in this chapter are, however, worth noting briefly.

The first of these is *Frontier Dispute (Burkina Faso/Niger)*, in which the Court drew on a French colonial administrative order (the '*Arrêté*') to determine the land boundary between the two parties in accordance with the principle of *uti possidetis juris*.[14] The *compromis* in that case referred to a prior agreement between the parties (the '1987 Agreement') which stated that the *arrêté* determined the land boundary in the relevant area.[15] In this respect, the *Burkina Faso/Niger* case differed from other cases in which the Court has drawn on colonial law in that the relevant boundary treaty explicitly identified the *arrêté* as the applicable law.[16] Even if the *arrêté* were to be considered as a domestic law,[17] the judgment is best characterised as an *application* of the administrative law of the colonial power, as mandated by the 1987 Agreement, rather than the use of such law to *interpret* that Agreement.

The second case that bears mention is the Court's judgment in *Jurisdictional Immunities*. In that case, the Court was called upon to interpret Article 31 of the European Convention on State Immunity, which excludes from the scope of the Convention 'anything done or omitted to be done by, or in relation to, its armed forces'.[18] The question of interpretation arose in the context of Italy's argument that states are not entitled to immunity in respect of acts committed abroad by their armed forces in times of armed conflict.[19] This was relevant because Article 11 of the European Convention enshrined the 'territorial tort exception' to state immunity, according to which:

---

[14] *Frontier Dispute (Burkina Faso/Niger), Judgment,* (2013) ICJ Rep 44, paras 64–7, 70 et seq.

[15] *Frontier Dispute (Burkina Faso/Niger),* para 2.

[16] Cf *Frontier Dispute (Benin/Niger), Judgment,* (2005) ICJ Rep 90 and *Frontier Dispute (Burkina Faso/Mali), Judgment,* (1986) ICJ Rep 554, in which there were no treaty that defined the applicable law to determine the boundary, in the same vein as the 1987 Agreement.

[17] See for example, the following, which define *arrêté* as a unilateral administrative act; R. Cabrillac (ed), *Dictionnaire du vocabulaire juridique 2014* (5th edn, LexisNexis 2013) 40 (defining *arrêté* as an 'acte unilatéral émanant d'une ou plusieurs autorités administratives'); S. Guinchard (ed), *Lexique des termes juridiques* (20th edn, Dalloz 2012) 71 (defining *arrêté* as an 'acte exécutoire à portée générale ou individuelle émanant d'un ou de plusieurs ministres ... ou d'autres autorités administratives').

[18] European Convention on State Immunity 1972, 16 May 1972, 1495 UNTS 182, Article 31.

[19] *Jurisdictional Immunities,* para 66.

> A Contracting State cannot claim immunity from the jurisdiction of
> a court of another Contracting State in proceedings which relate to redress
> for injury to the person or damage to tangible property, if the facts which
> occasioned the injury or damage occurred in the territory of the State of
> the forum, and if the author of the injury or damage was present in that
> territory at the time when those facts occurred.

It was in this context that the Court referred to judgments of the Belgian, Irish, Slovenian, Greek and Polish courts (which had all held that Article 11 does not affect the immunity of armed forces under Article 31) as support for its conclusion that, despite the inclusion of Article 11, 'Article 31 means that the immunity of a State for torts committed by its armed forces is unaffected'.[20]

It would be difficult to argue that the domestic judgments cited in *Jurisdictional Immunities* constituted 'subsequent practice' within the meaning of Article 31(3)(b) VCLT, as only one of the cited states is actually party to the Convention (Belgium).[21] However, it would be equally problematic to accept, as has been suggested, that the Court in effect used the domestic judicial decisions as a subsidiary source of law within the meaning of Article 38(1)(d) of the Court's Statute. The Court did not invoke domestic law as a means for the 'determination of rules of law', as subsidiary means of law are defined within Article 38(1)(d), but instead as support for a particular interpretation of the European Convention. The Court's invocation of domestic law in this case would therefore seem to fall outside of both the Statute of the Court and the provisions of the Vienna Convention, and is more akin to domestic courts' invocation of foreign law as non-binding, persuasive support for a particular proposition.[22]

In addition to these instances of the use of domestic law, the Court has invoked domestic law on three occasions to interpret unilaterally drafted legal instruments: twice to interpret declarations made under Article

---

[20] *Jurisdictional Immunities,* para 68.

[21] H. Thirlway, *The Sources of International Law* (OUP 2014) 126. It could be argued that the Court used the domestic laws as confirmation of its interpretation within the meaning of Article 32 of the Vienna Convention, which provides a non-exhaustive list of supplementary materials to which an interpreter may have recourse. However, it is notable that the Court did not justify its recourse to domestic law in such a manner.

[22] Cf M. Gelter & M. Siems, 'Citations to Foreign Courts – Illegitimate and Superfluous, or Unavoidable? Evidence from Europe', (2014) 62 American Journal of Comparative Law 35, 82 (stating that domestic courts cite foreign law 'to strengthen the authority of the court in the legal community by showing how well the opinion is researched, and thus to guard the court against criticism').

36(2) of the Court's Statute and once to interpret a reservation to a multilateral treaty.

3.2.1   Anglo-Iranian Oil

The first of these is the judgment in *Anglo-Iranian Oil*, rendered in 1952, in which the Court was called on to interpret a limitation *ratione temporis* to Iran's Optional Clause declaration. The Declaration, which was ratified on 19 September 1932, provided that Iran's consent to the jurisdiction of the Court applied to disputes 'arising after the ratification of the present declaration with regard to situations or facts relating directly or indirectly to the application of treaties or conventions accepted by Persia and subsequent to the ratification of this declaration'.[23] This phrase is syntactically ambiguous: the final limb of the sentence ('subsequent to the ratification of this declaration') could relate either to the words directly preceding it ('treaties or conventions accepted by Persia') or to the words at the start of the phrase ('situations or facts').

The Applicant in the case, the UK, contended that the latter was the correct interpretation and that the scope of the Court's jurisdiction was not therefore limited to treaties and conventions concluded after ratification of Iran's Declaration. Iran, on the other hand, argued that the jurisdiction of the Court was limited to the application of treaties accepted after ratification of the Declaration, noting that the temporal limitation followed directly after the expression 'treaties or conventions accepted by Persia'.[24] This question of interpretation was of importance to the case at hand because the UK's Application related to the nationalisation of the Anglo-Iranian Oil Company's assets in 1951 and Iran's

---

[23] *Anglo-Iranian Oil*, 103. Iran's Declaration was made under Article 36 of the Statute of the PCIJ, but was effective in relation to the ICJ by virtue of Article 36(5) of the latter's Statute, which provides that 'Declarations made under Article 36 of the Statute of the Permanent Court of International Justice and which are still in force shall be deemed, as between the parties to the present Statute, to be acceptances of the compulsory jurisdiction of the International Court of Justice for the period which they still have to run and in accordance with their terms.' See generally, M. Fartache, 'De la competence de la Cour Internationale de Justice dans l'affaire de l'Anglo-Iranien Oil Co.', (1953) 57 RGDIP 584; S. Pahuja & C. Storr, 'Rethinking Iran and International Law: The Anglo-Iranian Oil Company Case Revisited', in J. Crawford et al. (eds), *The International Legal Order: Current Needs and Possible Responses* (Brill 2017). For a factual background to the case, see F. P. Feliciano, 'The Anglo-Iranian Oil Dispute', (1951) 26 Philippine LJ 55.

[24] *Anglo-Iranian Oil*, 104.

subsequent refusal to arbitrate, acts which the UK claimed breached numerous treaties concluded between 1857 and 1928.[25]

The Court adopted an approach to interpretation that is in some ways strikingly similar to that which was subsequently enshrined in Articles 31 and 32 of the Vienna Convention. It rejected a purely textual interpretation,[26] stating that 'it must seek the interpretation which is in harmony with a natural and reasonable way of reading the text, having due regard to the intention of the Government of Iran at the time when it accepted the compulsory jurisdiction of the Court'.[27] A 'natural and reasonable' way of reading the text suggested that Iran's interpretation was to be preferred.

However, it was the circumstances in which Iran's Declaration was signed and ratified that played a larger role in the Court's reasoning and sounded the death knell for the British argument. The Court noted that Iran, on 10 May 1927 (i.e. approximately five years before the Iranian Declaration was ratified), denounced all treaties related to the capitulatory regime and had subsequently started treaty renegotiations with certain states.[28] In the view of the Court, it was thus 'reasonable to assume' that Iran must have intended to exclude disputes related to the capitulatory regime from the compulsory jurisdiction of the Court, and that it was this consideration that had motivated the limitation *rationae temporis* to Iran's Declaration. As a result, the Court accepted Iran's proposed interpretation as faithfully corresponding to the 'manifest intention of the Government of Iran [which] has found an adequate expression in the text of the Declaration as interpreted by the Court'.[29]

As confirmation of this intention, the Court invoked the Iranian law of 14 June 1931 which approved the Optional Clause Declaration. That law recounted the text of Article 36 of the Court's Statute and described the conditions that Iran had placed on its accession to the Optional Clause, including the limitation of the Court's jurisdiction to:

> all disputes arising out of situations or facts relating, directly or indirectly, to the execution of treaties and conventions which the Government will have accepted after the ratification of the Declaration.[30]

---

[25] *Anglo-Iranian Oil*, Application, paras 14–17.

[26] The Court stated that it cannot 'base itself on a purely grammatical interpretation of the text'; *Anglo-Iranian Oil*, 104. The Court nevertheless suggested that a textual interpretation would lean in Iran's favour.

[27] ibid.

[28] ibid., 105.

[29] ibid., 106.

[30] ibid.

It was particularly probative that the Iranian law recounted the condition that Iran had attached to its Declaration in slightly different, less ambiguous language to that which was actually adopted in the reservation to the Optional Clause. For the Court, this provided 'decisive confirmation' that the Iranian Government had intended to exclude the Court's jurisdiction for disputes related to conventions ratified prior to the ratification of its Declaration.[31]

Although acting only as confirmation, the invocation of Iran's domestic law was clearly a matter that divided the Court. The UK had claimed that the Iranian law should not be considered as admissible evidence of Iran's intention as it was a 'private document written only in the Persian language which was not communicated either to the League [of Nations] or to any of the other States which had made declarations'.[32] However, the majority of the Court took a different view:

> The Court is unable to see why it should be prevented from taking this piece of evidence into consideration. The law was published in the Corpus of Iranian laws voted and ratified during the period from January 15th, 1931, to January 15th, 1933. It has thus been available for the examination of other governments during a period of about twenty years. The law is not, and could not be, relied on as affording a basis for the jurisdiction of the Court. It was filed for the sole purpose of throwing light on a disputed question of fact, namely, the intention of the Government of Iran at the time when it signed the Declaration.[33]

Certain members of the Court were, however, more sympathetic to the British argument. President McNair declared that he 'should have preferred that it [the Iranian Law] should be excluded from the consideration of the Court ... [i]ts admissibility in evidence is open to question, and its evidentiary value slight'.[34] Judge Hackworth was more emphatic in his criticism of the Court's reference to the Iranian law, stating that 'it was not necessary or even permissible for the Court to rely upon Iranian Parliamentary Act of approval as evidence of the intention of the Iranian Government, since that was a unilateral act of a legislative body of which other nations had not been apprised'.[35] His principal concern was that the Court's approach may undermine the reliance that states justifiably put on the declarations of other states on the international level:

---

[31] ibid., 107.
[32] *Anglo-Iranian Oil, Oral Proceedings Concerning the Preliminary Objection*, 530 (Heald).
[33] *Anglo-Iranian Oil*, 107.
[34] *Anglo-Iranian Oil*, Separate Opinion of President McNair, 121.
[35] *Anglo-Iranian Oil*, Dissenting Opinion of Judge Hackworth, 137–8.

When a State deposits with an international organ a document, such as a declaration accepting compulsory jurisdiction of the Court, upon which other States are expected to rely, those States are entitled to accept that document at face value; they are not required to go back to the municipal law of that State for explanations of the meaning or significance of the international instrument. Such a procedure in many cases would lead to utter confusion. This is not a case of drawing upon the *travaux préparatoires* of a bilateral or multilateral agreement to explain ambiguities. Had the Act of Parliament been attached to the instrument of ratification filed by Iran with the League of Nations, a different situation would have been presented. Other States would thus have been on notice of the discrepancy between the Declaration and the act of approval. But this was not done.[36]

The Court's reasoning in *Anglo-Iranian Oil* is notable in several respects. First, domestic law played a subsidiary role in the reasoning of the Court, acting as confirmation of an interpretation that the Court made on other grounds. Whilst the Court considered the Iranian law to indicate the declaring state's intent, it considered other manifestations to be more probative, namely, the text of the Declaration and the circumstances in which it was drafted and submitted. Second, the disagreement that divided the Court rested on competing views regarding whether the intention of the declarant state or legal certainty should be privileged when interpreting the Declaration. Those that argued in favour of reference to the Iranian law took the view that it was probative evidence of Iran's intention at the time of ratification of the Declaration, whereas those against highlighted the instability that could be caused by attributing importance to an act that was neither notified to other states nor widely available in languages other than Persian. As we will see later in this chapter, similar concerns have been echoed when the Court has referred to domestic law in subsequent cases.

The latter issue raises a broader question regarding the extent to which the interpretation of Optional Clause declarations can be analogised to treaty interpretation, and how and why the rules of interpretation applicable to the two classes of legal instrument might differ.[37] Of particular

---

[36] ibid., 137.

[37] See for example, M. Shaw, *Rosenne's Law and Practice of the International Court: 1920–2015*, vol II (5th edn, Brill 2016) §209; G. Törbar, *The Contractual Nature of the Optional Clause* (Hart 2015) 125–63; R. Kolb, *The International Court of Justice* (Hart 2013) 456, 488–9; C. Tomuschat, 'Article 36', in A. Zimmerman et al. (eds), *The Statute of the International Court of Justice: A Commentary* (2nd edn, OUP 2012) 678; S. A. Alexandrov, 'Accepting the Compulsory Jurisdiction of the International Court of Justice with Reservations: An Overview of Practice with a Focus on Recent Trends and

relevance in this context is the rejection by the Court of the UK's argument that Optional Clause declarations should be interpreted as if they were treaties, as, once deposited, they create 'relations with other States'.[38] According to the UK, the contractual character of Optional Clause declarations meant that Iran's interpretation of its Declaration should be rejected because it would render certain words redundant – an argument that was based on the principle of treaty interpretation of *effet utile*.[39] The Court emphasised that, whilst *effet utile* might be relevant for the purposes of treaty interpretation, Iran's Declaration was 'not a treaty text resulting from negotiations between two or more States. It is the result of unilateral drafting by the Government of Iran, which appears to have shown a particular degree of caution when drafting the text of the Declaration'.[40] Whilst the first phrase of this quote might suggest that the Court considered the unilateral manner in which the legal obligation was created to be the factor that distinguishes Optional Clause declarations from treaties, the wording of the second sentence suggests that the Court actually considered the unilateral nature of the Declaration's drafting to be the more important element.[41] This point was made by Gerald Fitzmaurice, who, writing shortly after the judgment was rendered, suggested that the defining characteristic of certain kinds of declarations, like those made under Article 36(2) of the Court's Statute, is that they are unilateral in form (in that they are unilaterally drafted), but are

---

Cases', (2001) 14 LJIL 89, 94; M. Fitzmaurice, 'The Optional Clause System and the Law of Treaties', (1999) 20 Australian YBIL 127; *Anglo-Iranian Oil*, Dissenting Opinion of Judge Read, 142.

[38] Indeed, this was the view advanced by the UK in oral pleadings; *Oral Pleadings concerning the Preliminary Objection*, 528 (Heald). ('In fact, such declarations have a double character. Their drafting is unilateral. They are not an agreed text, and one is therefore justified in applying to them the *contra proferentem* rule. But once deposited they create relations with other States; accordingly, they must be interpreted upon the principles applicable to treaties.')

[39] The argument of the UK was that '[i]f the construction now suggested by Iran, namely, taking "*postérieurs*" as governing "*traités ou conventions*", is correct, the words "*qui s'élèveraient après la ratification de la présente déclaration*" are completely otiose'; Observations of the Government of the United Kingdom with regard to Jurisdiction of the Court to Deal with the Merits of the Case, para 35.

[40] *Anglo-Iranian Oil*, 105.

[41] G. Fitzmaurice, 'The Law and Procedure of the International Court of Justice 1951–4: Treaty Interpretation and Other Treaty Points', (1957) 33 BYIL 203, 230–1. See also, G. Fitzmaurice, 'The Law and Procedure of the International Court of Justice 1951–4: Questions of Jurisdiction, Competence and Procedure', (1958) 34 BYIL 1, 75–7. ('These declarations are not treaties, but they give rise to a quasi-treaty situation by creating a network of bilateral relationships between the various declarants'; ibid., 75.)

contractual in substance (in that they are dependent on the declarations of other states to establish the scope of the Court's jurisdiction).[42] Due to the interdependent nature of such declarations – forming part of a '*quid pro quo*' between states – he considered that the rules of treaty interpretation were to be applied, albeit with certain allowance made for 'the unilateral character of the Declaration in point of *form*, and more particularly the manner of its drafting'.[43]

3.2.2   Aegean Sea Continental Shelf

Some similarities can be found in the second judgment in which the Court drew on domestic law to interpret a legal instrument, the *Aegean Sea Continental Shelf* case, handed down in 1978. In that case, the Applicant, Greece, claimed that the Court had jurisdiction over a dispute with Turkey on the basis of Article 17 of the General Act for the Pacific Settlement of International Disputes of 1928, a compromissory clause that gave the Court jurisdiction over disputes between parties to the Act.[44] One of the central issues that the Court had to address related to the applicability of one of Greece's reservations to the General Act, which was invoked by Turkey in an earlier phase of proceedings.[45] The reservation at issue

---

[42] Fitzmaurice, 'The Law and Procedure of the ICJ: Treaty Interpretation', 230–1.

[43] ibid., 231. Cf Fitzmaurice, 'The Law and Procedure of the ICJ: Questions of Jurisdiction', 77 ('the Court, while in general applying ordinary principles of treaty interpretation, seems to have felt that voluntary and unilateral character of these declarations put them in a special position, in which it was necessary to have particular regard to the known, apparent or probable intentions of the State making the declaration'; *Anglo-Iranian Oil*, Dissenting Opinion of Judge Read, 142. ('I am unable to accept the contention that the principles of international law which govern the interpretation of treaties cannot be applied to the Persian Declaration, because it is unilateral. Admittedly it was drafted unilaterally. On the other hand, it was related, in express terms, to Article 36 of the Statute, and the declarations of other States which had already deposited, or which might in the future deposit, reciprocal declarations.')

[44] 93 LNTS 343. Article 17 of the General Act provided that 'disputes ... shall ... be submitted to the Permanent Court of International Justice'. By virtue of Article 37 of the Statute of the ICJ, treaties or conventions with compromissory clauses that provided the PCIJ with jurisdiction are applicable to the ICJ: '[w]henever a treaty or convention in force provides for reference of a matter to ... the Permanent Court of International Justice, the matter shall, as between the parties to the present Statute, be referred to the International Court of Justice'.

[45] *Aegean Sea Continental Shelf,* paras 43–7. NB Turkey did not file a preliminary objection nor did it take part in the oral proceedings. The only action of Turkey in response to Greece's Application was at the provisional measures phase, where, after being informed by the Registrar of its right to make observations on Greece's Request for the Indication of Provisional Measures, it submitted a document entitled 'Observations of the Government

excluded from the scope of the General Act 'disputes concerning questions which by international law are solely within the domestic jurisdiction of States, and in particular disputes relating to the territorial status of Greece, including disputes relating to its rights of sovereignty over its ports and lines of communication'.[46] This was relevant to the case at hand because Greece's Application related to the purported infringement by Turkey of continental shelf entitlements of certain Greek islands opposite the Turkish coast.

Greece argued that the two limbs of its reservation to the General Act – disputes 'solely within the domestic jurisdiction' and disputes 'relating to the territorial status' of Greece – should not be understood as two separate categories of dispute in respect of which it excluded the Court's jurisdiction.[47] Drawing on examples from several French dictionaries, Greece contended that the use of the phrase 'in particular' – '*et notamment*' in the original French version of the reservation – demonstrated that reference to 'disputes relating to the territorial status of Greece' was merely an illustrative example of disputes that were solely within its domestic jurisdiction of Greece.[48]

This argument was unlikely to succeed. The Court noted that Greece's grammatical argument would lead to 'a result which is legally somewhat surprising' by assimilating two categories of disputes which related to distinct legal concepts that were normally treated as such in both treaties and Optional Clause declarations.[49] Furthermore, if one were to read the two categories as being combined, one of those categories (disputes relating to the territorial status of Greece) would be completely deprived of effect.[50]

Whilst the Court outlined some grammatical arguments that undermined Greece's proposed interpretation,[51] the bulk of its reasoning related to what it termed 'a number of considerations of a substantive character' which demonstrated that the two categories mentioned in Greece's reservation to the General Act were intended to refer to two separate and autonomous classes of dispute.[52] Three considerations were

---

of Turkey on the request by the Government of Greece for provisional measures of protection dated The Hague, 10 August 1976'. It was in this document that Turkey raised the issue of Greece's reservation to the General Act; ibid., para 14.

[46] ibid., para 48.
[47] ibid., para 49.
[48] ibid., para 51.
[49] ibid., para 52.
[50] ibid., para 52.
[51] ibid., paras 53–4.
[52] ibid., para 55.

given particular importance in the reasoning of the Court: first, the enumeration of certain permissible reservations in the General Act; secondly, the existence of a similarly worded reservation to Greece's Optional Clause Declaration; and, thirdly, legislative documents that accompanied Greece's domestic ratification of the General Act.

In relation to the first of these considerations, Article 39(2) of the General Act, which specified the permissible reservations to the convention, listed the two categories of dispute separately.[53] This resulted in 'clearly a high probability, if not an actual presumption' that states would define the categories in their reservations in the same terms.[54] Second, the Court noted that Greece had appended a reservation to its declaration recognising the compulsory jurisdiction of the Court, according to which it excluded the Court's jurisdiction for 'disputes related to the territorial status of Greece'. The circumstances of conclusion of that reservation suggested that Greece's main preoccupation was to exclude a potential claim by Bulgaria for revision of the territorial settlement enacted by the Treaty of Neuilly of 1919 from the Court's jurisdiction.[55] Any dispute that could arise out of an attempt by Bulgaria to revisit the territorial settlements made following the First World War was, according to the Court, by its very nature, not 'legally capable of falling within the concept of questions of domestic jurisdiction'.[56] As this was the preoccupation that had motivated the reservation to Greece's Optional Clause declaration, which it submitted in 1929, the Court reasoned that similar motivations underpinned the reservation to Greece's accession to the General Act in 1931.[57] This being the case, the Court noted that it would defeat the very purpose of the Greek reservation if it were to be read as Greece suggested, insofar as any potential territorial dispute with Bulgaria would not be excluded from the scope of the General Act:

---

[53] Article 39(2) of the General Act 'exhaustively enumerated' the permitted reservations to the General Act, specifying '[d]isputes concerning questions which by international law are solely within the domestic jurisdiction of States' and '[d]isputes concerning particular cases or clearly specified subject-matters, such as territorial status . . . ' under subparagraphs (b) and (c), respectively.

[54] *Aegean Sea Continental Shelf*, para 55.

[55] By virtue of Article 42 of the Treaty of Peace between the Allied and Associated Powers and Bulgaria, signed at Neuilly-sur-Seine on 27 November 1919, Bulgaria renounced all title and rights to Thrace; (1920) 5 UK Treaty Series 81.

[56] *Aegean Sea Continental Shelf*, para 60.

[57] ibid., para 57.

by integrating its territorial status reservation into its reservation of questions of domestic jurisdiction, Greece would automatically deprived itself of the protection which the former reservation would otherwise have given it against attempts to use the General Act as a means of effecting a revision of the territorial settlement established by the Peace Treaties.[58]

For our purposes, the third 'substantive consideration' examined by the Court is the most interesting. In response to a request by the Court, Greece submitted various documents related to its accession to the General Act,[59] including a first draft of its domestic law ratifying accession to the Act and the accompanying explanatory notes (*exposé des motifs*). What put Greece's intention to make an autonomous reservation in relation to territorial disputes 'beyond doubt' was the Court's examination of the *exposé des motifs*, which stated that the reservation attached to Greece's instrument of accession replicated 'one of the two reservations which we [i.e. Greece] formulated when we accepted the compulsory jurisdiction of the Permanent Court'.[60] As acknowledged by the Agent of Greece in oral proceedings, this could only have referred to Greece's exclusion of territorial disputes from the Court's compulsory jurisdiction.[61]

As the domestic law that approved accession to the General Act was passed without change, the Court concluded that:

> when the Chambre des députés authorized the deposit of Greece's instrument of accession to the General Act, it could only have believed that Greece was making its accession subject to precisely the same reservation of disputes relating to its territorial status as the Chambre had previously authorized for its declaration under the optional clause.[62]

Thus, in the view of the Court, the Greek domestic law approving accession to the General Act and, more importantly, the *travaux préparatoires* of that law confirmed that the two categories specified in the Greek reservation were to be read separately.

---

[58] ibid., para 60. The Court also placed importance on a letter from Nicolas Politis, who was, at the time, the Rapporteur for the drafting of the General Act, to the Greek Foreign Minister, in which he recommended that Greece make several reservations to the Act, including in relation to territorial disputes, on the basis of 'an eventual application of Bulgaria on matters related to our territorial status'; ibid., para 62.

[59] *Aegean Sea Continental Shelf,* ICJ Pleadings 296.

[60] *Aegean Sea Continental Shelf,* para 66.

[61] ibid.

[62] ibid., para 67.

Unlike *Anglo-Iranian Oil*, the reference to the Greek law did not attract any dissent or criticism from individual judges. One factor that might explain this is that the interpretation of the reservation advanced by Greece was relatively straightforward to dismiss, unlike the syntactically ambiguous sentence at issue in *Anglo-Iranian Oil*. Indeed, it seems quite impossible to have a territorial dispute between states that is solely within the domestic jurisdiction of one state, as Greece contended. Perhaps the members of the Court therefore considered that the Greek domestic law was not as central to the reasoning of the Court as the Iranian law was in *Anglo-Iranian Oil*, and thus did not merit dissent.

However, the more important distinction between the two cases is the object of interpretation in each: in *Anglo-Iranian Oil*, a limitation *ratione temporis* in Iran's Optional Clause declaration was at issue, whilst in *Aegean Sea Continental Shelf*, the Court was called on to interpret a reservation to a multilateral treaty. The two instruments are to a certain extent similar in that both the Declaration and the Reservation were the products of a unilateral drafting process by one state. In this context, it is notable that the Court cited without qualification or explanation its judgment in *Anglo-Iranian Oil* as authority for the proposition that it could not adopt the grammatical interpretation that Greece advocated.[63]

However, whilst the unilateral drafting of the two instruments might be similar, the manner in which they acquire legal validity and the extent to which they have legal effect are different. Optional Clause declarations rely on a pre-existing conventional framework (i.e. the Statute of the Court) to have legal validity, but are ultimately put into force, modified, and revoked at the behest of one state.[64] Reservations, on the other hand, are only given full effect if they are not opposed by other states parties to the treaty.[65] In this respect, reservations depend on other states to

---

[63] ibid., para 55 (citing *Anglo-Iranian Oil*, para 55).

[64] Cf 'First Report on the Unilateral Acts of States, by Mr. Víctor Rodríguez Cedeño, Special Rapporteur', (1998) II [2] YBILC 332, paras 115–17 ('These declarations, although they take the form of unilateral acts, give rise to a treaty relationship. The declaration provided for in Article 36, paragraph 2, of the ICJ Statute produces effects only if a corresponding act has been performed ... [The] ICJ has concluded that such declarations are unilateral acts.') (hereinafter 'Cedeño First Report'). See also, 'First Report on the Law of Treaties by Mr H. Lauterpacht, Special Rapporteur', (1953) II YBILC 101, para 2. ('For it is clear that the totality of the declarations under Article 36 of the Statute of the Court constitutes a treaty as between the parties making the declaration. They have been so interpreted by the International Court of Justice.')

[65] Articles 20–1 VCLT, especially Article 20(4): 'In cases not falling under the preceding paragraphs and unless the treaty otherwise provides: (a) acceptance by another contracting State of a reservation constitutes the reserving State a party to the treaty in relation to

determine the extent of their legal effect, if any. Reference to domestic law to interpret a treaty reservation therefore presupposes that the other states parties to the convention have examined, or at least have had the opportunity to examine, the relevant domestic law at the time they were notified of the reservation, and thus that their objection to the reservation – or lack thereof – is based on knowledge, whether actual or constructive, of the domestic law ratifying the relevant treaty.[66] The bilateral or multilateral basis of the legal effect of reservations might lead to the conclusion that courts should be more cautious in referring to extraneous evidence of the state's intention, including relevant domestic laws, to interpret treaty reservations as opposed to Optional Clause declarations. In this regard, *Aegean Sea Continental Shelf* was an exceptional case

that other State if or when the treaty is in force for those States; (b) an objection by another contracting State to a reservation does not preclude the entry into force of the treaty as between the objecting and reserving States unless a contrary intention is definitely expressed by the objecting State; (c) an act expressing a State's consent to be bound by the treaty and containing a reservation is effective as soon as at least one other contracting State has accepted the reservation.' See also, I. Sinclair, *The Vienna Convention on the Law of Treaties* (2nd edn, Manchester UP 1984) 51 ('A reservation is a declaration which is external to the text of a treaty. It is unilateral at the time of its formulation; but it produces no legal effects unless it is accepted, in one way or another, by another State.'); 'Third Report on reservations to treaties, by Mr Alain Pellet, Special Rapporteur', (1998) II [1] YBILC 245, paras 120–1.

[66] Note that the issue of the knowledge of other states of extraneous evidence of the intention of the declaring or reserving state was raised in the ILC in relation to the interpretation of unilateral acts, but was reflected neither in the final commentaries to the ILC Guiding Principles Application to the Unilateral Declarations of States capable of creating legal obligations nor in the ILC Guide to Practice on Reservations of Treaties. See for example, 2695th Meeting of the ILC, (2001) I YBILC 187, para 6 (Pellet) ('In the case of treaties it was difficult to judge the exact role of preparatory work in the interpretation and the impossibility of access to some such work often meant that in practice it had to be disregarded. That was even more true with regard to unilateral acts, not only because the preparatory work did not always exist, or was not accessible, but also and chiefly because when it was accessible it was unequally accessible'); 187–8, paras 13–16 (Gaja) ('When other States were entitled to rely on unilateral acts, it would seem logical to limit the relevance of preparatory work to materials that were reasonably accessible to the other States, as Mr. Pellet had suggested'); 'Fourth Report on the unilateral acts of States, by Mr Víctor Rodríguez Cedeño, Special Rapporteur', (2001) II [1] YBILC 134, para 147 ('Preparatory work in the context of unilateral acts may take the form of the notes and internal memorandums of ministries for foreign affairs or other organs of State, which will not always be easy to obtain and whose value will not be easy to determine.') (hereinafter 'Cedeño Fourth Report'); 'Guiding Principles application to unilateral declarations of States capable of creating legal obligations, with commentaries thereto', (2006) II [2] YBILC 377–8; ILC, 'Guide to Practice on Reservations to Treaties', Report of the ILC, Sixty-third Session, 26 April–3 June and 4 July–12 August 2011, UN Doc. A/66/10/Add.1, 467–72.

insofar as the treaty reservation at issue closely mirrored a reservation to Greece's Optional Clause declaration and both were clearly motivated by a certain set of circumstances related to a potential claim by Bulgaria. Nevertheless, the question remains whether the legal character of Optional Clause declarations and treaty reservations affect the arguments in favour of use of domestic law in interpretation. This will be revisited in the following section.

One final difference is worth noting. In *Aegean Sea Continental Shelf*, the Court went further than it had done in *Anglo-Iranian Oil* by referring not just to the domestic law authorising accession to the General Act, but also to the statement of reasons that accompanied that law, putting more weight on the latter. This is significant because the explanatory notes accompanying a piece of domestic legislation are normally less widely accessible or publicised than the law itself. Thus, even if one presumes knowledge of a state's domestic law in relation to a certain matter, the same cannot be said to be true for the accompanying explanatory notes.

Despite the abovementioned differences, the Court's use of domestic law in both *Anglo-Iranian Oil* and *Aegean Sea Continental Shelf* is similar in certain respects. Notably, the Court invoked the Greek legislation merely to confirm an interpretation made on other grounds, just as the domestic law served as confirmation of the presumed intention of Iran in *Anglo-Iranian Oil*. Although it did not frame its reference to domestic law as such, one might say that the Court used the Greek law in an analogous manner to the supplementary means of interpretation provided for in Article 32 of the Vienna Convention.

3.2.3   *Fisheries Jurisdiction (Spain v. Canada)*

In *Fisheries Jurisdiction*, the Court drew on the two judgments examined above in order to interpret a reservation to Canada's Optional Clause Declaration. In doing so, the Court implied that the interpretation of reservations to multilateral treaties and declarations recognising the compulsory jurisdiction of the Court was comparable.[67] *Fisheries Jurisdiction* concerned a challenge by Spain to the legality of Canada's coastal fisheries protection legislation, referred to as Bill C-29,[68] and the boarding, seizure and prosecution of crew of a Spanish fishing vessel, the

---

[67] See generally, R. Churchill, '*Fisheries Jurisdiction Case (Spain v. Canada)*', (1999) 12 LJIL 597; B. Kwiatkowska, '*Fisheries Jurisdiction (Spain v. Canada)*', (1999) 93 AJIL 502.
[68] The Bill amended the Coastal Fisheries Protection Act.

Estai. Canada challenged Spain's reliance on Canada's Optional Clause Declaration as the basis of the jurisdiction of the Court, invoking a reservation to the Declaration that excluded disputes 'arising out of or concerning conservation or management measures taken by Canada with respect to vessels fishing in the NAFO [Northwest Atlantic Fisheries Organization] Regulatory Area, as defined in the Convention on Future Multilateral Co-operation in the North-west Atlantic Fisheries, 1978, and the enforcement of such measures' from the compulsory jurisdiction of the Court.[69]

As the challenge to the jurisdiction of the Court focussed on the rules of interpretation applicable to the reservation to Canada's Optional Clause Declaration and their application to the case at hand, a significant portion of the parties' written and oral pleadings was dedicated to the elaboration of their competing views regarding inter-pretation. For its part, Spain argued that any reservation to an Optional Clause declaration should be given 'the most limited scope permitted in the context of observing of the general rule of interpretation laid down in Article 31 of the Vienna Convention on the Law of Treaties',[70] as the purpose of the declarant state, 'in formulating reservations, is to limit as little as possible the jurisdiction in principle [that it] accepted'.[71] Canada, on the other hand, emphasised the unilateral nature of such declarations and reservations, and argued that the latter were to be interpreted in a natural way, in their context and with particular regard for the intention of the reserving state.[72]

The detail with which the parties laid out their respective arguments led the Court to explicate its approach to the interpretation of Optional Clause declarations with more specificity than it had done in previous cases. The Court started by highlighting the *sui generis* character of Optional Clause declarations, being both a unilateral act and a consensual bond with other states that have submitted declarations,[73]

---

[69] *Fisheries Jurisdiction,* para 14.
[70] CR 98/13, p. 30, para 23 (Remiro Brotóns).
[71] CR 98/13, p. 32, para 27 (Remiro Brotóns).
[72] *Fisheries Jurisdiction,* para 43. See further the Counter-Memorial of Canada, Chapter II (1).
[73] *Fisheries Jurisdiction,* para 46, citing *Land and Maritime Boundary between Cameroon and Nigeria (Cameroon* v. *Nigeria), Preliminary Objections,* (1998) ICJ Rep 275, para 25. See also, *Military and Paramilitary Activities in and around Nicaragua, (Nicaragua* v. *USA), Jurisdiction and Admissibility, Judgment,* (1984) ICJ Rep 392, para 59. ('Declarations of acceptance of compulsory jurisdiction of the Court are facultative, unilateral engagements, that States are absolutely free to make or not to make.')

and stated that the VCLT was only applicable by analogy to the extent compatible with the specific character of Optional Clause declarations.[74] In relation to the applicable rules of interpretation, it held that the regime applicable to the interpretation of declarations made under Article 36(2) of the Statute 'is not identical with that established for the interpretation of treaties by the Vienna Convention on the Law of Treaties'.[75] Although the Court did not state explicitly why and to what extent the rules of interpretation applicable to Optional Clause declarations differed from Articles 31 and 32 of the Vienna Convention, it stated that, referring to the judgment of the Court in *Anglo-Iranian Oil*, 'since a declaration under Article 36, paragraph 2, of the Statute *is a unilaterally drafted instrument*, the Court has not hesitated to place a certain emphasis on the intention of the depositing State'.[76]

To a certain extent, the prominence that the Court gave to the intention of the declarant state sits uneasily with the general approach to the interpretation of Optional Clause declarations in its jurisprudence, which emphasised the importance of the text of the declaration:

> The Court will thus interpret the relevant words of a declaration including a reservation contained therein in a *natural and reasonable way*, having due regard to the intention of the State concerned at the time when it accepted the compulsory jurisdiction of the Court. The intention of a reserving State may be deduced not only from the text of the relevant clause, but also from the context in which the clause is to be read, and an examination of the evidence regarding the circumstances of its preparation and the purposes intended to be served.[77]

It was at this juncture that the Court referred to its judgment in *Aegean Sea Continental Shelf* as authority for the proposition that the intention of the declarant state should be given due regard.[78] The Court's assimilation

---

[74] *Fisheries Jurisdiction,* para 46. On this point, the Court followed its previous judgment in *Cameroon and Nigeria,* para 30.

[75] ibid.

[76] *Fisheries Jurisdiction,* para 48, citing *Anglo-Iranian Oil,* 107 (emphasis added). The Court considered that the interpretation of declarations and reservations to declarations was identical, stating: 'the Court has in earlier cases elaborated the appropriate rules for *the interpretation of declarations and reservations.* Every declaration "must be interpreted as it stands, having regard to the words actually used" [citing *Anglo-Iranian Oil,* 105]' (emphasis added).

[77] ibid., para 49 (emphasis added). See also, ibid., para 44. ('All elements in a declaration under Article 36, paragraph 2, of the Statute which, read together, comprise the acceptance by the declarant State of the Court's jurisdiction, are to be interpreted as a unity.')

[78] ibid., para 49, citing *Aegean Sea Continental Shelf,* para 69.

of the interpretation of a reservation to a multilateral treaty and the interpretation of a reservation to a declaration accepting the compulsory jurisdiction of the Court is revealing. Although the Court did note that the submission of an Optional Clause declaration was a 'unilateral act of State sovereignty', it cannot be the unilateral legal effect of the declaration that dictates the rules of interpretation applicable to it, for such rules would clearly not also be applicable to reservations to multilateral treaties. Instead, the Court's equation of reservations and Optional Clause declarations leads one to the conclusion that it is the unilateral manner in which those instruments are drafted that justifies the importance placed on the intention of the state.

In *Fisheries Jurisdiction*, domestic law played a more prominent role in the reasoning of the Court than it did in either *Anglo-Iranian Oil* or *Aegean Sea Continental Shelf*. It is useful to distinguish two ways in which the Court drew on domestic law. First, it observed that the circumstances surrounding the submission of the reservation to Canada's Declaration were 'essential' to ascertain the intention of Canada. The fact that the reservation and Canada's new coastal fisheries protection legislation, which addressed the management and regulation of fish stocks in the NAFO Regulatory Area, were submitted to the Secretary-General of the United Nations and Canadian Parliament, respectively, on the same day, and used similar terms, led the Court to conclude that Canada must have been intended to exclude disputes relating to the fisheries legislation from the jurisdiction of the Court.[79] This was supported by transcripts of parliamentary debates and public statements of Canadian officials, which demonstrated that 'the purpose of the new declaration was to prevent the Court from exercising jurisdiction over matters which might arise with regard to the international legality of the amended legislation and its implementation'.[80] This presumed intention provided the background against which the Court examined the text of the reservation.

Certain members of the Court considered that the majority's emphasis on the intention of Canada, and, in particular, the prominence given to the

---

[79] ibid., para 60. This point was consistently argued by Canada in both its written and oral pleadings; see for example, Counter-Memorial of Canada, paras 5, 9, 104–14; CR 98/11, p. 15, paras 30–1 (Kirsch); CR 98/11 pp. 43–4, paras 62–4 (Hankey).

[80] ibid., para 60. The Court quoted the following statement made by the Canadian Minister of Foreign Affairs in the Senate: 'to protect the integrity of this legislation [Bill C-39], we registered a reservation to the International Court of Justice, explaining that this reservation would of course be temporary … '.

Canadian legislation as evidence of its intention, went too far.[81] Judge ad hoc Torres Bernárdez criticised the Court's recourse to extraneous evidence of Canada's intention, suggesting that the judgment took the Court's jurisprudence in the direct of 'extreme subjective interpretation' that threatened the legal certainty of the Optional Clause system.[82] He acknowledged that the circumstances surrounding the deposit of a Declaration might be a useful aid to interpretation, but considered that these should constitute merely supplementary means of interpretation.[83] In a similar vein, Judge Ranjeva argued that the majority, by departing from the traditional rules of treaty interpretation, failed to comprehend the network of relationships established by the submission of an Optional Clause declaration, which create a 'common intention of the two parties, as formed at the moment when the intention of the author of the reservation meets that of the applicant State'.[84]

Those that dissented from the reasoning of the majority on this point perhaps considered that the Court had given more prominence to the presumed intention of Canada than may be gleaned from the judgment. Although the Court highlighted the importance of the link between the legislation and reservation for the purposes of determining Canada's intention, this did not serve to displace the natural meaning of the words used in the reservation. Indeed, reference to Canada's intention played only a confirmatory role in the Court's reasoning. For example, in relation to whether the term 'measures' in the Canadian reservation covered legislative acts, the Court based its interpretation on the ordinary meaning of the term, as evidenced in international conventions.[85] It then added that '[m]oreover ... the purpose of the reservation was specifically to protect "the integrity" of the Canadian coastal fisheries protection legislation ... to take the contrary view [regarding the term "measures"] would be to disregard the evident intention of the declarant and to deprive the reservation of its effectiveness.'[86] Similarly, in relation to the phrase 'conservation and management measures', the Court based its interpretation on the natural and reasonable meaning of the phrase,

---

[81] See also, ibid., Dissenting Opinion of Judge Vereshchetin, para 19.

[82] ibid., Dissenting Opinion of Judge Torres Bernárdez, paras 227, 30.

[83] ibid., para 280. He did indicate, however, that the Court's recourse to domestic law in *Anglo-Iranian Oil* and *Aegean Sea Continental Shelf* were different insofar as those cases drew on domestic law that addressed the Optional Clause declaration and reservation to the General Act, respectively, directly; ibid., para 260.

[84] ibid., Dissenting Opinion of Judge Ranjeva, para 40.

[85] *Fisheries Jurisdiction,* para 66. The Court referred in particular to the use of the term in Articles 61 and 62 of the 1982 UN Convention on the Law of the Sea.

[86] ibid., para 67 (emphasis added). Similarly, see ibid., para 76.

which it induced from various international conventions and states' domestic laws (examined below). Again, the intention of Canada was merely a subsidiary element in the Court's interpretation:

> *Reading the words of the reservation in a 'natural and reasonable' manner,* there is nothing which permits the Court to conclude that Canada intended to use the expression 'conservation and management measures' in a sense different from that generally accepted in international law and practice. *Moreover, any other interpretation of that expression would deprive the reservation of its intended effect.*[87]

Nevertheless, there are certain inconsistencies in the Court's reasoning that cast doubt upon its search for the intention that underlay the reservation to Canada's Declaration. Most notable is the fact that Canada's legislation did not, at the time it submitted the reservation to its Optional Clause declaration on 10 May 1994, apply to Spanish vessels.[88] It was only after the Act was modified by its implementing regulations, on 3 March 1995, that Spanish vessels came within the scope of the coastal fisheries legislation.[89] Spain noted this point, and argued that this led to the conclusion that Canada had intended to exclude the compulsory jurisdiction of the Court only in relation to disputes related to stateless vessels or vessels flying a flag of convenience, a point that it considered to be supported by statements of Canadian officials and transcripts of legislative debates. Disputes regarding Spanish-flagged vessels, as was at issue in the case, fell outside the scope of the reservation.[90]

This argument was rejected by the Court, which stated that a 'natural and reasonable' reading of the text led to the conclusion that Canada intended to leave the term 'vessels' unqualified, a position for which it found support in the transcripts of debates in the Canadian House of Commons regarding the legislation at issue, and statements of the Minister of Fisheries and Oceans and Minister of Foreign Affairs.[91] These statements demonstrated, in the view of the Court, that Canada did not intend to limit the application of Bill C-39 to a certain category of vessel. Particularly probative was the fact that the Canadian officials did not exhaustively or exclusively enumerate a particular class of vessels to

---

[87] ibid., para 71 (emphasis added).

[88] CR 98/11, p. 9, para 7 (Kirsch). Although Canada introduced Bill C-29 to Parliament on the same day as it amended its Optional Clause declaration (i.e. 10 May 1994), the Bill only entered into force two days later, on 12 May 1994.

[89] *Fisheries Jurisdiction,* paras 15–18.

[90] See *Fisheries Jurisdiction,* Memorial of Spain, paras 108–29.

[91] *Fisheries Jurisdiction,* para 77.

which they considered the legislation to be applicable and that any examples of vessels to which the legislation applied were couched in illustrative terms.[92] The Minister of Fisheries and Oceans, for example, stated in the Canadian House of Commons, that:

> as to what is meant by 'vessels of a prescribed class', it is simply a reference that allows the government to prescribe or designate a class, a type or kind of vessel we have determined is fishing in a manner inconsistent with conservation rules and therefore against which conservation measures could be taken.
>
> *For example*, we could prescribe stateless vessels. Another example is that we could prescribe flags of convenience. That is all that is meant.[93]

The conclusion of the Court on this point is unconvincing for two reasons. First, it is the intention of the declarant state at the time of submission of its Optional Clause declaration that is relevant.[94] One might argue that 'vessels' is a generic term that was intended by Canada to evolve over time in line with the definition of vessels covered by Canada's coastal fisheries protection legislation.[95] In the absence of any subsequent changes to the Canadian regulations, such an argument might have been convincing.[96] However, in light of the amendment to *include* Spanish vessels almost 10 months after submission of its reservation, on 3 March 1995, it must be the case *a contrario* that the legislation did *not* apply to Spanish vessels prior to that date.[97] It is thus difficult to

---

[92] See also, the statement of the Minister for Foreign Affairs in the Senate, quoted at ibid., para 77 ('We have said from the outset, and Canada's representatives abroad in our various embassies have explained to our European partners and other parties, that this measure is directed *first of all* towards vessels that are unflagged or that operate under so-called flags of convenience.' Emphasis in judgment).

[93] ibid., para 77 (emphasis in judgment).

[94] ibid., para 49 ('The Court will thus interpret the relevant words of a declaration including a reservation contained therein in a natural and reasonable way, having due regard to the intention of the State concerned *at the time when it accepted the compulsory jurisdiction of the Court.*'; emphasis added).

[95] Cf the Court's interpretation of the term *'comercio'* in Article VI of the 1858 Treaty of Limits between Costa Rica and Nicaragua; *Dispute Regarding Navigational and Related Rights, Judgment,* (2009) ICJ Rep 213, paras 64–7.

[96] It should be noted that it was not the primary legislation itself that was amended, but the implementing regulations, the 'Coastal Fisheries Protection Regulations', which defined the prohibited vessels for the purposes of the primary Act; *Fisheries Jurisdiction,* paras 17–18.

[97] As the Court noted, the implementing regulation to Canada's legislation referred only to Belize, the Cayman Islands, Honduras, Panama, Saint Vincent and the Grenadines and Sierra Leone at the time Canada deposited its revised Optional Clause declaration; ibid., para 17.

avoid the conclusion that the Canadian coastal fisheries protection legislation did not apply to Spanish vessels at the time it submitted its
amended Declaration, including the reservation at issue in this case, to
the Court.[98]

Second, one could argue that the term 'vessels' within the primary
legislation should be understood as distinct from the application of that
term as governed by the implementing Regulations, which defined the
prescribed classes of vessels to which the Act applied. Thus, Canada's
intention should be understood in relation to the broad sense in which it
used 'vessels' in its primary legislation and reservation, as opposed to the
vessels to which the Coastal Fisheries Protection Act actually applied by
virtue of its implementing Regulations. This was implicit in the Court's
line of reasoning.[99] However, in a preceding paragraph in the judgment,
the Court recognised that primary legislation and implementing regulations frequently formed an indissoluble whole:

> The Court would further point out that, in the Canadian legislative system
> as in that of many other countries, a statute and its implementing regula-
> tions cannot be dissociated. The statute establishes the general legal
> framework and the regulations permit the application of the statute to
> meet the variable and changing circumstances through a period of time.
> The regulations implementing the statute can have no legal existence
> independently of that statute, whilst conversely the statute might require
> implementing regulations to give it effect.[100]

In light of the Court's recognition of the close link between the primary
legislation and implementing regulations, it is somewhat artificial to
maintain that it is the broad sense of the terms 'vessels' that should be
given effect in the reservation, as opposed to the class of vessel to which
Canada intended the Act to apply at the time it submitted the reservation
to its Optional Clause declaration. The inevitable conclusion is that
disputes concerning Spanish vessels – including the dispute that formed
part of the subject-matter of Spain's Application in the case – fall outside
the scope of Canada's reservation. The Court's use of a textual argument
to rebut this point is inconsistent with the emphasis that it places elsewhere on the intention of Canada.

---

[98] *Fisheries Jurisdiction,* Dissenting Opinion of Judge Torres Bernárdez, paras 320–2.
[99] *Fisheries Jurisdiction,* para 76. ('It would clearly have been simply enough for Canada, if
this had been its real intention [i.e. to limit its reservation to the classes of vessels to
which the Act applied by virtue of the Regulations], to qualify the word "vessels" so as to
restrict its meaning in the context of the reservation.')
[100] ibid., para 67.

The second manner in which the Court used domestic law was as evidence of the 'natural and reasonable' meaning of the phrase 'conservation and management measures' in the reservation to Canada's Optional Clause declaration.[101] The Court's reasoning on this point was prompted by Spain's contention that 'conservation and management measures' must be understood in accordance with international law, and, more specifically, that measures which fell outside the scope of the regulating state's jurisdiction could not be qualified as 'conservation and management measures' but were 'unlawful acts pure and simple'.[102] The Court rejected this as conflating two different issues (conformity with international law and the extent of a state's consent to the compulsory jurisdiction of the Court) and proceeded to examine the use of the phrase in numerous conventions and in the domestic practice of various states (specifically, the laws of Algeria, Argentina, Madagascar, New Zealand and the European Communities).[103] These demonstrated, in its view, that the natural meaning of a 'conservation and management measure' is a measure the purpose of which is to 'conserve and manage living resources and that, to this end, it satisfies various technical requirements'.[104]

The second way in which the Court used domestic law is certainly open to criticism. It is neither clear why the domestic law of certain states reflects the common usage of the term, nor is it evident that it was the intention of Canada to use the phrase in the manner that the cited states did in their domestic legislation. Furthermore, the Court referred to the domestic laws in the context of its examination of the meaning attributed to the term in international law.[105] Yet the relationship between the cited laws and international law is unclear. The Court was certainly not asserting that these domestic laws constituted state practice capable of forming a rule of customary international law. Nor would such an argument be very convincing in the absence of evidence that those states adopted a particular definition of 'conservation and management measures' because they considered themselves obligated to do so under international law.

More generally, the Court's use of domestic law raises the broader issue of whether and how an interpreter should evidence the conventional or

---

[101] *Fisheries Jurisdiction*, para 70.
[102] ibid., para 64.
[103] ibid., para 70.
[104] ibid.
[105] See the first and final sentences of para 70, which state '*According to international law* . . .' and 'International law *thus* characterizes "conservation and management measures" by reference to factual and scientific criteria' (emphasis added).

common meaning of a term, whether framed as the 'natural and reasonable' meaning, as in this case,[106] or the 'ordinary meaning' of a term, as in Article 31(1) of the Vienna Convention. If a court or tribunal supports the ordinary meaning that it attributes to a term by reference to certain materials, such as a dictionary entry[107] or the laws of certain states, it is susceptible to charges of cherry-picking or of misunderstanding the context in which the term is used in the selected jurisdictions. Yet, the alternative is simply to assert the ordinary meaning of a word with no supporting evidence. The latter may be criticised insofar as it would allow the judges to adopt what *they* considered to be the natural or ordinary meaning of a term, or, from a more sceptical viewpoint, to simply adopt the meaning they thought appropriate or preferable under the guise of the 'ordinary meaning'.[108] In the present case, it may have been more prudent for the Court simply to refer to international conventions that used the phrase 'conservation and management measures' as evidence of the usage of the term on the international plane; it added little to the line of reasoning to refer to the domestic practice of certain states.

3.3   The Interpretation of Unilaterally Drafted Instruments

It is difficult, if not rather ill-advised, to draw general lessons from the analysis of just three judgments of the Court. Nevertheless, certain commonalities between the cases examined above are noteworthy. The most evident is that in each case the Court's use of domestic law related to a legal instrument – whether that be an Optional Clause declaration or a reservation to a multilateral treaty – that was the product of the unilateral drafting of one state. This raises the question of how and why the rules of interpretation applicable to Optional Clause declarations and reservations to multilateral treaties differ to those applicable to the interpretation of treaties, and, in particular, why domestic law might be

---

[106]   ibid., paras 49, 71.

[107]   See in this respect the practice of the WTO Appellate Body; G. Cook, *A Digest of WTO Jurisprudence on Public International Law Concepts and Principles* (CUP 2015) 278.

[108]   Cf Comments of Myres McDougal, the US representative to the Vienna Conference on the Law of Treaties, UN Conference on the Law of Treaties, First Session, 26 March–24 May 1968, Official Records, Summary records of the plenary meeting and of the meetings of the Committee of the Whole, UN Doc. A/CONF.39/11, 168, para 48 ('The criterion of ordinary meaning, because of its ambiguity, opened the door to arbitrary interpretations of the text … '); M. Wählisch, 'Cognitive Frames of Interpretation in International Law', in A. Bianchi et al. (eds), *Interpretation in International Law* (OUP 2015) 344.

more relevant for the interpretation of those instruments than for the interpretation of treaties.

The question of the character of Optional Clause declarations and their relationship to the law of treaties is an issue that has long been debated.[109] For some, a declaration made pursuant to the Optional Clause is akin to a unilateral act,[110] which creates a series of latent bilateral relationships between that state and the other states that recognise the compulsory jurisdiction of the Court.[111] Certain commentators highlight that declarations are 'non-autonomous acts' that only have a legal effect because of the pre-existing conventional framework within which they are produced,[112] whilst others acknowledge the unique character of the

---

[109] Fitzmaurice, 'The Optional Clause System', 155 (stating that 'the main issue that continues to make the determination of the legal character of Optional Clause declarations so elusive is that of their relationship with treaties ... neither the Court nor international lawyers have yet produced a clear-cut definition of what an Optional Clause declaration is and how it relates to treaties'). See generally, Törbar, *The Contractual Nature of the Optional Clause*, Chapter 2; C. Eckhart, *Promises of States under International Law* (Hart 2012) 69–75; V. Lamm, *Compulsory Jurisdiction in International Law* (Edward Elgar 2014) 79–95.

[110] See for example, R. P. Anand, *Compulsory Jurisdiction of the International Court of Justice* (Asia Publishing House 1961) 147 ('though the making of a declaration is a unilateral act, entirely in the discretion of a state ... but which changes itself into a bilateral agreement when a dispute is concretized by the filing of an application before the Court'); H. Thirlway, *The International Court of Justice* (OUP 2016) 46 ('Declarations of this kind may be regarded as unilateral acts ... [i]n their operation, however, the declarations necessarily become bilateral'.). Cf A. P. Rubin, 'The International Legal Effects of Unilateral Declarations', (1977) 71 AJIL 1, 12 ('no basis is stated for characterizing the declarations as something like cross-offers and cross-acceptances'). It is interesting to note that the Optional Clause of the PCIJ was, in the words of Sir Robert Jennings, 'an *actual* "Optional Clause"' (*Military and Paramilitary Activities in and against Nicaragua (Nicaragua v. USA), Jurisdiction and Admissibility*, Separate Opinion of Sir Robert Jennings (1984) ICJ Rep 535) in that there was a '*disposition facultative*' attached to the Protocol of Signature of the Statute of the Permanent Court of International Justice – in other words, a clause that was distinct from the Statute of the Court – that states could sign if they so desired. See PCIJ Ser. D No. 1, 5–6.

[111] See for example, Cedeño First Report, para 116; H. Thirlway, 'The International Court of Justice', in M. D. Evans, *International Law* (4th edn, OUP 2014) 600; H. Kelsen, *The Law of the United Nations: A Critical Analysis of Its Fundamental Problems* (Stevens & Sons 1950) 521 ('The unilateral declaration of one state together with the unilateral declaration of another constitute an agreement.'); Lamm, *Compulsory Jurisdiction in International Law* 95 (the submission of the Optional Clause as a 'unilateral commitment regarding the Court's jurisdiction, which could create a bilateral legal relationship at a later stage').

[112] See for example, E. Suy, *Les actes juridiques unilatéraux en droit international public* (LGDJ 1962) 31; E. Suy, 'Unilateral Acts of States as a Source of International Law: Some

Optional Clause, labelling declarations made pursuant to it 'hybrid' insofar as they are unilateral in form, but bilateral in substance.[113]

The jurisprudence of the Court has been and, to a certain extent, remains ambiguous regarding the character of declarations made under the Optional Clause. In the words of one author, the Court has simply manifested the 'the ambivalent nature of the declarations'[114] themselves by expressing the tension that is inherent between, on the one hand, the unilateral origins of the declaration, and, on the other hand, its bilateral effects when viewed in relation to other states' declarations.[115] This has resulted in the qualification of declarations made under the Optional Clause as having a '*sui generis*' character, and, thus, that the law of treaties is only applicable by analogy to the extent compatible with the unique character of declarations.[116] The Court has, however, failed to specify the manner in which Optional Clause declarations are analogous to treaties, and hence which rules of the Vienna Convention may be relevant.

In relation to matters of interpretation, however, the Court has been less vague. From the Court's jurisprudence, one can readily identify how and why the rules of interpretation applicable to Optional Clause declarations diverge from those applicable to treaties. As noted in the preceding section, the Court has addressed the rules of interpretation applicable to

---

New Thoughts and Frustrations', in N. Angelet (ed), *Droit du pouvoir, pouvoir du droit: Mélanges offerts à Jean Salmon* (Bruylant 2007) 633.

[113] See for example, R. Kolb, *The International Court of Justice* (Hart 2013) 375, 454–6, 88–9; H. Waldock, 'Decline of the Optional Clause', (1955–6) 32 BYIL 244, 254.

[114] Kolb, *ICJ*, 455. See also, Fitzmaurice, 'The Optional Clause System', 155.

[115] Compare, for example, *Phosphates in Morocco, Preliminary Objections*, PCIJ Ser. A/B No. 74, p. 10 (a declaration under the Optional Clause is a 'unilateral act . . . which must on no account be interpreted in such a way as to exceed the intention of the States that subscribed') with *The Electricity Company of Sofia and Bulgaria, Preliminary Objection*, PCIJ Ser. A/B No. 77, p. 64 (a declaration under the Optional Clause may give rise to 'the establishment of the juridical bond between the two States under Article 36 of the Court's Statute'); *Military and Paramilitary Activities*, paras 59–60 ('Declarations of acceptance of the compulsory jurisdiction of the Court are facultative, unilateral engagements, that States are absolutely free to make or not to make . . . In fact, the declarations, even though they are unilateral acts establish a series of bilateral engagements with other States accepting the same obligation of compulsory jurisdiction'); *Cameroon v. Nigeria*, para 25; *Fisheries Jurisdiction*, para 46. See also, Fitzmaurice, 'The Optional Clause System', 155.

[116] *Fisheries Jurisdiction*, para 46 ('The Court observes that the provisions of that Convention may only apply analogously to the extent compatible with the *sui generis* character of the unilateral acceptance of the Court's jurisdiction.'); *Cameroon v. Nigeria*, para 30 ('the provisions of that Convention [the VCLT] may only be applied to declarations by analogy'); *Military and Paramilitary*, para 63 (treating the withdrawal of a declaration analogously to withdrawal from a treaty).

declarations made under the Optional Clause in detail,[117] adopting an approach that is broadly similar to that enshrined in Article 31(1) of the Vienna Convention[118] whilst placing emphasis on the intention of the declarant state as evidenced by the text and context of the declaration, the circumstances in which the declaration was prepared and the purposes intended to be served.[119] The focus on the intention of the declarant state is the main feature that distinguishes the Court's approach to interpretation of Optional Clause declarations when compared to the rules of interpretation applicable to treaties.[120]

The reason for this divergence from the normal rules of treaty interpretation is evident if one examines the reasoning of the Court. In *Fisheries Jurisdiction*, the principal case in which the Court outlined its approach to the interpretation of Optional Clause declarations, the Court stated that 'since a declaration under Article 36, paragraph 2, of the Statute is a *unilaterally drafted instrument*, the Court has not hesitated to place a certain emphasis on the intention of the depositing State'.[121] Similarly, in *Anglo-Iranian Oil*, the Court stated that 'the text of the Iranian declaration is not a treaty text resulting from negotiations between two or more States. *It is the result of unilateral drafting* by the Government of Iran . . . '[122] These statements lead to the conclusion that it is the unilateral nature of the drafting process that justifies emphasis on the intention of the declarant state.[123] Indeed, this feature is common to both Optional Clause declarations and reservations to multilateral treaties, which explains why the Court has readily referred to its jurisprudence relating to the interpretation of

---

[117] *Fisheries Jurisdiction*, paras 47–49. This approach was subsequently confirmed in *Aerial Incident of 10 August 1999 (Pakistan v. India)*, Jurisdiction of the Court, Judgment, (2000) ICJ Rep 12, para 42; *Whaling in the Antarctic (Australia v. Japan)*, Judgment, (2014) ICJ Rep 226, para 36.

[118] D. Caron, 'The Interpretation of National Foreign Investment Law as Unilateral Acts under International Law', in M. H. Arsanjani et al. (eds), *Looking to the Future: Essays on International Law in Honor of W. Michael Reisman* (Martinus Nijhoff 2010) 658.

[119] *Fisheries Jurisdiction*, para 49.

[120] Kolb, *ICJ*, 488; Tomuschat, 'Article 36', para 72. Cf P. Y. S. Chow, 'Reservations as Unilateral Acts? Examining the ILC's Approach to Reservations', (2017) 66 ICLQ 335, 360.

[121] *Fisheries Jurisdiction*, para 48 (emphasis added), citing *Anglo-Iranian Oil*, 107.

[122] *Anglo-Iranian Oil*, 105. See also, H. Lauterpacht, *The Development of International Law by the International Court* (Reprint, Grotius 1982) 345.

[123] M. Shaw, *Rosenne's Law and Practice of the International Court, 1920–2015*, vol II (5th edn, Brill 2016) §II, 209. See also, Fitzmaurice, 'The Law and Procedure of the ICJ: Treaty Interpretation', 230–1.

Optional Clause declarations when interpreting reservations to multilateral treaties and vice versa.[124]

The idea that the rules of interpretation applicable to Optional Clause declarations and reservations to multilateral treaties are analogous due to the unilateral nature of the drafting process is also found in the work of the International Law Commission (ILC) on unilateral acts and reservations to treaties. In his first report on unilateral acts, the Special Rapporteur of the ILC, Víctor Rodríguez Cedeño, excluded declarations recognising the compulsory jurisdiction of the Court from the ILC's work on the basis that '[t]hese declarations, although they take the form of unilateral acts, give rise to a treaty relationship ... [t]he legal relations stemming from an acceptance are contractual in nature'.[125] Yet, in subsequent reports, the Special Rapporteur considered that it was the unilateral *form* as opposed to the purportedly contractual *nature* of Optional Clause declarations that made the jurisprudence of the Court related to the interpretation of such declarations relevant to understanding the rules of interpretation applicable to unilateral declarations.[126] In his fifth report, the Special Rapporteur explained his reliance on these cases in more detail:

> In this connection the most recent opinion given by ICJ [i.e. the *Fisheries Jurisdiction* judgment] on declarations of acceptance of its compulsory jurisdiction should be noted. Although it might not be of a 'strictly unilateral nature', *it is a unilateral declaration from a formal point of view* and hence, as the Court itself indicated, a *sui generis* declaration.[127]

---

[124] See in particular, *Aegean Sea Continental Shelf,* para 55; *Fisheries Jurisdiction,* para 49.

[125] Cedeño First Report, para 116.

[126] Cedeño Fourth Report, para 121, citing *Anglo-Iranian Oil.* ('In other cases, the ICJ has considered unilateral declarations by States, such as those regarding acceptance of the Court's jurisdiction, which are of great value regardless of whether they can be considered as formal unilateral declarations made in the context of a treaty relationship.')

[127] Cedeño Fifth Report, para 123 (emphasis added). Ultimately, the principle that addressed interpretation in the ILC Guiding Principles to unilateral acts, Principle 7, was a significantly slimmed down version of that originally proposed by the Special Rapporteur as a result of disagreement within the Commission. That Principle provides that: 'A unilateral declaration entails obligation for the formulating State only if it is stated in clear and specific terms. In the case of doubt as to the scope of the obligations resulting from such a declaration, such obligations must be interpreted in a restrictive manner. In interpreting the content of such obligations, weight shall be given first and foremost to the text of the declaration, together with the context and the circumstances in which it was formulated.' On the disagreement within the Commission, see 'Ninth Report on the unilateral acts of States, by Mr Víctor Rodríguez Cedeño, Special Rapporteur', (2006) II [1] YBILC 177, para 157.

Similarly, in his work on Reservations to Treaties, the Special Rapporteur of the Commission, Alain Pellet, treated the jurisprudence of the Court regarding the interpretation of Optional Clause declarations as relevant for the interpretation of reservations to treaties, invoking the Court's judgment in *Fisheries Jurisdiction* – a case related to the interpretation of a reservation to Canada's Optional Clause declaration, not to a multilateral treaty – as authority for the proposition that the Court 'places emphasis on the intention of the author as one of the main elements on which interpretation of the *reservation* should be based'.[128] Although the analogy between the interpretation of Optional Clause declarations and reservations to treaties was not made explicit in the ILC's Guide to Practice on Reservations to Treaties, the latter, which explicitly followed the ILC's Guiding Principles applicable to unilateral declarations of States in relation to interpretation,[129] can only have been based on the assumption that any deviation from the rules of treaty interpretation is justified on the basis that both reservations and Optional Clause declarations are 'formally' unilateral acts produced by one state.

If one accepts that a certain emphasis on the intention of the drafting state is justified when interpreting unilaterally drafted instruments, the use of domestic law as extraneous evidence of a state's intent raises two further issues, which have been noted in the preceding section. First, to what extent should extraneous evidence of that state's intention be admitted if other states were not apprised – or could not even have been aware – of that document or statement? The idea that extraneous evidence of a state's intention should not be permitted, or should be permitted only when that evidence was reasonably available to other states, has been advanced both by individual judges in the ICJ and certain members of the ILC in the course of its discussions on unilateral acts.[130] Indeed, the competing considerations have been aptly summarised as follows:

---

[128] 'Guide to Practice on Reservations to Treaties', in Report of the International Law Commission, Sixty-Third Session (26 April–3 June and 4 July–12 August 2011), A/66/10/Add. 1, 468, para 5 (emphasis added).

[129] 'Guide to Practice on Reservations to Treaties', 467–8, para 2.

[130] See *Anglo-Iranian Oil,* Separate Opinion of President McNair, 121; *Anglo-Iranian Oil,* Dissenting Opinion of Judge Hackworth, 137–8; *Fisheries Jurisdiction,* Dissenting Opinion of Judge Torres Bernárdez, paras 228–30; 2695th Meeting of the ILC, (2001) I YBILC 187, para 6 (Pellet); 187–8, paras 13–16 (Gaja).

> The interpretation of unilateral acts presents us in raw form with the potentially competing effect of, on the one hand, an enquiry into the declaring State's true will, and, on the other, the interpretation of a legal document in accordance with the principles of trust and confidence, ie that every legal document must be understood in the manner in which a recipient reasonably could and should understand it.[131]

In assessing the extraneous evidence of a state's intention that should be admissible, the Court has not laid out clear rules; nor, indeed, should it have done so. It would seem to be impossible to determine *a priori* what kind of extraneous evidence of intent should be admitted. That is a question that can only be determined in light of the particular circumstances of the case at hand. Nevertheless, it is clear that the Court has considered that domestic law related to approval or accession of a unilaterally drafted legal instrument is potentially probative as evidence of intent, even if that law is not disseminated internationally or translated into other languages.[132]

The second issue is whether law that is passed on the domestic level reflects the intention of the state to be bound on the international level. Here, again, it is impossible to give an answer *a priori*. As the cases analysed above demonstrate, the Court has considered that domestic law may reflect the intention of a state regarding the scope of its international commitments, whether under the Statute of the Court or a multilateral treaty. However, it is only when one considers the language of the international instrument and the domestic law, the context in which they were concluded, and the circumstances in which they were drafted and approved, that one could give an informed response regarding whether the domestic law might be relevant to determine the intention of the state. In this context, the criticism in the preceding section regarding the Court's use of the Canadian Coastal Fisheries Protection Act and implementing regulations is particularly relevant.[133]

Aside from the formally unilateral nature of both Optional Clause declarations and reservations to treaties, there are two other common threads between the cases analysed in the section above that bear mention. The first is that the ICJ used domestic law as confirmation of an

---

[131] Kolb, *ICJ*, 488, n. 1341. See also, T. M. Franck, 'Word Made Law: The Decision of the International Court of Justice in the Nuclear Test Cases', (1975) 69 AJIL 612, 616 (' . . . intention cannot be determined solely by reference to the speaker's state of mind but must also take into account that of the listeners').

[132] Cf *Anglo-Iranian Oil*, 107.

[133] See section 3.2.3, above.

interpretation that was determined by another, predominantly textual or circumstantial, means of interpretation. This is particularly evident in *Anglo-Iranian Oil* and *Aegean Sea Continental Shelf*, in which the Court referred to the Iranian and Greek laws, respectively, at the end of its chain of reasoning. Indeed, the very terms the Court used to introduce the argument based on domestic law demonstrate the auxiliary, confirmatory role it played in the reasoning of the Court (as 'decisive confirmation' of the intention of the Government of Iran in *Anglo-Iranian Oil*,[134] and as putting the intention of Greece 'beyond doubt' in *Aegean Sea Continental Shelf*).[135] At first sight, it may appear that the Court attributed more weight to domestic law in the *Fisheries Jurisdiction* case. However, as noted, when one examines the reasoning of the Court, it is clear that it too only played a confirmatory role in the Court's interpretation. Whilst domestic law has therefore played a role in the Court's approach to interpretation, it has done so within relatively circumscribed confines.

Second, in each of the cases examined above, the domestic law cited by the Court was to the benefit of the state challenging the Court's jurisdiction, even if that state did not take part in that phase of the proceedings.[136] Although it is impossible to draw any causal link in this regard, and bearing in mind that the present Court has decisively rejected the application of a rule of restrictive interpretation in relation to titles of jurisdiction,[137] one might surmise that the Court would have been more hesitant to refer to a domestic law to assert its jurisdiction. In this respect, one might say (to para-

---

[134] *Anglo-Iranian Oil*, 107.

[135] *Aegean Sea Continental Shelf*, para 66.

[136] See n 45, above.

[137] See for example, *Fisheries Jurisdiction*, para 44 ('Conditions or reservations [of an Optional Clause declaration] thus do not by their terms derogate from a wider acceptance already given. Rather, they operate to define the parameters of the State's acceptance of the compulsory jurisdiction of the Court. There is thus no reason to interpret them restrictively.'). See more generally, *Navigational and Related Rights*, para 48 ('While it is certainly true that limitations of the sovereignty of a State over its territory are not to be presumed, this does not mean that treaty provisions establishing such limitations, such as those that are in issue in the present case, should for this reason be interpreted *a priori* in a restrictive way. A treaty provision which has the purpose of limiting the sovereign powers of a State must be interpreted like any other provision of a treaty, i.e. in accordance with the intentions of its authors as reflected by the text of the treaty and the other relevant factors in terms of interpretation.'). See also, Törbar, *The Contractual Nature of the Optional Clause*, 129–32; C. Tomuschat, 'Article 36', in A. Zimmerman et al. (eds), *Statute of the International Court of Justice* (2nd edn, OUP 2012) 657.

phrase the English courts) that domestic law has been used as a 'shield and not as a sword.'[138]

The issues that are raised by the ICJ's relatively scarce invocation of domestic law, such as the extent to which extraneous evidence of a state's intention should be admitted, are also relevant to the use of domestic law in the practice of the panels and Appellate Body of the WTO. It is to this that we now turn.

---

[138] *Combe* v. *Combe* [1951] KB 215, 218 (Denning LJ).

The Interpretation of Schedules of Commitments in the WTO

4.1 Introduction

The Dispute Settlement Mechanism (DSM) of the World Trade Organization (WTO) is the compulsory, binding inter-state adjudicatory system for disputes between member states related to WTO law.[1] The panels and the Appellate Body (AB) that work under the framework of the DSM have gained a reputation for judicious and effective dispute resolution in the international sphere, leading them to be hailed as a guiding light for other international courts and tribunals.[2] Although fact-intensive cases are the norm in the WTO DSM, the legal questions that come before panels and the AB are primarily questions of treaty interpretation and hence hold interest for any study of legal interpretation.[3]

---

[1] Article 1.1, Dispute Settlement Understanding (DSU) ('The rules and procedures of this Understanding shall apply to disputes brought pursuant to the consultation and dispute settlement provisions of the agreements listed in Appendix 1 to this Understanding (referred to in this Understanding as the "covered agreements") . . .'). The covered agreements referred to in Article 1.1 DSU include the Agreement Establishing the WTO, the Multilateral Agreements on Trade in Goods (including the General Agreement on Tariffs and Trade 1994, or GATT 1994) and the General Agreement on Trade in Services (GATS). See also, Panel Report, *US–Import Measures on Certain Products from the EC* WT/DS165/R (17 July 2000), para 6.23.

[2] See for example, the joint dissenting opinion of Judges Al-Khasawneh and Simma, *Case Concerning Pulp Mills on the River Uruguay (Argentina v. Uruguay)* (Judgment) (2010) ICJ Rep 14, 113. See also, J. Bacchus, 'WTO Appellate Body Roundtable' (2005) 99 ASIL Proceedings 175 (calling the Appellate Body 'an international tribunal of historical global achievement'); R. Howse, 'Adjudicative Legitimacy and Treaty Interpretation in International Trade Law: The Early Years of WTO Jurisprudence' in J. H. H. Weiler (ed), *The EU, the WTO and NAFTA: Towards a Common Law of International Trade?* (OUP 2001) 35.

[3] I. Van Damme, *Treaty Interpretation by the WTO Appellate Body* (OUP 2009) 3. It should be noted that the ultimate power to interpret the WTO legal texts lies with the Ministerial

Under Article 3.2 of the DSU, panels and the AB must interpret the covered agreements 'in accordance with the customary rules of interpretation of public international law'. This provision has been understood primarily – but not exclusively – to refer to Articles 31 to 33 of the VCLT.[4] Reference to the 'customary rules' of interpretation opens the door to the possibility that the applicable rules may diverge from those codified in the Vienna Convention, and the AB has in practice applied certain uncodified principles of interpretation, such as the principle of effectiveness or *effet utile*.[5] Nevertheless, the 'perception is that the Appellate Body has put its trust in strict adherence to the codified principles of treaty interpretation in the VCLT', augmenting the image of stability and predictability that such formal attachment provides.[6]

In principle, the provisions of the VCLT do not limit which materials may be consulted for the purposes of interpretation, instead limiting when certain materials may be ascribed significance for interpretation.[7] Within the framework of the Vienna Convention, domestic law could be used to evidence intention, ordinary meaning or the object and purpose of the treaty. However, in practice, the use of domestic law by panels and the AB has been circumscribed.[8] In the view of one commentator, this

---

Conference and the General Council of the WTO under Article IX:2 of the WTO Agreement.

[4] See for example, Appellate Body Report, *US–Standards for Reformulated and Conventional Gasoline* WT/DS2/AB/R (29 April 1996), 17; Appellate Body Report, *Japan–Taxes on Alcoholic Beverages* WT/DS8 & 10 & 11/AB/R (4 October 1996), 10; Appellate Body Report, *India–Patent Protections for Pharmaceutical and Agricultural Chemical Products* WT/DS50/AB/R (19 December 1997), para 46. See also, G. Cook, *A Digest of WTO Jurisprudence on Public International Law Concepts and Principles* (CUP 2015), Chapter 15. Cf Article 17(6)(ii), Anti-Dumping Agreement, which provides that 'the panel shall interpret the relevant provisions of the Agreement in accordance with customary rules of interpretation of public international law. Where the panel finds that a relevant provision of the Agreement admits of more than one permissible interpretation, the panel shall find the authorities' measure to be in conformity with the Agreement if it rests upon one of those permissible interpretations'.

[5] See for example, Appellate Body Report, *US–Continued Dumping and Subsidy Offset Act of 2000* WT/DS217 & 234AB/R (16 January 2003), para 271.

[6] Van Damme, *Treaty Interpretation*, 380. See also, ibid., 382 (stating that adherence to the provisions of the Vienna Convention was 'instrumental in justifying and making acceptable [the AB's] early choice to function as a court and thus to build its legitimacy as a judicial actor').

[7] See in relation to the *travaux préparatoires* of a treaty, J. D. Mortenson, 'The *Travaux* of *Travaux*: Is the Vienna Convention Hostile to Drafting History?' (2013) 107[4] AJIL 780. On the flexibility of the Vienna Convention provisions, see Chapter 2.

[8] One use of domestic law not elaborated in this chapter was by the Panel Report in *US–COOL*, in which the panel surveyed domestic law to confirm that consumer information

reticence is attributable to the fact that 'it would be inappropriate to characterize, for the purposes of applying multilateral treaty provisions, the same thing differently depending on its legal categorization within the jurisdictions of different States'.[9] Accordingly, panels and the AB have repeatedly emphasised that the provisions of the covered agreements refer to autonomous concepts that are distinct from the domestic law of any particular member state.[10]

Despite this general reluctance, domestic law has played a limited role in the reasoning of panels and the AB, often as a result of its invocation by one of the parties to the case. In *Section 110(5) of the US Copyright Act*, for example, the Panel used domestic law as evidence of the subsequent practice of states parties to a treaty, which is relevant under Article 31(3)(b) of the Vienna Convention insofar as it manifests a 'concordant, common and consistent'[11] sequence of acts that is sufficient to establish the agreement of the parties regarding the treaty's interpretation.[12]

---

provided by labelling should be recognised as a 'legitimate objective' under Article 2.2 of the TBT Agreement. Such recourse seems analogous to the ECtHR's use of domestic law to interpret standards of behaviour or justification, examined below in Chapter 6; Panel Report, *US–Certain Country of Origin Labelling (COOL) Requirements* WT/DS384 & 386/R (18 November 2011), para 7.638.

[9] Cook, *A Digest of WTO Jurisprudence*, 188.

[10] See for example, Panel Report, *US–Countervailing Measures on Certain EC Products* WT/DS212/R (31 July 2002), para 7.50 ('[t]he concept of benefit is independent of the legal business structure established pursuant to national corporate law'); Appellate Body Report, *US–Countervailing Measures on Certain EC Products* WT/DS212/AB/R (9 December 2002), para 115 ('the legal distinction between firms and their owners that may be recognized in a domestic legal context is not necessarily relevant, and certainly not conclusive, for the purpose of determining whether a 'benefit' exists under the SCM Agreement'); Appellate Body Report, *US–Corrosion-Resistant Steel Sunset Review* WT/DS244/AB/R (15 December 2003), fn 87 ('We observe that the scope of each element in the phrase "law, regulations and administrative procedures" must be determined for the purposes of WTO law and not simply by reference to the label given to various instruments under the domestic law of each WTO Member'); Appellate Body Report, *US–Softwood Lumber IV* WT/DS275/AB/R (19 January 2004), para 65 ('The concepts of "personal" and "real" property are, in the context Canada raises them, creatures of municipal law that are not reflected in Article 1.1(a)(1)(iii) itself. As we have said above, the manner in which the municipal law of a WTO Member classifies an item cannot, in itself, be determinative of the interpretation of provisions of the WTO covered agreements.'). See also, the AB's criticism of the panel's use of the domestic law in *US–Anti-Dumping and Countervailing Duties (China)* WT/DS379/AB/R (11 March 2011), para 335.

[11] Appellate Body Report, *Japan–Alcoholic Beverages II* WT/DS8 & 10 & 11/AB/R (4 October 1996), 13.

[12] Panel Report, *US–Section 110(5) of the US Copyright Act* WT/DS160/R (15 June 2000). That case related to whether parties to the Berne Convention had recognised a 'minor exceptions' doctrine, which allowed member states to place exceptions on the rights of copyright holders in certain instances of non-profit use, such as religious ceremonies or

Domestic law played an important role, however, in two cases that related to the interpretation of the schedules of commitments of WTO members: *EC–Chicken Cuts* and *Mexico–Telecoms*. Some commentators have suggested that the interpretation of schedules of commitments – documents that detail the trade concessions of each WTO member and which form an integral part of the WTO agreements – should be distinguished from the interpretation of multilateral conventions on the basis that they are not 'as multilateral as treaties'.[13] Drawing inspiration from the interpretation of unilateral acts in general public international law, these authors argue that the 'hybrid character of schedules'[14] justifies a different approach to interpretation that places more emphasis on the intention of the state that drafted the schedule. This chapter examines that claim in light of the relevant WTO jurisprudence and assesses whether domestic law is, or should be, given greater weight in the interpretation of schedules of commitments.

The structure of this chapter is as follows. Section 4.2 describes why schedules of commitments have been described as 'multilateral acts of a special character'[15] that are distinct from multilateral treaties, and contrasts schedules to the legal instruments examined in the preceding chapter (i.e. Optional Clause declarations and reservations to multilateral treaties). Section 4.3 examines the reasoning of the Panel and AB in the *EC–Chicken Cuts* case, in which EU law was considered to be a circumstance of conclusion of the WTO Agreement within the meaning of Article 32 of the VCLT. Section 4.4 analyses the use of domestic law by the Panel in *Mexico–Telecoms* in its assessment of the purported

---

military band performances. The USA defended the Copyright Act on the basis that an implicit minor exception doctrine had been accepted by subsequent practice of parties to the Berne Convention, which formed part of the *acquis* incorporated into the TRIPS Agreement under Article 9.1. The Panel found confirmation for its conclusion that a minor exceptions doctrine had been accepted in the practice of states parties to the Berne Convention, citing national laws that incorporated the minor exceptions doctrine into domestic law; ibid., fn 67. The Panel noted the domestic law of Australia, Belgium, Denmark, Finland, New Zealand, Philippines, India, Canada, South Africa and Brazil. Cf G. Nolte, 'First Report on Subsequent Agreements and Subsequent Practice in Relation to Treaty Interpretation' UN Doc. A/CN.4/660 (19 March 2013), paras 107–10 (identifying broad and narrow conceptions of subsequent practice).

[13] I. Van Damme, 'The Interpretation of Schedules of Commitments' (2007) 41[1] Journal of World Trade 1, 13. See also, F. Ortino, 'Treaty Interpretation and the WTO Appellate Body Report in *US–Gambling*: A Critique' (2006) 9 JIEL 117, 124.

[14] Van Damme, 'The Interpretation of Schedules', 19.

[15] Van Damme, 'The Interpretation of Schedules', 19–21 (Van Damme adopts the phrase from the dissenting opinion of Judge Alvarez in the *Anglo-Iranian Oil* case, examined in the preceding chapter).

special meaning of a term under Article 31(4) of the Vienna Convention. Section 4.5 identifies security and predictability as the main values underpinning the functioning of the DSM,[16] and argues that the limited use of domestic law has been deployed in pursuance of these values. Section 4.6 concludes.

4.2   Schedules of Commitments as Multilateral Acts of a Special Character

In order to comprehend fully the argument that schedules of commitments are distinct from multilateral treaties, it is necessary to understand the legal nature of a schedule under the WTO agreements and the negotiation process that leads to a member's schedule of commitments.

Schedules of commitments are documents that detail the trade concessions that a WTO member has negotiated with trading partners, not only as the result of multilateral trade rounds, such as the Uruguay Round, but also those agreed during bilateral and plurilateral negotiations, such as those covered by the Agreement on Government Procurement. In relation to goods, members' schedules generally record the maximum tariff level to which the member is bound under Article II of the GATT 1994.[17] In relation to services, schedules of commitments detail the specific sectors and modes of service for which the member has committed to liberalise trade.[18]

Schedules are, formally, part of the WTO agreements. By virtue of Article II:7 of the GATT 1994, members' schedules of commitments related to goods are 'an integral part' of the GATT.[19] In a similar vein, under Article XX:3 of the GATS, members' schedules related to services form an integral part of that agreement. This *de jure* incorporation has led panels and the AB

---

[16] Art 3.2, DSU ('[t]he dispute settlement system of the WTO is a central element in providing security and predictability to the multilateral trading system'). See also, GATT *Panel on Newsprint* L/5680-31S/114 (20 November 1984), para 52.

[17] In the case of agricultural goods, schedules of concessions also record tariff rate quotas, limits on export subsidies and commitments related to other domestic support. See further www.wto.org/english/tratop_e/schedules_e/goods_schedules_e.htm (accessed 24 August 2018).

[18] Pursuant to Article I:2, the GATS covers four modes of service: cross-border trade (mode 1); services consumed abroad (mode 2); a commercial presence that provides services in a foreign country (mode 3); and the presence of a natural person who provides services in a foreign country (mode 4).

[19] The GATT 1994 and GATS are in turn integral parts of the WTO Agreement by virtue of Article II:2 of that Agreement.

to treat schedules of commitments as treaties for the purposes of interpretation, applying Articles 31 to 33 of the Vienna Convention with little further enquiry into the legal nature of schedules.[20]

The formal designation of schedules of concessions as treaties, however, stands in tension with the process of negotiation that leads to those schedules. Those negotiations are characterised by both bilateral and multilateral discussions between trading partners and are somewhat distinct from the negotiation process that leads to the conclusion of a multilateral treaty.[21] In this respect, it is useful to recount the general format of negotiations during the Uruguay Round, which took place from September 1986 to April 1994.[22]

Whilst the format of tariff negotiations was discussed on a multilateral basis, the initial phase of negotiations in the Uruguay Round was characterised by its bilateral nature:

> [t]ariff concessions are often negotiated for a considerable period of time on a bilateral basis between WTO Members before the results of these negotiations are 'multilateralized' through the MFN principle [most-favoured nation principle under Article I GATT 1994] ... the negotiating process consists mostly of continuous (in the assumption that there is actual progress in the negotiations) exchanges of offers, which are bundles of concessions that are evaluated on a wide range of reciprocity criteria by the receiving negotiating and trading partner.[23]

As this process progressed, the negotiations became 'more multilateral through examinations of each tariff proposal by the entire group of participants in the negotiations, [and were] complemented by evaluations of all proposals by the (then) GATT Secretariat'.[24] Certain draft

---

[20] See Appellate Body Report, *EC–Computer Equipment*, para 109; Appellate Body Report, *EC–Measures Affecting Importation of Certain Poultry Products* WT/DS69/AB/R (13 July 1998), paras 82–3; Appellate Body Report, *EC–Customs Classification of Frozen Boneless Chicken Cuts* WT/269 & 286/AB/R (12 September 2005), paras 148, 175.

[21] On the mechanics of multilateral trade negotiations, see B. M. Hoekman & M. M. Kostecki, *The Political Economy of the World Trading System: The WTO and Beyond* (OUP 2009) Chapter 4; A. Hoda, *Tariff Negotiations and Renegotiations under the GATT and the WTO: Procedures and Practices* (CUP 2001) Chapter II.

[22] For a description of previous rounds of multilateral negotiations, see Hoda, *Tariff Negotiations*, 44–8.

[23] Van Damme, 'The Interpretation of Schedules', 5–6; Hoda, *Tariff Negotiations*, 48–52. Cf Appellate Body Report, *EC–Computer Equipment*, para 109 (stating that 'tariff negotiations are a process of reciprocal demands and concessions, of "give and take"').

[24] Van Damme, 'The Interpretation of Schedules', 3. Hoda, *Tariff Negotiations*, 49 (stating that the 'multilateral reviews supplemented the bilateral and plurilateral negotiations which constituted the core of the negotiations').

schedules that were revised pursuant to the multilateral examinations were then subject to further bilateral negotiations, as was the case in the Uruguay Round in relation to agricultural and industrial goods.[25] The final phase consisted in the verification of draft schedules by all members for accuracy, during which members also eliminated to a large extent any provisional conditions that were placed on their concessions.[26] The final schedules as agreed were annexed to the Marrakesh Protocol to the GATT 1994.

As Isabelle Van Damme has noted, the nature of the process of negotiation leading to the conclusion of schedules is rather different to that leading to the conclusion of multilateral treaties. Under Article 2(1) (a) of the Vienna Convention, the latter must be 'concluded between States', a notion that implies the agreement by consensus of all states parties to the treaty. However, in relation to schedules of commitments, the extent to which WTO members have actually reviewed and accepted the commitments detailed in other members' schedules is unclear. In the words of Van Damme:

> The notion of consensus [of states parties to a treaty] arguably implies the prerequisite of negotiations or at least a minimum exchange of views on the rights and obligations to which Members have committed. In the case of schedules of commitments, it is not entirely clear to what extent their drafting in effect included such – even minimal – exchange of views between WTO Members on each Member's schedules.[27]

Accordingly, she suggests, to the extent that the concept of a treaty rests on the idea that there is a 'meeting of the minds' of states parties, schedules of commitments are a *sui generis* category that is distinguished by 'a distinct qualifying unilateral characteristic'.[28] The argument that schedules of commitments do not enshrine the common intention of all WTO members is supported by the fact that not all WTO members have the right to participate in renegotiations should a member desire to change the commitments contained in its schedule.[29]

---

[25] Hoda, *Tariff Negotiations*, 49–50.

[26] Hoda, *Tariff Negotiations*, 51.

[27] Van Damme, 'The Interpretation of Schedules', 8.

[28] Van Damme, 'The Interpretation of Schedules', 21. See also, Appellate Body Report, *US–Measures Affecting the Cross-Border Supply of Gambling and Betting Services* WT/DS285/AB/R (7 April 2005), para 182.

[29] See Article XXVIII GATT 1994 (limiting renegotiations to 'any contracting party with which such concession was initially negotiated' and 'any other contracting party determined by the Contracting Parties to have a principal supplying interest').

The *sui generis* nature of schedules leads to the claim that more emphasis should be placed on the intention of the state whose schedule of commitments is being interpreted. Unlike multilateral treaties, it is this intention that has most clearly influenced and determined the text of the schedule. In a similar vein, Federico Ortino claims that 'instead of focusing on a *single* treaty text, identifying the common intention behind a member's concession cannot avoid taking into account the *unilateral* origin of such a concession as well as the existence of concessions of all other members'.[30]

A parallel can be drawn with Optional Clause declarations and reservations to multilateral treaties, which were examined in the previous chapter. In that chapter, it was suggested that the ICJ had justified placing greater emphasis on the intention of the declarant or reserving state on the basis that the legal instrument was drafted unilaterally. Schedules of commitments, however, seem to be different to both Optional Clause declarations and to multilateral reservations. They differ from the former because schedules require the acceptance of all WTO members, a condition that is not applicable for Optional Clause declarations. Schedules differ from multilateral reservations, on the other hand, because the latter do not result from a process of negotiation that involves multiple states parties. The question remains, therefore, the extent to which the interpretation of schedules does or should diverge from the interpretation of multilateral treaties. In this respect, it is instructive to examine two cases in which the WTO AB drew on domestic law to inform its interpretation of members' schedules.[31]

4.3   Domestic Law as a Circumstance of Conclusion

Perhaps the most interesting and illuminating use of domestic law within the WTO has been as a circumstance of conclusion of a treaty, recourse to which is permissible under Article 32 of the VCLT. Under Article 32, recourse to the preparatory works or circumstances of conclusion of a treaty is permitted either to confirm a meaning resulting from the application of Article 31 or to determine the meaning of a provision when the application of Article 31 leads to an ambiguous, obscure,

---

[30] Ortino, 'Treaty Interpretation and the WTO Appellate Body Report in *US–Gambling*: A Critique', 124.

[31] Cf Van Damme, 'The Interpretation of Schedules', 17 (stating that '[s]o far, the Appellate Body has rejected the relevance of national laws as means to establish the meaning of the WTO covered agreements').

manifestly absurd or unreasonable result. What constitutes the circumstances of conclusion of a treaty is not defined in the VCLT but, in the
words of one commentator, '[t]he circumstances that cause a treaty to be
drawn up, affect its content and attach to its conclusion are all factors
which are in practice taken into account'.[32] The possibility of recourse to
the circumstances of conclusion of a treaty allows the interpreter to step
into the shoes of parties to the treaty and 'to take into account all the work
which had led to the formation of that will – all material which the parties
had had before them when drafting the final text'.[33] They hence extend
further than the preparatory works of a treaty, as they 'are intended to
cover both the contemporary circumstances [of conclusion of the treaty]
and the historical context in which the treaty was concluded'.[34] The
broad scope and undefined character of the circumstances that may be
taken into account provides a wide degree of flexibility for the interpreter
to consult a variety of materials. As has been noted, '[d]epending on the
nature of the treaty, the interpreter could examine the political, economical, social, or other situation of the parties at the time of conclusion'.[35]

The AB has adopted a broad understanding of the circumstances of
conclusion of a treaty, stating that such circumstances could include any
'event, act, or instrument',

> not only if it has actually influenced a specific aspect of the treaty text in
> the sense of a relationship of cause and effect; it may also qualify as
> a 'circumstance of the conclusion' when it helps to discern what the
> common intentions of the parties were at the time of conclusion with
> respect to the treaty or specific provision … not only 'multilateral'
> sources, but also 'unilateral' acts, instruments, or statements of individual
> negotiating parties may be useful in ascertaining 'the reality of the situa
> tion which the parties wishes to regulate by means of the treaty' and,
> ultimately, for discerning the common intentions of the parties.[36]

This broad understanding of the circumstances of conclusion of
a treaty accommodates recourse to a wide range of material by the
interpreter. It was the acceptance that 'unilateral acts' could constitute
circumstances of the conclusion of a treaty that opened the door to the

---

[32] R. Gardiner, *Treaty Interpretation* (2nd edn, OUP 2015) 398.
[33] Statement of M. K. Yasseen, 873rd Meeting of the ILC, [1966] I(II) YBILC 205, para 25.
See also, Panel Report, *Chile–Price Band System and Safeguard Measures Relating to
Certain Agricultural Products* WT/DS207/R (3 May 2002), para 7.35.
[34] Waldock Third Report, 59, para 22 (emphasis added).
[35] Y. le Bouthillier, 'Article 32', in O. Corten & P. Klein (eds), *The Vienna Conventions on the
Law of Treaties: A Commentary* (OUP 2011) 860.
[36] Appellate Body Report, *EC–Chicken Cuts*, para 289.

use of domestic law – or, more precisely, the law of the European Union[37] – in the *EC–Chicken Cuts* case.

4.3.1 *EC–Chicken Cuts*

The dispute in *EC–Chicken Cuts* revolved around the interpretation of heading 02.10 of the EC Schedule of commitments, which covered 'salted' meat.[38] The complainants in that case, Brazil and Thailand, claimed that frozen salted chicken cuts exported to the EU were subject to a tariff over and above that contained in the EC schedule, breaching Articles II:1(a) and (b) of the GATT 1994.[39] The EU retorted that products falling under tariff heading 02.10 must have been salted for the purpose of long-term preservation, which the Brazilian and Thai products at issue were not.[40] The central issue before the Panel and AB was, therefore, to interpret heading 02.10 of the EC schedule: if 'salted' necessarily and exclusively meant meat salted for the purpose of long term preservation, then the products at issue did not fall under heading 02.10 and were not being afforded less favourable treatment.[41] This is an unglamorous topic if ever there was one, although one could scarcely

---

[37] The European Union has exclusive competence to conclude trade agreements on behalf of EU member states, and is a member of the WTO in its own right. Although all member states of the EU are separately members of the WTO, cases in the DSM are brought against the EU and not individual member states. In effect, therefore, EU law is analogous to the domestic law of other non-EU WTO members; see *Opinion 1/94 re WTO Agreement* [1994] ECR I-5267, codified in Articles 3(1)(e) and 3(2) of the Treaty on the Functioning of the European Union.

[38] Heading 02.10 of the EC Schedule covered 'Meat and edible offal, salted, in brine, dried, or smoked'.

[39] Articles II:1(a) and (b) of the GATT 1994 provide inter alia that a state shall not accord to imported goods less favourable treatment than that provided for in its schedule and that such goods shall be exempt from customs duties in excess of those set out in its schedule. Products falling in heading 02.10 of the EU Schedule were subject to an *ad valorem* tariff of 15.4 per cent. The products in question were classified by the EU under heading 02.07.41.10 (boneless frozen chicken), and were hence subject to a specific tariff of €102.4/100 kg as well as potentially being subject to safeguard measures under Article 5 of the Agreement on Agriculture. The complainants contended that this equated to an *ad valorem* equivalent of 40–60 per cent; WorldTradeLaw.net Dispute Settlement Commentary, 'Panel Report, *EC–Chicken Cuts*', 2.

[40] Panel Report, *EC–Customs Classification of Frozen Boneless Chicken Cuts* WT/269 & 286/R (30 May 2005), para 7.81.

[41] H. Horn & R. Howse, 'European Communities – Customs Classification of Frozen Boneless Chicken Cuts' in H. Horn & P. Mavroidis (eds), *The WTO Case Law of 2004–2005* (CUP 2008) 10.

imagine a case that so wholly revolved around interpretation, and one to which 280 pages of Panel and AB Reports were dedicated.

As noted in the preceding section, the schedules of WTO members are integral parts of the GATT 1994 by virtue of Article II:7, and hence, in the view of the Panel, 'must be considered treaty language'.[42] Accordingly, it recognised that Articles 31 and 32 of the VCLT 'comprise[d] the legal framework within which this interpretive exercise must take place'.[43] Neither the ordinary meaning nor the context of the word 'salted' led to the conclusion that salting must have occurred for the purpose of long-term preservation.[44] However, both the EC's 'consistent practice of classifying the products at issue under heading 02.10 during 1996–2002'[45] – which, in the view of the Panel, constituted subsequent practice under Article 31(3)(b) – and the 'security and predictability of the reciprocal and mutually advantageous [trade] arrangements'[46] led the Panel to conclude provisionally that 'salted' did not include a long-term preservation requirement.

In order to confirm this interpretation, the Panel turned to the circumstances of conclusion of the Uruguay Round, including EU law, judgments of the ECJ, EC explanatory notes to the schedule and previous classification practice.[47] Of particular importance was EC Regulation 535/94, which was adopted and published prior to the conclusion of the WTO Agreement, but after the conclusion of the EC tariff negotiations. The Regulation was adopted on 9 March 1994, published on 11 March 1994, and came into force on 1 April of that year (i.e. during the verification period of schedules, which took place from 15 February 1994 to the end of March 1994).[48] Despite pre-dating the conclusion of the WTO Agreement, the Panel found that the Regulation nevertheless formed part of the 'historical background' against which

---

[42] Panel Report, *EC–Chicken Cuts*, para 7.87.
[43] Panel Report, *EC–Chicken Cuts*, para 7.88.
[44] Panel Report, *EC–Chicken Cuts*, paras 7.116, 7.163.
[45] Panel Report, *EC–Chicken Cuts*, para 7.290.
[46] Panel Report, *EC–Chicken Cuts*, para 7.323.
[47] The Panel followed the AB Report in *EC–Computer Equipment*, which determined that the legislation of a WTO member could constitute part of the 'circumstances of conclusion' of a treaty; Appellate Body Report, *EC–Customs Classification of Certain Computer Equipment* WT/DS62 & 67 & 68/AB/R (5 June 1998), para 94. The Panel rejected the ECJ judgments as either irrelevant (*Dinter*) or ambiguous (*Gausepohl*), and used the other materials to support the conclusion reached on the basis of Regulation 535/94.
[48] Hoda, *Tariff Negotiations*, 50.

negotiations took place, and that the WTO membership could be considered to have 'constructive knowledge' of the measure.[49]

The purpose of the Regulation was to alter and clarify parts of the EC's tariff classification system – the Combined Nomenclature – to effect changes necessitated by the conclusion of the Uruguay Round negotiations. Specifically, Article 1 of the Regulation provided that 'For the purposes of heading No 02.10, the term "salted" means meat . . . having a total salt content of no less than 1.2% by weight'.[50] WTO members were hence presumed to have negotiated on the basis that this Regulation defined products that fell under heading 02.10, a finding that confirmed the Panel's preliminary conclusion.[51] In its view, this approach also accorded with the twin goals of security and predictability of the multilateral trading system:

> In reaching this conclusion, the Panel recalls that a fundamental object and purpose of the WTO Agreement and the GATT 1994 is that the security and predictability of reciprocal and mutually advantageous arrangements must be preserved. In the Panel's view, a Member's unilateral intention regarding the meaning to be ascribed to a concession that Member has made in the context of the WTO multilateral trade negotiations cannot prevail over the common intentions of all WTO Members as determined through an analysis undertaken pursuant to Articles 31 and 32 of the *Vienna Convention.*[52]

On appeal, the AB upheld the Panel's analysis under ordinary meaning, context and object and purpose of the treaty. However, it disagreed with the Panel that EC classification could qualify as subsequent practice under Article 31(3)(b).[53] Having found that interpretation under Article 31 was inconclusive, the AB moved to examine the circumstances surrounding the conclusion of the treaty 'to ascertain whether WTO Members have agreed on the preservation criterion advanced by the European Communities'.[54] The circumstances of conclusion relevant to interpretation did not, in the view of the AB, have to be 'directly linked' to the treaty itself, but could be determined by:

> [A] number of objective factors . . . [including] the type of event, document, or instrument and its legal nature; temporal relation of the

---

[49] Panel Report, *EC–Chicken Cuts*, para 7.361.
[50] Panel Report, *EC–Chicken Cuts*, para 7.366.
[51] Panel Report, *EC–Chicken Cuts*, para 7.340.
[52] Panel Report, *EC–Chicken Cuts*, para 7.427.
[53] Appellate Body Report, *EC–Chicken Cuts*, para 272.
[54] Appellate Body Report, *EC–Chicken Cuts*, para 281.

circumstance to the conclusion of the treaty; actual knowledge or mere access to a published act or instrument; subject matter of the document, instrument, or event in relation to the treaty provision to be interpreted; and whether or how it was used or influenced the negotiations of the treaty.[55]

Regulation 535/94 fit the bill: it was, in the words of the AB, a 'product description of 02.10' which reflected the common intentions of the parties in respect of tariff negotiations under that heading.[56] If a specific criterion of long-term preservation were to be included in heading 02.10, 'then there must be clear evidence that such a criterion was agreed upon by the parties for the European Communities' WTO Schedule'.[57] This criterion was not present in any of the materials before the AB, including Regulation 535/94.

For the purposes of the present study, it is notable that the Appellate Body stated that WTO members' legislation, as well as the judgments of domestic courts, could be relevant to the interpretation of a schedule insofar as those are relevant circumstances of conclusion within the meaning of Article 32 of the VCLT.[58] This leads us back to the question posed at the outset of this chapter; namely, does domestic law have a role to play in the interpretation of WTO members' schedules, and, if so, why?

4.3.2   Reasonable Reliance

From a normative standpoint, it seems justifiable to emphasise the intention of the member whose schedule is being interpreted, including – if relevant – that member's domestic law. However, it would be wrong to premise this argument on an analogy between unilateral acts and schedules of commitments, as some have suggested.[59] For unilateral acts, reference to the sole intent of the committing state is based on the fact that the intent of the declaring state alone imbues the act with legal significance (although whether unilateral acts even have legal significance is unclear).[60] This is not the case with schedules. Schedules might be

---

[55] Appellate Body Report, *EC–Chicken Cuts*, para 291.
[56] Appellate Body Report, *EC–Chicken Cuts*, para 314.
[57] Appellate Body Report, *EC–Chicken Cuts*, para 344.
[58] Appellate Body Report, *EC–Chicken Cuts*, paras 308–9.
[59] Cf A. Orakhelashvili, *The Interpretation of Acts and Rules in Public International Law* (OUP 2008) 477–80.
[60] See for example, H. Thirlway, 'The Sources of International Law', in M. D. Evans (ed), *International Law* (4th edn, OUP 2014) 112; H. Thirlway, *The Sources of International Law* (OUP 2014) 21.

concessions on the part of one WTO member state that are negotiated bilaterally, plurilaterally or multilaterally, but they only have legal force because they have been accepted by all members as an element of the 'package' that constitutes the WTO Agreement. If one looks at the practice of tariff negotiations, it is indeed a fallacy to say that every concession represents a 'meeting of minds' of all members.[61] Without the ultimate consent of all parties, however, schedules would have no legal value.

If the source of legal normativity does not suggest an analogy with unilateral acts, could one nevertheless argue that schedules are unilaterally drafted and hence that the intent of the drafting state should be privileged? To do so would be wrong for two reasons. First, the text of the schedule might have been unilaterally drafted but it certainly was not unilaterally determined. Rather, it was the result of negotiations with myriad trading partners, resulting in the agreement of the entire membership.[62] As noted above, this fact distinguishes schedules of commitments from the Optional Clause declarations and reservations to multilateral treaties examined in the previous chapter. Second, in relation to instruments that are the result of a process of negotiation between multiple states, the identity of the drafting party has never played a role in limiting the task of the interpreter. Legally, it is irrelevant which party drafted the text; the fact to be borne in mind when interpreting the text is that it embodies an agreement between parties.

If the analogy with unilateral acts does not hold, why might we be interested in the domestic law of the member state whose schedule is under interpretation? An examination of the reasoning of the panel and AB in the *Chicken Cuts* case is instructive. The intention of the member state is not *in se* more important than the intention of any other member. What is important, on the other hand, are the external manifestations of intent that could have been reasonably relied upon by other WTO members in the process of negotiating and concluding the Uruguay Round.

In *Chicken Cuts*, the panel and AB were at pains to emphasise the relevance of Regulation 535/94, based on inter alia its temporal and substantive relationship to the conclusion of the treaty. The factors of relevance expounded by the AB – the type of act, its temporal relation to conclusion of the treaty, its subject matter, actual knowledge or mere

---

[61] Van Damme, *Treaty Interpretation*, 98.

[62] Appellate Body Report, *EC–Computer Equipment*, para 109.

access to the document or act, and whether it is actually used in negotiations – reflect the likelihood that other WTO members relied upon the particular event, act or instrument in their acceptance of the tariff concession. Although interpreting to give effect to the legitimate expectations of the exporting member has been explicitly rejected by the AB,[63] one would be tempted to frame the use of domestic law in the interpretation of schedules as giving effect to the *common* legitimate expectations of the WTO membership.[64] Put another way, it helps construct what the WTO membership reasonably thought that they were agreeing to.[65] As the Panel stated, this approach accords with one of the professed objectives of the DSM; namely, to provide security and predictability for the multilateral trading system.[66]

Despite serving this function, does reference to domestic law in this case place an 'unacceptable and unworkable burden' on the WTO membership to know the domestic law of all members?[67] Clearly, it would not be appropriate to place an obligation on a state to be omniscient of the domestic law of all WTO members. However, in some cases it may be acceptable to presume knowledge of the domestic law of a contracting party. The dividing line between when it is acceptable and when would be too burdensome to presume such knowledge inevitably depends on the facts of the case. However, the factors of relevance for circumstances of conclusion expounded by the AB in *Chicken Cuts* provide a useful framework within which the burden of knowledge of domestic law can be analysed.

---

[63] Appellate Body Report, *India–Patents* WT/DS/50/AB/R (16 January 1998), para 45; Appellate Body Report, *EC–Computer Equipment*, paras 80–4.

[64] On the construction of the 'reasonable' common intention of WTO members, although not using domestic law, see Appellate Body Report, *US–Gambling*, para 180, fn 219 (on the reasonable inferences members can draw from the mutual exclusivity of schedule headings); Panel Report, *China–Publications and Audiovisual Products* WT/DS363/R (12 August 2009), paras 7.1205 (mutual exclusivity of schedule headings), 7.1237, 7.1246 (both on the relevance of technical possibility of electronic recording distribution in China). This is to be distinguished from the concept of 'reasonable expectation' relevant to non-violation complaints under Article XXIII of the GATT; see Appellate Body Report, *India–Patents*, WT/DS50/AB/R (16 January 1998), paras 36, 41.

[65] Cf Panel Report, *US–Gambling*, para 6.125 ('[a USITC document] is undoubtedly one element in the body of evidence that the Panel can and must consider when assessing the common intentions of Members for the purpose of interpreting the scope and meaning of the US Schedule').

[66] See Panel Report, *EC–Chicken Cuts*, para 7.320; Appellate Body Report, *EC–Computer Equipment*, para 82; Appellate Body Report, *EC–Chicken Cuts*, para 243.

[67] Van Damme, 'Interpretation of Schedules', 17.

Let us take a hypothetical example to demonstrate this. Consider a bilateral treaty between State A and State B, whose trade was previously not legally regulated. The sole obligation in the simple treaty is that both states will lower tariffs on product X. The definition of, and current tariffs applicable to, product X are provided for in recent domestic statutes in both states which pre-date the conclusion of the treaty. Evidently, this treaty has been negotiated on the basis of several presumptions enshrined in domestic law; namely, how product X is defined and what the current tariffs on the product are. In such a case, discerning the common intentions of the parties cannot proceed without reference to domestic law. Adopting the framework of relevance laid down by the AB in *Chicken Cuts*, the domestic law that classified product X and detailed the previously applicable tariffs has both temporal and subject relevancy, and must have been used as the basis for negotiation of the treaty. In this case, it is clear that it would be acceptable to have reference to the domestic law as the circumstances of conclusion of the treaty. To do so would not place an 'unacceptable and unworkable burden' of knowledge upon either state. In the context of WTO schedules, however, the criteria of relevance – the type of act, its temporal and subject-matter proximity to conclusion of the treaty, actual knowledge or mere access to the document or event, and whether it is actually used in negotiations – will clearly be more difficult to fulfil than in the case of the hypothetical bilateral treaty.

To conclude, in *Chicken Cuts*, domestic law was used to uphold the agreement to which the WTO membership reasonably thought that they consented to, in pursuance of the objectives of security and predictability of international trade. The factors of relevance for circumstances of conclusion of a treaty expounded by the AB in *Chicken Cuts* provide a useful framework within which to consider whether contracting parties might reasonably be expected to have relied on domestic law in any given case.

4.4   Domestic Law as Agreement: Special Meaning

In *Mexico–Telecoms*, the Panel drew on domestic law to determine whether a special meaning should be attributed to a term under Article 31(4) of the VCLT.[68] This provision has been described by some as the

---

[68] Article 31(4) of the VCLT provides: 'A special meaning shall be given to a term if it is established that the parties so intended.'

'reintegration' of the intentions of the parties back into the general rule of interpretation enunciated in Article 31, overriding the presumption that the ordinary meaning of the text constitutes the best embodiment of the common understanding struck by the parties.[69] To label Article 31(4) in such terms, however, overemphasises the uniqueness of the provision and neglects other expressions of the intention of the parties that are integrated into the other sections of the 'general rule', such as subsequent agreements and practice under Articles 31(3)(a) and (b), respectively.

In the academic literature and case law, the term 'special meaning' has been used to refer to two similar but nevertheless distinct concepts.[70] The first of these uses is 'cases in which the term at issue is a technical one that is in common use in its field, and which the parties can be presumed to have been aware of'.[71] The second use of 'special meaning' is to refer to terms that are given a particular meaning by the parties to a treaty which diverges from the commonly understood meaning or meanings of the terms.[72] Certainly, the first of these uses of the term seems capable of being understood as the ordinary usage of a term in a particular, technical context.[73] The line between the ordinary meaning of a term in its context under Article 31(1) and the special meaning of a term under Article 31(4) is hence blurred. The main difference between the two provisions is the allocation of the burden of proof required to evidence a special meaning, which lies with the party advancing that meaning.[74] This was the primary consideration that advocated in favour of a separate provision for 'special meanings', distinguishing it from interpretation under Article 31(1).[75]

There is no reason in principle why the materials used to evidence agreement on a special meaning should be different from those used in

---

[69] J.-M. Sorel & V. Boré Eveno, 'Article 31' in O. Corten & P. Klein (eds), *The Vienna Convention on the Law of Treaties: A Commentary* (OUP 2011) 828.

[70] Gardiner, *Treaty Interpretation*, 334.

[71] Panel Report, *Mexico–Measures Affecting Telecommunications Services* WT/DS204/R (2 April 2004), para 7.169.

[72] J. Stone, 'Fictional Elements in Treaty Interpretation – A Study in the International Judicial Process', (1955) 1[3] Sydney Law Review 344, 356; Gardiner, *Treaty Interpretation*, 334.

[73] Gardiner, *Treaty Interpretation*, 334.

[74] ILC, *Draft Articles of the Law of Treaties with commentaries* [1966] II YBILC 177, 222.

[75] ILC, *Draft Articles of the Law of Treaties*, 222. See also, [1966] I [II] YBILC 198, para 3. Initially, it was also proposed that a special meaning could only be established in light of 'decisive proof'; Waldock Third Report, 57. This was later dropped following protestations by the USA; see ILC, Law of Treaties: Comments by Governments on Parts I, II and III of the Draft Articles on the Law of Treaties drawn up by the Commission at its fourteenth, fifteenth and sixteenth sessions [1966] II YBILC 93.

the context of other sub-paragraphs of Article 31, such as Articles 31(3) (a) and (b), as all are considered to be manifestations of the intention of the parties that displace the ordinary meaning of the term. Whilst it has not explicitly defined the materials it considers relevant to an enquiry under Article 31(4), the WTO AB has stated, in the context of Article 31(3)(b), that it will consider all materials that permit the interpreter to discern a 'pattern implying the agreement of the parties regarding [the treaty's] interpretation'.[76] Clearly, this does not preclude reference to domestic law; instead, an examination of the national law of states parties to the agreement may be instructive in assessing whether the parties intended a term to have a special meaning.

4.4.1   Mexico–Telecoms

In *Mexico–Telecoms*, the Panel was called upon to interpret provisions of the Telecommunications Reference Paper, which formed an integral part of Mexico's schedule of commitments under the GATS. The Telecommunications Reference Paper was negotiated by WTO members and lays out principles of competition regulation in the telecoms sector. It is not formally an integral part of the GATS, but has been accepted – either partially or in its totality – by 69 WTO members, including Mexico, which have inscribed the Paper (or sections thereof) into their schedules of commitments under Article XVIII GATS.[77]

The Panel was required to interpret whether Mexico's commitment to liberalise telecommunications services was limited to domestic interconnections, or also covered cross-border provision of services (for example, from a US telecoms firm inbound to a Mexican firm). The terms that were the focus of the interpretative enquiry, and which supposedly qualified the telecommunications commitments of Mexico, were 'linking' and 'interconnection'. Mexico contended that those terms referred only to domestic connections, thereby excluding Mode 1 provision of

---

[76] Appellate Body Report, *Japan–Alcoholic Beverages*, 13. Recourse to *travaux préparatoires* is in principle not permissible to demonstrate a special meaning under Article 31(4); Gardiner, *Treaty Interpretation*, 340. ('Where a special meaning is recorded in the preparatory work, its effect on interpretation is probably no different from that of other statements or declarations in preparatory work, but confirmation of this is not readily found.')

[77] See further, D. J. Neven & P. C. Mavroidis, '*Mexico–Measures Affecting Telecommunications Services* (WT/DS204/R: DSR 2004:IV, 1537): A Comment on "El mess in TELMEX"' in H. Horn & P. C. Mavroidis (eds), *The American Law Institute Reporters' Studies on WTO Case Law: Legal and Economic Analysis* (CUP 2007) 765.

services (cross-border supply) from the purview of Mexico's commitments.[78] This was at issue because the USA argued that Mexico had failed to ensure that American telecommunications suppliers were provided with a cross-border connection on a cost-oriented basis and with reasonable rates, terms and conditions.[79]

After noting that the ordinary meaning of 'linking' did not limit the commitments to domestic service producers, the Panel examined if 'interconnection' could circumscribe Mexico's commitment.[80] Blurring the two different conceptions of 'special meaning' identified at the start of this section, the Panel noted that:

> Interconnection is, however, a term which may be given a 'special mean-ing', according to Article 31.4 of the Vienna Convention, 'if it is estab-lished that the parties so established'. Since the provision is a technical one that appears in a specialized service sector, we are entitled to examine what 'special meaning' it may have in the telecommunications context, and whether the 'linking' referred to in Section 2.1 is circumscribed by that special meaning.[81]

In order to elucidate this special meaning, the Panel examined a telecommunications dictionary before stating that 'the term "intercon-nection" also appears as a technical term with a possible "special mean-ing" in national laws and regulations'.[82] Of particular importance in this context were Mexico's Federal Telecom law and rules issued by the Mexican Federal Communications Commission, neither of which lim-ited interconnection with foreign networks from the scope of the term.

In the view of the Panel, this confirmed that 'the term "interconnec-tion" is used by Mexico *in its domestic affairs* for interconnection between domestic networks, *and* between domestic and foreign networks'.[83] It continued to state that it had 'not been provided evidence of laws or regulations of other Members which offer definitions or usage that indicate that the definition of "interconnection"' suggests limitation to solely domestic connections.[84] On the contrary, the Panel had before it

---

[78] Panel Report, *Mexico–Telecoms*, paras 4.9, 4.16.
[79] Panel Report, *Mexico–Telecoms*, para 4.1
[80] Panel Report, *Mexico–Telecoms*, para 7.108. The Panel treated 'interconnection' as an element of the context of 'linking'; however, the term was itself subject to interpretation on its own.
[81] Panel Report, *Mexico–Telecoms*, para 7.108.
[82] Panel Report, *Mexico–Telecoms*, para 7.110.
[83] Panel Report, *Mexico–Telecoms*, para 7.110 (emphasis added).
[84] Panel Report, *Mexico–Telecoms*, para 7.111.

evidence that other members defined the term broadly, which it illustrated by reference to the EU Market Access Directive.[85] This interpretation was confirmed by the Panel's subsequent analysis under Articles 31
and 32 of the Vienna Convention.

The reasoning of the Panel raises some interesting points regarding
interpretation under Article 31(4). First, the Panel's assessment of the
term 'interconnection' seems somewhat muddled. As noted above, whilst
the Panel asserted that interconnection was capable of having a special
meaning if the parties 'so intended', it continued to state that 'since the
provision is a *technical one* that appears in a specialized service sector, we
are entitled to examine what "special meaning" it could have in the
telecommunications context ... '[86] This conflates two distinct lines of
enquiry: special meaning intended by the parties and special meaning
that results from the use of a term in a particular context.[87] The latter
variant – perhaps more appropriately called a 'technical' meaning – may
be elucidated without reference to Article 31(4). This is particularly so in
the context of the WTO as the AB has taken a wide approach to the
relevant context that should be taken into account when determining the
ordinary meaning of a term under Article 31(1).[88] The special meaning of
interconnection in the context of telecommunications need not therefore
make reference to the intentions of parties or Article 31(4).

It may be questioned why reference to domestic law took place under
the rubric of Article 31(4) and not under Article 32, as it was in the
Chicken Cuts case. This was necessitated by the argument of Mexico. As
noted above, within the framework of the VCLT recourse to the circumstances of conclusion of a treaty is only possible if interpretation under
Article 31 leaves the meaning obscure, ambiguous or leads to an absurd
or unreasonable result. In *Mexico–Telecoms*, neither scenario was

---

[85] Panel Report, *Mexico–Telecoms*, para 7.111. The EU Directive defined interconnection as
'the physical or logical linking of public communications networks used by the same or
a different undertaking in order to allow users of one undertaking to communicate with
users of the same or another undertaking, or to access services provided by another
undertaking'. It was the USA that invoked the EC Directive before the Panel; ibid.,
para 4.13.

[86] Panel Report, *Mexico–Telecoms*, para 7.108 (emphasis added).

[87] Cf Van Damme, *Treaty Interpretation*, 351.

[88] See in particular, the acknowledgement of the pertinence of 'factual context' by the AB in
EC–Chicken Cuts; Appellate Body Report, *EC–Chicken Cuts*, paras 175–6. See also,
Appellate Body Report, *US–Definitive Safeguard Measures on Imports of Wheat Gluten
from the European Communities* WT/DS166/AB/R (22 December 2000) para 105; Panel
Report, *US–Import Prohibition of Certain Shrimp and Shrimp Products (Article 21.5)* WT/
DS58/RW (15 June 2001) para 5.51; Van Damme, *Treaty Interpretation*, 269–72.

present: the ordinary meaning of the term in its context was clear. Instead, it was Mexico's argument that this meaning should be displaced. Article 31 allows for divergence from the ordinary meaning in cases of authentic interpretation under Articles 31(3)(a), (b) and 31(4), should parties be in agreement. Mexico's domestic law was hence assessed in the context of the search for an agreement that might displace the ordinary meaning under Article 31(1).

4.4.2   The Utility of Domestic Law under Article 31(4) of the VCLT

What lessons can we draw from the Panel Report in *Mexico–Telecoms*? First, the Report demonstrates that domestic law may be relevant for interpretation carried out under the rubric of Article 31. Although there is no reason in principle why domestic law cannot assist in elucidating an ordinary meaning under Article 31(1), it has very rarely – if ever – been used to do so in the WTO.[89] The reason for this is evident: it is more efficacious to find the ordinary meaning of a term by other means than surveying the use of the term by all WTO members. In the words of one commentator, a dictionary essentially plays the role of a 'statistical report' in this sense.[90] On the other hand, when a different meaning or an authentic interpretation might have displaced the ordinary meaning of the term, an enquiry into the intention of parties – possibly evidenced by domestic law – is called for. This was the case with *Mexico–Telecoms*. The absence of a restrictive definition of interconnection in Mexico's federal telecommunications law precluded it from successfully advancing a claim of 'special meaning' under Article 31(4).

Second, *Mexico–Telecoms* supports the conclusion drawn in Section 4.3; namely, that the domestic law of the member whose schedule is

---

[89] One potential example of the use of domestic law to evidence an ordinary meaning is the report of the AB in *US–FSC (Article 21.5)*, in which the AB was called upon to interpret 'foreign-source income' in footnote 59 of the SCM Agreement. Finding that international instruments did not define the term uniformly, the AB derived 'assistance from [the] widely recognized principles which many States generally apply in the field of taxation'; Appellate Body Report, *US–Tax Treatment for 'Foreign Sales Corporations' (Article 21.5 – EC)* WT/DS108/AB/RW (14 January 2002), paras 141–2, fn 121.

[90] S. Fish, 'Intention is All There Is: A Critical Analysis of Aharon Barak's Purposive Interpretation in Law' (2008) 29(3) Cardozo L Rev 1109, 1123. See for example, Panel Report, *US–Measures Affecting the Cross-Border Supply of Gambling and Betting Services (Article 21.5)* WT/DS285/RW (30 March 2007), para 6.13; Van Damme, *Treaty Interpretation*, 227 et seq.

under interpretation might be particularly relevant in certain circumstances. Unlike *EC–Chicken Cuts, Mexico–Telecoms* provides us not
with an example of when the domestic law supports a certain interpretation, but rather illustrates how domestic law might be used to
preclude an interpretation posited by one party. This is clearer if we
consider the counterfactual scenario. As noted above, if interconnection was defined restrictively under Mexican domestic law, WTO
members might reasonably be considered to have accepted Mexico's
GATS commitments on the basis of that definition. This would have
called for an analysis of the circumstances surrounding the domestic
law in a manner analogous to the 'relevance' test for circumstances of
conclusion espoused by the AB in *EC–Chicken Cuts*, which was not
necessary on the facts of the case.

4.5   Security and Predictability in International Trade

The question posed at the outset of this chapter was whether domestic
law is or should be given greater weight in the interpretation of schedules
of commitments, as opposed to the interpretation of multilateral treaties.
The examples examined in the previous sections demonstrate that the
WTO panels and AB have, in very limited instances, considered domestic
law to be probative of the intention of the WTO membership. However,
was it the supposedly *sui generis* character of schedules of commitments
that led to this comparative reasoning?

Whilst it is difficult to draw any general conclusions, the jurisprudence examined above suggests that it was not the character of
schedules *per se* that justified examining domestic law. Rather, it
was the desire to ensure that any manifestations of intent on which
the WTO membership may reasonably have relied were given effect.
The circumstances in which it may have been reasonable to rely on
a state's domestic law very much depends on the facts of the case.
However, the indices of relevance set out by the AB in *Chicken Cuts*
provide an indication of the considerations that may be useful to
take into account.

This conservative use of domestic law accords with the general interpretative approach of the AB, which places paramount importance on the
stability and predictability of international trade. This was clearly
expressed by the AB in *Japan–Alcoholic Beverages II*, in which it stated
that:

WTO rules are reliable, comprehensible and enforceable ... They will serve the multilateral trading system best if they are interpreted with that in mind. In that way, we will achieve the 'security and predictability' sought for the multilateral trading system by the Members of the WTO ...[91]

In the words of Georges Abi-Saab, the process of interpretation within the WTO has been conceived of as 'a rigid sequence of autonomous or discrete steps, each of which has to be explicitly addressed and 'exhausted' before moving onto the next one'.[92] Unlike the crucible approach envisaged by Waldock and the ILC, this step-by-step approach examines sequentially the ordinary meaning of the term, then the context, the object and purpose, other elements of Article 31 that might be relevant to the case in hand (such as subsequent practice or the intention of parties to adopt a special meaning) and – if necessary – subsidiary material permitted under Article 32.[93] By approaching the provisions of the Vienna Convention thus, the AB creates not only the impression of security but also renders the interpretative demarche of the AB more predictable for parties within the DSM.[94] The emphasis placed on contextualised ordinary meaning as the presumptive meaning of a text, to be displaced only if convincing evidence is adduced that demonstrates divergence from this meaning is justified, enables WTO members to reasonably foresee the result of an interpretative question that might arise in the DSM.

To sum, the panels and AB of the WTO have referred to domestic law in cases when it may evidence the agreement of the parties or constitute a 'relevant' circumstance of the conclusion of the treaty. By using

---

[91] Appellate Body Report, *Japan–Alcoholic Beverages II*, 31. See also, Appellate Body Report, *EC–Computer Equipment*, para 82; Appellate Body Report, *US–Corrosion-Resistant Steel Sunset Review* WT/DS224/AB/R (15 December 2003), para 82; Appellate Body Report, *US–Stainless Steel (Mexico)* WT/DS344/AB/R (30 April 2008), para 160. See also, J. T. Fried, '2013 in WTO Dispute Settlement: Reflections from the Chair of the Dispute Settlement Body', www.wto.org/english/tratop_e/dispu_e/jfried_13_e.htm; P. Lamy, 'The AWCL at Ten – Looking Back, Looking Forward' (4 October 2011), www.wto.org/english/news_e/sppl_e/sppl207_e.htm.

[92] G. Abi-Saab, 'The Appellate Body and Treaty Interpretation', in G. Sacerdoti et al. (eds), *The WTO at Ten: The Contribution of the Dispute Settlement System* (CUP 2006) 459.

[93] See for example, Appellate Body Report, *EC–Chicken Cuts*, paras 170–346; Appellate Body Report, *US–Softwood Lumber IV*, paras 58–67; Appellate Body Report, *US–Gambling*, paras 164–7, 179–213.

[94] Van Damme, *Treaty Interpretation*, 382. See also, J. Klabbers, 'On Rationalism in Politics: Interpretation of Treaties and the World Trade Organization', (2005) 74 Nordic JIL 405, 412–13.

domestic law within these limits, the panels and AB have acted to further the security and predictability of the world trading system by giving effect to the agreements that members intended to agree to, or those that they reasonably thought that they were agreeing to.

4.6   Domestic Law under the Rubric of the VCLT

The two examples analysed in this chapter highlight how domestic law has been used within the framework of the Vienna Convention articles to promote a certain value; in this case, security and predictability. It demonstrated how the use of domestic law has been acknowledged as relevant to establish the agreement of the parties within the scope of Article 31(4). The AB also recognised the use of 'relevant' domestic law as a circumstance of conclusion within the meaning of Article 32. 'Relevance' in this sense was understood to be determined by reference to a number of factors, including: the type of legal instrument; its temporal and subject proximity to the treaty matter; knowledge of or access to the domestic law by other parties; and actual influence of the domestic law on treaty negotiations. The limited use of domestic law within the framework of these articles promotes the security and pre-dictability of the multilateral trading system by giving effect to the understanding of a treaty term that was established by the agreement of the parties (either prior or subsequent to the conclusion of the treaty), or giving effect to the understanding of a treaty term that parties could reasonably have relied on in the context of treaty negotiations.

The inter-state dispute settlement bodies examined in this and the preceding chapter have manifested a certain reticence in referring to the domestic laws of states, only doing so in relation to legal instruments that were unilaterally drafted. The following chapters analyse the practice of courts and tribunals that deal with cases brought by an individual against a state. These jurisdictions demonstrate more willingness to refer to domestic laws, and provide an interesting comparison to the practice of the ICJ and WTO panels and AB.

International Investment Law and the
Public Law Analogy

5.1 Introduction

The relative novelty of the international investment regime has led authors to draw analogies with a range of other systems, from international commercial arbitration[1] to human rights law,[2] in order to respond to the host of theoretical and practical challenges the regime poses.[3] Of these analogies, perhaps the most interesting is the parallel drawn with domestic public law.[4] Advocates of the analogy argue that investment disputes are 'regulatory dispute[s] arising between the state (acting in a public capacity) and an individual who is subject to the exercise of public authority by the state'[5] in much the same way as public and administrative law disputes relate to the exercise of public authority in domestic legal

---

[1] See e.g., *Pope & Talbot Inc.* v. *Canada* (Merits, Phase 2) (10 April 2001) para 79. See further, C. Brower, 'W(h)ither International Commercial Arbitration', (2008) 24 Arbitration International 181; W. Mattli, 'Private Justice in a Global Economy: From Litigation to Arbitration', (2001) 55 International Organization 919.

[2] See e.g., *Mondev International Ltd* v. *United States of America*, ICSID Case No. ARB(AF)/99/2, Award (11 October 2002) paras 143–4. See further, G. Van Harten, *Investment Treaty Arbitration and Public Law* (OUP 2008) 136–43; V. Vadi, *Analogies in International Investment Arbitration* (CUP 2016) 217–19.

[3] See generally, A. Roberts, 'Clash of Paradigms: Actors and Analogies Shaping the Investment Treaty System', (2013) 107 AJIL 45. Cf M. Paparinskis, 'Analogies and Other Regimes of International Law', in Z. Douglas et al. (eds), *The Foundations of International Investment Law: Bringing Theory into Practice* (OUP 2014).

[4] D. Schneiderman, *Constitutionalizing Economic Globalization: Investment Rules and Democracy's Promise* (CUP 2008); S. W. Schill (ed), *International Investment Law and Comparative Public Law* (OUP 2010); S. Montt, *State Liability in Investment Treaty Arbitration: Global Constitutional and Administrative Law in the BIT Generation* (Hart 2012); Van Harten, *Investment Treaty Arbitration*.

[5] G. Van Harten and M. Loughlin, 'Investment Treaty Arbitration as a Species of Global Administrative Law', (2006) 17 EJIL 121, 148.

systems.[6] They contend that this functional similarity means that it is beneficial to look to domestic public law to fill gaps, resolve ambiguities or understand the nature of the international investment regime.[7]

One of the ways to operationalise the public law analogy is through treaty interpretation.[8] Arbitrators could draw on comparative surveys of domestic public and administrative law in order to guide the interpretation of the vague provisions and broad standards that are invariably incorporated in investment treaties.[9] Proponents argue that the benefits of drawing on comparative public law in this way are manifold: it would enable the investment law regime to benefit from the experience that domestic legal systems have in dealing with analogous legal issues,[10] restrain arbitrators' discretion in interpreting treaties[11] and enhance the perceived legitimacy of investment arbitration.[12] Yet, despite enjoying growing support in academia and in practice,[13] the use of comparative public law to interpret investment treaties has recently been criticised on both methodological and practical grounds.[14]

This chapter argues that much of the debate regarding the use of comparative public law to interpret investment treaties is to a certain

---

[6] See S. W. Schill, 'International Investment Law and Comparative Public Law – An Introduction', in Schill (ed), *International Investment Law*, 17; Roberts, 'Clash of Paradigms', 64–5 (distinguishing between the public action and public interest theories of international investment law).

[7] Roberts, 'Clash of Paradigms', 46.

[8] See e.g., S. W. Schill, 'The Sixth Path: Reforming Investment Law from Within', (2014) 11 Transnational Dispute Management.

[9] Schill, 'Introduction', 36.

[10] ibid.

[11] Montt, *State Liability*, 343–4.

[12] Vadi, *Analogies*, 241.

[13] *International Thunderbird Gaming Corporation v. The United Mexican States*, UNCITRAL, Separate Opinion of Thomas Wälde (1 December 2005) para 13; *Noble Ventures, Inc. v. Romania*, ICSID Case No. ARB/01/11, Award (12 October 2005) para 178; *Joseph Charles Lemire v. Ukraine*, ICSID Case No. ARB/06/18, Decision on Jurisdiction and Liability (14 January 2010) para 506; *Total S.A. v. The Argentine Republic*, ICSID Case No. ARB/04/01, Decision on Liability (27 December 2010) paras 111, 129; *Toto Costruzioni Generali S.p.A. v. The Republic of Lebanon*, ICSID Case No. ARB/07/12, Award (7 June 2012) para 166; *Occidental Petroleum Corporation and Occidental Exploration and Production Company v. The Republic of Ecuador*, ICSID Case No. ARB/06/11, Award (5 October 2012) para 403; *Gold Reserve Inc. v. Bolivarian Republic of Venezuela*, ICSID Case No. ARB(AF)/09/1, Award (22 September 2014) para 576.

[14] J. E. Alvarez, 'Is Investor–State Arbitration "Public"?', (2016) 7 JIDS 534; see also, J. E. Alvarez, '"Beware: Boundary Crossings" – A Critical Appraisal of Public Law Approaches to International Investment Law', (2016) 17 JWIT 171.

extent based on a false premise. One of the central strands of argument adduced in favour of such comparative reasoning is that domestic law is relevant insofar as it may reflect a general principle of law that is applicable by virtue of Article 31(3)(c) of the Vienna Convention on the Law of Treaties (VCLT).[15] Practice, however, demonstrates that domestic law is commonly used by courts and tribunals as an interpretative aid outside the framework of Article 31 VCLT and outside the formal sources of law enumerated in Article 38 of the Statute of the International Court of Justice (ICJ). Investment tribunals that have drawn on domestic law have done so not because it embodies a general principle of law, but rather because it constitutes a 'benchmark' against which investment protection is to be assessed,[16] or provides the 'background' for the interpretation of a provision,[17] or because it demonstrates the fairness of a regulatory measure.[18] As subsequent chapters demonstrate, similar uses of domestic law play a role in the reasoning of other international courts and tribunals, particularly in the domains of human rights law and international criminal law.[19] The existing literature fails to address the normative and methodological issues that are raised by the tribunals' actual use of comparative law.

This chapter is composed of four sections. Section 5.2 traces the development of the public law analogy and the debate surrounding the use of comparative public law in the literature, highlighting the centrality of the 'general principles method'. Section 5.3 examines the awards of international investment tribunals in order to demonstrate that comparative law has been used either as confirmation for a conclusion made on other grounds or as a means of substantiating a treaty standard, such as the obligation to accord fair and equitable treatment (FET) to foreign investors. Section 5.4 explores the complex normative, methodological and evaluative considerations that are raised by investment tribunals' use of comparative law. Section 5.5 concludes by suggesting that investment lawyers need to step outside of the framework of the VCLT in order to

---

[15] Vienna Convention on the Law of Treaties, 23 May 1969, 1155 UNTS 331.

[16] *Toto Costruzioni Generali S.p.A.* v. *The Republic of Lebanon*, ICSID Case No. ARB/07/12, Award (7 June 2012) para 193.

[17] *Occidental Petroleum Corporation and Occidental Exploration and Production Company* v. *The Republic of Ecuador*, ICSID Case No. ARB/06/11, Award (5 October 2012) para 404.

[18] *Joseph Charles Lemire* v. *Ukraine*, ICSID Case No. ARB/06/18, Decision on Jurisdiction and Liability (14 January 2010) para 506.

[19] See Chapters 6 and 7.

understand and account for the current and future use of comparative law in investment treaty interpretation.

5.2   The Public Law Analogy: Rationales, Function and Legal Basis

The interpretation of the broad standards and vague provisions that are commonplace in international investment agreements (IIAs) is an issue that is of a relatively recent vintage. Whilst IIAs were concluded at a moderate pace for the three decades following the first bilateral invest-ment treaty in 1959,[20] it was not until the mid-1980s that the pace of treaty-making picked up significantly, culminating in the creation of a network of over 3,300 IIAs that exist today.[21] As the number of IIAs increased, so too did the number of investment disputes that could make use of the dispute settlement mechanisms contained in those treaties. The first known example of international investment arbitration was initiated in 1987[22] and since then a total of 817 arbitral awards have been initiated, with over 50 new arbitrations initiated each year for the past five years.[23]

The increased activity of the investment law regime put into sharp relief the legal issues that the nascent regime faced. Systemically, increased recourse to investor–state dispute settlement (ISDS) raised questions about the legitimacy of the system, particularly regarding the neutrality and accountability of arbitrators.[24] However, the increased use of arbitration also raised more specific procedural and substantive questions that had until then not arisen. Should, for example, a state that prevails in arbitration have to bear its own costs, or should the losing claimant investor be ordered to cover the respondent state's costs?[25] What standard should be used to determine whether a measure is 'necessary' to protect a state's essential

---

[20] Z. Elkins et al., 'Competing for Capital: The Diffusion of Bilateral Investment Treaties, 1960–2000', (2006) 60 International Organization 811, 815.

[21] UNCTAD, World Investment Report 2016, xii.

[22] Asian Agricultural Products Ltd (AAPL) v. Republic of Sri Lanka, ICSID Case No. ARB 87/3, 27 June 1990.

[23] UNCTAD, Investment Dispute Settlement Navigator, available at http://investmentpoli cyhub.unctad.org/ISDS (accessed 19 June 2018). Note that this dataset includes only information about investment arbitrations that are public.

[24] See in particular, Van Harten, Investment Treaty Arbitration. For an elaboration of these criticisms in the context of the European Union's ongoing Multilateral Investment Court project, see European Commission Staff Working Document Impact Assessment, 'Multilateral reform of investment dispute resolution', 13 September 2017, 11–15.

[25] e.g., ADC Affiliate Ltd v. Republic of Hungary, ICSID Case No. ARB/03/16, Award (2 October 2006), para 532.

security interests or to maintain public order?[26] Should *amicus curiae* briefs be admitted by investment tribunals?[27] It was in response to these systemic, procedural and interpretative challenges that commentators and tribunals drew analogies with other legal regimes as a way to conceptualise and to develop international investment law. One way in which they did so was by drawing an analogy with domestic public law.[28]

Anthea Roberts identifies two rationales for drawing a parallel between international investment law and public law.[29] The first, termed the 'public action theory', draws on the traditional idea, elaborated in the context of sovereign immunity, that a state can act in both public and private capacities. This creates a 'bright-line test' according to which 'investment treaty arbitrations are public law disputes because the state acted in its public capacity when entering into the treaty, and, accordingly, liability for treaty breaches should also be understood as public'.[30] The seemingly clear distinction between public and private is somewhat muddied when one takes into account the existence of 'umbrella clauses' in many IIAs, which provide (public) treaty protection to (private) contractual obligations.[31]

According to a second theory, termed the 'public interest theory', the basis of the public law analogy rests on the fact that disputes regarding both domestic public law and international investment law may involve adjudicating upon acts that 'involve significant matters of public concern that transcend the private rights and obligations of the disputing parties'.[32] Whilst there may be disagreement regarding which matters

---

[26] e.g., *Enron Creditors Recovery Corp. & Ponderosa Assets L.P.* v. *Argentine Republic*, ICSID Case No. ARB/01/3 (22 May 2007) paras 322–45; *CMS Gas Transmission Co.* v. *Argentine Republic*, ICSID Case No. ARB/01/8 (12 May 2005) paras 353–78. Cf *Continental Casualty Co.* v. *Argentine Republic*, ICSID Case No. ARB/03/9 (5 September 2008) paras 189–230.

[27] *Aguas del Tunari S.A.* v. *The Republic of Bolivia*, ICSID Case No. ARB/03/02 (21 October 2005) paras 15–18. Cf *Suez, Sociedad General de Aguas de Barcelona, S. A. and Vivendi Universal S.A.* v. *Argentine Republic*, ICSID Case No. ARB/03/19, Order in Response to a Petition by Five Non-Governmental Organizations for Permission to Make an Amicus Curiae Submission (12 February 2007).

[28] Roberts, 'Clash of Paradigms', 46.

[29] Roberts, 'Clash of Paradigms', 64–5. Cf Alvarez, 'Is Investor–State Arbitration "Public"?', 535–6 (identifying 10 reasons why the international investment regime is purportedly 'public').

[30] Roberts, 'Clash of Paradigms', 64–5.

[31] ibid., 65. As Roberts notes, the public v. private distinction is also complicated by the existence of stabilisation clauses in contracts, which provide for compensation for certain regulatory acts.

[32] Roberts, 'Clash of Paradigms', 65. See also, Burke-White and von Staden, 'Private Litigation in a Public Sphere: The Standard of Review in Investor–State Arbitrations',

fall within this category, certain investment disputes, such as those related to the environment, human rights or a state's economy, clearly may have ramifications that go beyond the individual dispute.[33]

A third theory, which I will call the 'functionalist approach', emphasises the functional similarity of the two regimes. According to this theory, international investment law is akin to public law because it imposes restraints on a state's exercise of powers vis-à-vis private actors in much the same way that domestic public law imposes restraints on the state's exercise of powers over those within its jurisdiction.[34] In the domain of dispute settlement, international investment tribunals apply standards that constrain the sovereign actions of a state's legislature, executive and judiciary, at the behest of a natural or legal person. As such, they are considered to function in an analogous manner to domestic courts exercising judicial review over the acts of the executive branch of government.[35]

Whilst this theory recognises that international investment law imposes additional restrictions on the sovereignty of a state, it also

288. ('The arbitrations that we would classify as falling within the public law sphere are those in which the outcome-determinative issue in the arbitration requires a determination of the state's power and legal authority to undertake regulation in the public interest.')

[33] Roberts, 'Clash of Paradigms', 65. For what might be considered a paradigm example, see *Methanex v. USA*, Final Award on Jurisdiction and Merits (3 August 2005). That case related to a ban on methyl tertiary butyl ether (MTBE), which California claimed contaminated drinking water supplies and posed a significant risk to human health and the environment.

[34] Schill, 'Introduction', 17. See also, Van Harten, *Investment Treaty Arbitration*, 4; Montt, *State Liability*, 12–17; S. W. Schill, 'Deference in Investment Treaty Arbitration: Reconceptualising the Standard of Review', (2012) 3 JIDS 577, 587; Van Harten and Loughlin, 'Investment Treaty Arbitration', 148; T. Wälde & A. Kolo, 'Environmental Regulation, Investment Protection and "Regulatory Taking" in International Law', (2001) 50 ICLQ 811 ('Comparative constitutional law seems to provide the most suitable analogy and precedent since treaties in effect set up a similar system of higher-ranked controls over domestic law-making . . . '). See also, the Submission of the European Union on 'Possible Reform of investor–state dispute settlement (ISDS)' to UNICTRAL Working Group III, 12 December 2017, UN Doc. A/CN.9/WG.III/WP.145, para 5. ('These public international law treaties deal with the *sovereign capacity of states to regulate*, by providing certain protections which are enforceable by investors. This creates a situation similar to public or constitutional law, in which individuals are protected from acts of the state and can act to enforce those protections. It is important to recall that the state is acting in its sovereign capacity, both in approving these treaties and as regards the acts challenged.')

[35] Van Harten and Loughlin, 'Investment Treaty Arbitration', 146–8 (describing the international investment system as 'akin to domestic judicial review in that it keeps public authorities within the bounds of legality and provides enforceable remedies to individuals harmed by unlawful state conduct').

acknowledges that the state is in a peculiar position in relation both to foreign investors and to those within its jurisdiction. In the words of Santiago Montt:

> the state possesses the constitutional power to redefine and readjust the relationship between private interests and the public interest. Put differently, it has the constitutional duty to allocate burdens and benefits across society in its permanent quest for the public good. The constant upsetting of the status quo, hence, is part of the essence of the regulatory state . . . [36]

As a consequence of this regulatory function, the state can legally encroach on private rights without necessarily incurring liability for actions that fall within its prerogative.[37] A necessary corollary of this power is the possibility of judicial review of legislative and/or administrative acts. However, it also implies that the state should be accorded deference when its actions are reviewed by courts or tribunals.[38]

Regardless which theory is adopted (and whether it is adopted wholesale or piecemeal),[39] the analogy with public law provides the basis for responses to a variety of systemic and substantive challenges that investment law raises.[40] On a general level, it acts as a normative benchmark against which one can evaluate the current system of international

---

[36] Montt, *State Liability*, 7–8.

[37] ibid. (stating that '[s]omething more than a demonstration of economic damages is needed in order to successfully demand that the government pay compensation'). See also, J. Arato, 'The Margin of Appreciation in International Investment Law', (2014) 54 Virginia JIL 545, 548–9 (stating that 'it is uncontroversial that state action cannot be considered unfair or inequitable just because it affects a foreign investor's bottom line . . . States retain significant authority to regulate in the public interest, even if such authority is curtailed by their treaty obligations, and it will often happen that legitimate regulatory measures will reduce the value of an investment without entailing any violation of the foreign investor's rights').

[38] W. W. Burke-White and A. von Staden, 'Private Litigation in a Public Sphere: The Standard of Review in Investor–State Arbitrations', (2010) 35 Yale JIL 283, 345; Arato, 'The Margin of Appreciation', 549.

[39] Some authors recognise certain elements of the public law analogy as valid, but do not adopt the public law analogy wholesale. Instead, they characterise the investment regime as a public/private hybrid or as a *sui generis* regime; see e.g., Roberts, 'Clash of Paradigms', 94; Alvarez, 'Is Investor–State Arbitration "Public"?', 576; J. Maupin, 'Public and Private in International Investment Law: An Integrated Systems Approach', (2014) 54 Virginia JIL 367; Paparinskis, 'Analogies and Other Regimes'; Z. Douglas, 'The Hybrid Foundations of Investment Treaty Arbitration', (2003) 54 BYIL 151.

[40] See e.g., Schill, 'Introduction', 24 (calling the public law analogy the 'standard methodology of thinking about issues in international investment law, both as regards the interpretation of the often vague standards of investment protection and also in addressing concerns about the institutional and procedural structure of investor–state dispute'). See

investment arbitration and as inspiration for the development of international investment law.[41] For Gus Van Harten, for example, those that adjudicate public law matters should be accountable and independent, and their decision-making should be both open and coherent. The present system of investor–state arbitration squarely fails, in his opinion, to live up to these ideals.[42] For others, such as Stephan Schill and Santiago Montt, the analogy with public law plays a more direct role, providing arbitrators with a repository of solutions to specific issues on which investment treaties are vague, ambiguous or silent.

One of the challenges that domestic public law has been called upon to address is the interpretation of provisions of a 'Delphic economy of language'[43] that invite 'an almost infinite range of arguments'.[44] Take the obligation to accord FET – a standard fixture in almost all investment treaties – as an example.[45] Whilst the terms 'fair' and 'equitable' provide the interpreter with a significant degree of flexibility to account for the particularities of the case at hand, they have quite correctly been deemed to be 'almost devoid of any substantial meaning'.[46] Nor do Articles 31 and 32 of the VCLT provide interpreters with much assistance in interpreting FET.[47] Tribunals have thus been left with precious little to address the 'fundamental and practical question that every arbitral tribunal must answer: by what criteria, standard or test is an arbitral

---

also, S. W. Schill, 'Editorial: Towards a Normative Framework for Investment Law Reform', (2014) 15 JWIT 795.

[41] Schill, 'Introduction', 26; Van Harten, *Investment Treaty Arbitration*, Chapter 7. This is termed comparison on the 'macro' level by Roberts and Vadi; Roberts, 'Clash of Paradigms', 47; Vadi, *Analogies*, Chapters 4 and 5.

[42] Van Harten, *Investment Treaty Arbitration*, Chapter 7.

[43] *Lemire*, para 246.

[44] R. Kläger, *'Fair and Equitable Treatment' in International Investment Law* (CUP 2011) 3.

[45] See e.g., Denmark–Ethiopia BIT, Article 3(1) ('Each Contracting Party shall in its territory accord to investments made by investors of the other Contracting Party fair and equitable treatment . . . '); Thailand–Argentina BIT, Article 4(1)(a) ('Investments of investors of one Contracting Party in the territory of the other Contracting Party, and also the returns therefrom, shall receive treatment which is fair and equitable . . . ').

[46] R. Kläger, 'Fair and Equitable Treatment: A Look at the Theoretical Underpinnings of Legitimacy and Fairness', (2010) 11 JWIT 435, 438. Cf M. Paparinskis, *The International Minimum Standard and Fair and Equitable Treatment* (OUP 2013) 112–14.

[47] Roberts, 'Clash of Paradigms', 51; Kläger, 'Fair and Equitable Treatment', 438 (stating that a literal interpretation would be 'doomed to failure from the outset'). See also, *Suez, Sociedad General de Aguas de Barcelona S.A., and InterAgua Servicios Integrales del Aguas v. Argentina*, ICSID Case No. ARB/03/19, Decision on Liability, 30 July 2010, para 202 (stating that the FET obligation is 'not judicially operational in the sense that they lend themselves to being readily applied to complex, concrete investment fact situations').

tribunal to determine whether the specific treatment accorded to investments of a particular foreign investor in a given context is or is not "fair and equitable"?'[48]

A range of methods for the operationalisation of the public law analogy have been suggested. At one end of the spectrum is a 'methodologically loose' use of comparative law,[49] akin to the 'learning' argument that is commonly invoked by those defending the use of foreign law by domestic courts.[50] According to this argument, comparative surveys of public law may open arbitrators' eyes to the range of possible interpretations of IIAs that are available, allowing them to consider how and why certain approaches have been taken in domestic systems and whether such an approach is suitable for the international level.[51] Such use of comparative law entails no obligation to follow the solution adopted by domestic law: '[c]omparative public law thus can be an eye-opener in raising awareness of possible interpretations of investment treaties without controlling that interpretation'.[52]

At the other end of the spectrum is a more ambitious use of comparative law, which I will call the 'general principles method'. According to this method, the interpreter is obliged, by virtue of Article 31(3)(c) VCLT,[53] to take into account comparative surveys of domestic public law insofar as these surveys elucidate relevant general principles of law within the meaning of Article 38(1)(c) of the Statute of the ICJ.[54] This allows investment tribunals to concretise both the minimum and maximum levels of protection afforded by IIAs, such as developing 'standards [to which] administrative proceedings have to conform under fair and equitable treatment, or develop[ing] methods and thresholds for determining when non-

---

[48] *Suez, Sociedad General de Aguas de Barcelona S.A.*, para 202.

[49] S. W. Schill, 'Sources of International Investment Law: Multilateralization, Arbitral Precedent, Comparativism, Soft Law', in S. Besson & J. d'Aspremont (eds), *The Oxford Handbook on the Sources of Law* (2017) 1107–8.

[50] See e.g., Justice Breyer in N. Dorsen, 'A Conservation between US Supreme Courts Justices' (2005) 3 International Journal of Constitutional Law 519, 523; V. Jackson, 'Constitutional Comparisons: Convergence, Resistance, Engagement' (2005) 119 Harvard LR 109, 114; R. Bader Ginsburg, 'Looking Beyond our Borders: The Value of a Comparative Perspective in Constitutional Adjudication' (2003) 40 Idaho LR 1.

[51] Schill, 'Introduction', 26, 33; Montt, *State Liability*, 343–4.

[52] Schill, 'Introduction', 26.

[53] Article 31(3)(c) of the VCLT provides: 'There shall be taken into account, together with context . . . any relevant rules of international law application in the relations between the parties.'

[54] Schill, 'Deference', 594–5; Montt, *State Liability*, 344.

compensable regulation turns into a regulatory taking requiring compensation'.[55]

For public international lawyers, the clear route of legal reasoning that runs through Article 38 of the ICJ Statute and Article 31 of the VCLT seems to provide an obvious pathway through which comparative law – with its attendant benefits – could be incorporated into investment law jurisprudence. The premise underlying this approach is that IIAs are creatures of international law and thus their implementation, interpretation and application is controlled by the sources of law and rules of interpretation of public international law. Schill puts this clearly when he states that:

> given that investment treaty tribunals are constituted under international investment treaties, public international law has a controlling function for how arbitral tribunals can make use of comparative public law. They can only do so to the extent to which the applicable international legal sources leave interpretive leeway to arbitral tribunals.[56]

However, even amongst public international lawyers, the general principles method is contentious. One of the most critical voices has been that of José Alvarez, who has forcefully denounced the general principles method on both practical and methodological grounds, whilst also more broadly criticising the public law analogy itself.[57]

From a practical perspective, Alvarez argues that the prospects of finding general principles of public law that could be applicable to investment law 'would appear to be very scant indeed'[58] as 'national public laws regarding property rights are notoriously context-dependent and driven by cultural and other social values'.[59] In his view, the heterogeneity of domestic laws was the very basis for the creation of autonomous investor rights in international investment law.[60] Accordingly, Alvarez argues that the drafters of IIAs must have intended treaty terms to have a meaning that is autonomous from national law, an intention that would be undermined by the adoption of the general principles method.

---

[55] Schill, 'Introduction', 33.
[56] Schill, 'Deference', 594–5.
[57] ibid., 535, 542–5. Alvarez himself considers the method to be more appropriately conceived of as a hybridised form of public and private law dispute settlement; ibid., 540, 576.
[58] ibid., 565.
[59] ibid., 565.
[60] ibid., 566.

Methodologically, Alvarez notes that 'diverse and inconsistent' conceptions of general principles have plagued international law scholarship and practice for years. Whilst some scholars claim that general principles must be induced from municipal legal orders, others argue that general principles should be those 'derived from the specific nature of the international community', and yet another group contends that general principles should be those 'inherent to the idea of law'.[61] In relation to the general principles method specifically, Alvarez argues that it is unclear how many jurisdictions need to be surveyed to induce a general principle, whether one could adopt a convenience sampling method (for example, on the basis of 'legal families'),[62] and how one should account for the context in which the domestic law operates.[63] This lack of methodological clarity opens the door to courts and tribunals to conduct superficial comparative surveys of a select group of countries, presenting an opportunity for adjudicators to mask their subjective preferences with 'careless comparativism'.[64] Such an approach would, in his view, constitute a 'considerable expansion of the third source in Article 38 of the Statute of the ICJ'[65] that may 'become a politically charged route for a *de facto* (and unauthorized) return to the Calvo Clause'.[66]

Alvarez's scepticism regarding the use of general principles from other regimes in investment law has not gone unchallenged. Commenting on a previous paper published by Alvarez,[67] Alec Stone Sweet and Giacinto della Cananea contend that his analysis constitutes 'elaborate wishful thinking'[68] that 'fails to explain actual judicial practice'.[69] The authors point to the dissemination of proportionality

---

[61] ibid., 564 (citing O. Schachter, *International Law in Theory and Practice* (Springer 1991) 50–5).

[62] For more on the concept of 'legal families', see R. David, C. Jauffret-Spinosi & M. Goré, *Les grands systèmes de droit contemporains* (12th edn, Dalloz 2016); K. Zweigert & H. Kötz, *An Introduction to Comparative Law* (3rd edn, OUP 1998); N. Jain, 'Judicial Lawmaking and General Principles of Law in International Criminal Law', (2016) 57 Harvard Intl L J 111, 134–7; M. Pargendler, 'The Rise and Decline of Legal Families', (2012) 60 American J Comp L 1043.

[63] Alvarez, 'Is Investor–State Arbitration "Public"?', 568. J. Ellis, 'General Principles and Comparative Law', (2011) 22 EJIL 955–8, 962–6.

[64] Alvarez, 'Is Investor–State Arbitration "Public"?', 569.

[65] ibid., 564.

[66] ibid., 569.

[67] Alvarez, 'Beware Boundary Crossings'.

[68] A. Stone Sweet & G. della Cananea, 'Proportionality, General Principles of Law, and Investor–State Arbitration: A Response to José Alvarez', (2014) 46 NYU J Intl L & Pol 911, 943.

[69] ibid., 916.

analysis in the courts of the European Union, the European Court of Human Rights and the World Trade Organization to demonstrate that general principles have moved freely between domestic and international jurisdictions without being 'bound by originalism or the constraints of micro-institutional, comparative analysis' that Alvarez claims should preclude their diffusion.[70]

Stone Sweet and della Cananea are right to identify the core of Alvarez's argument regarding general principles as normative and prescriptive, rather than descriptive, and are also correct to point to the dissemination of certain general principles, such as proportionality, as evidence of the breach of such normative precepts. However, their argument aims to respond to different elements of Alvarez's argument than the present study. Specifically, they aim to show that the intention of states parties to a treaty and inter-regime differences have not in practice precluded the spread of general principles.[71] The authors do not aim to answer the different, but related, question of whether and how investment tribunals use comparative law.[72] As such, whilst Stone Sweet and della Cananea's description of the use of general principles might be valid for the principles that are the subject of their study, it does not engage with the theoretical and methodological questions raised by the use of comparative law by tribunals.

Alvarez's criticisms – and the debate surrounding the general principles method more generally – focus on the wrong questions by relying on idealised normative constructions of general principles and presumptions about the use of comparative law. Although the general principles method might strike international lawyers as an obvious (if not somewhat convoluted) method of incorporating comparative law into investment jurisprudence, an examination of the awards in which comparative law has been invoked shows that this is not how tribunals in fact use domestic law. Instead, the way in which tribunals use comparative law raises different theoretical and methodological questions that have not yet been addressed in the literature.

---

[70] ibid., 943.
[71] ibid.
[72] The authors note in passing that tribunals have 'largely refrained' from adducing general principles from comparative surveys of domestic law; ibid., 951.

5.3   Comparative Law in the Case Law of Investment Tribunals

To date, investment tribunals have principally drawn on domestic law in one of two ways. First, in the rare instances in which the use of comparative public law has been linked to general principles of law, its use has not been justified *because* the domestic law manifests a general principle of law, but rather because the treaty provision being interpreted is itself *derived from* a general principle of law. Such reasoning is markedly different from the general principles method described above. Second, in a number of cases, comparative public law plays an auxiliary role in the reasoning of the Tribunal, acting to confirm or support a conclusion that has been made on other grounds. Each of these uses raises different theoretical and methodological issues that will be explored in the following section.

5.3.1   Fair and Equitable Treatment as Derived from a General Principle of Law

The first strand of case law that draws on comparative public law does so in a way that is notably distinct from the general principles method propounded in the literature. These awards reason that FET is derived from the general principle of good faith, and that, because of this origin, it is justifiable to examine comparative public law in order to substantiate the content of the obligation.

The first instance of this reasoning was the Decision on Liability in *Total* v. *Argentina*,[73] in which the Claimant argued that Argentina had breached FET by frustrating its legitimate expectations. In its Decision, the Tribunal spelled out in more depth why, in its view, comparative public law was instructive when interpreting the FET obligation:

> In determining the scope of a right or obligation, Tribunals have often looked as a benchmark to international or comparative standards. Indeed, as is often the case for general standards applicable in any legal system (such as 'due process'), a comparative analysis of what is considered generally fair or unfair conduct by domestic public authorities in respect of private firms and investors in domestic law may also be relevant to identify the legal standards under BITs. Such an approach is justified because, factually, the situations and conduct to be evaluated under

---

[73] *Total S.A.* v. *The Argentine Republic*, ICSID Case No. ARB/04/01, Decision on Liability (27 December 2010).

a BIT occur within the legal system and social, economic and business environment of the host State. Moreover, *legally, the fair and equitable treatment standard is derived from the requirement of good faith which is undoubtedly a general principle of law under Article 38(1) of the Statute of the International Court of Justice.*[74]

The *Total* Tribunal proceeded to accept the argument that the doctrine of legitimate expectations was based on the general principle of good faith, and hence 'that a comparative analysis of the protection of legitimate expectations in domestic jurisdictions is justified'.[75] Acknowledging that 'the scope and legal basis of the principle varies' between domestic systems, the Tribunal claimed nevertheless that 'it has been recognized lately in both civil law and in common law jurisdictions within well defined limits',[76] citing Argentinian and English court decisions, as well as scholarly writings, as authority. However, when it came to define the scope of the doctrine, the Tribunal relied solely on secondary sources as authority for the proposition that:

> in domestic legal systems the doctrine of legitimate expectations supports 'the entitlement of an individual to legal protection from harm caused by a public authority retreating from a previous publicly stated position, whether that be in the form of a formal decision or in the form of a representation'.[77]

Two subsequent arbitral awards have referred to the *Total* Tribunal's Decision as authority for the proposition that comparative public law can assist in the interpretation of FET. In *Toto* v. *Lebanon*,[78] the Tribunal was called on to adjudicate a purported breach of FET under Article 3(1) of the Italy–Lebanon BIT. The Tribunal in that case drew on previous arbitral awards to elaborate what is entailed by FET and the doctrine of

---

[74] ibid., para 111 (emphasis added, citations omitted).

[75] *Total*, para 128.

[76] ibid.

[77] ibid., para 129. The secondary source from which the quote is drawn from is C. Brown, 'The Protection of Legitimate Expectations as a "General Principle of Law": Some Preliminary Thoughts', (2009) 1 Transnational Dispute Management, available at www .transnational-dispute-management.com/article.asp?key=1303. Brown himself in turn relies on the comparative surveys carried out by Jürgen Schwarze (J. Schwarze, *European Administrative Law* (Sweet & Maxwell 2006)) and Søren Schønberg (S. Schønberg, *Legitimate Expectations in Administrative Law* (OUP 2000)) to reach the conclusion that 'there is only a modest amount of common ground'.

[78] *Toto Costruzioni Generali S.p.A.* v. *The Republic of Lebanon*, ICSID Case No. ARB/07/12, Award (7 June 2012). Note that the Tribunal also cited the *Lemire* v. *Ukraine* and *Noble* v. *Romania* awards (examined below) as authority; ibid., fn 129.

legitimate expectations, adding that '[t]he fair and equitable treatment standard of international law does not depend on the perception of the frustrated investor, but should use public international law and comparative domestic public law as a benchmark[, a]s was recently also confirmed in *Total S.A.* v. *Argentina*'.[79]

Whilst the Tribunal reiterated that 'fair and equitable treatment has to be interpreted with international and comparative standards as a benchmark', it found that Toto had not furnished the Tribunal with any evidence that Lebanon had actually fallen below such standards.[80] It is notable that the Tribunal did not in its analysis refer to any domestic law or any comparative survey in order to concretise the scope of the doctrine of legitimate expectations.

The most recent award to refer to comparative public law – and the one that seems to be most closely aligned to the general principles method – is *Gold Reserve* v. *Venezuela*.[81] That case related inter alia the alleged breach of FET under Article II(2) of the Canada–Venezuela BIT by Venezuela. Like the tribunals in *Total* and *Toto*, the Tribunal commenced its analysis by reviewing the investment awards that had elaborated FET, paying particular attention to 'a few cases whose factual circumstances appear to be closer to the facts of the present case'.[82] It noted that:

> Article 54 of the ICSID Arbitration (Additional Facility) Rules directs ICSID tribunals to apply 'such rules of international law as may be applicable' unless otherwise agreed by the parties. This reference may be considered to include the 'general principles of law recognized by civilized nations' referred to in Article 38 of the Statute of the International Court of Justice ...
>
> With particular regard to the legal sources of one of the standards for respect of the fair and equitable treatment principles, i.e. the protection of 'legitimate expectations', these sources are to be found in the comparative analysis of many domestic legal systems. This has been succinctly stated recently by other ICSID tribunals, for example in *Total* v. *Argentina* and in *Toto Construzioni SpA* v. *Republic of Lebanon*.[83]

[79] ibid., para 166.
[80] ibid., para 193. See also, paras 205, 224.
[81] *Gold Reserve Inc.* v. *Bolivarian Republic of Venezuela*, ICSID Case No. ARB(AF)/09/1, Award (22 September 2014).
[82] ibid., para 568.
[83] ibid., paras 575–6 (citations omitted). It should be noted that this is not, in fact, what Article 54 of the Additional Facility Rules provides. Article 54(1)(a) of the Rules provides that, failing the designation of applicable law by the parties, tribunals shall apply 'such rules of international law as the Tribunal considers applicable'.

The Tribunal continued to cite German, French, English, Argentinian and Venezuelan law to demonstrate that the doctrine of 'legitimate expectations is found in different legal traditions according to which some expectations may be reasonably or legitimately created for a private person by the constant behaviour and/or promises of its legal partner, in particular when this partner is the public administration on which this private person is dependant'.[84]

This strand of case law is open to criticism on several grounds. First, the *Toto* and *Gold Reserve* Awards expressly refer to the Tribunal's Decision in *Total* as authority for their invocation of comparative law.[85] Yet that Award does not bear close scrutiny. The paragraph of the *Total* Decision on which the *Toto* and *Gold Reserve* Tribunals rely states that '[T]ribunals have often looked as a benchmark [of what constitutes FET] to international or comparative standards',[86] citing two awards as authority: the first Partial Award in *S.D. Myers, Inc.* v. *Canada* and the Award in *Genin and Others* v. *Estonia*. However, when one refers back to those awards, there is neither reference to comparative public law nor is there any discussion regarding its use to interpret the relevant treaty provisions.[87] Indeed, the *Genin* Award seems, if anything, to be authority for the rather different proposition that domestic law and the FET standard are autonomous, stating that '[w]hile the exact content of [the FET] standard is not clear, the Tribunal understands it to require an "international minimum standard" *that is separate from domestic law*'.[88] The subsequent awards are seemingly oblivious to the fact that the assertion upon which their use of comparative public law is based is nothing but a juristic sleight of hand.[89]

Second, despite the Tribunals' attempts to justify the use of comparative public law to interpret treaty standards, their comparative surveys

---

[84] ibid., para 576.

[85] NB the *Gold Reserve* Award incorrectly cites para 11 of the *Total* Award. In fact, para 11 describes procedural aspects of the case; the correct citation is to para 111.

[86] *Total*, para 111.

[87] See *S.D. Myers, Inc.* v. *Government of Canada*, First Partial Award (13 November 2000), paras 263–4; *Alex Genin, Eastern Credit Limited, Inc. and A.S. Baltoil* v. *The Republic of Estonia*, ICSID Case No. ARB/99/2, Award (25 June 2001), paras 367 et seq. The *Total* Decision later cites the *Noble* Award as authority for the same; *Total*, fn 106. As noted below, the Decision in *Noble* was not based on an analysis of comparative public law, but on the facts.

[88] *Genin*, para 367.

[89] The *Gold Reserve* Award also cites several academic works (including Schill) as authority for the proposition that the source of legitimate expectations is to be found in comparative surveys of domestic legal systems; *Gold Reserve*, fn 474.

provide little detail as to how analogous matters are in fact dealt with under domestic law. Indeed, the *Toto* Tribunal failed to cite *any* domestic law, whilst the *Total* and *Gold Reserve* Tribunals used perfunctory surveys of comparative law to demonstrate merely that the doctrine of legitimate expectations is recognised in some form or another in multiple domestic jurisdictions.[90] As such, it would be correct to say that the comparative surveys adduced failed to shape meaningfully the Tribunals' approach to FET or legitimate expectations, or to determine the outcome of the case.

Third, the most notable feature of these awards is the absence of any claim that comparative public law manifests a relevant general principle of law that is applicable by virtue of Article 31(3)(c) of the Vienna Convention. The Tribunals scarcely enquired into the commonalities that exist between domestic jurisdictions (except the general notion that legitimate expectations are protected), nor did they draw on Article 31(3)(c) of the VCLT as the basis for invoking comparative law. Instead, the reasoning pursued was essentially the inverse of the general principles method: rather than comparative public law constituting a general principle of law and thus being relevant to the interpretation of the treaty, the treaty provision's origins as a general principle of law justified recourse to comparative public law.

This rationale bears a close resemblance to the approach recently adopted by Campbell McLachlan and his co-authors.[91] Whilst the Tribunal in *Total* considered FET to be derived from the general principle of good faith,[92] McLachlan et al. consider the obligation to give 'modern expression' to a *general principle of due process*',[93] which they understand to be synonymous with the 'minimum requirements of the rule of law'.[94] Leaving aside the question whether FET is based on good faith, due process or any other general principle, the authors are right to point out that 'the voluntary acceptance of the principle by treaty transforms the question from one of obligation to one of content'.[95] In other words, recourse to comparative law becomes necessary to flesh out the

---

[90] *Total*, paras 129–30.

[91] C. McLachlan et al., *International Investment Law: Substantive Principles* (2nd edn, OUP 2017).

[92] Although cf ibid., §7.183, where McLachlan et al. acknowledge that tribunals have linked the doctrine of legitimate expectations to the general principle of good faith.

[93] ibid., §7.15.

[94] ibid., §7.16.

[95] ibid., §7.19.

content of FET, rather than to establish its character as a rule of law.[96] As such, even if one accepts that FET is derived from a general principle, the methodological criticisms that Alvarez raises in relation to the use of comparative public law are still relevant.

5.3.2   Comparative Public Law as Auxiliary Reasoning

The abovementioned awards are exceptional in that they are the only three awards to link the use of comparative public law to general principles of law. Other tribunals have drawn on comparative law as confirmation of a conclusion reached on other grounds.[97] Whilst not dispositive of the Tribunals' reasoning, this use of comparative law nevertheless merits close analysis. In particular, the awards raise the question whether, from the point of view of methodology or principle, it matters that comparative law plays a merely confirmatory role, as opposed to forming the operative part of the reasoning of a tribunal.

One of the first arbitral awards to refer to comparative public law was *Noble* v. *Romania*,[98] in which the Tribunal was faced with the question of whether judicial insolvency proceedings constituted 'arbitrary' or 'discriminatory' measures that fell foul of Article II(2)(b) of the US–Romania BIT. As the Treaty gave no definition of arbitrary or discriminatory measures, the Tribunal found the definition of arbitrary treatment given by the International Court of Justice (ICJ) in the *ELSI* case to be instructive; namely, that an arbitrary action was 'something opposed to the rule of law . . . [in the sense that it] is a wilful disregard of due process of law, an act which shocks, or at least surprises, a sense of judicial propriety'.[99] In light of the facts of the case at hand (namely, the jobs at

---

[96]   ibid. Cf J. E. Alvarez, 'The Public International Law Regime Governing International Investment', (2009) 344 Recueil des cours 193, 362–3 (stating that the 'treatification' of investment protection does not necessarily result in increased precision).

[97]   One could also place the Award in *Occidental* v. *Ecuador* in this category, in which the Tribunal cited comparative public law, alongside WTO law and other international investment awards, as authority for the proposition that the principle of proportionality is relevant for investment disputes. The Tribunal only noted in passing that '[i]t is very well-established law in a number of European countries that there is a principle of proportionality' before analysing proportionality in other investment awards in depth. *Occidental Petroleum Corporation and Occidental Exploration and Production Company* v. *The Republic of Ecuador*, ICSID Case No. ARB/06/11, Award (5 October 2012), paras 402–9.

[98]   *Noble Ventures, Inc.* v. *Romania*, ICSID Case No. ARB/01/11, Award (12 October 2005).

[99]   ibid., para 176, citing *Elettronica Sicula S.p.A. (ELSI) (United States of America* v. *Italy)*, [1989] ICJ Rep 15, para 128.

stake, the factual insolvency of the company and the likelihood of debt restructuring), the Tribunal concluded that 'there are sufficient grounds not to regard the proceedings as arbitrary'[100] and that 'the proceedings were at the time the only short term solution for the "social crisis"'[101] that had engulfed the town in which the mill at issue was located.

It was only *after* having arrived at this conclusion that the Tribunal referred to comparative law. Harking back to the definition of arbitrariness adopted by the ICJ in *ELSI*, the Tribunal stated that '[s]uch proceedings [i.e. the judicial insolvency proceedings at issue] *are provided for in all legal systems* and for much the same reasons. One therefore cannot say that they were "opposed to the rule of law" ... [the Claimant] was in a situation that would have justified the initiation of comparable proceedings *in most other countries*. Arbitrariness is therefore excluded'.[102] Like the Tribunal in *Toto*, the *Noble* Tribunal failed to point to any specific domestic law or comparative law study as authority for its statement.

Comparative public law played a similarly auxiliary role in the reasoning of the Tribunal in *Plama* v. *Bulgaria*. One argument advanced by the Claimant in that case was that taxes imposed by Bulgaria as the result of debt restructuring breached the FET obligation enshrined in Article 10(1) of the Energy Charter Treaty (ECT).[103] This claim was dismissed by the Tribunal on procedural grounds.[104] However, after noting that the claim was inadmissible, the Tribunal nevertheless continued to address Plama's argument under the FET obligation, finding that 'no action by Respondent ... comes anywhere near to being unfair or inequitable treatment', as the Claimant was, or should have been, aware of the tax implications of the debt restructuring.[105] It was only then, after having rejected Plama's FET claim on both procedural grounds and on the merits, that the Tribunal noted *obiter* that:

> Respondent produced evidence which shows that the tax laws of many countries around the world treat debt reductions, as were negotiated in

---

[100] ibid., para 177.
[101] ibid., para 177.
[102] ibid., para 178 (emphasis added).
[103] Energy Charter Treaty, 17 December 1994, 2080 UNTS 95.
[104] Plama had not referred the matter to Bulgarian tax authorities, as required under Article 21(5) of the ECT. The Tribunal therefore could not 'see how this claim gives rise to a violation of Bulgaria's obligations under the ECT'; *Plama Consortium Limited* v. *Republic of Bulgaria*, ICSID Case No. ARB/03/24, Award (27 August 2008) para 266.
[105] ibid., paras 267–8.

this case, as income taxable to the beneficiary . . . [i]t cannot therefore be said that Bulgaria's law in this respect was unfair, inadequate, inequitable or discriminatory. It was part of the generally applicable law of the country like that of many other countries.[106]

A final example is the Decision on Jurisdiction and Admissibility in *Lemire* v. *Ukraine*,[107] in which the Tribunal was called upon to decide if a Ukrainian regulation that required radio stations to play at least 50 per cent Ukrainian music was a prohibited local content requirement under Article II.6 of the US–Ukraine BIT. The Tribunal accepted Ukraine's argument that a state has the right to regulate its affairs for the public good, especially in matters related to culture or language:

> As a sovereign State, Ukraine has the inherent right to regulate its affairs and adopt law in order to protect the common good of its people . . . The *'high measure of deference that international law generally extends to the right of domestic authorities to regulate matters within their own borders'* is reinforced in cases when the purpose of the legislation affects deeply felt cultural or linguistic traits of the community.[108]

Noting that other countries, such as France and Portugal, had adopted similar requirements for radio stations, the Tribunal stated that such a measure 'cannot be said to be unfair, inadequate, inequitable, or discriminatory, when it has been adopted by many countries in the world'.[109] However, it went on to state that 'this conclusion is really *obiter dicta*' as the Claimant had challenged the measure as a prohibited local content requirement, not as a breach of FET.[110] On the facts, the Tribunal found that the regulation did not have a protectionist purpose and therefore did not breach Article II.6 of the US–Ukraine BIT.

Several points regarding these awards are worthy of note. First, the Tribunals' use of comparative law does not live up to the threshold they themselves set. In both *Plama* and *Lemire*, the Tribunals stated that an

---

[106] ibid., para 269. It should be noted that the Award does not reproduce the evidence adduced by the Respondent as an annex to the Award. The Tribunal went on to reject Plama's claim on another two grounds, noting that Plama had not adduced any evidence showing that it had actually paid the tax and that it had not shown that the tax liability precluded it from obtaining financing to reopen the plant; ibid., para 271.

[107] *Joseph Charles Lemire* v. *Ukraine*, ICSID Case No. ARB/06/18, Decision on Jurisdiction and Liability (14 January 2010).

[108] ibid., para 505 (quoting *SD Myers*, First Partial Award, para 263).

[109] ibid., para 506. Note that the *Lemire* Tribunal cited para 269 from the *Plama* Award as authority for this proposition.

[110] ibid., para 507.

action could not be 'unfair, inadequate, inequitable or discriminatory' if it also existed in 'many' other countries. Yet those Tribunals cited, respectively, no domestic laws and the laws of just two countries. To claim that the measure at issue in those cases is in line with a significant body of domestic practice is therefore mere assertion that is unsupported by evidence. Furthermore, as a matter of principle, it is not evident why the domestic laws of other countries should affect our understanding of what constitutes a discriminatory or arbitrary measure. As has been pointed out in the context of the human rights law, deferring to the majority view of states in relation to a particular issue risks undermining the very rights that the international legal regime was established to protect.[111] In the context of investment law, referring to the domestic laws of 'many countries' fails to protect investors' rights if those laws are themselves arbitrary, discriminatory, unfair or inequitable.

Second, as in the preceding section, none of the awards examined drew on domestic law because it constituted a general principle of law. Rather, in each case, comparative public law was drawn on because it allowed the tribunal to substantiate a standard in the relevant treaty, such as what is 'arbitrary' (*Noble*) or 'unfair, inadequate, inequitable or discriminatory' (*Plama, Lemire*). The most notable feature of these awards is that the Claimant's argument was dismissed without relying on comparative public law at all, whether on the facts (*Noble, Lemire*) or because of failure to fulfil procedural requirements (*Plama*). Comparative public law did not signal the death knell for the claimant's argument; rather, it acted as confirmation for a decision that had already been made on other grounds.

5.4 Engaging with Practice

Whilst certain authors claim that tribunals should conduct a survey of domestic law from which they can induce general principles, in reality reference to comparative law is less pivotal to the reasoning of tribunals – and less methodologically rigorous – than the general principles method suggests. Examining the use of comparative law in light of tribunals' practice puts into sharp relief questions of significant theoretical and practical complexity. This section addresses two of the issues that are

---

[111] See e.g., E. Benvenisti, 'Margin of Appreciation, Consensus, and Universal Standards', (1999) 31 NYU JILP 843; G. Letsas, *A Theory of Interpretation of the European Convention on Human Rights* (OUP 2007). See further the discussion on the use of consensus analysis by the European Court of Human Rights in Chapter 6, section 6.4(ii).

raised by tribunals' use of comparative law: first, how might we explain why tribunals use comparative law, and, second, what methodological constraints are incumbent upon its use? This is not intended to be an exhaustive examination of the issues raised by the practice of investment tribunals; rather, it flags areas that have not yet been addressed thoroughly by the literature and may be worthy of further investigation.

5.4.1   The Interpretation of Standards

The general principles method purports both to explain why tribunals have recourse to comparative law and to normatively justify such use. From a descriptive standpoint, the cases examined in the preceding section demonstrate that tribunals' use of comparative law cannot be explained by the general principles method. A different – and more convincing – explanation why tribunals draw on comparative law can be given by focussing on the object of interpretation.

In each of the awards examined in the previous section, comparative law was adduced in order to interpret a standard.[112] In legal theory, standards are distinguished from rules on the basis of both their form and their function.[113] In relation to form, the distinction drawn is between the relative determinacy of certain legal norms (rules) and the relative vagueness of others (standards).[114] Rules bind 'a decisionmaker to respond in a determinate way to the presence of delimited triggered facts'.[115] The classic example given is that of a speed limit: in the UK, if

---

[112]   I. Tudor, *The Fair and Equitable Treatment Standard in the International Law of Foreign Investment* (OUP 2008) 131.

[113]   F. Schauer, 'The Convergence of Rules and Standards', (2003) NZLR 303, 305–6 (stating that the distinction between rules and standards has 'a wide currency in legal theory'). See also, D. Kennedy, 'Form and Substance in Private Law Adjudication', (1976) 89 Harvard LR 1685, 1685–7; H. M. Hart & A. Sacks, *The Legal Process: Basic Problems in the Making and Application of Law* (Foundation Press 1994) 139–41. For an elaboration of a theory of standards in international law, see Y. Radi, *La standardisation et le droit international: Contours d'une théorie dialectique de la formation du droit* (Bruylant 2013).

[114]   Schauer, 'The Convergence of Rules and Standards', 305 (referring to the distinction between '(comparatively) specific rules and (comparatively) vague ones as the distinction between rules (specific) and standards (vague)'). See also, Radi, *La standardisation et le droit international*, 40–2.

[115]   K. M. Sullivan, 'The Supreme Court 1991 Term, Foreword: The Justices of Rules and Standards', (1992) 106 Harvard LR 22, 58. See also, P. Schlag, 'Rules and Standards', (1985) 22 UCLA LR 379, 382–3 (stating that rules have 'a hard empirical trigger and a hard determinate response' and standards 'a soft evaluative trigger and a soft modulated response').

a driver travels faster than 70 miles per hour on a motorway, they have violated the law. Standards, on the other hand, are vague legal directives that 'collapse decisionmaking back in to the direct application of the background principle or policy to a fact situation'.[116] As an example, take a law requiring drivers to travel 'no faster than is reasonable'.[117] Instead of referring to a particular speed, an adjudicator must take into account a range of relevant factors (driving conditions, the age and condition of the car, the presence of schools in the vicinity, etc.) to determine the level of risk that is acceptable to society (and thus reasonable) in the case at hand. The formal difference between rules and standards is admittedly one of degree: they denote two 'extremes of a continuous spectrum of "ruleness", with rules representing the maximum and standards the minimum'.[118] Nevertheless, despite the fact that rules are 'not infinitely precise and standards not infinitely vague',[119] the distinction is analytically useful.[120]

Rules and standards are also distinguished on the basis of the function that they play in the legal system. H. L. A. Hart recognised that the use of standards was one method by which a legal system could cater for the inability to anticipate with certainty scenarios that may arise in the future.[121] In his view, standards are adopted when a legislature cannot determine *a priori* the interests that should be privileged in any given situation. In a similar vein, Neil MacCormick describes standards as seeking 'to strike a balance that takes account of [an] apparently irreducible plurality of values',[122] deferring the assessment of the competing values in play to adjudication of particular cases.[123] To illustrate, one

---

[116] Sullivan, 'Foreword', 58.

[117] R. B. Korobkin, 'Behavioral Analysis and Legal Form: Rules vs. Standards Revisited', (2000) 79 Oregon L Rev 23. Note that this is not a mere hypothetical example: in the 1990s, Montana had a law requiring drivers to be 'reasonable and prudent'. The law was later invalidated on the grounds of vagueness; see *State v. Stanko*, 974 P 2d 1132 (1998).

[118] Schauer, 'The Convergence of Rules and Standards', 309. See also, Korobkin, 'Behavioural Analysis', 26.

[119] Schauer, 'The Convergence of Rules and Standards', 309.

[120] See e.g., Korobkin, 'Behavioural Analysis', 30; Schauer, 'The Convergence of Rules and Standards', 305.

[121] H. L. A. Hart, *The Concept of Law* (3rd edn, OUP 2012) 130–1. The other option identified by Hart to address this was to delegate to administrative authorities the task of specifying what was required by the law; ibid., 131.

[122] N. MacCormick, *Rhetoric and the Rule of Law* (OUP 2005) 167.

[123] Cf O. Corten, 'Motif légitime et lien de causalité suffisant: un modèle d'interprétation rationnel du "raisonnable"' (1998) Annuaire français de droit international 187, 188. Corten argues that the interpretation of 'reasonable' by international courts and tribunals does not automatically depend on 'la seule subjectivité de l'interprète, mais qu'il est

might give the example of the standard of due care in Anglo-American negligence law, which only takes definite form when considered by an adjudicator in light of the circumstances of the case at hand. Rules, on the other hand, are characterised by the 'fact that certain distinguishable actions, events, or states of affairs are of such practical importance to us, as either things to avert or to bring about, that very few concomitant circumstances incline us to regard them otherwise'.[124] One example is the (relatively determinate) crime of murder, which reflects the fact that few countervailing considerations would require balancing against the heinousness of killing.[125] The determinacy of rules allows individuals to know *ex ante* the interests that the legal system will privilege in a certain scenario.

In the context of investment law, the form and the function of FET, as well as the prohibitions on arbitrary and discriminatory treatment, bear the hallmarks of a standard. The obligations are broad and indeterminate, and their adoption defers the evaluation of the myriad different factors that may be relevant to the question of what constitutes 'fair and equitable', 'arbitrary' or 'discriminatory' conduct to particular cases.[126] It acknowledges that the law simply cannot determine *a priori* which interests should take precedence in relation to certain questions.[127] The fact that domestic law has predominantly been invoked to interpret

---

susceptible de faire l'objet d'un contrôle par des tiers, et ce à l'aide de jugements de fait, et non par l'affirmation péremptoire de jugements de valeurs'. This is optimistic – Corten, for example, considers that the second stage in reasonableness analysis is the identification of a 'legitimate reason' for the act under review. Clearly, the qualification of an act as 'legitimate' or not is a subjective act, even if legitimate reasons are enumerated in the treaty provision. ibid., 189.

[124] Hart, *The Concept of Law*, 133.

[125] ibid.

[126] Cf *Total*, para 107 (stating that 'it is difficult, if not impossible "to anticipate in the abstract the range of possible types of infringements upon the investor's legal position"'; quoting C. Schreuer, 'Fair and Equitable Treatment in Arbitral Practice', (2005) 6 Journal of World Trade 357, 365). See also, *Mondev International Ltd v. United States of America*, ICSID Case No. ARB(AF)/99/2 (11 October 2002), para 118 ('a judgment of what is fair and equitable cannot be reached in the abstract; it must depend on the facts of the particular case. It is part of the essential business of courts and tribunals to make judgments such as these.'); *Waste Management Inc. v. Mexico*, ICSID Case No. ARB(AF)/00/3 (30 April 2004), para 99. ('Evidently the standard is to some extent a flexible one which must be adapted to the circumstances of each case.')

[127] Cf R. Y. Jennings, 'State Contracts in International Law', (1961) 37 BYIL 156, 180–1. ('It is perhaps also a mistaken notion to set too much store by the method of establishing minimum international standards by comparative researches into selected municipal laws.')

a standard, as opposed to rules, raises the question whether there is something about the form or the function of those norms that justifies – or perhaps necessitates – different interpretative techniques.

Standards are commonplace in international treaties that cover a wide range of subject-matter. The practice of other international courts and tribunals, in particular that of the European Court of Human Rights and International Criminal Tribunal for the former Yugoslavia, shows that investment tribunals are not alone in interpreting treaty standards by reference to domestic law.[128] The methodological and normative considerations raised by the use of comparative law is therefore not just limited to the domain of investment law but raises issues of relevance to international law more generally.

The idea that standards are interpreted differently is not new. Legal philosophers have argued that deductive reasoning is particularly inapt to describe how lawyers interpret standards. John Wisdom captured this peculiarly legal form of reasoning in a famous essay, stating that:

> In such cases we notice that the process of argument is not a *chain* of demonstrative reasoning. It is presenting and representing of those features of the case which *severally cooperate* in favour of the conclusion, in favour of saying what the reasoner wishes, in favour of calling the situation by the name by which he wishes to call it. The reasons are like the legs of a chair, not the links of a chain ... [T]he reasoning is not vertically extensive but horizontally extensive – it is the matter of the cumulative effect of several independent premises, not of the repeated transformation of one or two. And because the premises are severally inconclusive the process of deciding the issue becomes a matter of weighing the cumulative effect of another group of severally inconclusive items against the cumulative effect of another group of severally inconclusive items ... It has its own sort of logic and its own sort of end – the solution of the question at issue is a decision, a ruling by the judge.[129]

---

[128] See Chapter 6, section 6.3. Interestingly, in the process of the drafting of the Report of the Secretary-General on the ICTY, Canada suggested explicitly that 'Reference could be made to appropriate national law, if necessary, for interpretive purposes.' Letter Dated 13 April 1993 from the Permanent Representative of Canada to the United Nations Addressed to the Secretary-General 14 April 1993 S/25594, para 11. See also, *Prosecutor v. Tadić*, Decision on the Prosecutor's Motion Requesting Protective Measures for Victims and Witnesses (10 August 1995), paras 31–42, 47–8, 55, 60–7, 71; *Prosecutor v. Strugar* (Trial Chamber Decision on Defence Motion to Terminate Proceedings) IT-01–42-T (26 May 2014), paras 29–34; *Prosecutor v. Strugar* (Appeals Chamber Judgement) IT-01–42-A (17 July 2008), paras 52–4.

[129] J. Wisdom, 'Gods' (1945) 45 Proceedings of the Aristotelian Society 185, 194.

This description, whilst certainly not valid for all forms of legal reasoning, 'captures exactly and vividly the way in which we must bring a plurality of factors together into consideration when ... we seek to pass judgement upon the reasonableness of some decision'.[130] When interpreting standards, various factors, singularly incapable of supporting a particular conclusion, combine in order to provide (arguably) persuasive reasoning that supports the desired result. In the absence of clearly defined rules that lend themselves to syllogistic application, such reasoning fulfils the requirement that arbitrators provide a reasoned decision.[131]

The theory that standards are interpreted using 'horizontally extensive' reasoning accords with the practice of the tribunals examined in the preceding section, each of which adduced comparative law as just one element of reasoning – normally alongside arbitral awards and judgments of other international courts and tribunals – in support of its conclusion.[132] To adopt Wisdom's analogy, comparative law plays the role of a chair leg without which the reasoning might be more unstable but would not falter entirely.

The use of comparative law also responds to what some have called the 'tyranny of choice'.[133] The discretion left to the rule-applier in the case of a standard is not always welcome, and not every decision-maker 'has the time, energy, or inclination to engage in the "from the ground up" process that unconstrained discretion and unspecified standards require'.[134] As a result, they have a tendency to structure their choice to make it more manageable by, for example, creating 'guidelines' or 'per se rules' that apply to the standard.[135] In the same vein, decision-makers might refer to precedents interpreting the particular standard as a way to

---

[130] MacCormick, *Rhetoric*, 181.

[131] See Article 48(4), Convention on the Settlement of Investment Disputes between States and Nationals of Other States, 18 March 1965, 575 UNTS 160 ('ICSID Convention').

[132] See e.g., *Total*, paras 109–10 (citing other arbitral awards, the judgment of the ICJ in *ELSI* and Judge Higgins' Separate Opinion in *Oil Platforms* in support of its interpretation of fair and equitable treatment); *Gold Reserve*, paras 569–74 (citing other arbitral awards that recognised the protection of legitimate expectations).

[133] Schauer, 'The Convergence of Rules and Standards', 315–16. See also, F. Schauer, 'The Tyranny of Choice and the Rulification of Standards', (2005) 14 Journal of Contemporary Legal Issues 803.

[134] ibid., 316.

[135] See also, Schlag, 'Rules and Standards', 413 (stating that when we consider how standards are applied in practice 'it becomes apparent that these tests merely defer the constraints on judicial decision making to some external source such as precedent ... Inflexibility is just as much a part of standards as their supposed flexibility').

structure their reasoning and limit their discretion. In adopting these techniques,

> [f]or the decision-maker concerned about efficiency, docket-clearing (even in a non-judicial context), allocation of his or her own competence to its highest and best use, and apportioning time between more or less important decisions, a way of narrowing the range of factors to be considered from what might be available under an open-ended 'justice' or 'reasonableness' standard is highly appealing.[136]

Comparative law is one mechanism by which arbitrators constrain the otherwise unfettered freedom that FET and other standards give them. By referring to comparative law, as well as to arbitral decisions, treaties and case law of other international courts and tribunals, arbitrators are able to construct some benchmark of fairness and equitableness to which they can adhere, structuring their reasoning and absolving them of the responsibility and burden of substantiating the standard from scratch. This seems to be particularly relevant to international investment regime, in which the neutrality of arbitrators is frequently called into question.[137] By drawing on an external source of law upon which to base their reasoning, arbitrators provide a veneer of objectivity to what would otherwise be a wholly subjective decision.

The character of standards may, to a certain extent, answer the question why arbitrators have drawn on comparative law to interpret treaty provisions. A different – and more difficult – question is normative: which domestic jurisdiction(s) should they rely on? The selection of jurisdictions cannot be dissociated, in my view, from the role that comparative law plays in the reasoning of the tribunal. The following section elaborates on this.

5.4.2 The Selection of Jurisdictions and Methodological Diversity

Whilst the general principles method mandates a comprehensive (or at least representative) survey of domestic jurisdictions, recognition that

---

[136] Schauer, 'The Convergence of Rules and Standards', 316.

[137] See for example, Van Harten, *Investment Treaty Arbitration*, 167–75; G. Van Harten, 'Arbitrator Behaviour in Asymmetrical Adjudication (Part Two): An Examination of Hypotheses of Bias in Investment Treaty Arbitration', (2016) 53 Osgoode Hall LJ 540, 545; F. De Ly et al. 'Who Wins and Who Loses in Investment Arbitration? Are Investors and Host States on a Level Playing Field? The Lauder/Czech Republic Legacy', (2005) 6 JWIT 59, 60; O. Chung, 'The Lopsided International Investment Law Regime and Its Effect on the Future of Investor–State Arbitration', (2007) 47 Virginia JIL 953, 976.

comparative law plays both a role in the interpretation of standards and a confirmatory role in the reasoning of tribunals raises the question whether this does – or should – impact the methodology of the comparative survey that is carried out. A parallel can be drawn with the use of foreign law by domestic courts, which has been the subject of renewed interest following a string of highly politicised judgments delivered by the US Supreme Court in the early 2000s.[138]

One characteristic of the debate regarding the use of foreign law by domestic courts is the recognition that there is a plurality of ways in which such law can be invoked, each of which entails different normative and methodological considerations.[139] Consider the argument that foreign laws are used as a method of 'testing [an] understanding of one's own traditions and possibilities by examining them in reflection of others'.[140] Where judges are prohibited from publicly discussing pending cases because of concerns regarding neutrality and impartiality, decisions from another jurisdiction might act as a 'partial intellectual substitute' for discussion regarding the issues in a case, providing judges with 'a testing from outside that may be particularly helpful on the most controversial

---

[138] *Roper* v. *Simmons*, 543 US 551 (2005); *Lawrence* v. *Texas*, 529 US 558 (2003); *Graham* v. *Florida*, 560 US 48 (2010); *Atkins* v. *Virginia*, 536 US 304, 321 (2002). See further, J. Toobin, *The Nine: Inside the Secret World of the Supreme Court* (Anchor Books 2007) 225–32. Amongst the voluminous literature, see in particular, G. Sitaraman, 'The Use and Abuse of Foreign Law in Constitutional Interpretation' (2009) 32 Harvard Journal of Law and Public Policy 653; V. Jackson, 'Constitutional Comparisons: Convergence, Resistance, Engagement' (2005) 119 Harvard LR 109; J. Waldron, 'Foreign Law and the Modern *Ius Gentium*' (2005) 119 Harvard LR 129; E. A. Young, 'Foreign Law and the Denominator Problem' (2005) 119 Harvard LR 148; N. Dorsen, 'The Relevance of Foreign Legal Materials in US Constitutional Cases: A Conversation between Justice Antonin Scalia and Justice Stephen Breyer' (2005) 3 International Journal of Constitutional Law 519; S. Calabresi & S. Zimdahl, 'The Supreme Court and Foreign Sources of Law: Two Hundred Years of Practice and The Juvenile Death Penalty Decision' (2005) 47 William & Mary LR 743; M. D. Ramsey, 'International Materials and Domestic Rights' (2004) 98 AJIL 69; A. -M. Slaughter, 'A Global Community of Courts' (2003) 44 Harvard International Law Journal 191.

[139] One of the most interesting works conducted on the use of foreign law by domestic courts is that of Martin Gelter and Matthias Siems, who conducted an empirical analysis of 636,172 decisions of domestic courts; M. Gelter & M. Siems, 'Networks, Dialogue or One-Way Traffic? An Empirical Analysis of Cross-Citations between Ten of Europe's Highest Courts' (2012) 8 Utrecht LR 88, 89. Gelter & Siems' work surveys the practice of the courts of Austria, Belgium, England and Wales, France, Germany, Ireland, Italy, the Netherlands, Spain and Switzerland. They find a total of 1,430 judgments that cite foreign law.

[140] Jackson, 'Constitutional Comparisons', 114. See also, J. Bell, 'The Argumentative Status of Foreign Legal Arguments' (2012) 8 Utrecht LR 8, 17.

and apparently value-laden choices'.[141] This use of foreign law does not constitute unjustified deference to the will of 'like-minded foreigners',[142] but rather prompts deeper reflection on whether the 'current interpretations live up to our own constitutional commitments'.[143]

The diversity of uses of foreign law clearly has methodological implications. Take the familiar 'cherry-picking' argument as an example.[144] The cherry-picking argument rests on the assumption that in order to be successful the comparative survey of foreign law conducted must be exhaustive (or at least representative) to meet the expected standard of 'scientific rationality and objectivity'.[145] Yet, there is nothing to say that this standard is valid and applicable to the use of foreign law by domestic courts. Rather, it has been rightly recognised as the 'mechanical projection' of 'the aims of (scholarly) scientific research and corresponding precision required therein into the judicial use of comparative arguments'.[146] The breadth and depth of the comparative survey required depends on the exact argument proffered for the use of foreign law.[147] Judges that wish to look to domestic laws simply for inspiration or to use them as a 'sounding board', for example, 'need (in fact quite shallow) inspiration or argumentative support, not deep-level contextualised scientific "truth"'.[148] For these judges, there is nothing 'magic' about absolute comprehensiveness: 'we can learn from foreign decisions one by one or in clusters or in something approaching a world consensus'.[149] That is not to say that the cherry-picking critique has no validity, but rather that its purchase depends on the particular justification proffered for the use of foreign law.

To return to the use of comparative law by investment tribunals, whilst the general principles method would require a representative survey of domestic jurisdictions, there is no reason in principle why this should be the case for other uses of comparative law. Take the idea that domestic law can illuminate the intention of the parties to a treaty, for

---

[141] Jackson, 'Constitutional Comparison', 119.
[142] *Roper*, 608 (Scalia J, dissenting).
[143] Jackson, 'Constitutional Comparisons', 127.
[144] See Alvarez, 'Is Investor–State Arbitration "Public"?', 567.
[145] M. Bobek, *Comparative Reasoning in European Supreme Courts* (OUP 2013) 243.
[146] ibid., 242.
[147] Waldron, 'Foreign Law', 175.
[148] Bobek, *Comparative Reasoning*, 242–3. For an example, see the UK House of Lords' judgment in *Fairchild* v. *Glenhaven Funeral Services* [2002] UKHL 22, paras 23–32 (per Lord Bingham); para 168 (per Lord Rodger). See also, the US Supreme Court case of *Washington* v. *Glucksberg*, 521 US 702 (1997) 734–5 (Rehnquist CJ, for the Court).
[149] Waldron, 'Foreign Law', 175.

example.[150] Implicitly, this was the basis on which the Tribunal in *Saar Papier* v. *Poland* drew on the domestic law of the states parties to interpret a provision of the Germany–Poland BIT that prohibited 'measures equivalent to expropriation'.[151] If one accepts the somewhat dubious premise that Germany and Poland intended to give indirect expropriation under Article 4 of the BIT the same meaning as in their domestic administrative law, there would be no reason to search further than the case law of the two states parties to the treaty.

If comparative law is used to interpret a standard or as an auxiliary or confirmatory argument for a particular approach, what implications does this have for the methodology? The reason for citing comparative law in support of a particular argument rests on two premises: first, that the public law analogy is valid; and, second, that the jurisdictions cited are analogically relevant, in that they uphold the same values as the international investment regime does or should do. The first of these premises does not have implications for *which* domestic laws are cited, but only for whether comparative law is used at all. The second premise, on the other hand, holds the key to the question of methodology for the use of comparative law. It makes no difference whether the tribunal cites the laws of 1, 15 or 100 jurisdictions – what matters is the approval of the values embodied by that domestic legal system that is implicit in the citation. The use of comparative law as a general matter is in that sense 'neutral'; the real question is *which* domestic laws should be used. In this context, some authors have criticised arbitrators for adopting Eurocentric approaches, privileging domestic legal systems with which they are familiar over those from other parts of the world.[152]

Intimately linked with this argument is the criticism that arbitrators can obfuscate their subjective biases with comparative law.[153] It is worth pausing

---

[150] The *Saar Papier* Tribunal is not alone in using domestic law to discern the intentions of parties; see e.g., Panel Report, *Mexico–Measures Affecting Telecommunications Services*, WT/DS204/R (2 April 2004), para 7.110; *Anglo-Iranian Oil Co., Preliminary Objections*, [1952] ICJ Rep, pp. 106–7.

[151] *Saar Papier Vertriebs GmbH* v. *Poland*, UNCITRAL, Final Award (16 October 1995) para 79 ('To interpret the Treaty administrative law practice in Germany and Poland would be helpful.'). *Saar Papier* is the only award released to date in which comparative law plays more than a subsidiary role.

[152] Alvarez, 'Beware: Boundary Crossings', 220–2; Schill, 'Sources', 1109. See also, Ellis, 'General Principles', 955–8.

[153] Alvarez, 'Is Investor–State Arbitration "Public"?', 569. Cf US Senate Committee on the Judiciary, 'Confirmation Hearing on the Nomination of John G. Roberts, Jr. to be Chief Justice of the United States, September 12–15, 2005', Serial No. J-109-37, 201 ('Foreign Law. You can find anything you want. If you don't find it in the decisions of France or

to consider why, specifically, it is bad for judges to make such a selection. Judges select all the time: they select precedents,[154] historical sources[155] and separate or dissenting opinions to use as authority. They select to such an extent that one judge has commented that the 'very process of adjudication implies a selection'.[156] Adjudicators will undoubtedly select the domestic or foreign law that supports their view; in fact, the selective use of foreign law by domestic judges has been empirically proven.[157] So why, a sceptic might ask, should the selection of domestic or foreign laws be singled out as a particularly egregious manifestation of subjective bias?

The fact that arbitrators do not command a Herculean knowledge of comparative law necessitates selection, but that fact says nothing *in se* about the desirability of the approach that the arbitral tribunal takes. An arbitral panel that invokes the administrative laws of North Korea and Zimbabwe to justify its understanding of FET is unlikely to convince many people of the desirability of its approach. But it is not the use of comparative law *per se* that is objectionable, but the values that the domestic law, or the comparative survey more generally, represents. The assessment entails consideration of the fundamental values underpinning the investment regime and whether the domestic jurisdictions live up to those ideals. The question is, ultimately, one of political values.

5.5 The General Principles Fallacy

The use of comparative law cannot be explained or dismissed as easily as it has been in the literature to date. The practice of investment tribunals

---

Italy, it's in the decisions of Somalia or Japan or Indonesia or wherever. As somebody said in another context, looking at foreign law for support is like looking out over a crowd and picking out your friends . . . It allows the judge to incorporate his or her own personal preferences, [and] cloak them with the authority of precedent.'). See also, R. A. Posner, 'The Supreme Court 2004 Term – Foreword: A Political Court' (2005) 119 Harvard LR 32, 86.

[154] Waldron, 'Foreign Law', 172.

[155] J. S. Sutton, 'The Role of History in Judging Disputes about the Meaning of the Constitution' (2009) 41 Texas Tech LR 1173, 1185.

[156] Justice Moseneke in U. Bentele, 'Mining for Gold: The Constitutional Court of South Africa's Experience with Comparative Constitutional Law' (2009) 37 Georgia Journal of International and Comparative Law 219, 239.

[157] R. C. Black et al., 'Upending a Global Debate', (2014) 103 Georgetown LJ 1, 43–4; B. Flanagan & S. Ahern, 'Judicial Decision-Making and Transnational Law', (2011) 60 ICLQ 1, 23–4. Cf Comments of G. Kodek of the Austrian Supreme Court in M. Gelter & M. Siems, 'Citations to Foreign Courts – Illegitimate and Superfluous, or Unavoidable? Evidence from Europe' (2014) 62 AJCL 35, 64.

examined in this chapter demonstrates that comparative law has not been used because it manifests a general principle of law and is thus applicable by virtue of Article 31(3)(c) VCLT. Instead, comparative law has been used to substantiate treaty standards or to confirm an interpretation made on other grounds. In the context of international investment law, the use of comparative law relates mainly to the obligation to accord FET to investors.

Discussion of the general principles method and the attendant theoretical and methodological problems have to a certain extent diverted attention from the host of issues raised by the actual use of comparative law by tribunals. From a descriptive standpoint, the general principles method fails to explain why tribunals use comparative law. A more convincing explanation focusses on the object of interpretation for which comparative law is invoked: standards. Standards, unlike rules, lend themselves to a different, non-deductive form of legal reasoning, in which comparative law can act alongside other factors to justify a particular interpretative approach. In terms of methodology, the general principles method suggests that a comprehensive or representative survey is required, much in the same vein as a comparative law academic would approach inducing a general principle from domestic jurisdictions. Yet there is nothing to say that such an approach is necessary if comparative law is used in other ways. In particular, there is no reason that such a methodology would be required if comparative law is adduced to interpret a standard or to support a conclusion made on other grounds. Instead, those that wish to evaluate the use of comparative law in such a scenario must engage with the approval that such citation implies.

Whilst this chapter has attempted to address some of the issues regarding the use of comparative law in international investment law, there are still many matters left to address. Two seem to be of particular importance. First, could one argue that the rules of interpretation or the sources of law that are applicable to international investment law have evolved to account for the use of comparative law? Put another way, how does the practice of tribunals examined here fit within a positive legal framework, if it does at all? Second, what makes referring to a particular jurisdiction normatively preferable or justifiable as opposed to another? This is a question of crucial importance to the evaluation of comparative law in the future. In order to determine whether such use of comparative law is 'bad' or 'good', we have to make a searching enquiry into the values that we want the investment regime to uphold and how those are furthered by referring to domestic jurisdictions. In this respect, one cannot help but agree with Neil MacCormick's observation that 'the whole enterprise of explicating and expounding criteria and forms of good legal reasoning has to be in the context of the fundamental values that we impute to legal order'.[158] That task is both necessary and unavoidably subjective.

[158] N. MacCormick, *Rhetoric and the Rule of Law* (OUP 2005) 1.

6

Consensus Doctrine in the European Court of Human Rights

6.1 Introduction

The European Convention on Human Rights and Fundamental Freedoms (ECHR, or 'the Convention') was adopted in 1950 by 12 member states of the Council of Europe and entered into force three years later.[1] The Convention was a direct response to the Second World War,[2] and aimed to give effect to the rights enounced in the Universal Declaration of Human Rights, adopted by the UN General Assembly in 1948.[3] The Convention and its associated 15 Protocols protect mainly the civil and political rights of citizens of the member states of the Council of Europe.[4] These rights are enforceable by judicial procedure under Articles 33 and 34 of the Convention, which provide the European Court of Human Rights (ECtHR, or 'the Court') with jurisdiction over inter-state disputes and applications from aggrieved individuals, respectively.[5]

---

[1] Convention for the Protection of Human Rights and Fundamental Freedoms, 4 November 1950, 213 UNTS 221 (ECHR).

[2] B. Rainey et al., *The European Convention on Human Rights* (6th edn, OUP 2014) 3.

[3] See Preamble, alinea 2, ECHR.

[4] A 16th protocol, Protocol No. 15, is yet to enter into force. Protocol No. 16 entered into force on 1 August 2018 in respect of the states which have signed and ratified it.

[5] Prior to the entry into force of Protocol 11, which created a single full-time Court, two organs – the European Commission of Human Rights and the European Court of Human Rights – were entrusted to 'ensure the observance of the engagements undertaken by the High Contracting Parties' (former Article 19 ECHR). The former Commission received initial complaints, and – if it found the complaint to be admissible – produced a report on the matter. If this did not result in settlement of the matter within three months of transmission of the report to the Committee of Ministers, the application could be referred to the Court for judicial determination (former Articles 47–9 ECHR).

It has been said that many of the rights enumerated in the Convention are 'general, vague and often uncertain as to their import'.[6] However, this has not prevented cases from being brought to the Strasbourg court; indeed, the Convention and Court have been called 'the most effective human rights regime in the world'.[7] Since its establishment in 1959, the Court has delivered over 20,600 judgments, finding violations in 84 per cent of cases.[8] Unsurprisingly, then, the practice of the Court is a veritable treasure-trove for the interpretative methodologist.

The Court has a long heritage of referring to the domestic laws of states parties to the ECHR when interpreting the Convention. Most commonly carried out under the rubric of the 'consensus doctrine', domestic laws are often examined in order to ascertain the existence or absence of a common approach amongst Council of Europe states on a certain issue: for example, the legal recognition of transsexuals, the criminal prohibition of homosexual acts or the rights of conscientious objectors to military service. Broadly speaking, the existence of consensus will push the Court towards an interpretation that is in line with the prevailing approach amongst contracting states, whereas the absence of consensus will result in deference to the respondent state.[9]

The interaction between domestic law and the Convention has held a prominent place in political discourse regarding the protection of human rights in Europe in recent years. In response to the perceived activism of the Court, Council of Europe states have issued a series of declarations reaffirming the primacy of the national protection of human rights and the subsidiarity of the Convention mechanism.[10] This was

---

[6] J. L. Murray, 'Consensus: Concordance, or Hegemony of the Majority?' in European Court of Human Rights, *Dialogue between judges* (Council of Europe 2008) 41.

[7] A. Stone-Sweet & H. Keller, 'The Reception of the ECHR in National Legal Orders', in H. Keller & A. Stone-Sweet (eds), *A Europe System of Rights: The Impact of the ECHR on National Legal Systems* (OUP 2008) 3.

[8] European Court of Human Rights, *ECHR: Overview 1959–2017* (Council of Europe 2017) 3.

[9] On evolutionary treaty interpretation generally, see E. Bjorge, *The Evolutionary Interpretation of Treaties* (OUP 2014); G. Nolte (ed), *Treaties and Subsequent Practice* (OUP 2013); J. Arato, 'Subsequent Practice and Evolutive Interpretation: Techniques of Treaty Interpretation over Time and their Diverse Consequences', (2010) 9 Law & Practice of International Courts and Tribunals 443.

[10] See High Level Conference on the Implementation of the European Convention of Human Rights, Our Shared Responsibility, Brussels Declaration, 27 March 2015, paras 2 and 7; High Level Conference on the Future of the European Court of Human Rights, Brighton Declaration, 19–20 April 2012, paras 3, 11 and 12. See also, High Level Conference on the Future of the European Court of Human Rights, Izmir Declaration, 27 April 2011, para 4; High Level Conference on the Future of the European Court of

formalised in Protocol 15 to the Convention, which will add a recital to the preamble to the Convention that explicitly enshrines the principle of subsidiarity and the doctrine of the margin of appreciation.[11] The Protocol, which requires accession of all states parties to the Convention, has not yet entered into force.

Academic commentary on the use of consensus has been divided, with some authors claiming that consensus obfuscates the values that under-pin decision making, whilst others argue that consensus augments the legitimacy of the judgments that the Court delivers. However, a fresh insight is to be gained by approaching the question from a different perspective; namely, focussing upon the character of the treaty obligation being interpreted. As was the case with investment tribunals' use of domestic law, examined in the preceding chapter, the majority of cases in which domestic laws are referred to by the ECtHR pertain to the interpretation of legal standards;[12] for example, what is 'necessary in a democratic society', 'fair' or 'duly diligent'. These standards are inevi-tably embedded in the society to which they refer. Whilst the fictional passenger on the Clapham omnibus represents the anthropomorphised standard of conduct expected of a member of society in English law,[13] the standards accepted by Council of Europe member states – as manifested in their domestic law – are both more accessible and more verifiable than societally accepted standards within domestic jurisdictions.

This chapter is composed of four sections. Section 6.2 outlines the origins of the consensus doctrine and notes its purported incoherence. The following section (Section 6.3) examines judgments of the Grand Chamber over the 10-year period 2005–15 in order to ascertain how the Chamber has used comparative law. It demonstrates that in the vast

Human Rights, Interlaken Declaration, 19 February 2010, para 4; A. Mowbray, 'Subsidiarity and the European Convention on Human Rights', (2015) Human Rights LR 313.
[11] Protocol No. 15 amending the Convention on the Protection of Human Rights and Fundamental Freedoms, 24 June 2013, Article 1 (adding the following preambular paragraph to the Convention: 'Affirming that the High Contracting Parties, in accordance with the principle of subsidiarity, have the primary responsibility to secure the rights and freedoms defined in this Convention and the Protocols thereto, and that in doing so they enjoy a margin of appreciation, subject to the supervisory jurisdiction of the European Court of Human Rights established by this Convention'). See also, Protocol 16 on the Protection of Human Rights and Fundamental Freedoms, 2 October 2013.
[12] In this chapter, I adopt the definition of standards given in the preceding chapter; see Chapter 5, section 5.4.1.
[13] *Healthcare at Home Limited* v. *The Common Services Agency* [2014] UKSC 49, para 12 (*per* Lord Reed).

majority of cases, comparative law has been adduced in order to interpret standards incorporated in the Convention. Section 6.4 addresses
the methodological and principled arguments that have been made
against the use of comparative law, as well as addressing the arguments
that support its use. The following section (Section 6.5) examines the
Court's use of comparative law in light of the interpretation of standards in domestic legal systems, and assesses the theoretical justifications that may be advanced for interpreting standards in light of the
domestic laws of member states of the Council of Europe. Section 6.6
concludes.

6.2   The Consensus Doctrine

For almost 40 years, the Court has acknowledged the import of the
'practice of European States reflecting their common values'[14] when
interpreting the Convention, in order to render the protection given by
the Convention effective in light of the prevailing social and political
conditions. The 'practice of European States' in this context means the
domestic laws and international legal obligations of states, which are
presumed to manifest the contemporary values of members of the
Council of Europe. The comparative analysis of these elements is frequently called the 'doctrine of consensus'.[15] In keeping with the focus of
this book, the remit of this chapter is limited to the use of domestic law by
the Court.[16]

---

[14] *Demir and Baykara* v. *Turkey*, 12 November 2008, App. No. 34503/97, para 85. For an
examination of the relationship between the Strasbourg Court and national courts more
generally, see P. Mahoney, 'The Relationship between the Strasbourg Court and the
National Courts', (2014) 130 LQR 568.

[15] The use of the terms 'comparative analysis' and 'comparative method' in relation to the
ECtHR have been criticised on the basis that 'there appears to be little analysis and even
less method involved'; P. G. Carozza, 'Uses and Misuses of Comparative Law in
International Human Rights: Some Reflections on the Jurisprudence of the European
Court of Human Rights', (1998) 73 Notre Dame Law Review 1217, 1219, fn 8. See also,
P. Mahoney, 'The Comparative Method in Judgments of the European Court of Human
Rights: Reference Back to National Law', in G. Canivet et al., *Comparative Law Before the
Courts* (BIICL 2005) 149; P. Mahoney & R. Kondak, 'Common Ground: A Starting Point
or Destination for Comparative-Law Analysis by the European Court of Human Rights?',
in M. Andenas & G. Canivet (eds), *Courts and Comparative Law* (OUP 2015) 121–2 (on
the Court's use of the term 'consensus').

[16] For a typology of other forms of consensus, see K. Dzehtsiarou, *European Consensus and
the Legitimacy of the European Court of Human Rights* (CUP 2015) 39–55.

Whilst the Court has held certain terms to be 'autonomous concepts' that are to be understood in isolation from domestic legal systems,[17] consensus often 'constitutes the primary determining factor as to whether a right is one protected by the Convention',[18] enabling the Court to strike the 'delicate balance between national sovereignty and international obligation'.[19] In the years since the three pioneering consensus cases of *Tyrer*,[20] *Marckx*[21] and *Dudgeon*,[22] the Court has had frequent recourse to consensus analysis in the interpretation of a wide range of Convention rights,[23] normally with the effect that:

> where there is no European consensus, the margin of appreciation will be wider ... [and] where the Court affirms the existence of European consensus, the margin of appreciation will narrow, and the Court will proceed to an

---

[17] See for example, *Sramek v. Austria*, 22 October 1984, App. No. 8790/79, para 36; *Bochan v. Ukraine (No. 2)*, 5 February 2015, App. No. 22251/08, para 43; *Chiragoc and Others v. Armenia*, 16 June 2015, App. No. 13216/05, para 206 ('The notions of "private life", "family life" and "home" under Article 8 are, like "possessions" under Article 1 of Protocol No. 1, autonomous concepts; their protection does not depend on the classification under domestic law, but on the factual circumstances of the case.'). The doctrine of autonomous concepts is to be distinguished from the consensus doctrine insofar as the former relates to the irrelevance of the classification under the domestic law of the respondent state in the case at hand.

[18] J. L. Murray, 'Consensus: Concordance, or Hegemony of the Majority?' in European Court of Human Rights, *Dialogue between judges* (Council of Europe 2008) 27.

[19] R. St. J. MacDonald, 'The Margin of Appreciation', R. St. J. MacDonald et al., *The European System for the Protection of Human Rights* (Martinus Nijhoff 1993) 123.

[20] *Tyrer v. UK*, 25 April 1978, App. No. 5856/72. In *Tyrer*, the Court said that 'the Convention is a living instrument which, as the Commission rightly stressed, must be interpreted in the light of present-day conditions. In the case now before it the Court cannot but be influenced by the developments and commonly accepted standards in the penal policy of the member States of the Council of Europe in this field', ibid., para 31. This was the first time in which the Court referred to the Convention as a 'living instrument' – a phrase that perhaps came from a paper presented by Max Sørensen at the 1975 ECHR colloquium; E. Bates, *The Evolution of the European Convention of Human Rights: From Its Inception to the Creation of a Permanent Court of Human Rights* (OUP 2010) 329.

[21] *Marckx v. Belgium*, 13 June 1979, App. No. 6833/74. *Marckx* reaffirmed the living instrument approach taken in *Tyrer*, placing importance on the recognition by contracting parties of the equality of children born into and out of wedlock.

[22] *Dudgeon v. UK*, 22 October 1981, App. No. 7525/76. In *Dudgeon*, the acceptance of homosexual practices in the 'great majority of the member States of the Council of Europe' led the Court to the conclusion that 'it is no longer considered to be necessary or appropriate to treat homosexual practices' as criminal conduct; ibid., para 60.

[23] L. Wildhaber et al., 'No Consensus on Consensus? The Practice of the European Court of Human Rights', (2013) 33 Human Rights LJ 248, 257.

evolutive interpretation of the Convention and as a rule will find a violation.[24]

A clear demonstration of the 'orthodox effect' of consensus is the case of *M.C. v. Bulgaria*.[25] In that case, the victim of an alleged incident of rape brought a case before the Court claiming that Bulgaria had failed to fulfil its positive obligations under Articles 3 and 8 by failing to pursue the prosecution of her attackers. The Court acknowledged that member states enjoyed a 'wide margin of appreciation' in ensuring adequate protection against rape, but this diminished in line with 'any evolving convergence as to the standards to be achieved'.[26] On the basis of comparative surveys carried out by the Court and an NGO, Interights,[27] which demonstrated a 'universal trend' towards recognising lack of consent as the basis of the crime of rape, the Court stated that:

> [A]ny rigid approach to the prosecution of sexual offences, such as requiring proof of physical resistance in all circumstances [as was claimed to be *de facto* the case in Bulgaria], risks leaving certain types of rape unpunished and thus jeopardising the effective protection of the individual's sexual autonomy. In accordance with contemporary standards and trends in that area, the member States' positive obligations under Articles 3 and 8 of the Convention must be seen as requiring the penalisation and effective prosecution of any non-consensual sexual act, including in the absence of physical resistance by the victim.[28]

The jurisprudence is clear, however, that consensus is not dispositive of a particular interpretation: the Court has ruled contrary to the consensus approach on a number of occasions, determining that countervailing considerations – such as the state's prerogative to protect public

---

[24] Wildhaber et al., 'No Consensus on Consensus?', 250. For examples of the Court interpreting in line with consensus, see *M. C. v. Bulgaria*, 4 March 2004, App. No. 39272/98, paras 154–5; *Vo v. France*, 8 July 2004, App. No. 53924/00, para 82.

[25] *M.C. v. Bulgaria*, 4 March 2004, App. No. 39272/98.

[26] *M.C.*, paras 154–5.

[27] *M.C.*, paras 88–108 (Court study surveying Belgium, the Czech Republic, Denmark, Finland, France, Germany, Hungary, Ireland, Slovenia, the UK and cases from the ICTY, a Recommendation of the Committee of Ministers of the Council of Europe, and a Recommendation of the UN Committee on the Elimination of Discrimination against Women), 130–47 (Interights study surveying Belgium, Denmark, Ireland, the UK, the USA, Australia, Canada and South Africa).

[28] *M.C.*, para 166. The Court did 'also note' that 'the member States of the Council of Europe, through the Committee of Ministers, have agreed that penalising non-consensual sexual acts, "[including] in cases where the victim does not show signs of resistance", is necessary for the effective protection of women against violence'; ibid., para 162. On the question of inferring lack of consent from proof of physical resistance, see ibid., para 180.

morals – outweigh the importance of adopting the consensus approach.[29] Consensus hence provides a rebuttable presumption that the Court will interpret the Convention in line with the approach adopted in the majority of Council of Europe member states.[30]

The variable weight given by the Court to the consensus approach has resulted in criticism of its use.[31] Given this seeming lack of a coherent approach, how should we better understand the Court's use of comparative law?

6.3   Standards of Conduct and the Use of Domestic Law

Whilst commentators have bemoaned the lack of consistency of the Court, few have methodologically examined how the Court uses consensus in its reasoning. In the 10-year period from 1 January 2005 to 1 January 2015, the Grand Chamber of the ECtHR delivered 183 judgments, of which it used comparative law in 60 judgments (33 per cent of judgments).[32] In 73.3 per cent of these (44 judgments), the Court used comparative law to interpret standards, such as necessity, fairness or due diligence. In only 10 per cent of judgments did the court use comparative law outside of these four categories.[33]

This section outlines the four types of standard in relation to which the Court has made reference to domestic law: cases in which a standard of acceptable conduct is explicitly provided for (e.g., Article 6); cases in which limitations to a right are explicitly permitted (Articles 8–11); cases in which implied limitations to a right have been accepted by the Court

---

[29] See for example, *A, B, C* v. *Ireland*, 16 December 2010, App. No. 25579/05, paras 235–41; *Christine Goodwin* v. *UK*, 11 July 2002, App. No. 28957/95, paras 85–90.

[30] Dzehtsiarou, *European Consensus*, 36–7. Quite how many states is necessary to establish consensus is unclear. However, it is clear that the approach need not be unanimous. For further discussion, see Section 6.4.1 of this chapter.

[31] P. Martens, 'Perplexity of the National Judge Faced with Vagaries of European Consensus', in European Court of Human Rights, *Dialogue between judges* (Council of Europe 2008) 54 (stating that consensus is 'sometimes positive, sometimes negative, sometimes descriptive, sometimes prescriptive'). Cf J. A. Brauch, 'The Dangerous Search for an Elusive Consensus: What the Supreme Court Should Learn From the European Court of Human Rights', (2009) 52 Howard LJ 277, 278 ('Despite hundreds of cases and over thirty years of experience, the ECHR has still not made clear what a European consensus is, or even how one would identify the consensus if it existed.').

[32] The sample of judgments examined in this book is limited to the Grand Chamber of the ECtHR as it would be difficult to survey all judgments of the Court in the same period, which total 11,872 judgments.

[33] *Söderman* v. *Sweden*, 12 November 2013, App. No. 5786/08, para 105.

(e.g., Articles 2–3 of Protocol No. 1); and cases in which consensus has been used to specify the remit of a purportedly absolute right (in particular, Articles 2 and 3). In 10 of the 60 cases examined, the Grand Chamber outlined the approaches taken in domestic jurisdictions but did not rely on this in its operative reasoning,[34] whereas in only six cases did the Grand Chamber rely on comparative law to justify evolutive interpretation outside of the four categories of standard outlined below.[35]

6.3.1   Explicit Standards

The first of these four categories accounts for five of the 60 judgments in which the Grand Chamber drew on comparative law. The case of *Taxquet* v. *Belgium* illustrates the use of comparative law to interpret what constitutes a 'fair' hearing under Article 6(1).[36] In that case, the applicant argued that the absence of reasons accompanying a Belgian lay jury's guilty verdict infringed his Article 6 right. The Court stated that, in the absence of a reasoned verdict:

> Article 6 requires an assessment of whether sufficient safeguards were in place to avoid any risk of arbitrariness and to enable the accused to understand the reasons for his conviction. Such procedural safeguards may include, for example, directions or guidance provided by the

---

[34] *Anheuser-Busch Inc.* v. *Portugal*, 11 January 2007, App. No. 73049/01, paras 39–40; *D. H. and Others* v. *Czech Republic*, 13 November 2007, App. No. 57325/00, paras 105–7; *Burden* v. *UK*, 29 April 2008, App. No. 13378/05, paras 25–8; *A.* v. *UK*, 19 February 2009, App. No. 3455/05, paras 111–13; *Sergey Zolotukhin* v. *Russia*, 10 February 2009, App. No. 14939/03, para 79; *Perdigao* v. *Portugal*, 16 November 2010, App. No. 24768/06, paras 47–50; *Serife Yiğit* v. *Turkey*, 2 November 2011, App. No. 3976/05, paras 41–4; *El-Masri* v. *The Former Yugoslav Republic of Macedonia*, 13 December 2012, App. No. 39630/09, paras 106–7; *Nada* v. *Switzerland*, 12 September 2012, App. No. 10593/08, paras 94–101; *Allen* v. *UK*, 12 July 2013, App. No. 25424/09, paras 73–7.

[35] *Stec and Others* v. *UK*, 12 April 2006, App. No. 65731/01 & 65900/01, paras 64–5; *Evans* v. *UK*, 10 April 2007, App. No. 6339/05, para 79; *Micallef* v. *Malta*, 15 October 2009, App. No. 17056/06, paras 78–81; *Lautsi and Others* v. *Italy*, 18 March 2011, App. No. 30814/06, para 70; *Söderman* v. *Sweden*, 12 November 2013, App. No. 5786/08, para 105; *Hämäläinen* v. *Finland*, 16 July 2014, App. No. 37359/09, paras 73–5.

[36] *Taxquet* v. *Belgium*, 6 November 2010, App. No. 926/05. Article 6(1) provides, in relevant part, that 'In the determination of his civil rights and obligations or of any criminal charge against him, everyone is entitled to a fair and public hearing within a reasonable time by an independent and impartial tribunal established by law.' See also, *Kyprianou* v. *Cyprus*, 15 December 2005, App. No. 73797/01, para 124; *Gäfgen* v. *Germany*, 1 June 2010, App. No. 22978/05, para 174; *Nejdet Şahin and Perihan Şahin* v. *Turkey*, 20 October 2011, App. No. 13279/05, para 82; *Al-Khawaja and Tahery* v. *UK*, 15 December 2011, App. No. 26766/05 & 22228/06, para 139.

presiding judge to the jurors on the legal issues arising or the evidence adduced.[37]

To illustrate what may constitute sufficient procedural safeguards, the Court referred to a previous section of the judgment, entitled 'Comparative Law', in which it outlined the approaches taken in 38 Council of Europe member states. It considered that these laws provided illustrative examples of the procedural safeguards that may be necessary to protect an individual's right under Article 6(1): 'Such procedural safeguards may include, for example, directions or guidance provided by the presiding judge to the jurors on the legal issues arising or the evidence adduced . . .'[38]

On the facts, the questions presented to the jury by the presiding judge were not of sufficient detail to allow the applicant to comprehend the evidence that had led to his conviction.[39] Comparative law was hence used as an aid to substantiate what 'fairness' within the context of Article 6 demanded from the contracting parties' judicial systems.

6.3.2   Proportionality in Express Limitations

Examples abound of the use of comparative law by the Court to determine whether a state's actions constitute justified infringements on Convention rights under the second paragraphs of Articles 8–11. For each of these, the Court carries out a three-fold analysis: first, it determines if the interference is prescribed by law; second, the Court decides if the aim of interference is legitimate within the meaning of the particular article; and, third, it establishes whether the interference is 'necessary in a democratic society'.[40] It is within this final leg that the Court undertakes a test of proportionality, assessing if the interference is a proportionate response to the pressing social need faced by the state. Comparative law has been predominantly used within this limb of the test; in other words, in order to substantiate what is

---

[37] *Taxquet*, para 92, referring to the comparative survey carried out in paras 43–60.

[38] The comparative survey examined the laws of Albania, Andorra, Armenia, Azerbaijan, Bosnia and Herzegovina, Cyprus, Latvia, Lithuania, Luxembourg, Moldova, the Netherlands, Romania, San Marino, Turkey, Bulgaria, Croatia, the Czech Republic, Denmark, Estonia, Finland, France, Germany, Greece, Hungary, Iceland, Italy, Liechtenstein, Monaco, Montenegro, Norway, Poland, Portugal, Serbia, Slovakia, Slovenia, Sweden, 'the former Yugoslav Republic of Macedonia', Ukraine, Austria, Belgium, Georgia, Ireland, Malta, Russia, Spain, Switzerland and the UK.

[39] *Taxquet*, paras 93–100.

[40] See for example, *Dudgeon*, para 43.

'necessary in a democratic society'.[41] These constitute 32 per cent of cases in which the Grand Chamber invoked comparative law in the period under review.

An illustrative example is the case of *Demir and Baykara* v. *Turkey*.[42] In that case, the applicants were civil servants that were prohibited from joining trade unions under the Turkish law. The Court recognised that this prohibition could constitute an inference with the applicants' right to freedom of association under Article 11[43] and moved to address whether such a prohibition could be considered as a legitimate interference under Article 11(2); in particular, it assessed whether the Turkish ban could be considered as a lawful prohibition imposed on members of the administration of the state.[44]

The Court adduced several arguments to reject Turkey's claim that placing restrictions on civil servants' ability to join trade unions answered a 'pressing social need', as required under the proportionality test. The Court noted that: first, Turkey had not specified what the 'pressing social need' was that justified this restriction; second, Turkey had signed

---

[41] See also, *Leyla Sahin* v. *Turkey*, 10 November 2005, App. No. 44774/98, para 109; *Sørensen and Rasmussen* v. *Denmark*, 11 January 2006, App. No. 52562/99 & 52560/99, para 70; *Üner* v. *the Netherlands*, 18 October 2006, App. No. 59450/00, paras 39–55; *Dickson* v. *UK*, 4 December 2007, App. No. 44362/04, para 81; *Stoll* v. *Switzerland*, 10 December 2007, App. No. 69698/01, paras 107, 155; *S. and Marper* v. *UK*, 4 December 2008, App. No. 30562/04 & 30566/04, paras 107–12; *Brosset-Triboulet and Others* v. *France*, 29 March 2010, App. No. 34078/02, para 93; *A, B, C* v. *Ireland*, 16 December 2010, App. No. 25579/05, paras 235–6; *Neulinger and Shuruk* v. *Switzerland*, 6 July 2010, App. No. 41615/07, para 135; *Bayatyan* v. *Armenia*, 7 July 2011, App. No. 23459/03, paras 122–3; *Palomo Sánchez and Others* v. *Spain*, 12 September 2011, App. No. 28955/06 & 28957/06 & 28959/06 & 28964/06, para 75; *S. H. and Others* v. *Austria*, 3 November 2011, App. No. 57813/00, paras 95–6; *Herrmann* v. *Germany*, 26 June 2012, App. No. 9300/07, paras 79–80; *Van der Heijden* v. *the Netherlands*, 3 April 2012, App. No. 42857/05, para 61; *Animal Defenders International* v. *UK*, 22 April 2013, App. No. 48876/08, para 123; *Sindicatul 'Pastorul cel Bun'* v. *Romania*, 9 July 2013, App. No. 2330/09, para 171; *Fernández Martínez* v. *Spain*, 12 June 2014, App. No. 56030/07, para 143; *S. A. S.* v. *France*, 1 July 2014, App. No. 43835/11, para 156.

[42] *Demir and Baykara* v. *Turkey*, 12 November 2008, App. No. 34503/97. See also, R. Nordeide, '*Demir & Baykara* v. *Turkey*', (2009) 103 AJIL 567.

[43] The Grand Chamber also recognised that the ban could be considered as a failure on the part of Turkey to 'comply with its positive obligation to secure the applicants' rights under this provision'; *Demir and Baykara*, para 116.

[44] Article 11(2) provides that 'No restrictions shall be placed on the exercise of these rights other than such as are prescribed by law and are necessary in a democratic society in the interests of national security or public safety, for the prevention of disorder or crime, for the protection of health or morals or for the protection of the rights and freedoms of others. This Article shall not prevent the imposition of lawful restrictions on the exercise of these rights by members of the armed forces, of the police or of the administration of the State.'

Convention No. 87 of the International Labour Organization, which recognised this right; and third, Turkey had confirmed its willingness to recognise this right by actions of both the legislature and the judiciary.[45] Crucially, however, the Court placed importance on the fact that international, regional and comparative materials (including the domestic laws of *all* Council of Europe states) overwhelmingly recognised the right of civil servants to form and join trade unions.[46]

To be sure, the use of comparative law was not the sole determinant of the necessity of the measure at issue in this case. However, it did assist the Court in determining what constituted the acceptable standard of conduct at the relevant time: in this case, whether the 'non-recognition of the right of the applicants, as municipal civil servants, to form a trade union' fell within the express limitation to Article 11.[47]

6.3.3   Proportionality in Implied Limitations

Analogous lines of reasoning can be found where implied limitations to certain rights have been recognised by the Court, notably under Article 14 of the Convention, and Articles 2 and 3 of Protocol 1. Under these provisions, states may discriminate or interfere with a Convention right if that discrimination or interference pursues a legitimate aim and is proportionate, despite the absence of a specific clause allowing such infringement. The interpretation of implied limitations constitutes 27 per cent of the cases in which the Grand Chamber has adduced comparative law in the period under review.

Consider, for example, the case of *Tănase* v. *Moldova*.[48] The applicant in that case claimed that the Moldovan law prohibiting those holding dual nationality from becoming members of Parliament breached his

---

[45] *Demir and Baykara*, paras 120–4.
[46] *Demir and Baykara*, para 122.
[47] *Demir and Baykara*, para 121.
[48] *Tănase* v. *Moldova*, 27 April 2010, App. No. 7/08. See also, *Hirst (No. 2)* v. *UK*, 6 October 2005, App. No. 74025/01, para 81; *Yumak and Sidak* v. *Turkey*, 8 July 2008, App. No. 10226/03, paras 129–32; *Georgian Labour Party* v. *Georgia*, 8 July 2008, App. No. 9103/04, paras 103–4; *Kozacioglu* v. *Turkey*, 19 February 2009, App. No. 2334/03, para 71; *Paksas* v. *Lithuania*, 6 January 2011, App. No. 34932/04, para 106; *Depalle* v. *France*, 29 March 2010, App. No. 34044/02, para 89; *Stummer* v. *Austria*, 7 July 2011, App. No. 37452/02, para 109; *Kart* v. *Turkey*, 3 December 2009, App. No. 8917/05, paras 97–8; *Konstantin Markin* v. *Russia*, 22 March 2012, App. No. 30078/06, paras 140, 147; *Scoppola* v. *Italy (No. 3)*, 22 May 2012, App. No. 126/05, paras 95, 101; *Sitaropoulos and Giakoumopoulos* v. *Greece*, 15 March 2012, App. No. 42202/07, para 74; *Stanev* v. *Bulgaria*, 17 January 2012, App. No. 36760/06, para 243; *Fabris* v. *France*, 7 February 2013, App. No.

right to stand for election under Article 3 of Protocol 1 to the European Convention.[49] The Court noted that:

> a review of practice across Council of Europe member States reveals a consensus that where multiple nationalities are permitted, the holding of more than one nationality should not be a ground for ineligibility to sit as an MP, even where the population is ethnically diverse and the number of MPs with multiple nationalities may be high.[50]

However, it considered that 'notwithstanding this consensus, a different approach may be justified where special historical or political considerations exist which render a more restrictive practice necessary'.[51] The Court recognised that Moldova, as a newly independent state, might legitimately want to place restrictions on those involved in its nascent democratic institutions for reasons of 'loyalty' to the state. However, the fact that it had only put in place these restrictions 17 years after independence rendered such arguments 'less persuasive'.[52] The Court continued to highlight the universal condemnation of the law by intergovernmental bodies and the unduly burdensome effect that the measure had on opposition parties to conclude that the prohibition was disproportionate.

Consensus in this case set a standard of acceptable interference with the right, albeit one from which derogations were permitted. This idea of consensus as a *prima facie* standard was clearly expounded by the Court in its exposition of the view that '[w]here there is a common standard which the respondent State has failed to meet, this may constitute a relevant consideration for the Court when it interprets the provisions of the Convention in specific cases'.[53]

6.3.4 Defining Absolute Rights

In the abovementioned cases, consensus played a role in determining the proportionality of an interference with an enumerated right. However, in

---

16574/08, para 58; *Vallianatos and Others* v. *Greece*, 7 November 2013, App. No. 29381/09 & 32684/09, para 91; *X and Others* v. *Austria*, 19 February 2013, App. No. 19010/07, para 149.

[49] Although Article 3, Protocol 1 does not explicitly mention a 'right to stand for election', the Court has interpreted the provision as encompassing both an 'active' element (right to vote) as well as the 'passive' right to stand for election; see for example, *Ždanoka* v. *Latvia*, 16 March 2006, App. No. 58278/00.

[50] *Tănase*, para 172.

[51] *Tănase*, para 172.

[52] *Tănase*, para 173.

[53] *Tănase*, para 176.

a small number of cases (5 per cent of the total number of cases in which comparative law was used in the period under review), it was a factor in shaping the right itself. Articles 2 and 3 enshrine the right to life and the prohibition of torture or inhuman and degrading treatment, respectively. Whilst these are recognised as absolute rights from which no derogations are permitted, the Court in practice undertakes an evaluation of factors (including comparative law) when interpreting the positive obligations incumbent on a contracting state under Article 2, or what constitutes 'inhuman or degrading treatment' for the purposes of Article 3.[54] Reference to several cases will illustrate this point.[55]

In *Opuz* v. *Turkey*, the applicant claimed that the Turkish authorities had not fulfilled their positive obligations under Article 2 by failing to safeguard her mother from a foreseeable threat to her life.[56] The murderer, the applicant's husband, had a history of perpetrating domestic violence against his wife and mother-in-law, rendering further attacks 'not only possible, but foreseeable'.[57] The Turkish law in force at the time provided that a complaint lodged by the victim was necessary for the prosecution of acts of violence, unless the attack rendered the victim incapable of working for more than 10 days, in which case public prosecution (i.e. without the complaint of the victim) could be pursued.[58]

The Court recognised that there was an obligation to show due diligence on the part of the state to protect the lives of its citizens under Article 2. In substantiating what constituted 'due diligence', the Court made reference to the domestic laws of 39 contracting parties regarding

---

[54] Natasa Mavronicola distinguishes between two criteria that help explain the Court's reasoning regarding absolute rights. The first – 'applicability' – provides that, where the right is found to apply, no derogation or exception is permitted. The second – 'specification' – sets the boundaries for the application of absolute rights. Only 'legitimate specifications' may be taken into account; that is, the Court must draw on 'ordinary concepts' that manifest principles underpinning the Convention and that do not collapse into consequentialism. N. Mavronicola, 'What is an Absolute Right? Deciphering the Absoluteness in the Context of Article 3 of the European Convention on Human Rights', (2012) 12 [4] Human Rights Law Review 723.

[55] See also, *Vinter and Others* v. *UK*, 9 July 2013, App. No. 66069/09, 130/10 & 3896/10, para 117; *Nachova and Others* v. *Bulgaria*, 6 July 2005, App. No. 43577/98 & 43579/98, para 100; *Jalloh* v. *Germany*, 11 July 2006, App. No. 46410/99, paras 77–8. For an earlier example of the use of comparative law to define an absolute right, see *T.* v. *UK*, 16 December 1999, App. No. 24724/94, paras 70–2.

[56] *Opuz* v. *Turkey*, 9 June 2009, App. No. 33401/02.

[57] *Opuz*, para 142.

[58] *Opuz*, para 70.

public prosecution of violent domestic crimes.[59] It detailed the factors commonly taken into account by contracting parties to the Convention when deciding whether to pursue public prosecution, such as the seriousness of the offence; whether the victim's injuries are physical or psychological; if the defendant used a weapon; if the defendant has made any threats since the attack; if the defendant planned the attack; the effect (including psychological) on any children living in the household; the chances of the defendant offending again; the continuing threat to the health and safety of the victim or anyone else who was, or could become, involved; the current state of the victim's relationship with the defendant and the effect on that relationship of continuing with the prosecution against the victim's wishes; the history of the relationship, particularly if there had been any other violence in the past; and the defendant's criminal history, particularly any previous violence.

Although the Court recognised that no general consensus existed regarding when to pursue public prosecution, it nevertheless considered that '[i]t can be inferred from [the practice of the states surveyed] that the more serious the offence or the greater the risk of further offences, the more likely that the prosecution should continue in the public interest, even if victims withdraw their complaints'.[60] On this basis, the Court concluded that the local authorities did not sufficiently consider these factors when repeatedly deciding to discontinue the criminal proceedings against the applicant's husband.

Similarly, the Court had recourse to comparative law in order to substantiate when a penal sentence would amount to inhuman and degrading treatment under Article 3 of the Convention. In *Harkins and Edwards* v. *UK*,[61] an extradition request had been submitted by the United States to the UK for transfer of the applicants to face charges of murder for separate offences. The applicants argued that, if extradited,

---

[59] *Opuz*, paras 87–8, 138. The comparative study surveyed Albania, Austria, Bosnia and Herzegovina, Estonia, Greece, Italy, Poland, Portugal, San Marino, Spain, Switzerland, Andorra, Armenia, Azerbaijan, Belgium, Bulgaria, Cyprus, the Czech Republic, Denmark, England and Wales, Finland, 'the former Yugoslav Republic of Macedonia', France, Georgia, Germany, Hungary, Ireland, Latvia, Luxembourg, Malta, Moldova, the Netherlands, the Russian Federation, Serbia, Slovakia, Sweden, Turkey, Ukraine and Romania.

[60] *Opuz*, paras 138–9.

[61] *Harkins and Edwards* v. *UK*, 12 January 2012, App. No. 9146/07 & 32650/07. This was followed in *Babar Ahmed and Others* v. *UK*, 10 April 2012, App. No. 24027/07, 11949/08, 36742/08, 66911/09 & 67354/09. It should be noted that this is *not* a judgment of the Grand Chamber.

they faced risk of being sentenced to death or to a life sentence without parole, which – they contended – breached the UK's positive obligation to protect the Article 2 and 3 rights of those within its jurisdiction. After accepting assurances from US state prosecutors that they would not seek the death penalty, the Court moved to consider whether a penal sentence could constitute inhuman or degrading treatment, and – if so – the attributes that would give it that character. The Court stated that the comparative materials it was presented 'demonstrate that "gross disproportionality" is a widely accepted and applied test for determining when a sentence will amount to inhuman or degrading punishment, or equivalent constitutional norms'.[62] The Court continued:

> *Consequently*, the Court is prepared to accept that while, in principle, matters of appropriate sentencing largely fall outside the scope of Convention, a grossly disproportionate sentence could amount to ill-treatment contrary to Article 3 at the moment of its imposition. However, the Court also considers that the comparative materials set out above demonstrate that 'gross disproportionality' is a strict test and, as the Supreme Court of Canada observed in *Latimer*, it will only be on 'rare and unique occasions' that the test will be met.[63]

In the face of criticisms of incoherence, the use of comparative law in interpretation shows surprising consistency. It is invoked to interpret standards of conduct, providing a rebuttable presumption that states' domestic laws manifest what is, for example, necessary, fair, or inhuman or degrading. It is with this understanding of the doctrine in mind that the following section analyses the academic commentary on consensus.

6.4   No Consensus on Consensus

Criticisms of the use of consensus have been generally advanced on two fronts: those that take issue with the methodology of the Court when using consensus, and those that have principled qualms with its invocation. None of those criticisms, however, convincingly rebuts the utility of consensus doctrine as a matter of principle.

---

[62] *Harkins and Edwards*, para 133. The Court made reference to the laws of Austria, Belgium, the Czech Republic, Estonia, Germany, Lithuania, Luxembourg, the Netherlands, Norway, Poland, Portugal, Romania, Russia, Slovakia, Slovenia, Spain, Switzerland, Turkey, the UK, Canada, the USA, South Africa, Belize, Mauritius, Namibia, Hong Kong and New Zealand; *Harkins and Edwards*, paras 59–61, 66–81.
[63] *Harkins and Edwards*, para 133 (emphasis added).

6.4.1   Methodological Criticisms

The main issue identified by commentators is that the use of comparative law by the ECtHR lacks methodological rigour: it is unclear how many states must be surveyed, how many states constitute 'consensus', and whether contextual factors are taken into account in the Court's comparative survey.[64] Underpinning this criticism is the idea that consensus is mere subterfuge for the judges' own values, enabling their subjective preferences to be cloaked in a veil of formal law. In the words of one author, 'vague references to emerging national standards, which are not empirically verifiable, undermine [the Court's] credibility and sow the seeds of suspicion that they are engaged in an unfounded judicial activism'.[65]

To a certain extent, the sting of this critique may be alleviated with the increased detail of comparative surveys provided in recent judgments of the Court. Although the pre-Protocol 11,[66] part-time ECtHR lacked the personnel and resources to carry out thorough comparative research,[67] transparency has increased with the advent of the full-time Court and the newly created Research Division.[68] As a result, the use of comparative law by the Court has generally – although not uniformly – become 'visibly more professional and detailed'.[69] For example, the Chambers and Grand Chamber of the 'new' Court readily detail the comparative law analyses undertaken in 75.4 per cent of judgments.[70] This has allowed

---

[64] See Carozza, 'Uses and Misuses of Comparative Law', 1233; Dzehtsiarou, *European Consensus*, 78–82; Helfer, 'Consensus, Coherence and the European Convention on Human Rights', 133–41.

[65] Y. Arai-Takahashi, *The Margin of Appreciation Doctrine and the Principle of Proportionality in the Jurisprudence of the ECHR* (Intersentia 2002) 192–3. Cf Mahoney & Kondak, 'Common Ground', 120.

[66] Protocol 11, concluded on 1 May 1994, established the current, full-time ECtHR, abolishing the former two-tier adjudicatory system of the Commission and the Court.

[67] Wildhaber et al., 'No Consensus on Consensus?', 257. Previously, comparative research fell to the judges themselves: 'Luzius Wildhaber [former Judge and President of the ECtHR] remembers that in the early 1990ies, the Registry wrote letters to the Judges and asked them to help explore issues of domestic law relevant for consensus analysis'; ibid.

[68] K. Dzehtsiarou, 'Consensus from within the Palace Walls', UCD Working Papers in Law, Criminology & Socio-Legal Studies, Research Paper No. 40/2010, 5–6. Dzehtsiarou, *European Consensus*, 88.

[69] Wildhaber et al., 'No Consensus on Consensus', 257. For more detail, see Mahoney & Kondak, 'Common Ground', 125–7 (stating that 'In 2014 we can no longer speak of "suboptimal methodology or flimsy or even incorrect evidence".').

[70] Wildhaber et al., 'No Consensus on Consensus?', 258. See for example, *Bayatyan*, paras 46–9. See also, Mahoney & Kondak, 'Common Ground'.

commentators to induce from the case law that, although the 'actual criterion [for consensus] remains a mystery',[71] the Court 'frequently, but not consistently, opts against the existence of consensus, as long as some 6 to 10 States adhere to solutions which differ from the majority view'.[72] With the increased transparency of the Court's reasoning, the ability for consensus to obscure the subjective choices of the bench diminishes. By detailing the comparative methodology, the Court is forced situate itself and its judgment in relation to that survey, expressly adhering to the consensus view or disavowing it.[73]

It should be noted that a full, comprehensive, contextualised comparative survey would demonstrate to the addressees of the judgment, and to the wider community, that the Court's use of comparative law is not simply a matter of 'looking out over a crowd and picking out your friends'.[74] However, time and budget restraints might well preclude such work.[75] Moreover, if such studies were carried out, it seems highly unlikely that such a voluminous work could or should be included in its entirety in the final judgment.

The methodological critique does not claim that the use of domestic law is, as a matter of principle, unjustified. Indeed, quite on the contrary, the advancement of a methodological critique presupposes that there is utility to the use of domestic law if correctly deployed.[76] Principled critiques, on the other hand, claim that the pernicious use of domestic law undermines the very basis of human rights protection, and it is to those claims that we now turn.

---

[71] H. Senden, *Interpretation of Fundamental Rights in a Multilevel Legal System: An Analysis of the European Court of Human Rights and the Court of Justice of the European Union* (Intersentia 2011) 395.

[72] Wildhaber et al., 'No Consensus on Consensus', 259. The authors also conclude that in 56 per cent of post-1998 judgments that discuss consensus, 60–67 per cent or more of member states are surveyed; in 12.3 per cent of cases, around half of the 47 member states are examined; and in 7 per cent of cases, less than a quarter of the member states. In 24.6 per cent of cases, the new Court adopts the approach of the old Court, and does not explicitly say which countries it has taken into account; ibid., 258.

[73] Compare *M. C.*, para 166 with *A, B, C*, paras 235–41.

[74] A. Scalia, *A Matter of Interpretation: Federal Courts and the Law* (Princeton UP) 36.

[75] Dzehtsiarou, *European Consensus*, 88 (noting that the Research Division still has a 'heavy workload').

[76] Most clearly, this is the position of Kanstantin Dzehtsiarou; Dzehtsiarou, *European Consensus*, 72–114, 209.

6.4.2 Principled Criticisms

Of the principled critiques of consensus, perhaps the most damning are those that criticise the Court for abdicating its duties to protect minorities from the tyranny of the majority and to uphold universal moral truths.

The most vociferous and detailed principled criticism of consensus has been advanced by George Letsas. He invokes a strand of case law in which the Court uses the lack of consensus amongst contracting states on 'public morals' to defer to the judgement of the respondent state regarding legitimate incursions on, for example, free speech.[77] The use of the absence of consensus to defer to the state is, he argues, a manifestation of the tyranny of the majority – precisely what human rights should protect against. In other words, by using the consensus doctrine as a reason not to question the legality of a law, the Court fails to fulfil its duty to protect minorities that could be persecuted by the majoritarian legislature in their state.[78] 'Needless to say', he contends, 'no plausible theory of human rights, at least one with liberal-egalitarian aspirations, would ever allow moralistic preferences to constitute a legitimate restriction on liberty'.[79]

This strand of Letsas' argument has merit, but the dangers are overemphasised. Undoubtedly, the scenario he envisages could eventuate and in such instances the use of consensus is to be deplored. However, there are two reasons to doubt the general applicability of his argument. First, it works on the basis that the challenged law is consonant with the consensus approach in the other Council of Europe states or that the Court defers to the respondent state on the basis of an absence of consensus. As such, the oppressed minority in the respondent state is provided with no relief by the Court due to the consensus in other Council of Europe states. Put another way, it is the tyranny of the democratic majority confirmed by the tyranny of the majority by consensus.

But this need not be the case – the Court has used consensus as a reason to find the domestic law to be illegal, protecting the oppressed minority in the contracting state.[80] Take the case of *Bayatyan* v. *Armenia*,

---

[77] *Handyside* v. *UK*, 7 December 1976, App. No. 5493/72, para 48; *Müller and Others* v. *Switzerland*, 24 May 1988, App. No. 10737/84, para 35; *Wingrove* v. *UK*, 25 November 1996, App. No. 17419/90, para 58; *Murphy* v. *Ireland*, 10 July 2003, App. No. 44179/98, para 67.

[78] Letsas, *A Theory of Interpretation*, 121–3.

[79] Letsas, *A Theory of Interpretation*, 121.

[80] Note that this is the case even if we focus upon Letsas' example of the interpretation of 'public morals' under Article 10(2). That consensus could be used in the face of nationalist

for example.[81] In that case, the applicant was a Jehovah's Witness that conscientiously objected to the compulsory military service in Armenia. He brought a case to the ECtHR claiming that the compulsory conscription breached his Article 9 right to freedom of thought, conscience and belief. The Court recognised that the 'overwhelming majority' of Council of Europe states recognised the possibility of conscientious objection, with only Armenia, Azerbaijan and Turkey not recognising such an option.[82] In light of this consensus, as well as the existence of certain international instruments that recognised the right to conscientious objection, the Court decided that by not providing the applicant with any non-military alternative service, the interference with his Article 9 right was not 'necessary in a democratic society'. In a particularly pertinent passage, the Court stated that:

> Although individual interests must on occasion be subordinated to those of a group, democracy does not simply mean that the views of a majority must always prevail: a balance must be achieved which ensures the fair and proper treatment of people from minorities and avoids any abuse of a dominant position. Thus, respect on the part of the State towards the beliefs of a minority religious group like the applicant's by providing them with the opportunity to serve society as dictated by their conscience might, far from creating unjust inequalities or discrimination as claimed by the Government, rather ensure cohesive and stable pluralism and promote religious harmony and tolerance in society.[83]

In this case, therefore, Letsas' argument that consensus analysis panders to the majority view to the detriment of the minority is contradicted.

intransigence was recognised at the start of the twentieth century by François Geny, who loquaciously stated that 'derrières les phénomènes psychologiques d'imitation, qui représente l'action extérieure réciproque des droits de divers pays, se révèle sans peine l'idée, qu'une règle, dégagée du consensus des systèmes juridiques, places à un même niveau de civilisation, a, pour elle, une sorte de conscience juridique collective, plus large que celle qui ne se manifeste qu'au sein d'un pays déterminé, et capable, par suite, de vaincre, au besoin, certaines résistances nationales'; F. Gény, *Méthode d'interprétation et sources en droit privé positif* vol II (2nd edn, LGDJ 1919) 274.

[81] *Bayatyan v. Armenia*, 7 July 2011, App. No. 23459/03.

[82] *Bayatyan*, paras 48, 103–9, 124–9. The comparative study surveyed the UK, Denmark, Sweden, the Netherlands, Norway, Finland, Germany, France, Luxembourg, Belgium, Italy, Austria, Portugal, Spain, Poland, the Czech Republic, Hungary, Croatia, Estonia, Moldova and Slovenia, Cyprus, the former Federal Republic of Yugoslavia (which in 2006 divided into two member states: Serbia and Montenegro, both of which retained that right) and Ukraine, Latvia, Slovakia and Switzerland, Bosnia and Herzegovina, Lithuania, Romania, Georgia, Greece, Bulgaria, 'the former Yugoslav Republic of Macedonia', Russia, Albania, Azerbaijan and Turkey.

[83] *Bayatyan*, para 126 (emphasis added, citations omitted).

It seems to be incontrovertible that, in some instances at least, consensus analysis is used to protect minority rights in a state. Similarly, the domestic law challenged might protect minorities but be unpopular with, and challenged by, other groups in society. In such a scenario, the Court could use consensus to defeat the challenge to the law protecting the minority.

Second, Letsas neglects to take into account that consensus has been used to promote the progressive evolution of domestic legislation to provide *better protection* for the rights of minorities. An illustrative example is the *Goodwin* case. In that case, the Court decided that the UK could no longer maintain that full legal recognition of transsexuals was within its margin of appreciation in light of 'an increase in the [global] social acceptance of the phenomenon of transsexualism and a growing recognition of the problems with which transsexuals are confronted'.[84] This evolution in social values was confirmed by a comparative survey.[85] Shortly after the judgment, the UK Parliament passed the Gender Recognition Act 2004, which allowed transsexuals to gain full legal recognition upon assessment by a Gender Recognition Panel. In the Explanatory Notes to the Act, which specifically cites the ECtHR judgment in *Goodwin*, the Government recognised that it 'ha[d] a positive obligation under international law to secure the Convention rights and freedoms and must rectify these ongoing breaches [those identified in *Goodwin*]'.[86] Although it is impossible to attribute decisive influence to the Court's use of consensus, Letsas himself recognises that the *Goodwin* judgment gives effect to the principles of legality and equality, yet he ignores the purported reasons for which it did so.[87]

Letsas advances another criticism of consensus, which is based on the Court's case law regarding the legal recognition of transsexuals, culminating in *Goodwin*.[88] He claims that:

---

[84] *Christine Goodwin* v. *UK*, 11 July 2002, App. No. 28957/95, para 92.

[85] The judgment cited the change of position in Singapore, Canada, South Africa, Israel, Australia and New Zealand, as well as all but two of the states of the United States; *Goodwin*, para 56.

[86] *Gender Recognition Act 2004: Explanatory Notes* (HMSO 2004), para 6, available at www .legislation.gov.uk/ukpga/2004/7/pdfs/ukpgaen_20040007_en.pdf.

[87] Letsas, *A Theory of Interpretation*, 124.

[88] *Rees* v. *UK*, 17 October 1986, App. No. 9532/81, para 37; *Cossey* v. *UK*, 27 September 1990, App. No. 10843/84, para 37; *Sheffield and Horsham* v. *UK*, 30 July 1998, App. No. 31–32/ 1997/815–816/1018–1019, para 52; *Christine Goodwin* v. *UK*, 11 July 2002, App. No. 28957/95, para 72; *I* v. *UK*, 11 July 2002, App. No. 25680/94, para 52.

> [T]he idea [of the use of consensus in the line of cases] seems to be that the Court should wait for a consensus within Contracting States to be established before it rules something to be a violation. This is because it is felt that the Court should not rush into finding the majority of states in breach of the Convention whenever there is a new evolving standard. Rather, it should first warn them that a new standard is evolving and allow them time to reform their policies gradually, in line with present-day conditions.[89]

This 'piecemeal evolution', he claims, cannot be justified either by the notion that consensus provides state consent regarding the interpretation of the Convention, nor can it be justified by the realist argument that consensus analysis increases the likelihood of compliance and hence safeguards the authority of the Court.[90] In fact, the denial of legal recognition of transgender people prior to the *Goodwin* case 'treated the applicants in an unprincipled manner ... [which] deeply offends the values of legality and equality'.[91]

This criticism is based on a certain view of human rights and a certain view of the appropriate interpretative practice of the ECtHR, which need to be outlined in order to fully understand Letsas' point. He believes that the rights enshrined in the European Convention are transcendental and universal: that they are extant 'abstract moral truths' which bind states regardless of any convention obligation, and the retrieval and protection of which is the job of the Court.[92] This belief in the transcendental nature of certain rights accords well, he claims, with the interpretative practice of the European Court. For him, it explains why the Court eschews a textualist or intentionalist approach, and instead focusses on an examination of 'the substance of the human right at issue and the moral value

---

[89] Letsas, *A Theory of Interpretation*, 123. For similar arguments, see S. Dothan, 'Judicial Deference Allows European Consensus to Emerge', (2018) 18 Chicago JIL 393, 398, 411–13 ('This exercise [the Court's judgments in the cases that pre-dated *Goodwin*] allowed the ECHR to signal to European countries that they can make their laws independently without fearing a finding of violation prior to being warned. To the extent that this maneuver was successful, it may have incentivized countries to make their policies independently without guessing what policy the majority of the countries would opt for and thereby facilitated the finding of a genuine European consensus by the ECHR.'); Y. Shany, 'All Roads Lead to Strasbourg?: Application of the Margin of Appreciation Doctrine by the European Court of Human Rights and the UN Human Rights Committee', (2018) 9 JIDS 180, 184–5.

[90] F. de Londras & K. Dzehtsiarou, 'Managing Judicial Innovation in the European Court of Human Rights', (2015) 15 Human Rights Law Review 541–4.

[91] Letsas, *A Theory of Interpretation*, 124.

[92] Letsas, 'Strasbourg's Interpretive Ethic', 540.

it serves in a democratic community'.[93] In Letsas' view, therefore, there already exist goals – 'abstract moral truths' – against which the adequacy of the jurisprudence of the Court can be assessed, and in reference to which its case law most makes sense.[94] Set against this theory of interpretation, consensus has no place – it is superfluous: 'the Court applie[s] a first-order moral reading of the ECHR rights, adding hesitant and redundant remarks about this being somehow commonly accepted'.[95]

Leaving aside the rather contentious suggestion that rights are objective moral truths that can be retrieved from the ether,[96] the second strand of Letsas' argument falls short on two counts. First, it assumes that his theory of interpretation – that the Court has interpreted the Convention as if on some intractable march towards the realisation of perfect rights – is valid, and that consensus analysis is just an anomaly. But this just does not square with the consistent and continuous use of consensus by the Court over the past 35 years. Letsas seems to ignore the fact that the invocation of comparative law is not just a singular aberration on an otherwise smooth road to the discovery of objective moral truth. Instead, it seems to be something more fundamental to the interpretative practice of the Court, something that cannot be explained away as an error or a superfluity. Second, Letsas recognises that consensus does sometimes coincide with an evolution towards moral truth. To illustrate this, he gives the example of the *Dudgeon* case, stating that:

> [T]here is an apparent effort in the [judgment] to base its reasoning on what is now believed in the great majority of the member states, it is equally striking that the Court takes contemporary understanding to be *better* and not merely different from that at the time when anti-homosexual legislation was enacted . . . the change to affect the interpretation of an ECHR right must constitute an improvement, moving closer to the truth of the substantive protected right.[97]

If consensus pushes the Court towards this 'better' interpretation of the Convention, is it still to be disregarded or deemed superfluous? At the

---

[93] Letsas, 'Strasbourg's Interpretive Ethic', 520. Extrapolating from the heavy influence that Dworkin seems to have exerted on Letsas, it seems to be that this view of the interpretative practice of the ECtHR is his attempt to frame the case law of the Court in its 'best light'.

[94] Letsas, 'Strasbourg's Interpretive Ethic', 528; 'The Court is more interested in the moral value the Convention rights serve and what arguments best support it rather than on whether such agreements are widely shared across the Council of Europe.'

[95] Letsas, 'Strasbourg's Interpretive Ethic', 531.

[96] See for example, L. Henkin, 'The Universality of the Concept of Human Rights', (1989) 506 Annals of the American Academy of Political and Social Science 10, 12.

[97] Letsas, 'Strasbourg's Interpretive Ethic', 531.

very least, then, Letsas must admit that consensus analysis is useful if it facilitates a movement towards the protection of abstract moral rights. However, this possibility is not admitted in his critique of the 'piecemeal evolution' of the Convention culminating in the *Goodwin* case. If the Court 'is to discover, over time and through persuasive moral argument, the moral truth about these fundamental rights',[98] there seems to be no reason why consensus analysis cannot contribute to the strength of the moral arguments proffered.

Eyal Benvenisti is also critical of the use of the consensus by the Court, claiming that, from a theoretical perspective, it 'can draw its justification only from nineteenth century theories of State consent'.[99] Whilst Benvenisti rightly recognises that consent-based theories of international law are outmoded, it is not clear that consensus analysis is in fact the search for state consent. Perhaps most obviously, the laws examined by the Court inevitably pertain to the domestic relationship between the state and its citizens, and do not manifest *opinio juris* regarding the state's international obligations.[100] Take, for example, the abovementioned case of *M.C.* v. *Bulgaria*, in which domestic laws on rape were surveyed.[101] Those criminal statutes did not directly pertain to international law nor did they provide implicit consent to any international legal standard regarding criminalisation of conduct. One might argue that the use of consensus is 'apologetic' to states, attributing undue importance to the state's exercise of its prerogative to enact domestic law. This criticism might have purchase but it does not rely on the concept of state consent nor does it make sense to conceptualise the use of comparative law as a form of 'updated consent', as other authors have suggested.[102]

Whilst raising valid concerns, the substantive criticisms of the use of comparative law in the ECtHR do not rule out its utility as a matter of

---

[98] Letsas, 'Strasbourg's Interpretive Ethic', 540.
[99] E. Benvenisti, 'Margin of Appreciation, Consensus, and Universal Standards', (1999) 31 NYU JILP 843, 852. More recently, Benvenisti has stated that 'the recent jurisprudence of the court suggests that the court has indeed seized the new rationale for qualified deference to the political process by examining closely the quality of the parliamentary process that has led to the policy in question'. In his view, this approach 'allows the court to seize the principle of subsidiarity to properly address the internal democratic deficits that may arise in the Member States'; E. Benvenisti, 'The Margin of Appreciation, Subsidiarity and Global Challenges to Democracy', (2018) 9 JIDS 240, 252.
[100] The practice of states as it pertains to their international obligations is also important as subsequent practice under Article 31(3)(b) VCLT or as state practice for the purposes of custom.
[101] *M.C.*, paras 88–108, 130–47.
[102] Dzehtsiarou, *European Consensus*, 152.

principle, instead focussing on potential pitfalls that have not, as yet, eventuated in practice. The next section turns to examine the arguments made in favour of the use of consensus.

6.4.3 Defences of Consensus

Those that defend the Court's use of consensus often base their arguments on the legitimacy afforded to the Court by the use of comparative law. For Kanstantin Dzehtsiarou, legitimacy results from the increased acceptability to states of a judgment that adopts consensus analysis.[103] Consensus, Dzehtsiarou contends, 'is designed to ensure the consent of States, convince the general public, and secure obedience'.[104] In his view, the fact that a state is more likely to comply with a judgment that uses consensus analysis is all that is necessary to justify the interpretative technique. The crux of Dzehtsiarou's claim is that judgments that are based on consensus are 'persuasive because [they are] based on the decisions that are made by democratically elected bodies'.[105]

This is questionable on three counts. First, if consensus were *only* persuasive because it refers to decisions of democratically elected bodies, then – as Letsas and Benvenisti point out – the Court would be led down the path of pandering to the will of the minority-oppressing majority in contracting states. Second, if consensus provides legitimacy to a judgment *tout court*, why does the Court not adopt consensus analysis in each and every judgment? Clearly, this is not the case. However, Dzehtsiarou does not elaborate upon the circumstances in which consensus might augment the legitimacy of the judgment and why it might do so. Finally, he adduces no evidence to support the claim that consensus actually does make judgments more acceptable to states.

---

[103] K. Dzehtsiarou, 'Does Consensus Matter? Legitimacy of European Consensus in the case law of the European Court of Human Rights', (2011) Public Law 534, 536. In his monograph-length treatment of the topic, Dzehtsiarou bases legitimacy variously on state consent (Dzehtsiarou, *European Consensus*, 155), facilitation of dialogue between international and national legal systems (ibid., 158), consistency, coherence, predictability and certainty (ibid., 159–60), and even adherence to the traditional sources doctrine in international law (ibid., 161). Cf Mahoney & Kondak, 'Common Ground', 123.

[104] Dzehtsiarou, 'Does Consensus Matter?', 539.

[105] Dzehtsiarou, 'Does Consensus Matter?', 553. It seems as though Strasbourg judges, at least, consider that consensus potentially plays a legitimating role; *ibid.*, 544–5. Cf Benvenisti, 'The Margin of Appreciation, Subsidiarity and Global Challenges to Democracy', 252.

Paul Mahoney, a former Registrar and Judge of the ECtHR, takes a more nuanced view of the legitimising power of consensus. He argues that the use of comparative law forestalls the claim that the ECtHR is involved in judicial legislation:

> [T]he anchoring of an evolved meaning to empirical evidence, namely the perceivable changes in the legislative patterns of the contracting States, is a counter to the argument that the Strasbourg judges are trespassing into the Treaty-amendment domain of the contracting States or are simply relying on their own personal sense of justice to make new law.[106]

Moreover, he claims that it is 'natural' for the Court to draw on the domestic laws of contracting states when one bears in mind the shared values that motivated the drafting and conclusion of the ECHR. '[S]ince the ECHR is a kind of fusion of national constitutional principles safeguarding human rights in Europe', Mahoney argues, 'having regard to the common character – or lack of it – of those legislations is surely legitimate when interpreting the ECHR'.[107] Consensus has a place as a non-binding interpretative aid in the repertoire of the Court, albeit that 'comparative law considerations constitute only one element in a complex law-making process'.[108]

Former Judge and President of the Court, Luzius Wildhaber, also adheres to the legitimacy justification of consensus, but refutes the idea that monocausal explanations can fully capture 'the richness, the variety and the recurrent inconsistencies of the Court's case-law'.[109] Instead, he and his co-authors emphasise that the use of consensus encompasses both a 'rein' effect, which provides a check on aberrant states, and a 'spur' effect that promotes change in reticent states. This multifaceted view of consensus

---

[106] Mahoney, 'The Comparative Method in Judgments of the European Court of Human Rights', 147. See also, Mahoney & Kondak, 'Common Ground', 120 ('Convincing and reliable interpretative techniques, such as the search for common European ground, brings as much objectivity to the exercise as possible and serve to justify any law-making accomplished by the Court when filling interpretative gaps left in the Convention law. The comparative-law process thereby adds legitimacy to the judgments of the Court.').

[107] Mahoney, 'The Comparative Method in Judgments of the European Court of Human Rights', 147.

[108] R. Bernhardt, 'Comparative Law in the Interpretation and Application of the European Convention on Human Rights', in S. Busuttil (ed), *Mainly Human Rights: Studies in Honour of J. J. Cremona* (Fondation Internationale Malte 1999) 36, quoted in Mahoney, 'The Comparative Method in Judgments of the European Court of Human Rights', 150.

[109] Wildhaber et al., 'No Consensus on Consensus', 251.

rebuts the criticisms that consensus either inevitably privileges the status quo or that it leads the Court to 'overreaching' its judicial function.[110]

An altogether different justification for reference to domestic law has been suggested by the International Law Commission in the course of its work on subsequent agreements and subsequent practice in treaty interpretation. In his reports on the topic, the Special Rapporteur, Georg Nolte, draws a distinction between 'narrow' and 'broad' conceptions of the subsequent practice of states in the application of a treaty.[111] The 'narrow' conception is 'subsequent practice in the application of a treaty which establishes the agreement of the parties regarding its interpretation',[112] within the meaning of Article 31(3)(b) of the VCLT, whereas the 'broad' conception acknowledges that subsequent practice may be relevant even if it does not reflect an agreement regarding interpretation by all the parties.[113] Whether it fits within the broad or narrow conception of the term, Nolte recognises that subsequent practice must be undertaken 'in the application of the treaty'.[114]

Whilst Nolte correctly recognises that the ECtHR has often 'referred to the legislative practice of member States without explicitly mentioning article 31(3)(b) of the Vienna Convention',[115] his analysis of the practice of the ECtHR is somewhat ambiguous. At some points, he frames the consensus doctrine as subsequent state practice (presumably within the broad meaning of the term):

> the Court has confirmed that uniform, or largely uniform national legislation, and even domestic administrative practice, *can in principle constitute relevant subsequent practice* and may have effects which can go even

---

[110] See for example, Martens, 'Perplexity of the National Judge Faced with Vagaries of European Consensus', 95; T. Zwart, 'More Human Rights than Court: Why the Legitimacy of the European Court of Human Rights Is in Need of Repair and How It Can Be Done' in S. Flogaitis et al. (eds), *The European Court of Human Rights and Its Discontents* (Edward Elgar 2013) 89–93.

[111] This is also reflected in the distinction between subparagraphs 2 and 3 of draft conclusion 4; see G. Nolte, 'Fifth Report on Subsequent Agreements and Subsequent Practice in Relation to the Interpretation of Treaties', UN Doc A/CN.4/715 (28 February 2018), draft conclusion 4. The narrow conception of subsequent practice must be taken into account by an interpreter by virtue of Article 31(3)(b), whereas subsequent practice within the broad meaning of the term is relevant as a supplementary means of interpretation under Article 32 of the VCLT.

[112] G. Nolte, 'First Report on Subsequent Agreements and Subsequent Practice in Relation to Treaty Interpretation' UN Doc A/CN.4/660 (19 March 2013), para 107.

[113] Nolte, 'First Report', paras 107–10.

[114] ibid., para 111.

[115] Nolte, 'First Report', para 37. See also, para 98.

beyond that of being merely a means of interpretation according to article 31(3)(b) of the Vienna Convention.[116]

However, Nolte also acknowledges that the domestic laws to which the Court refers do not necessarily directly relate to the interpretation or application of the Convention:

> when describing the domestic legal situation in the member States, the Court rarely asks whether this legal situation results from a legislative process during which the possible requirements of the Convention were discussed. The Court nevertheless presumes that the member States, when legislating or otherwise acting in a particular way, are conscious of their obligations under the Convention, and that they act in a way which reflects their bona fide understanding of their obligations.[117]

It seems tenuous to suggest that the practice cited by the ECtHR reflects how states parties interpret or apply their obligations under the ECHR, nor is it clear that there is even a more attenuated link between the practice cited and the state's awareness of its obligations under the Convention, as the passage quoted above suggests. Instead, it seems as though the ECtHR's use of consensus analysis falls outside the scope of the provisions of the VCLT insofar as it does not concern the 'application of the treaty'.[118] It would seem to be hard, in most instances, to rationalise the Court's consensus analysis in terms of the provisions of the Vienna Convention.

In conclusion, even if one grants that consensus may, in some circumstances, ingrain the tyranny of the majority or obstruct the Court's interpretative path to objective 'moral truths', one cannot maintain that this will inevitably obviate the potential utility of consensus. At the opposite end of the spectrum, the main issue with the authors that advocate the use of consensus is the lack of a theory of *when* and *why* the Court uses consensus, and *how* it provides legitimacy or authority to its judgments, or evidence that it in fact does. The examination of the case law of the Grand Chamber in the preceding section demonstrates a pattern that may explain how and why consensus analysis might be desirable, and it is upon this that the following section will build.

---

[116] Nolte, 'First Report', para 37 (emphasis added; citations omitted). See also, paras 98, 134.

[117] G. Nolte, 'Second Report on Subsequent Agreements and Subsequent Practice in Relation to Treaty Interpretation' UN Doc A/CN.4/671 (26 March 2014), para 14.

[118] Nolte, 'First Report', para 114.

6.5 Standards of Conduct (Revisited)

In the preceding chapter, it was noted that international investment tribunals have invoked comparative law to interpret treaty standards, such as the obligation to accord fair and equitable treatment to investors, or the prohibition of arbitrary or discriminatory measures. This has clear parallels with the use of comparative law by the ECtHR identified in the present chapter. This section will explore two potential justifications for the use of consensus analysis by the Court. The first builds on a topic addressed in the previous chapter; namely, the use of domestic law to structure judicial discretion. The second explores a possible justification for reference to domestic law that has its origins in international legal theory; namely, the interactional theory of international law developed by Jutta Brunnée and Stephen Toope.

6.5.1 Structuring Discretion

It will be recalled that one justification posited for the use of domestic law by international investment tribunals in the previous chapter was that it provided arbitrators with material that structured their broad discretion vis-à-vis broad treaty standards.[119] As such, they could approach the interpretation of standards with a modicum of objectivity, insulating themselves (to a certain extent) from charges of bias or partiality. As noted above, certain commentators explicitly identify this as one of the principal functions of the ECtHR's recourse to consensus.[120]

In this context, it is useful to contrast the approach taken by the ECtHR and investment tribunals to the interpretation of standards in domestic legal systems as a means to think about why and how reference to actual behaviour might structure judicial discretion and the limits to this function. Although not representative of the approach taken in all national systems, the UK Supreme Court's judgment in *Healthcare at Home Limited* v. *The Common Services Agency* provides an interesting comparison. In that case, the UK Supreme Court was called upon to interpret 'reasonableness' in the context of EU law.[121] Lord Reed, delivering judgment for the Court, stated that:

---

[119] See Chapter 5.

[120] Mahoney & Kondak, 'Common Ground', 120; Mahoney, 'The Comparative Method in Judgments of the European Court of Human Rights', 147.

[121] Note that this is an undefined standard. Cf the UK Unfair Contract Terms Act 1977, section 11(2) and Schedule 2, which specify factors to be taken into account when

> [I]t would be misconceived for a party to seek evidence from actual passengers on the Clapham omnibus as to how they would have acted in a given situation or what they would have foreseen, in order to establish how the reasonable man would have acted or what he would have foreseen. Even if the party offered to prove that his witnesses were reasonable men, the evidence would be beside the point. The conduct of the reasonable man is not established by the evidence of witnesses, but by the application of a legal standard by the court. The court may require to be informed by evidence of circumstances which bear on its application of the standard of the reasonable man in any particular case; but it is then for the court to determine the outcome, in those circumstances, of applying that impersonal standard.[122]

Three reasons for substantiating standard of conduct tests without reference to actual conduct are present in the *Healthcare at Home* judgment. First, explicit reference to an individual or group of individuals would, in the words of the UK Supreme Court, 'violate equality of treatment' of citizens.[123] In domestic law, a court is faced with a pool of at least hundreds of thousands of individuals (or, in most Council of Europe states, millions) from which standards of conduct could be induced. Considering that it would be impossible for a court to survey a sufficiently large section of the population to claim objectivity or representativeness, any lesser survey would give undue weight to the behaviour of those sampled. In other words, any attempt to substantiate the legal standard of conduct will necessarily breach the principle of equality. The judge is hence endowed with the responsibility to substantiate the attributes of the reasonable man on the assumption that they will be able to rise above their own biases to expound an objective standard.

Second, the absence of reference to actual conduct accords legal certainty to a standard, which 'would be undermined by a standard which depended on evidence of the actual or subjective ability of particular [individuals]'.[124] For example, if what was considered as 'reasonable' were to be assessed in relation to a select group of individuals, the

---

    determining whether a contract term purporting to exempt a party from their contractual liabilities is reasonable.

[122] *Healthcare at Home Limited*, para 3.

[123] *Healthcare at Home Limited*, para 12.

[124] *Healthcare at Home Limited*, para 12. See also, Advocate General Sharpston in *Lämmerzahl GmbH* v. *Freie Hansestadt Bremen* (Case C-241/06) [2008] 1 CMLR 19, para 66.

ability of the public to assess the standard of conduct to which they were held would be significantly diminished.

Third, and relatedly, the doctrine of *stare decisis* allows the English courts to substantiate the reasonableness test in relation to concrete cases that will, unless overruled, be subsequently followed.[125] The ability to refer to prior cases in the course of the Court's reasoning allows the objective standard to be constructed incrementally, alleviating claims of subjectivity that might otherwise be levelled at the bench.

There is one crucial premise upon which the UK Supreme Court's arguments are based, which does not hold true for the international level. Whilst there are only 47 states in the Council of Europe, there are over 65 million people in the UK. What is considered to be a 'fair' trial, or what is 'necessary in a democratic society' is more readily discernable if the relevant pool of actors is only 47, and not millions.[126] This places the onus on the judge to justify their interpretation of the standard, as what is considered 'reasonable', 'fair' or 'necessary' is more readily verifiable than in domestic law. Put another way, if the position of the Court is out of line with the prevailing views of states in the Council of Europe, it will be more noticeable. Subjective bias has the potential to manifest itself more clearly because – unlike domestic judges – the international judiciary cannot justify their interpretation of a standard of conduct in reference to an amorphous constituency of hundreds of thousands, or millions.[127]

This structural difference renders the 'equality of treatment' and 'legal certainty' arguments advanced by the UK Supreme Court inapplicable. The fact that the constituent elements of the pertinent society are few in number allows for a representative or comprehensive survey of the actual standard in society to be undertaken, as well as providing an observable standard that – if followed in law – will provide legal certainty.[128] This is not to say every deviation from a generally accepted standard of conduct is a result of judges' biases: for example, normative considerations could,

---

[125] The doctrine of *jurisprudence constante* works analogously, although not identically, in the French system.

[126] Of course, this justification presupposes that the principal group to which the Court wishes to demonstrate its objectivity – and hence the community in relation to which it justifies its interpretation – is Council of Europe member states, and not the individuals under their jurisdiction. This seems to be a reasonable assumption in light of recent declarations of the Council of Europe member states, which have challenged the perceived activism of the Court. See the declarations cited at fn 10, above.

[127] Cf Dzehtsiarou, *European Consensus*, 164, 172; Mahoney, 'The Comparative Method in Judgments of the European Court of Human Rights', 147.

[128] Note that this presupposes a predictably stable methodology for examining consensus.

and do, play a role in a judicial interpretation of what constitutes an acceptable standard.[129] But it does place the onus on the judge to explicate the legal standard in relation to the actual standards of conduct observable in society.

6.5.2   The Importance of Shared Values

Whilst consensus may shield the Court from criticisms of subjectivity, the idea that the application of law should take into account the behaviour of those in the society it regulates is not alien to international legal theory. In particular, the interactional theory of international law of Jutta Brunnée and Stephen Toope attempts to demonstrate that normative alignment, or – in their terminology – 'shared understandings', is pivotal for the functioning of law.[130] This theory offers one of the most promising avenues for a solid theoretical justification for the consensus doctrine. As such, this section examines the theory in some detail, tracing its origins to the jurisprudence of Lon Fuller. It argues that Brunnée and Toope's theory fundamentally differs from Fuller's, but nevertheless both highlight an important aspect of the interpretation of standards.

The genesis of the interactional theory of Brunnée and Toope is Lon Fuller's classic work, *The Morality of Law*.[131] For Fuller, a legal system does not simply create positive law but rather legal rules must to some extent fulfil eight principles of legality, termed the 'inner morality of law' (such as the generality, promulgation and non-retroactivity of laws).[132] Brunnée and Toope adopt Fuller's eight criteria as the basis for their interactional theory of law, claiming that 'adherence to the eight criteria of legality (a "practice of legality") produces law that is legitimate in the eyes of the persons to whom it is addressed'.[133] This 'legal legitimacy' produces a feeling of *legal* obligation, and it is this sense of obligation that is the 'value added', and the identifying characteristic, of law.[134] Declared

---

[129]   Notably in this context, see *A, B, C*, paras 235–41. See also, *Tanase*, para 172; *Republican Party of Russia v. Russia*, 12 April 2011, App. No. 12976/07, para 126.

[130]   J. Brunnée & S. Toope, *Legitimacy and Legality in International Law: An Interactional Account* (CUP 2010).

[131]   L. L. Fuller, *The Morality of Law* (Revised edn, Yale UP 1969).

[132]   Fuller's eight principles of legality are: generality of laws; promulgation of laws; non-retroactivity of laws; comprehensibility of legal rules; coherence of laws; non-impossibility of compliance with laws; stability of laws; and congruence between laws as announced and as actually applied.

[133]   Brunnée & Toope, *Legality and Legitimacy*, 27.

[134]   Brunnée & Toope, *Legality and Legitimacy*, 37.

laws that do not meet any of the eight criteria do not command voluntary compliance through felt obligation, and hence do not function as 'law'.

Of Fuller's eight principles of legality, Brunnée and Toope place a great deal of importance on the final criterion, 'congruence'.[135] For Fuller, this criterion refers to congruence between official actions (including the police, courts and government officials) and the law 'as declared':[136]

> This congruence may be destroyed or impaired in a great variety of ways: mistaken interpretation, inaccessibility of the law, lack of insight into what is required to maintain the integrity of the legal system, bribery, prejudice, indifference, stupidity, and the drive toward personal power.[137]

However, in Brunnée and Toope's theory, the transposition of this criterion to the international level alters its character. No longer is it congruence between official actions and law, but rather in the case of international law, it is the congruence between the actions of states and international rules that is relevant.[138] In other words, '[w]hen explicit rules are unrelated to how states and other international actors actually behave, fidelity [to the law] is destroyed'.[139]

Brunnée and Toope's reformulated criterion of congruence 'reflects and operationalizes the [authors'] emphasis on shared understandings as a basis of international normativity'.[140] At a basic level, these shared understandings constitute the informal social practices necessary for law to be intelligible, such as the linguistic conventions that make legal rules comprehensible.[141] However, Brunnée and Toope claim that the importance of shared understandings goes further than this: actors within the international legal system also share the understanding that norms meeting the criteria of legality engender legal obligation, as well as sharing more 'rich and substantive' understandings regarding certain values that law must protect, such as the right to property.[142] In their view, international law is dependant upon 'a background of shared understandings that make it intelligible, *and* upon broad congruence with the patterns and practices in

---

[135] See N. Krisch, 'Review of Jutta Brunnée and Stephen Toope, *Legality and Legitimacy in International Law: An Interactional Account*', (2012) 106 AJIL 203, 204.

[136] Fuller, *The Morality of Law*, 81–91.

[137] Fuller, *The Morality of Law*, 81.

[138] Brunnée & Toope, *Legality and Legitimacy*, 35.

[139] ibid.

[140] Krisch, 'Review of Jutta Brunnée and Stephen Toope', 206.

[141] For more on the conventionality of language, see A. Marmor, *Social Conventions: From Language to Law* (Princeton UP 2009), Chapters 3–5.

[142] Brunnée & Toope, *Legality and Legitimacy*, 68–9.

international society'.[143] The authors work on the assumption that these patterns and practices reflect substantive shared understandings of states.[144] To illustrate this point, they provide the example of the Migrant Workers Convention as a 'law-making project' that was 'markedly at odds with – or ahead of – social background understandings', resulting in a low number of ratifications.[145] Whilst deep, substantive shared values within a 'community of practice' are not necessary, if present, they cannot be transgressed.[146]

This reformulation of the congruence criterion has drawn criticism. According to Krisch, 'the analogy here [between Fuller's and Brunnée and Toope's congruence criterion] is fragile at best, and this fragility may explain why the criterion of congruence proves particularly problematic most of the case studies in the book'.[147] As should be immediately apparent, by basing legal normativity on shared understandings anchored in the practice of states, the authors run the risk of taking an 'apologetic' stance with regards to the legality of state actions: if enough states act in an illegal way then it ceases to be illegal. Such a statement is unexceptional in the context of customary international law. However, the authors also contend that treaty law and even *jus cogens* norms cannot be incongruent with the 'patterns and practices in international society'.[148] Indeed, this forms the basis of Brunnée and Toope's striking conclusion that the prohibition on torture does not form part of international law.[149]

It is neither clear why shared understandings must be shoehorned into the criteria of congruence in quite the way that Brunnée and Toope do, nor is it evident that recourse must be had to constructivist IR literature to argue that shared understandings are important. In order to examine

---

[143] Brunnée & Toope, *Legality and Legitimacy*, 75 (emphasis added). Note that in other parts of their book, the authors seem to endorse Emanuel Adler's statement that members of a community of practice must share an understanding of 'what they are doing and why'. However, it is unclear whether the authors consider shared understandings regarding the purpose of law to be a pre-requisite; ibid., 80.

[144] This transposal of values to practices is not something that is fleshed out in Brunnée and Toope's work, leaving one to wonder if one really can induce the values of a state from its practice. An analogous issue is induction of *opinio juris* from state practice for the purposes of elucidating a rule of custom; see for example, *North Sea Continental Shelf (F. R. G. v. Denmark; F. R. G. v. The Netherlands)* (Judgment) [1969] ICJ Rep 3, 44, para 76.

[145] Brunnée & Toope, *Legality and Legitimacy*, 76.

[146] Brunnée & Toope, *Legality and Legitimacy*, 86–7.

[147] Krisch, 'Review of Jutta Brunnée and Stephen Toope', 206.

[148] Brunnée & Toope, *Legality and Legitimacy*, 75.

[149] Brunnée & Toope, *Legality and Legitimacy*, 269.

Brunnée and Toope's claim that congruence with the shared values of a community is a pre-requisite for law, it is instructive to trace the idea back to its Fullerian origins.

The most convincing analysis of this element of Fuller's jurisprudence has been conducted by Gerald Postema, who elucidates why and in what respects shared understandings are pivotal to the functioning of the law.[150] Postema distinguishes between the 'vertical interaction' thesis and the 'congruence' thesis, both of which are present in Fuller's work. These theses are predicated on two crucial points: first, that law provides citizens with reasons to act a certain way which factor into their deliberations; and, second, that the practical import of a norm can only be understood in relation to others in society.

With regard to the first element, this 'self-directed action' is the mechanism by which law fulfils its function. Laws seek to 'influence deliberation in a wholesale fashion, not through detailed step-by-step instructions, but through general norms that agents must interpret and apply to their specific practical situations'.[151] As a result, an individual faced with a legal rule must work out the practical import of a norm in order for it to factor into their deliberation.[152] This leads to the second point: for an individual to discern the practical import of a norm, they must be reasonably certain that they can predict how others will interpret and act in relation to the norm. Driving on the left-hand side of the road, for example, rests on the assumption that other road users understand the concepts of right and left in the same way as us. As a result, the practical import of a norm must be 'publicly accessible' and not subjectively imputed to the law by each individual.

The vertical interaction thesis pertains to the publicly accessible nature of the practical import of laws and the interaction of state and citizen.[153] In the words of Postema, this thesis entails that:

> [The] law-givers must shape the rules they enact or interpret in anticipation of how citizens are likely to understand, the language they use, and

---

[150] G. Postema, 'Implicit Law', (1994) 13 Law and Philosophy 361. See also, G. Postema, 'Conformity, Custom and Congruence' in M. Kramer (ed), *The Legacy of H. L. A. Hart* (OUP 2008).

[151] Postema, 'Implicit Law', 370.

[152] As Postema notes, the practical import of a norm in turn depends on 'a capacity to work out the correct applications of the norm and a capacity to appreciate the reason for acting in the way indicated and to relate it in an appropriate way to other reasons the agent might have'; Postema, 'Implicit Law', 370.

[153] Postema, 'Implicit Law', 368–72; Postema, 'Conformity, Custom and Congruence', 58.

the decisions they make. Likewise, citizens will understand announced rules and decisions in light of how they expect officials and their fellow citizens to understand and apply the rules.[154]

It is hence in the vertical interaction thesis that Fuller's eighth criterion of congruence between official actions and declared law finds its place, forming a crucial part of the 'relatively stable reciprocity of expectations between the law-giver and subject'.[155]

Postema identifies a second, 'more robust' claim regarding informal social practices in Fuller's work – and one that accords more readily with some elements of the theory of Brunnée and Toope – which he terms the 'congruence thesis'. According to the congruence thesis, a legal system cannot function if it is sealed off from background social practices.[156] That is not to say that laws can never diverge from social norms, but rather that they cannot be 'systematically at odds or radically isolated from ordinary, informal social practices and conventions'.[157] An example neatly illustrates this: consider a sign stating 'Dogs must be carried on the escalator'.[158] We understand this injunction because we know something about the nature of dogs (they have small feet), escalators (they are powerful machines), and can understand the likely concerns of people regarding the interaction of the two. We do not read the sign as obliging us to find multiple dogs in order to be able to use the escalator, nor that, should we intend to carry a dog, we must do so on an escalator.[159]

The steps in the argument for the congruence thesis are relatively straightforward. First, if laws are broadly congruent with the underlying social practices, then their practical import is publicly accessible. Without these practices, however, one must rely on the text of the law to convey its meaning, and either on fear of sanction, deference to the authority of the law-giver or the 'reasonableness' of the law, to give the 'reason-giving' force of the law. Fuller rejects outright the idea that the text of a law can determine meaning for the purposes of self-directed action. To illustrate, take the (now) well-worn example of a law prohibiting vehicles in a park: a 'vehicle' can only be understood in the context in which it is used, which

---

[154] Postema, 'Implicit Law', 372.
[155] Fuller, *The Morality of Law*, 209.
[156] Postema, 'Conformity, Custom and Congruence', 58–60.
[157] Postema, 'Implicit Law', 374. For a critique of the traditional Lewisian approach to conventionality, see A. Marmor, *Social Conventions: From Language to Law* (Princeton UP 2014).
[158] N. E. Simmonds, 'Between Positivism and Idealism', (1991) 50 CLJ 308, 311–14.
[159] See also, P. Schlag, 'No Vehicles in the Park', (1999) 23 Seattle University LR 381, 387.

enables one to discern the practical import of the law. We 'know that there is no need to worry about the difference between Fords and Cadillacs ... [but what] if some local patriots wanted to mount on a pedestal a truck used in World War II?'[160] It is the understanding that the law is aimed at preserving peace and quiet or preventing injury that leads one to the conclusion that automobiles are banned, not any meaning inherent in the word 'vehicle'.

As a result of the inherent indeterminacy of text and absent any link to informal social practices, the individual cannot determine what the law requires, hence precluding the effect of the 'reason-giving' force of the norm: 'Practical force supplied by sanction or authority or some other external source may adequately motivate compliance with norms once it is publicly clear what complying with them consists in, but they cannot help in determining the public content of those norms.'[161] Informal social practices are hence publicly accessible pools of information from which individuals collectively draw to discern the practical import of norms and alter their behaviour accordingly. Divorced from these norms, the mechanism by which law functions – its ability to factor into citizens' self-directed action – is substantially undermined.

Understood thus, the congruence theses of Fuller and Brunnée and Toope function on fundamentally different levels. On the one hand, Fuller's thesis is based on the idea that law cannot be hermetically sealed from social practices because to do so would render it unintelligible. The thesis of Brunnée and Toope, on the other hand, goes much further. As noted above, they argue that divergence of the law from 'rich, substantive' shared values, such as abhorrence of the death penalty, would result in the decay or desuetude of the law.[162] Whilst framing this contention in terms of Fullerian congruence, it seems that the rationale for such a claim

---

[160] L. L. Fuller, 'Positivism and Fidelity to Law: A Reply to Professor Hart', (1958) 71 Harvard LR 630, 663. This was a counter-example to Hart's proposition that a law prohibiting vehicles in a park would 'plainly' apply to automobiles; H. L. A. Hart, 'Positivism and the Separation of Law and Morals', (1958) 71 Harvard LR 593, 607. Fuller's characterisation of Hart's position might be unfair considering the debt Hart owed to the Ordinary Language School of philosophy, which based the meaning of words in practice. The argument here would be that Hart's 'core' meanings referred rather to the 'core' usages of the word vehicle within society, rather than the meanings intrinsic to the word itself. See A. Marmor, *Interpretation and Legal Theory* (2nd edn, Hart 2005) 100–1; A. Lefebvre, 'Hart, Wittgenstein, Jurisprudence', (2011) 154 Telos 99, 100.

[161] Postema, 'Implicit Law', 376.

[162] Brunnée & Toope, *Legality and Legitimacy*, 66–9, 86–7.

must come from elsewhere.[163] If the death penalty is enacted in a society that is unanimous in its condemnation of such a penalty, the lack of congruence is not a question of intelligibility but rather of fundamental values. In reality, the authors' requirement of congruence appends a new criterion of legality onto Fuller's criteria, yet we are left without a sufficiently robust explanation for why congruence commands such a stranglehold over legal normativity.

Whilst at first sight seeming to offer a solid jurisprudential foundation for the ECtHR's use of consensus, Brunnée and Toope's theory ultimately adds little to the observation that laws should reflect the fundamental values of the society that they regulate.[164] Understood thus, the consensus doctrine presupposes that domestic legal systems embody the values that should be reflected and protected by the Convention. Indeed, this point has been explicitly acknowledged by a former judge of the ECtHR: 'one reason why the Court follows national patterns is because the Convention converts into an international obligation observance of those fundamental rights which pre-exist in domestic legal systems founded on political democracy and the rule of law'.[165] The consensus doctrine acts as a link between the fundamental values protected by the Court and those acknowledged as being of importance within Council of Europe member states.

It is, however, open to question whether and to what extent the fundamental values protected by Council of Europe member states still reflect the values that are, or should be, protected by the Convention. This is especially so in light of the movement towards populism, nationalism and 'illiberal democracy' within some Council of Europe states in recent years.[166] As these fundamental values diverge, the justification and reasoning proffered by the Court to refer to certain domestic legal systems should become clearer and more precise. Such reasoning will

---

[163] Cf Krisch, 'Review of Jutta Brunnée and Stephen Toope', 206.

[164] Cf N. MacCormick, *Rhetoric and the Rule of Law* (OUP 2005) 1.

[165] Mahoney & Kondak, 'Common Ground', 120.

[166] See for example, Hungarian Prime Minister Viktor Orbán's Speech at the 25th Bálványos Summer Free University and Student Camp, 26 July 2014, available at www.kormany.hu /en/the-prime-minister/the-prime-minister-s-speeches/prime-minister-viktor-orban -s-speech-at-the-25th-balvanyos-summer-free-university-and-student-camp ('the new state that we are constructing in Hungary is an illiberal state, a non-liberal state'). See also, F. Zakaria, 'The Rise of Illiberal Democracy', (1999) 76 Foreign Affairs 22 (defining a liberal democracy as 'a political system marked not only by free and fair elections, but also by the rule of law, a separation of powers, and the protection of basic liberties of speech, assembly, religion, and property').

not only demonstrate that the Court is not foisting its own conception of the Convention upon member states, but it will also show that the Court is committed to upholding the liberal democratic values that motivated the creation of the Convention in the first place.

6.6 The Function of the Consensus Doctrine

This chapter has demonstrated that the ECtHR has drawn on comparative law when interpreting standards that are enshrined in the Convention. It has been suggested that this serves to structure the discretion afforded to the Court by the Convention, a point that is particularly important in light of recent criticism of the Court. Without reference to the accepted standards of conduct within the community, it would be impossible for the Court to maintain that it was not foisting its own conception of the appropriate means by which Convention rights are to be protected upon the contracting parties. Presented with broad, undefined standards of conduct, comparative law provides an objectively verifiable benchmark against which the Court can assess the proportionality, necessity or fairness of a state's actions.[167]

Although the function of the consensus doctrine is to structure the discretion of the Court when interpreting the Convention, the underlying theoretical justification for the doctrine lies in the presumed consonance of fundamental values between Council of Europe states and the Convention. However, the divergence between the liberal democratic values enshrined in the Convention and the legal systems of some Council of Europe members calls for a more detailed and considered approach to consensus. The Court should explicitly acknowledge the values that domestic jurisdictions enshrine and identify those values as being consistent with the liberal democratic ideals of the Convention.

The next chapter moves to address the use of comparative law by the International Criminal Tribunal for the former Yugoslavia. Unlike the courts and tribunals examined in preceding chapters, this Tribunal neither used domestic law as an indication of the intention of a state, nor did it draw on domestic law principally to elaborate standards incorporated in legal instruments. Instead, the Tribunal was forced to draw on domestic law to interpret crimes and rules of procedure and evidence in the absence of any relevant international precedent.

---

[167] Cf Dzehtsiarou, *European Consensus*, 210.

Domestic Law and System Building
in the ICTY

7.1 Introduction

In the late spring of 1992, the Secretary-General of the UN delivered a report to the Security Council that captured the attention of the international community. Yugoslavia – from which Croatia and Slovenia had declared independence less than a year before – had fallen into a pitched civil war fuelled by bitter ethnic tensions between Serb, Croat and Muslim communities. Nestled in the centre of the former unified state, the nascent republic of Bosnia-Herzegovina became the scene of atrocities not seen since the Second World War.[1] The Serbs of Bosnia-Herzegovina, the Secretary-General reported, were making a 'concerted effort ... to create "ethnically pure" regions' in the Republic,[2] employing tactics that 'were as brutal as they were effective'.[3] Reports on the situation documented the grim scene: the killing or displacement of 2.1 million Bosnians by the summer of 1993,[4] the systematic rape of women and girls and the operation of 715 detention centres in which rape, torture and execution was commonplace.[5]

The gravity of such acts led to the creation of the International Criminal Tribunal for the former Yugoslavia (ICTY),[6] which came

---

[1] At the time of the referendum on independence, the Bosnian population consisted of 43 per cent Slavic Muslims, 31 per cent Serbs and 17 per cent Croats: V. Morris & M. P. Scharf, *An Insider's Guide to the International Criminal Tribunal for the former Yugoslavia* (Transnational Publishers 1995) vol 1, 19.

[2] Further Report of the Secretary-General pursuant to Security Council Resolution 749 (1992), UNSCOR, 1992, UN Doc S/23900 at para 5.

[3] Morris & Scharf, *Insider's Guide to the ICTY*, 22.

[4] ibid.

[5] Final Report of the Commission of Experts Established Pursuant to Security Council Resolution 780 (1992), UNSCOR, 1994, UN Doc S/1994/674, paras 216–53.

[6] See T. Meron, 'Rape as a Crime under International Humanitarian Law', (1993) 87 AJIL 424.

into existence on 25 May 1993.[7] It was hoped that the Tribunal would facilitate the restoration of peace and stability in the area, providing a forum in which those guilty of grave breaches of international humanitarian law could be brought to justice.[8] As the first international criminal tribunal to be established since the Nuremberg and Tokyo international military tribunals in the wake of the Second World War,[9] the ICTY was faced with a statute that contained 'not much more than the skeletons of crimes' within its jurisdiction,[10] as well as procedural rules that had scant precedent to draw on.[11] By establishing an international tribunal 'on the basis of a laconic statute, a brief preparatory report and a few pages of debates, the Security Council left the judges with little choice but to innovate'.[12]

In an attempt to bridge the gap between vague rules and concrete application, the Tribunal had frequent recourse to domestic law in the interpretation of its Statute and Rules of Procedure and Evidence (RPE).[13] This chapter does not attempt to describe exhaustively these uses of domestic law by the Tribunal, which has been ably done by

[7] Resolution 827 (1993), SC Res 827, UNSCOR, 48th Session, UN Doc S/Res/827 (1993). On the appropriateness of establishing the ad hoc tribunals by Security Council resolution, as opposed to convention or resolution of the UN General Assembly, see Morris & Scharf, *Insider's Guide to the ICTY*, 40–8; M. C. Bassiouni, *The Law of the International Criminal Tribunal for the former Yugoslavia* (Transnational Publishers, 1996) at 220; Report of the Secretary-General pursuant to Paragraph 2 of Security Council Resolution 808 (1993), UNSCOR, 1993, UN Doc S/25704, paras 19–29; M. Swart, *Judges and Lawmaking at the International Criminal Tribunals for the former Yugoslavia and Rwanda* (PhD Thesis, Leiden University, 2006) 43–9.

[8] Resolution 808 (1993), SC Res 808, UNSCOR, 1993, UN Doc S/RES/808; Resolution 827.

[9] The International Military Tribunal at Nuremberg was established in August 1945 by virtue of a conventional agreement, Agreement for the Prosecution and Punishment of Major War Criminals of the European Axis (The London Agreement), 8 August 1945, 82 UNTS 279. The International Military Tribunal for the Far East, on the other hand, was established by military order in January 1946: Special Proclamation by the Supreme Commander for the Allied Powers at Tokyo, 19 January 1946, 4 Bevans 20.

[10] G. Mettraux, *International Crimes and the ad hoc Tribunals* (OUP 2005) at 5.

[11] *Prosecutor v. Dusko Tadić*, IT-94-1, Decision on the Prosecutor's Motion Requesting Protective Measures for Victims and Witnesses (10 August 1995), para 20.

[12] W. A. Schabas, 'Interpreting the Statutes of the ad hoc Tribunals' in L. C. Vohrah et al. (eds), *Man's Inhumanity to Man: Essays on International Law in Honour of Antonio Cassese* (Kluwer Law International 2003) 847, 848.

[13] 'Letter Dated 13 April 1993 from the Permanent Representative of Canada to the United Nations Addressed to the Secretary-General' UNSCOR, UN Doc S/25594, (1993), at para 11. Interestingly, in the process of the drafting of the Report of the Secretary-General on the ICTY, Canada suggested explicitly that reference could be made to appropriate national law, if necessary, for interpretative purposes.

others.[14] Instead, it focusses on illustrative examples to demonstrate and analyse the methodological and theoretical issues raised by the Tribunal's reasoning. This chapter examines three such examples: first, the Tribunal's use of domestic law to interpret the crime of rape in the cases of *Furundžija* and *Kunarac*; second, the elaboration of the criteria for a valid guilty plea by the Tribunal in *Erdemović*; and, third, the case of *Blaškić*, in which the Tribunal drew on domestic law to interpret its power to issue subpoenas. These cases will be placed in their temporal context in order to demonstrate that the use of domestic law has had an indelible effect on the international criminal law, including on the law and practice of the International Criminal Court (ICC).

This chapter is divided into six substantive parts. Section 7.2 describes the historical and legal background of the ICTY. Section 7.3 details the use of domestic law by the trial and appeals chambers of the ICTY to interpret the crime of rape in the cases of *Furundžija* and *Kunarac*, highlighting the importance of these judgments to the development of the crime within the context of the ICC. Section 7.4 analyses the Tribunal's use of comparative law to interpret legal institutions that have been imported from certain (common) legal systems in the cases of *Erdemović* and *Blaškić*. Section 7.5 moves to assess the reasoning of the Tribunal in light of the conception of the principle of legality that obtained at the time of the *Furundžija* and *Kunarac* judgments. Section 7.6 examines other criticisms of the Tribunal's use of domestic law; namely, methodological criticisms and insensitivity to the *sui generis* nature of international criminal law. Section 7.7 contextualises the Tribunal's use of domestic law and contrasts its position within the international criminal law landscape to that of the ICC. The chapter concludes by suggesting that domestic law was used as the interpretative aid of last resort, which allowed the Tribunal to adjudicate upon crimes within its subject-matter jurisdiction in the absence of all other relevant material. Section 7.8 concludes.

The jurisprudence of the ICTY provides a rich repository of instances in which domestic law has been invoked to interpret international crimes or rules of procedure.[15] Yet despite the frequency with which the

---

[14] See in particular, F. O. Raimondo, *General Principles of Law in the Decisions of International Criminal Courts and Tribunals* (Martinus Nijhoff Publishers 2008).

[15] *Prosecutor v. Dusko Tadić*, Decision on the Prosecutor's Motion, paras 38–42, 47–8, 60–71; *Prosecutor v. Kupreškić*, IT-95-16-A, Appeals Chamber Judgement (23 October 2001), paras 34–41 (when reliance on visual identification of the perpetrator is unsafe (Article 21)); *Prosecutor v. Limaj et al.*, IT-03-66-T, Trial Chamber Judgement

Tribunal adopted this technique, it remains 'the most varied and unexplained' use of any interpretative aid by the Tribunal.[16] This chapter aims to address some of those questions.

7.2 A Brief History of the ICTY

In the wake of the Secretary-General's Report regarding the situation in the former Yugoslavia, the Security Council formed a Commission of Experts tasked with investigating potential grave breaches of international humanitarian law.[17] The Commission documented and collated information relevant to the purported breaches which ultimately totalled over 65,000 pages.[18] The Interim Report of the Commission noted the possibility of establishing an international tribunal, adding to an increasing number of voices that had made similar recommendations in late 1992 and early 1993.[19] On the same day that the Commission's Interim Report was released, the Conference on Security and Co-operation in

(30 November 2005), para 17 (when reliance on visual identification of the perpetrator is unsafe (Article 21)); *Prosecutor* v. *Naletilić*, IT-98-34-A, Appeals Chamber Judgement (3 May 2006) at n 465 (the extent to which defendants have a right to confront witnesses under Article 21(4)(e)); *Prosecutor* v. *Strugar*, IT-01-42-A, Appeals Chamber Judgement (17 July 2008) at paras 52–4 (on the requirement to be fit to stand trial 'implicit in Articles 20 and 21 of the Statute').

[16] L. Grover, *Interpreting Crimes in the Rome Statute of the International Criminal Court* (CUP 2014) 65. For notable exceptions, see N. Jain, 'Judicial Lawmaking and General Principles of Law in International Criminal Law', (2016) 57 Harvard Intl L J 111; N. Jain, 'Comparative International Law at the ICTY: The General Principles Experiment', (2015) 109 AJIL 486.

[17] Resolution 780 (1992), SC Res 780, UNSCOR, 1992, UN Doc S/RES/780. The Commission of Experts was formed, inter alia, on the recommendation of the newly appointed Special Rapporteur for the Human Rights Commission: Report on the situation of human rights in the territory of the former Yugoslavia submitted by Mr Tadeusz Mazowiecki, Special Rapporteur of the Commission on Human Rights, pursuant to paragraph 14 of the Commission Resolution 1992/S-1/1, UNSCOR, 1992, Annex, UN Doc S/24516, para 70.

[18] Final Report pursuant to Res 780, para 20.

[19] Interim Report of the Commission of Experts Established Pursuant to Security Council Resolution 780 (1992), UNSCOR, 1993, Annex I, UN Doc S/25274, para 74. 'The Commission was led to discuss the idea of the establishment of an ad hoc international tribunal . . . The Commission observes that such a decision would be consistent with the direction of its work'; see also, Report on the situation of human rights in the territory of the former Yugoslavia prepared by Mr Tadeusz Mazowiecki, Special Rapporteur of the Commission on Human Rights, pursuant to para 15 of the Commission Resolution 1992/S-1/1 and Economic and Social Council decision 1992/305 annexed to The situation of human rights in the territory of the former Yugoslavia – Note by the Secretary-General, UNSCOR, 1992, UN Doc A/47/666, para 140; Report of the Secretary-General on the

Europe (CSCE) circulated a report examining the possibility of establishing an international tribunal at a meeting of the UN Human Rights Commission in Geneva,[20] with France and Italy making their own proposals for an international tribunal shortly thereafter.[21]

As impetus for the creation of an international tribunal amongst UN member states and civil society mounted, the Security Council passed Resolution 808 on 22 February 1993, which provided that 'an international tribunal shall be established for the prosecution of persons responsible for serious violations of international humanitarian law committed in the territory of the former Yugoslavia', as well as formally requesting the Secretary-General of the UN to submit a report on 'all aspects of this matter, including specific proposals [regarding the establishment of an international tribunal]'.[22]

Taking into account suggestions from member states, the Report of the Secretary-General proposed a statute for an ad hoc tribunal in May 1993, which was unanimously approved by the Security Council in Resolution 827 (1993).[23] The Security Council thus established, as 'an enforcement measure under Chapter VII of the UN Charter, a subsidiary organ within the terms of Article 29 of the Charter, but one of a judicial nature'.[24]

One overriding consideration was that the Tribunal should not be perceived to breach the principle of *nullum crimen sine lege*, or the principle of legality.[25] This was clearly reflected in paragraph 29 of the Report of the Secretary-General, which stated that:

Activities of the International Conference on the former Yugoslavia, UNSCOR, 1993, UN Doc S/25221, para 9.

[20] Morris & Scharf, *Insider's Guide to the ICTY*, vol 2, 211–310.

[21] 'Letter Dated 10 February 1993 from the Permanent Representative of France to the United Nations Addressed to the Secretary-General' UNSCOR, UN Doc S/25266, (1993); 'Letter Dated 18 February 1993 from the Permanent Representative of Italy to the United Nations Addressed to the Secretary-General' UNSCOR, UN Doc S/25300, (1993). In the following four months, a further 13 proposals for an international tribunal were circulated by states, international organisations and non-governmental organisations; for a full list including reproductions of the proposals, see Morris & Scharf, *Insider's Guide to the ICTY* vol 2, 209–480.

[22] Resolution 808 (1993), para 2.

[23] Report pursuant to SC Res 808; Resolution 827.

[24] Report pursuant to SC Res 808, para 28, emphasis added. By determining that this situation (the conflict in the former Yugoslavia) continues to *constitute a threat to international peace and security*, the Security Council framed the situation so that it came within its primary responsibility under Article 24(1) of the Charter of the United Nations and enabled measures to be taken under Chapter VII; Resolution 827.

[25] See A. Cassese et al., *Cassese's International Criminal Law* (3rd edn, OUP 2013) at 22 et seq. See Section 7.6, below, for more detail.

[i]t should be pointed out that, in assigning to the International Tribunal the task of prosecuting persons responsible for serious violations of international humanitarian law, the Security Council would not be creating or purporting to 'legislate' that law. Rather, the International Tribunal would have the task of applying existing international humanitarian law.[26]

As such, the applicable law of the Tribunal was limited to that which was 'beyond any doubt part of customary law'.[27] The Report recommended that the Tribunal have subject-matter jurisdiction over grave breaches of the Geneva Conventions of 1949, which constituted 'the core of customary international law applicable in international armed conflicts';[28] violations of the law or customs of war, as reflected in the 1907 Hague Convention (IV) and annexed regulations;[29] genocide, as codified in the 1948 Genocide Convention;[30] and crimes against humanity, encompassing murder, torture and rape.[31] Jurisdiction over these matters was enshrined in Articles 2 to 5 of the Statute of the International Criminal Tribunal of the former Yugoslavia (Statute of the ICTY). In the Statute of the ICTY, domestic law is only mentioned explicitly in relation to sentencing and is only applicable insofar as it constitutes 'general practice regarding prison sentences in the courts of the former Yugoslavia'.[32]

---

[26] Report pursuant to SC Res 808. See also, *Prosecutor v. Hadžihasanović*, IT-01–47-AR72, Decision on Interlocutory Appeal Challenging Jurisdiction in Relation to Command Responsibility (16 July 2003), para 55. Matters of personal, territorial, temporal and concurrent jurisdiction are not pertinent for the subject matter of this chapter, and will not be outlined here. For more information, see Morris & Scharf, *Insider's Guide to the ICTY*, 89–136.

[27] Report pursuant to SC Res 808, para 34. The limitation of the law applicable by the Tribunal to customary law was 'so that the problem of adherence of some but not all States to specific conventions does not arise'; the Secretary-General did, however, consider that 'some of the major conventional humanitarian law has become part of customary international law'; ibid., paras 33–5.

[28] Report pursuant to SC Res 808, para 37.

[29] ibid., paras 41–4.

[30] ibid., paras 45–6.

[31] ibid., paras 47–9.

[32] Updated Statute of the International Criminal Tribunal for the former Yugoslavia, Article 24(1). Cf the proposals by the CSCE, Amnesty International and Slovenia, which all permitted – to a greater or lesser extent – application of domestic law; Morris & Scharf, *Insider's Guide to the ICTY*, vol 1, 369–70. A similar demarche led to the creation of the International Criminal Tribunal for Rwanda 18 months later, the Statute of which is largely based on the Statute of the ICTY with only minor modifications; Report of the Secretary-General Pursuant to Paragraph 5 of Security Council Resolution 955 (1994), UNSCOR, 1995, UN Doc S/1995/134, para 9; V. Morris & M. P. Scharf, *The International Criminal Tribunal for Rwanda* (Transnational Publishers, 1998) vol 1, fn 466; W. Schabas,

Two points regarding the establishment of the ICTY are noteworthy. First, the Statute of the Tribunal, for reasons of efficacy, was incorporated in an annex to a resolution of the UN Security Council and not a convention. That distinguishes the object of interpretation in the present chapter from many of the other examples examined in this book.[33] Second, the subject-matter jurisdiction of the ICTY was based on what the Secretary-General considered to be extant and partially codified rules of customary international law.[34] The subsequent case law of the Tribunal demonstrates that these rules ultimately proved to be insufficiently defined for application. However, that does not detract from the fact that the normative authority of the legal rules had been recognised, which obviates the need to establish the legal proposition as a formally valid rule of international law prior to its application.[35] This supports the view, which is also borne out by case law, that when the Tribunal defined or substantiated the legal concepts examined below – whether an international crime or a procedural rule – it was *interpreting* the rule, as opposed to enquiring as to its validity. These are two qualitatively different processes.[36] Whilst domestic laws may form the basis of the validity of legal propositions if the laws either demonstrate the *opinio juris* of that state in the case of customary law[37] or if the laws manifest a general principle of law,[38] in the cases examined domestic law played

---

The UN International Criminal Tribunals: The Former Yugoslavia, Rwanda and Sierra Leone (CUP 2006) 30.

[33] It is questionable whether the interpretation of a UN Security Council resolution differs, to any great extent, from the interpretation of treaties; see M. Wood, 'The Interpretation of Security Council Resolutions', (1998) 2 Max Planck Yearbook of UN Law 73.

[34] In the case of Article 3 of the Statute of the ICTY, 'Violations of the laws or customs of war', the Statute enumerates a non-exhaustive list of prohibited acts, leaving the door open for the ICTY to ascertain novel custom. A similar non-exhaustive list is included in Article 4 of the Statute of the ICTR, 'Violations of Article 3 common to the Geneva Conventions and of Additional Protocol II'.

[35] See UNSCOR, 1993, 3217th Mtg, UN Doc S/PV.3217 [provisional], statement by the representatives of the United Kingdom, New Zealand and Brazil to the Security Council, reiterating that the ICTY is limited to applying extant legal norms.

[36] Cf J. d'Aspremont, 'The Multidimensional Process of Interpretation: Content-Determination and Law-Ascertainment Distinguished', in A. Bianchi et al. (eds), *Interpretation in International Law* (OUP 2015) 117.

[37] See *Jurisdictional Immunities of the State (Germany v. Italy: Greece Intervening)*, [2012] ICJ Rep 99, paras 70–8; the International Court of Justice examined domestic laws to assess whether a customary rule of immunity for state officials' tortious acts in other states existed.

[38] *Procès-Verbaux of the Proceedings of the Committee of Jurists, June 16th–July 24th 1920 with Annexes* at 335; *The Corfu Channel Case (Albania v. UK)*, [1949] ICJ Rep 4, 18.

neither of these roles. Instead, it was drawn on in a stage of reasoning when the question of legal validity had already been settled.

7.3   The Development of the Crime of Rape

7.3.1   The Evolution of the Crime of Rape

One of the most controversial uses of domestic law by the ICTY was the interpretation of the crime of rape under Article 3 of its Statute. The earliest legal prohibition of rape in times of war can be traced back to the fourteenth and fifteenth-century war ordinances of Richard II (1385) and Henry V (1419),[39] although its modern form is normally traced to the US Lieber Code of 1863, which provided that 'all rape, wounding, maiming, or killing of such inhabitants are prohibited under the penalty of death ... '.[40] After the Second World War, rape was successfully prosecuted at the Tokyo War Crimes Tribunal[41] and was included as a crime against humanity in Council Control Law No. 10, which regulated the Occupying Powers' individual war crimes courts operating in Germany.[42] Despite numerous conventional provisions prohibiting rape in times of war – notably, Article 27 of the fourth Geneva Convention of 1949, and Articles 76(1) and 4(2)(e) of Additional Protocols I and II of 1977, respectively[43] – doubts persisted in the latter half of the twentieth

---

[39] These ordinances are reprinted in T. Twiss, *The Black Book of the Admiralty* (CUP 1871) vol 1, 468; it was also mentioned in A. Gentili, *De Iure Belli Libri Tres*, translated by J. C. Rolfe (Clarendon Press 1933), section 421: '[T]o violate the honour of women will always be held to be unjust'. See generally, T. Meron, *Henry's Wars and Shakespeare's Laws: Perspectives on the Law of War in the Later Middle Ages* (Clarendon Press 1994), Chapters 6 and 8.

[40] *Instructions for the Government of Armies of the United States in the Field*, USC Article 44 (Government Printing Office 1898) online: avalon.law.yale.edu/19th_century/lieber.asp #sec2.

[41] Meron, 'Rape as a Crime', 426.

[42] *Council Control Law No. 10*, (1946), Article 2(1)(c). Rape was not, however, included in the subject-matter jurisdiction of the Nuremberg Tribunal: *Procès des Grands Criminels de Guerre Devant Le Tribunal Militaire International Tome 1: Documents Officiels* (Secretariat of the International Military Tribunal, 1947).

[43] *Geneva Convention Relative to the Protection of Civilian Persons in Time of War (Fourth Geneva Convention)*, 12 August 1949, 75 UNTS 287, Article 27 (entered into force 21 October 1950); *Protocol Additional to the Geneva Convention of 12 August 1949, and Relating to the Protection of Victims of International Armed Conflicts (Protocol I)*, 12 December 1977, 1125 UNTS 3, Article 76(1) (entered into force 7 December 1978); *Protocol Additional to the Geneva Convention of 12 August 1949, and Relating to the Protection of Victims of Non-International Armed Conflicts (Protocol II)*, 8 June 1977, 1125 UNTS 609, Article 4(2)(e) (entered into force 7 December 1978).

century as to whether rape constituted a 'grave breach' of the Geneva Conventions that was capable of giving rise to individual criminal responsibility.[44]

However, by the time of the Yugoslav conflict, any hesitation to recognise rape as a war crime or a grave breach of the Geneva Conventions had started to dissipate.[45] In late 1992, the International Committee of the Red Cross (ICRC) stated that rape constituted a grave breach under the fourth Geneva Convention, a sentiment that was echoed shortly after by the United States, which considered that 'the legal basis for prosecuting troops for rape is well established under the Geneva Conventions and customary international law'.[46] In early 1993, during negotiations regarding the formation of the ICTY, the widespread and systematic nature of rape and sexual assault in the former Yugoslavia became apparent.[47] The concern of the international community was reflected in the proposals for the statute of the Tribunal that were advanced: proposals from the United States and France both classified rape as a grave breach of the Geneva Conventions, whereas the proposals of Italy, the Netherlands, the Organization of the Islamic Conference and the Secretary-General of the UN re-affirmed rape as a crime against humanity.[48] At the suggestion of the Secretary-General,[49] rape was explicitly included in the list of crimes against humanity over which the ICTY has jurisdiction.[50] As a reflection of the fact that these crimes can also be committed in non-international armed conflicts, the

---

[44] *Geneva Convention*, Article 147; *Geneva Convention Protocol I*, Articles 11, 85. Rape was not explicitly included in the 'grave breaches' provisions of the Conventions; N. Hayes 'Creating a Definition of Rape in International Law: The Contribution of the International Criminal Tribunals' in S. Darcy & J. Powderly (eds), *Judicial Creativity at the International Criminal Tribunals* (OUP 2010) 129, 130.

[45] Meron, 'Rape as a Crime', 426; see further, G. Harbour, 'International Concern Regarding Conflict-related Sexual Violence in the Lead-up to the ICTY's Establishment', in S. Brammertz & M. Jarvis (eds), *Prosecuting Conflict-Related Sexual Violence at the ICTY* (OUP 2016) 19.

[46] Cited in Meron, 'Rape as a Crime', fn 22.

[47] UNSCOR 3217th Mtg: 'We must ensure that the voices of the groups most victimized are heard by the Tribunal. I refer particularly to the detention and systematic rape of women and girls, often followed by cold-blooded murder' – statement of the Permanent Representative of the United States of America. See further, G. Harbour, 'International Concern Regarding Conflict-related Sexual Violence'.

[48] Morris & Scharf, *Insider's Guide to the ICTY*, 379–83. The report of the Commission of Experts, as well as proposals by the National Alliance for Women's Organizations ('NAWO'), Amnesty International and the Lawyers Committee for Human Rights also considered rape as a crime against humanity.

[49] Report pursuant to SC Res 808, para 48.

[50] Statute of the ICTY, Article 5(g).

Statute of the International Criminal Tribunal for Rwanda (Statute of the ICTR) explicitly classifies rape as a crime against humanity, as well as recognising that rape may constitute a serious violation of common Article 3 and the Additional Protocol I of the Geneva Conventions.[51]

7.3.2   Interpretation of Rape by the ICTY

Whilst the prohibition on rape had been indubitably recognised as a rule of international criminal law, the question of which acts constituted rape had neither been defined in conventional nor customary law, nor in judicial practice.[52] The first judgment to address the issue was *Akayesu*, delivered by the Trial Chamber of the ICTR in September 1998.[53] In order to understand the legal context in which the ICTY functioned, it is necessary to examine briefly that judgment.

Akayesu was *bourgemestre* of a commune in Rwanda, charged with 'the performance of executive functions and maintenance of public order within his commune'.[54] In 1994, hundreds of Tutsi civilians sought refuge in the *bureau communal* of Akayesu's commune, only to be subjected to beatings, sexual assault, rape and murder at the hands of local militia and the police.[55] The Prosecutor of the ICTR charged Akayesu inter alia with rape as a crime against humanity, and as a violation of Common Article 3 and the Second Additional Protocol of the Geneva Conventions.[56] In addressing these charges, the Trial Chamber acknowledged that:

> there is no commonly accepted definition of [rape] in international law. While rape has been defined in certain national jurisdictions as non-consensual intercourse, variations on the act of rape may include acts which involve the insertion of objects and/or the use of bodily orifices not considered to be intrinsically sexual.[57]

---

[51] Statute of ICTR, SC Res 955, UNSCOR, 1994, UN Doc S/RES/955 (1994).

[52] See Boon, 'Rape and Forced Pregnancy', 647.

[53] *Prosecutor v. Jean-Paul Akayesu*, ICTR-96-4-T, Trial Chamber Judgment, (2 September 1998) (*International Criminal Tribunal for Rwanda*).

[54] ibid., para 4.

[55] ibid., para 12A.

[56] N. Pillay, 'Equal Justice for Women: A Personal Journey', (2008) 50 Arizona LR 657, 665–6. The charge of rape was included on an amended indictment which was modified following questioning from the Bench which brought to light evidence of rape and sexual assault.

[57] *Akayesu*, para 596.

Moving away from the traditional approaches to defining rape commonly found in domestic law, which specify *actus reus* and *mens rea* requirements,[58] the Trial Chamber considered that it was more useful to focus on the 'conceptual frame work of state sanctioned violence',[59] and opted for a broad conception of rape that defined the crime as 'a physical invasion of a sexual nature, committed on a person under circumstances which are coercive'.[60] This definition has been widely praised for shifting the focus to 'the overwhelming [coercive] circumstances which are knowingly exploited by the perpetrator, rather than [restricting] the context and criminality of the act to the internal acquiescence of the victim'.[61]

The conceptual definition of rape enunciated in *Akayesu* was followed two months later in the *Celebici* case, the first case involving rape to be heard by the ICTY.[62] In addition to being the first ICTY Chamber to broach the question of the definition of rape, the *Celebici* case broke new ground in other respects. Of particular note is the Trial Chamber's determination that rape in situations of armed conflict may constitute torture, a position that was followed by chambers in subsequent cases.[63]

---

[58] See e.g., Sexual Offences Act 2003 (UK) c 42, section 1, which defines rape as follows:

(1) A person (A) commits an offence if:

    (a) he intentionally penetrates the vagina, anus or mouth of another person (B) with his penis,
    (b) B does not consent to the penetration, and
    (c) A does not reasonably believe that B consents.

[59] *Akayesu*, para 597.

[60] ibid., para 598. See also, ibid., para 597 (stating that 'The Chamber considers that rape is a form of aggression and that the central elements of the crime of rape cannot be captured in a mechanical description of objects and body parts.').

[61] Hayes, 'Creating a Definition of Rape', 134; See also, Pillay, 'Equal Justice for Women', 666–7. Pillay, herself one of the judges in the Trial Chamber in *Akayesu*, stated that, 'I must say that the testimony of one of the witnesses motivated me to reexamine traditional definitions of rape. Witness "JJ" was being asked by the prosecutor, in respect of each of the multiple rapes she endured, whether there was penetration: "I am sorry to keep on asking you each time – did your attacker penetrate you with his penis"? Her answer was: "That was not the only thing they did to me; they were young boys and I am a mother and yet they did this to me. It's the things they said to me that I cannot forget"'. See also, P. Weiner, 'The Evolving Jurisprudence of the Crime of Rape in International Criminal Law', (2013) 54 Boston College LR 1207, 1210.

[62] *Prosecutor* v. *Delalic* ('*Celebici* case'), IT-96–21-T, Trial Chamber Judgment (16 November 1998), para 478.

[63] ibid., para 496. This followed the approach of the ICTR Trial Chamber in *Akayesu*; see *Akayesu*, para 597.

Just one month after the *Celebici* judgment, the ICTY was again required to interpret the crime of rape in the case of *Furundžija*.[64] The reasoning of the Trial Chamber in *Furundžija* is one of the clearest examples of recourse to domestic law that exists in international case law. In that case, the defendant was leader of the Jokers, a special unit within the armed forces of the Croatian Community of Herzeg-Bosna, who raped and tortured a female Bosnian Muslim civilian.[65] The Trial Chamber implicitly rejected the *Akayesu* definition for want of specificity,[66] and, stating that 'no definition of rape can be found in international law',[67] reasoned that:

> [to] arrive at an accurate definition of rape based on the criminal law principle of specificity (Bestimmtheitgrundsatz, also referred to by the maxim 'nullum crimen sine lege stricta'), it is necessary to look for principles of criminal law common to the major legal systems of the world. These principles may be derived, with all due caution, from national laws.[68]

This reliance was subject to two caveats: first, that reference should not be made solely to jurisdictions belonging to one 'legal family', such as common or civil law; and second, that account must be taken of the 'specificity of international criminal proceedings when utilising national law notions'.[69] The Chamber surveyed the definition of rape in 18 legal systems,[70] noting that 'most legal systems in the common and civil law worlds consider rape to be the forcible sexual penetration of the human body by the penis or the forcible insertion of any other object into either the vagina or the anus'.[71] Although the Tribunal did not find a universal definition of rape in criminal systems throughout the world – indeed, it explicitly acknowledged significant divergence between jurisdictions

---

[64] *Prosecutor v. Furundžija*, IT-95–17/1-T, Trial Chamber Judgment (10 December 1998).
[65] ibid., paras 121–30.
[66] ibid., para 177.
[67] ibid., para 175.
[68] ibid., para 177.
[69] ibid., para 178.
[70] ibid., fns 207–14. The comparative survey examined the laws of Chile, China, Germany, Japan, the Socialist Federal Republic of Yugoslavia, Zambia, Austria, France, Italy, Argentina, Pakistan, India, South Africa, Uganda, New South Wales, the Netherlands, England and Wales and Bosnia and Herzegovina.
[71] ibid., paras 181, 183. Domestic laws did not, however, agree as to whether forced oral penetration constituted rape. The Chamber adopted a teleological approach with regard to this point, stating that the *raison d'être* of international humanitarian law is to protect dignity, and forced oral penetration constituted 'a most humiliating and degrading attack upon human dignity'. As such, it was to be included within the definition of rape.

regarding whether forced oral sex constituted rape – it recognised that rape attached 'to a growing category of sexual offences, provided of course they meet certain requirements, chiefly that of forced penetration'.[72] Drawing from this conclusion, the Chamber defined rape as:

> (i) the sexual penetration, however slight: (a) of the vagina or anus of the victim by the penis of the perpetrator or any other object used by the perpetrator; or (b) of the mouth of the victim by the penis of the perpetrator; (ii) by coercion or force or threat of force against the victim or a third person.[73]

Both the first sentence of the *actus reus* (that rape covers vaginal and anal penetration with a penis or any other object) and the second limb of the test (the requirement of coercion or threat or use of force) are drawn from the Chamber's examination of the laws of rape in domestic jurisdictions.

Whilst the *Furundžija* definition of the crime of rape was affirmed on appeal,[74] the ICTR subsequently re-affirmed the *Akayesu* definition, which in its view 'clearly encompasse[d] all the conduct described in the definition of rape set forth in *Furundžija*'.[75] In light of the continued divergence between the 'conceptual' *Akayesu* and the more 'mechanistic' *Furundžija* definitions of rape, the issue was raised again in the case of *Kunarac* before the ICTY.[76]

In *Kunarac*, the three accused – members of the Bosnian Serb military accused of participating in the Foča 'Rape Camps'[77] – were charged with rape as a crime against humanity and as a breach of the laws or customs of war. The Trial Chamber acknowledged that the *Furundžija* definition provided the *actus reus* element of the crime of rape in international law

---

[72] ibid., para 179.

[73] ibid., para 185.

[74] *Prosecutor v. Furundžija*, IT-95–17/1-A, Appeals Chamber Judgment (21 July 2000), paras 211–12. The issue of the definition of rape was touched on incidentally in relation to the purported bias of one of the Trial Chamber judges; see ibid., paras 206–8.

[75] *Prosecutor v. Musema*, ICTR-96–13-T, Trial Chamber Judgment and Sentence, para 227 (27 January 2000). As Hayes notes, this adherence to the *Akayesu* definition was unsurprising 'given that the Trial Chamber contained the same three judges as in *Akayesu*'; Hayes, 'Creating a Definition of Rape', 140.

[76] *Prosecutor v. Kunarac*, IT-96-23-T & IT-96-23/1-T, Trial Chamber Judgment (22 February 2001).

[77] For more information on the Foča 'Rape Camps', see M. Fiori, '"The Foča 'Rape Camps'": A Dark Page Read through the ICTY's Jurisprudence' (2007) 2 Hague Justice Journal 9.

but that 'in the circumstances of the present case the Trial Chamber considers that it is necessary to clarify its understanding of the element in paragraph (ii) of the *Furundžija* definition'.[78] The Chamber continued:

> [i]n stating that the relevant act of sexual penetration will constitute rape only if accompanied by coercion or force or threat of force against the victim or a third person, the Furundžija definition does not refer to other factors which would render an act of sexual penetration non-consensual or non-voluntary on the part of the victim, which . . . is in the opinion of this Trial Chamber the accurate scope of this aspect of the definition in international law.[79]

As it did in *Furundžija*, the Trial Chamber turned to explain why reference to domestic laws could aid the interpretation of the crime of rape:

> the value of these sources is that they may disclose 'general concepts and legal institutions' which, if common to a broad spectrum of national legal systems, disclose an international approach to a legal question which may be considered as an appropriate indicator of the international law on the subject.[80]

The Chamber considered that the 'common denominator' of rape, as found in the domestic laws of 38 jurisdictions,[81] was wider than the requirement of force, threat of force or coercion proposed by the Trial Chamber in *Furundžija*. In the opinion of the Trial Chamber, the true common denominator of the surveyed jurisdictions was that 'serious violations of sexual *autonomy* are to be penalised'.[82] Thus, whilst accepting the *actus reus* limb of the *Furundžija* definition, the Trial Chamber considered that the 'coercion or force or threat of force' requirement should be expanded to criminalise the specified sexual acts 'where such sexual penetration occurs without the consent of the victim. Consent for

---

[78] *Kunarac* Trial Chamber, para 438.
[79] ibid. (footnotes omitted).
[80] ibid., para 439 (emphasis added).
[81] ibid., paras 443–5, 447–52, 453–6. The comparative study surveyed the laws of Bosnia and Herzegovina, Germany, South Korea, China, Norway, Austria, Spain, Brazil, the United States (New York, Maryland, Massachusetts, California), Switzerland, Portugal, France, Italy, Denmark, Sweden, Finland, Estonia, Japan, Argentina, Costa Rica, Uruguay, Philippines, England and Wales, Canada, New Zealand, Australia (New South Wales, Victoria, ACT, Western Australia, South Australia), India, Bangladesh, South Africa, Zambia and Belgium.
[82] ibid., para 457.

this purpose must be consent given voluntarily as a result of the victim's free will, assessed in the context of the surrounding circumstances'.[83]

Comparative law was again drawn on in the appeals phase in *Kunarac*, in which the Appeals Chamber considered whether true consent was ever possible when the victim was a detainee in an armed conflict. It examined the domestic laws of Germany and the USA, which classified sexual acts between prisoners and inmates as crimes of strict liability, or stated that such relations carry a presumption of non-consent.[84] The Chamber interpreted rape in international criminal law in accordance with these laws, recognising the possibility that there could be circumstances that 'were so coercive as to negate any possibility of consent'.[85]

7.3.3   The Legacy of the ICTY Approach: The ICC Elements of Crimes

The interpretation of the crime of rape in *Kunarac* has become 'the most widely used definition in the ICTY, ICTR and Special Court for Sierra Leone',[86] and the antecedent upon which it is based, *Furundžija*, forms

---

[83] ibid., para 460.

[84] *Prosecutor v. Kunarac*, IT-96–23 & IT-96–23/1-A, Appeals Chamber Judgment (12 June 2002), para 131, citing laws from Germany and the United States (California, New Jersey, the District of Columbia).

[85] ibid., para 132.

[86] V. Oosterveld, 'The Influence of Domestic Legal Traditions on The Gender Jurisprudence of International Criminal Tribunals', (2013) 2 Cambridge Journal of International and Comparative Law 825, 831; M. Eriksson, *Defining Rape: Emerging Obligations for States under International Law?* (Martinus Nijhoff Publishers, 2011) 407, 424; see *Prosecutor v. Kvocka*, IT-98–30/1-T, Judgement (2 November 2001), paras 177–9 (International Criminal Tribunal for the former Yugoslavia, Trial Chamber); *Prosecutor v. Semanza*, ICTR-97–20-T, Judgement (15 May 2003), paras 344–6 (International Criminal Tribunal for Rwanda, Trial Chamber); *Prosecutor v. Kajelijeli*, ICTR-98-44A-T, Judgement and Sentence (1 December 2003), paras 910–15 (International Criminal Tribunal for Rwanda, Trial Chamber); *Prosecutor v. Kamuhanda*, ICTR-95-54A-T, Judgement and Sentence (22 January 2004), paras 705–9 (International Criminal Tribunal for Rwanda, Trial Chamber); *Prosecutor v. Taylor*, SCSL-03–01-T, Judgement (18 May 2012), para 415 (Special Court for Sierra Leone, Trial Chamber). Cf *Prosecutor v. Niyitegeka*, ICTR-96–14-T, Judgement and Sentence (16 May 2003) at para 456 (International Criminal Tribunal for Rwanda, Trial Chamber); the ICTR Trial Chamber in *Muhimana* effectively held the *Kunarac* definition to be an elaboration of the *Akayesu* definition; *Prosecutor v. Muhimana*, ICTR-95-1B-T, Judgement and Sentence (28 April 2005), paras 550–1 (International Criminal Tribunal for Rwanda, Trial Chamber). Subsequently, the ICTR Appeals Chamber in *Gacumbitsi* followed the *Kunarac* definition; *Prosecutor v. Gacumbitsi*, ICTR-2001–64-A, Judgement (7 July 2006), paras 151–2 (International Criminal Tribunal for Rwanda, Appeals Chamber).

the basis for the definition of rape in the Elements of Crimes of the ICC.[87] At the time of the Trial Chamber judgment in *Furundžija*, it was clear that a conventional definition of rape in international criminal law was unlikely to come to fruition. This was particularly evident as the case was decided just a few months after conclusion of the Rome Statute of the International Criminal Court, which failed to define the crime due to the fundamentally different philosophical, legal and cultural approaches of the delegates to sexual offences, and to rape in particular.[88]

However, where the delegates to the Rome conference failed, the Preparatory Commission for the ICC Elements of Crimes succeeded, elaborating a definition of rape that was confirmed by the first Assembly of States Parties in 2002.[89] This definition drew upon the jurisprudence of the ICTY and ICTR, giving most weight to the definition expounded by the Trial Chamber in *Furundžija*. This was thought to be 'particularly persuasive because its definition of rape was based on a survey of municipal rape law and thus came with the authority of timeliness and neutrality'.[90] Indeed, the influence of the *Furundžija* definition is shown by the fact that the proposal for the definition of rape put forward by Costa Rica, Hungary and Switzerland mirrored word-for-word the definition laid down by the Trial Chamber.[91] Absent the definition of the crime of rape provided by the ICTY, the Preparatory Commission of

[87] Weiner, 'The Evolving Jurisprudence of the Crime of Rape', 1217. See Rome Statute of the International Criminal Court, 17 July 1998, 2187 UNTS 90, Article 7(1)(g); Official Records of the Assembly of States Parties to the Rome Statute of the International Criminal Court, ICC, 1st Session, ICC Doc ASP/1/3 (2002).

[88] W. A. Schabas, *An Introduction to the International Criminal Court*, 4d (CUP 2011) 117. Note that a definition of rape was originally considered in the 1996 Preparatory Committee for the Rome Statute, which defined rape as 'causing a person to engage in or submit to a sexual act by force or threat of force': M. C. Bassiouni, *The Legislative History of the International Criminal Court: An Article-by-Article Evolution of the Statute from 1994–1998* (Transnational Publishers, 2005) vol 2 at 53. See also, K. Boon, 'Rape and Forced Pregnancy under the ICC Statute: Human Dignity, Autonomy, and Consent' (2001) 32 Columbia Human Rights LR 625, 644.

[89] Pursuant to Article 9 of the Rome Statute, the Elements of Crimes is a document that assists the Court in the interpretation and application of Articles 6, 7 and 8 of the Statute. The document must be passed by a two-thirds majority of states parties.

[90] Boon, 'Rape and Forced Pregnancy under the ICC Statute', 646.

[91] Preparatory Commission for the International Criminal Court, Working Group on Elements of Crimes, 2nd Session, *Proposal Submitted by Costa Rica, Hungary and Switzerland on Certain Provisions of Article 8 para 2(b) of the Rome Statute of the International Criminal Court: (viii), (x), (xiii), (xiv), (xv), (xvi), (xxi), (xxii), (xxvi)*, PCNICC/1999/WGEC/DP.8 (1999); Boon, 'Rape and Forced Pregnancy under the ICC Statute', fn 95.

the Elements of Crimes may well have been back in the position of paralysis in which the states parties to the Rome Statute found themselves.

In March 2016, the ICC delivered its first conviction for rape as a war crime and a crime against humanity in the *Bemba* case, sentencing the defendant to 18 years of imprisonment.[92] In its verdict, the Trial Chamber adopted the gender-neutral definition of rape contained in the Elements of Crimes, citing the Trial Chamber judgment in *Furundžija* as authority for the proposition that forced oral sex may also constitute rape. The judgments of the tribunals, and in particular that of the *Furundžija* Trial Chamber, enabled international criminal law to move past the social, cultural and moral divides that stymied a conventional definition of rape.

Despite the influence of the ICTY's jurisprudence, the definition of rape in international criminal law is far from settled. Suffice for our purposes to note certain inconsistencies regarding the role of consent. Formally, the absence of consent is not a requirement in the definition of rape in the ICC Elements of Crimes, a fact that was explicitly recognised by the *Bemba* Trial Chamber.[93] However, echoing the *Kunarac* Appeal Chamber judgment, the Trial Chamber also held that when the perpetrator took advantage of a 'coercive environment' to commit rape the prosecution does not need to prove the victim's lack of consent.[94]

These two positions give rise to some conceptual problems: whilst formally not part of the definition of rape, the importance placed on the existence of coercive circumstances is based on the fact that there could be, in the words of the *Kunarac* Appeals Chamber, 'circumstances that were so coercive as to negate any possibility of consent'.[95] In other

---

[92] *Prosecutor v. Jean-Pierre Bemba Gombo,* ICC-01/05–01/08, Judgment pursuant to Article 74 of the Statute (21 March 2016) (International Criminal Court, Trial Chamber). These convictions were subsequently overturned by the Appeals Chamber of the ICC; see *Prosecutor v. Jean-Pierre Bemba Gombo,* ICC-01/05–01/08 A, Appeal against Trial Chamber's Judgment pursuant to Article 74 of the Statute (8 June 2018) (International Criminal Court, Appeals Chamber), paras 197–8. The Court did address the question of rape in the *Katanga* case, in which the defendant was acquitted of sexual violence charges; *Prosecutor v. Germain Katanga,* ICC-01/04–01/07–3436, Judgment pursuant to Article 74 of the Statute (7 March 2014) (International Criminal Court, Trial Chamber).

[93] *Bemba,* para 105.

[94] ibid., para 106. See also, Rule 70, Rules of Procedure and Evidence, Assembly of States Parties to the Rome Statute of the International Criminal Court, 1st Session, New York, 3–10 September 2002, ICC-ASP/1/3.

[95] *Prosecutor v. Kunarac,* IT-96–23& IT-96–23/1-A, Judgement (12 June 2002), para 132 (International Criminal Tribunal for the former Yugoslavia, Appeals Chamber).

words, coercive circumstances are important because they allow chambers to induce the absence of consent from circumstantial evidence. It seems therefore that despite protestations to the contrary, the absence of consent remains implicit in the definition of the crime of rape.[96] The relevant question is how that absence of consent may be evidenced.

Whilst certain questions regarding the definition of the crime of rape remain, the influence of the ICTY's judgments in *Furundžija* and *Kunarac* unquestionably shaped the approaches taken by subsequent chambers of the Tribunal, the ICTR and the ICC in relation to rape. Section 7.5, below, considers whether the Tribunal's interpretation of the crime was made in accordance with the principle of legality.

7.4   Interpreting Imported Legal Institutions

This section examines the use of domestic law to interpret legal institutions or concepts that were imported from common law jurisdictions into the Statute or RPE of the ICTY.[97] Two such examples are examined: the use of domestic law to develop the criteria of a valid guilty plea, and the use of domestic law to elaborate the limits of the Tribunal's power to issue subpoenas/binding orders. These cases raise different issues to those raised by the judgments in the preceding section, in particular, regarding the *sui generis* nature of the international criminal regime and the transposition of domestic law to the international sphere.

7.4.1   Elaborating the Guilty Plea

The first judgment handed down by the ICTY provides us with an illustrative example of such reasoning by the Tribunal. The defendant in that case was Drazen Erdemović, a member of the 10th Sabotage Detachment of the Bosnian Serb Army which partook in the summary execution of 1,200 Bosnian Muslim men in Srebrenica in 1995.[98] After

---

[96] Cf E. Dowds, 'Conceptualizing the Role of Consent in the Definition of Rape at the International Criminal Court: A Norm Transfer Perspective', (2018) International Feminist Journal of Politics 1.

[97] See also, *Prosecutor v. Popovic* (Trial Chamber Judgement) IT-05–88-T (10 June 2010) paras 872–4, 2122 (referring to common laws on conspiracy, as 'the concept of criminal conspiracy incorporated into the Genocide Convention derived from the common law approach . . .').

[98] *Prosecutor v. Erdemović* (Appeals Chamber Judgement) IT-96-22-A (7 October 1997), para 1. The judgment in this case also uses domestic laws in order to establish whether duress is a complete defence under international criminal law; this is not dealt with here

being transferred to The Hague to give pre-trial evidence in the cases of Radovan Karadzic and Ratko Mladic, Erdemović confessed to his participation in the Srebrenica massacre,[99] estimating that he alone had murdered about 70 men.[100] Charged with crimes against humanity and violations of the law or customs of war,[101] Erdemović pled guilty to crimes against humanity at his first appearance before the Trial Chamber.[102] However, he qualified his plea with the following words:

> Your Honour, I had to do this. If I had refused, I would have been killed together with the victims. When I refused, they told me: 'If you are sorry for them, stand up, line up with them and we will kill you too'. I am not sorry for myself but for my family, my wife and son who then had nine months, and I could not refuse because then they would have killed me. That is all I wish to add.[103]

This statement raised the question whether equivocal guilty pleas may nevertheless be accepted as valid. The possibility to plead guilty is not specifically provided for in the Statute of the ICTY. However, Article 20(3) of the Statute provides that 'The Trial Chamber shall . . . instruct the accused to enter a plea', implicitly recognising the possibility. On the other hand, Rule 62 of the RPE explicitly notes that a defendant may enter a guilty plea but does not elaborate what constitutes a valid guilty plea.[104]

Whilst the Trial Chamber accepted Erdemović's guilty plea,[105] the Appeals Chamber raised, *proprio motu*, the issue 'of interpreting the

---

as it does not involve the interpretation of any provision, but rather the establishment of a general principle of law.

[99] *Prosecutor* v. *Erdemović*, (Trial Chamber Sentencing Judgement), IT-96–22-T (29 November 1996), para 1; Schabas, *The UN International Criminal Tribunals*, 424.

[100] *Erdemović*, (Trial Chamber Sentencing), para 78.

[101] *Erdemović*, (Trial Chamber Sentencing), para 2.

[102] *Erdemović*, (Trial Chamber Sentencing), para 3.

[103] *Prosecutor* v. *Erdemović* (Trial Chamber Transcript) IT-96–22-T (31 May 1996), 9.

[104] Rule 62: 'The Trial Chamber shall: (iii) call upon the accused to enter a plea of guilty or not guilty on each count; should the accused fail to do so, enter a plea of not guilty on his behalf'. At the time of Erdemović's first trial, the applicable Rules of Procedure and Evidence were those of 5 July 1996; *Rules of Procedure and Evidence* 5 July 1996 IT/53/ Rev. 9.

[105] Nevertheless, the Trial Chamber, presided by a French judge, seemed to be 'uncomfortable with the whole business of guilty pleas' – a distinctly common law concept; Schabas, *The UN International Criminal Tribunals*, 424. Interestingly, the Trial Chamber recognised that pleading guilty could be 'one of the elements which constitutes . . . a defence strategy', thus leaving the possibility open that a Chamber may accept a guilty plea even when the defendant maintains their innocence; see *North Carolina* v. *Alford* 400 US 25

meaning of the guilty plea as it exists within the Statute and the Rules'.[106] The joint separate opinion of Judges McDonald and Vohrah, with whom Judge Stephen explicitly agreed on this point,[107] elaborated the reasoning of the majority, in which they expounded a general three-stage inter- pretative process. First, the judges stated that interpretation should take place according to the rules laid down in Articles 31 and 32 of the Vienna Convention on the Law of Treaties.[108] Should that prove unfruitful, the 'second step in the proper interpretation of the Statute and the rules involves a consideration of international law authorities' if such autho- rities are consistent with the 'spirit, object and purpose of the Statute and Rules'.[109] Quite what 'international authorities' meant is unclear – the term has potential to cover interpretations of analogous rules in different contexts, international jurisprudence or even doctrinal writings that may elucidate the provision.[110] The third and final step in the judges' triad of interpretative techniques deserves quoting at length:

> In the event that international authority is entirely lacking or is insuffi-
> cient, recourse may then be had to national law to assist in the interpreta-
> tion of terms and concepts used in the Statute and the Rules. We would
> stress again that no credence may be given to such national law authorities

---

(1970); J. R. W. D. Jones & S. Powles, *International Criminal Practice* (3rd edn, OUP 2003) §8.5.257.

[106] *Erdemović* (Appeals Chamber Judgment), Joint Separate Opinion of Judge McDonald and Judge Vohrah, para 3. Intimately bound with this issue was the question of the existence of duress as a complete defence to the murder of innocent civilians in inter- national law – if duress existed as such, and if a guilty plea could not be equivocal, any plea that suggested that the defendant was under duress would be inadmissible.

[107] *Erdemović* (Appeals Chamber Judgment) Separate and Dissenting Opinion of Judge Stephen, para 5. The very fact that Judges McDonald and Vohrah elaborated their reasoning in a separate opinion demonstrates that their reasoning did not command the support of *all* members of the majority. I note that this is different from the reasoning of Judges McDonald and Vohrah regarding duress as a defence to murder, in relation to which they also invoked domestic law. However, they explicitly based this use of domestic law on the fact that it might elucidate 'general principles of law recognized by civilized nations'. This was not the case in relation to their interpretation of the guilty plea. See ibid., paras 56–66. For analysis of their reasoning in relation to duress, see Jain, 'Judicial Lawmaking and General Principles of Law', 121–4.

[108] *Erdemović* (Appeals Chamber Judgement), Joint Separate Opinion of Judge McDonald and Judge Vohrah, para 3.

[109] *Erdemović* (Appeals Chamber Judgement), Joint Separate Opinion of Judge McDonald and Judge Vohrah, para 4.

[110] In *Furundžija*, however, the Tribunal seems to understand 'international law authorities' as referring to the case law of other international courts and tribunals that have dealt with analogous issues; *Prosecutor* v. *Furundžija* (Trial Chamber Judgement) IT-95–17/ 1-T (10 Dec 1998), para 177.

> if they do not comport with the spirit, object and purpose of the Statute and the Rules ... In our observation, there is no stricture in international law which prevents us from making reference to national law for guidance as to the true meaning of concepts and terms used in the Statute and the Rules.[111]

After expounding this approach to interpretation, Judges McDonald and Vohrah failed to follow the carefully reasoned methodology they had just laid out. Instead, the judges placed emphasis on the common law origins of the guilty plea in the Statute of the ICTY.[112] Accordingly, they were of the view:

> that we may have regard to national common law authorities for guidance as to the true meaning of the guilty plea and as to the safeguards for its acceptance. The expressions 'enter a plea' and 'enter a plea of guilty or not guilty', appearing in the Statute and the Rules which form the infrastructure for our international criminal trials *imply necessarily*, in our view, a reference to the national jurisdictions from which the notion of the guilty plea was derived.[113]

McDonald and Vohrah continued to examine the conditions for entering a valid guilty plea in Canada, the United States, Malaysia and England and Wales,[114] to conclude that three criteria must be met: a valid plea must be voluntary, informed and unequivocal.[115] Following this judgment, Rule 62 *bis* was adopted by the ICTY, which codified the *Erdemović* requirements for a valid guilty plea.[116] Similarly, Rule 62 of the RPE of the ICTR was amended after delivery of the

---

[111] *Erdemović* (Appeals Chamber Judgment), Joint Separate Opinion of Judge McDonald and Judge Vohrah, para 5.

[112] *Erdemović* (Appeals Chamber Judgment), Joint Separate Opinion of Judge McDonald and Judge Vohrah, para 6. See also, Rule 15 of *Suggestions Made by the Government of the United States of America, Rules of Procedure and Evidence for the International Criminal Tribunal for the Prosecution of Persons Responsible for Serious Violations of International Humanitarian Law Committed in the former Yugoslavia*; reprinted in Morris & Scharf, *Insider's Guide to the ICTY*, vol 2, 531–2.

[113] *Erdemović* (Appeals Chamber Judgment), Joint Separate Opinion of Judge McDonald and Judge Vohrah, para 6 (emphasis added).

[114] *Erdemović* (Appeals Chamber Judgment), Joint Separate Opinion of Judge McDonald and Judge Vohrah, paras 10–31.

[115] *Erdemović* (Appeals Chamber Judgment), Joint Separate Opinion of Judge McDonald and Judge Vohrah, para 8.

[116] ICTY, *Rules of Procedure and Evidence*, 14th Plenary Session 20 October 1997 & 12 November 1997 IT/32/Rev. 12, 43–4. The requirement that a guilty plea be informed was added subsequently at the 19th Plenary Session; ICTY, *Rules of Procedure and Evidence*, 19th Plenary Session 3 & 4 December 1998 IT/32/Rev. 14, 43.

Appeals Chamber judgment to reflect the *Erdemović* requirements for a valid guilty plea.[117]

7.4.2   Interpreting Subpoena Powers/Binding Orders

Another example of the use of domestic laws to interpret a transplanted legal institution is the *Blaškić* case.[118] In that case, Croatia challenged the ability of the ICTY to issue a *subpoena* to Croatia and its defence minister, compelling them to produce evidence before the Tribunal.[119] The ICTY has the ability to issue *subpoenas* pursuant to Rule 54 of the RPE, which elaborates the Tribunal's powers of discovery under Article 19 of the Statute.[120] Rule 54 provides that the ICTY 'may issue such orders, summonses, subpoenas, warrants and transfer orders as may be necessary for the purposes of an investigation or for the preparation or conduct of the trial'.[121]

The Trial Chamber of the ICTY adduced domestic law in response to two questions:[122] first, when is a *subpoena* considered to be 'required' for a trial, and hence fall within the Tribunal's powers under Article 19/Rule

---

[117] ICTR, *Rules of Procedure and Evidence* 8 June 1998, Rule 62 www.unictr.org/Portals/0/English%5CLegal%5CEvidance%5CEnglish%5C010698.pdf. Cf ICTR, *Rules of Procedure and Evidence* 6 June 1997, Rule 62 www.unictr.org/Portals/0/English%5CLegal%5CEvidance%5CEnglish%5C970606e.pdf. Note that the ICC takes a different position to that of the ad hoc tribunals with regards to a guilty plea. A Trial Chamber of the ICC may accept an 'admission of guilt' or order a more complete presentation of the facts, if it considers that this is required 'in the interests of justice, in particular the interests of the victims'; ICC Statute Article 65; ICC RPE Rule 139. The requirements for a valid 'admission of guilt' are nevertheless similar to those elaborated in *Erdemović*; ICC Statute Article 65(1). For a detail of the minor differences, see G. Boas et al. *International Criminal Law Practitioner Library, Volume III: International Criminal Procedure* (CUP 2011) 225–7.

[118] *Prosecutor* v. *Blaškić* (Trial Chamber), Decision on the Objection of the Republic of Croatia to the Issuance of *Subpoenae Duces Tecum* (18 July 1997).

[119] Specifically, the requested evidence was 'notes and writings including military orders and directives between the Croatian Defence Ministry and the Ministry of Defence of the Croatian Community in Herzog Bosna' from the Republic of Croatia and Its Defence Minister; K. A. A. Khan et al., *Principles of Evidence in International Criminal Justice* (OUP 2010) 580.

[120] Article 19(2) provides that 'Upon confirmation of an indictment, the judge may, at the request of the Prosecutor, issue such orders and warrants for the arrest, detention, surrender or transfer of persons, and any other orders as may be required for the conduct of the trial.'

[121] The stipulation that an order be 'required' stems from the wording of Article 19(2) of the ICTY Statute.

[122] The Trial Chamber grounded the ICTY's ability to issue *subpoenas* to states on the basis of Article 29 of the ICTY Statute, and to individuals on the basis that it was necessary to

54? Second, may the Tribunal review states' claims that the requested evidence is subject to national security privilege, thus relieving the state from the obligation to hand over the evidence? With regards to the former, the Chamber stated that 'there is little guidance to be found discussing that which is "required" for trial' in the documents related to the establishment of the Tribunal.[123] It continued:

> Although the use of the term 'subpoena' by the International Tribunal does not incorporate its full meaning as expressed in any national system, because the common law provides for the issuance of subpoenas, it is appropriate to look at the manner in which they are utilized in common law systems as well as its limitations.[124]

The Trial Chamber proceeded to review the law of the USA, England, Malaysia, the Iran–US Claims Tribunal and the European Court of Justice, concluding that a *subpoena* is to be considered necessary only if the information requested pertains to the charge being investigated and is 'limited to that which is relevant, necessary, or in some cases, desirable'.[125] In US and English law, the question of what is necessary is not dealt with at the time of issuance of the order, but is typically confronted in response to a challenge from the subject of the subpoena.[126] In the opinion of the Chamber, '[s]imilar procedures should apply in the International Tribunal' in order to avoid the 'unnecessary' and inefficient task of attempting *a priori* to determine what evidence was to be considered necessary.[127]

In relation to the claim that the Tribunal must defer to Croatia's invocation of national security privilege, the Trial Chamber once again drew on domestic law in the interpretation of its Rule 54 powers.[128] It surveyed cases from the USA, the UK, Canada, Pakistan, Yugoslavia and Australia, as well as analogous international jurisprudence, all of which provided for the review of national security claims by the courts.[129] The

---

fulfill the function of the Tribunal; *Blaškić*, Decision on *Subpoenae Duces Tecum*, paras 66, 81, 86.

[123] *Blaškić*, Decision on *Subpoenae Duces Tecum*, para 98.

[124] *Blaškić*, Decision on *Subpoenae Duces Tecum*, para 99.

[125] *Blaškić*, Decision on *Subpoenae Duces Tecum*, para 100.

[126] *Blaškić*, Decision on *Subpoenae Duces Tecum*, para 104.

[127] *Blaškić*, Decision on *Subpoenae Duces Tecum*, para 105.

[128] 'In view of the inconclusive nature of the existing jurisprudence in international law, an examination of the question of whether national courts have authority to review claims of national security may provide some guidance'; *Blaškić*, Decision on *Subpoenae Duces Tecum*, para 140.

[129] *Blaškić*, Decision on *Subpoenae Duces Tecum*, paras 141–6.

Chamber concluded that it is for the Tribunal, in closed session if appropriate, to determine whether the requested evidence should be exempt from the discovery powers of the Tribunal.[130]

The decision of the Trial Chamber was challenged by Croatia before the Appeals Chamber three months later, which is examined in more detail in Section 7.6.[131] The Appeals Chamber took a different approach to that of the Trial Chamber, rejecting the utility of recourse to domestic law to interpret Rule 54. Instead, it noted that Article 29 did not provide any exceptions to states' obligation to comply with orders of the Tribunal, and that to hold otherwise would jeopardise the very functioning of the Tribunal.[132]

Following the *Blaškić* case, the ICTY adopted a new rule, Rule 54 *bis*, codifying the procedural requirements that had been elaborated by the Trial and Appeals Chambers, including the obligation for parties submitting a request for a subpoena to specific why it is 'necessary for a fair determination of that matter'[133] and the procedures to be followed if a state invokes national security privilege.[134]

7.5   An Affront to the Principle of Legality?

Domestic law played an important role in the jurisprudence of the ICTY. However, its invocation is vulnerable to certain criticisms. This section will examine one of the most strident criticisms: that the Tribunal's interpretation of the crime of rape breached the principle of legality.

Although the principle of legality has various iterations,[135] it is commonly understood to comprise the prohibition of the *ex post facto* criminalisation of acts (or *nullum crimen sine lege*),[136] as well as the strict interpretation of law in favour of the accused, and the requirement of specificity of criminal legislation.[137] One rationale that is commonly

---

[130] *Blaškić*, Decision on *Subpoenae Duces Tecum*, para 149.

[131] *Prosecutor v. Blaškić* (Appeals Chamber) Judgement on the Request of the Republic of Croatia for Review of the Decision of Trial Chamber II of 18 July 1997 (29 October 1997).

[132] *Blaškić*, Judgement on the Request of the Republic of Croatia for Review of the Decision of Trial Chamber, para 47.

[133] Rule 54 *bis* (A)(ii), ICTY RPE (7 December 1999), IT/32/Rev. 17.

[134] Rule 54(F), ICTY RPE (7 December 1999), IT/32/Rev. 17.

[135] For other variants of the principle of legality, see K. S. Gallant, *The Principle of Legality in International and Comparative Law* (CUP 2009) at 11–14.

[136] T. Meron, 'Remarks on the Principle of Legality in International Criminal Law', (2009) 103 Proceedings of the ASIL Annual Meeting 107.

[137] See A. Mokhtar, '*Nullum Crimen, Nulla Poena Sine Lege*: Aspects and Prospects', (2005) 26 Statute LR 41; Jain, 'Judicial Lawmaking and General Principles of Law', 115; S. Darcy, 'The Principle of Legality at the Crossroads of Human Rights and International Criminal

adduced in support of the principle of legality is that it provides individuals with fair warning of what is forbidden, allowing them to modify their behaviour accordingly.[138]

One might argue that the Tribunal's interpretation of the crime of rape, examined in Section 7.3 above, breached the principle of legality insofar as it criminalised conduct that would not have fallen within the definition of rape under domestic law.[139] In the period over which the ICTY had temporal jurisdiction, the penal law of Bosnia and Herzegovina defined rape as forcible sexual intercourse and required force or threat of force to the victim or someone 'close to her'.[140] The ICTY's interpretation of the crime of rape departed from this definition in two ways: first, in *Furundžija*, the Trial Chamber included forced oral sex in the definition of rape; and, second, in *Kunarac*, the Appeal Chamber expanded the requirement of 'coercion or threat or use of force' to the absence of consent 'assessed in the context of the surrounding circumstances'. As such, one might argue that the ICTY in effect retroactively criminalised conduct, breaching *nullum crimen sine lege* by failing to provide the accused of fair warning of the criminal nature of their conduct.

When the cases are examined in detail, however, it becomes evident that this argument is more complex – and more problematic – than it initially seems. First, in *Furundžija*, the expansive interpretation which brought oral sex under the definition of rape did *not* result from the survey of domestic law. In fact, as noted above, the Trial Chamber explicitly noted that 'a major discrepancy may, however, be discerned in the criminalization of forced oral penetration' in domestic systems.[141] Instead, the Chamber brought oral sex within the definition of the crime of rape using a purely teleological methodology. It reasoned that forced

---

Law', in M. M. deGuzman & D. M. Amann (eds), *Arcs of Global Justice: Essays in Honour of William A. Schabas* (OUP 2018) 204.

[138] See J. C. Jeffries, 'Legality, Vagueness, and the Construction of Penal Statutes', (1985) 71 Virginia LR 189, 205–12.

[139] Cf I. Bantekas, 'Reflections on Some Sources and Methods of International Criminal and Humanitarian Law', (2006) 6 International Criminal LR 121, 126; M. Swart, 'Judicial Lawmaking at the ad hoc Tribunals: The Creative Use of the Sources of International Law and "Adventurous Interpretation"', (2010) 70 ZaöRV 459, 468.

[140] *Furundžija* Trial Chamber, n 214 (The Penal Code of Bosnia and Herzegovina (1988) Chapter XI states that '[w]hoever coerces a female person with whom he is not married to, into sexual intercourse by force of threat to endanger her life or body or that of someone close to her will be sentenced to between one to ten years in prison').

[141] ibid., para 182.

oral sex constitutes 'a most humiliating and degrading attack on human dignity'; that the very purpose of international humanitarian and human rights law was to protect human dignity; and, *therefore*, that 'it is consonant with this principle that such an extremely serious sexual outrage as forced oral penetration should be classified as rape'.[142] Whilst this expansive interpretation might be critiqued, such criticism cannot be placed at the foot of the Trial Chamber's use of domestic law.[143]

The argument has slightly more purchase with regards to the reasoning of the Trial Chamber in *Kunarac*. Recall that the Chamber used domestic law to reason that absence of voluntary consent, and not just coercion or the threat or use of force, constituted the second limb of the definition of rape.[144] This departed from both the *Furundžija* definition of rape and the crime under the penal law of Bosnia and Herzegovina in force at the time. This question was pertinent because one victim, 'DB', had initiated sexual intercourse with Kunarac without coercion or the threat or use of force on his part.[145] However, evidence was presented that another soldier, 'Gaga', had threatened the victim with death if she did not have intercourse with Kunarac. The defendant himself had therefore not used or threatened to use force or coerced the victim to have sexual intercourse with him, and his actions thus fell outside the *Furundžija* definition of rape.

However, to argue that this use of domestic law breached the principle of legality is erroneous. Neither was a strict principle of legality recognised as a rule of international criminal law in the pertinent period, nor was the application of such a principle acknowledged (or respected) in the practice of the ad hoc tribunals. From Nuremberg up until the inclusion of a strong principle of legality in the Rome Statute,[146] the principle has been treated 'as a flexible principle of justice that can yield to competing imperatives ... the condemnation of brutal acts, ensuring victim accountability, victim satisfaction and rehabilitation, the preservation of world order, and deterrence'.[147] As international criminal law

---

[142] ibid., para 183.

[143] ibid., para 184. The Trial Chamber went on to pre-empt the criticism that its teleological reasoning breached the principle of legality by arguing that the acts would in any case have been considered as sexual assault under the domestic law of Bosnia and Herzegovina. As long as the defendant was sentenced on this basis, the Chamber was of the opinion that the categorisation of the act was unimportant.

[144] *Kunarac*, Trial Chamber, para 460.

[145] See especially, ibid., paras 219, 647.

[146] Rome Statute, Articles 11, 22, 23, 24.

[147] B. Van Schaack, 'The Principle of Legality & International Criminal Law', (2009) 103:1 Proceedings of the ASIL Annual Meeting 101. See also, A. Cassese, *International*

has developed, what has been considered as protected by the principle of legality has evolved. This is best captured by characterising the change as a move from legality in law ascertainment in the Statute of the ICTY to legality in content determination in the Rome Statute.[148] The former encompasses non-retroactivity in the creation of crimes, as evidenced by the limitation of the subject-matter jurisdiction of the ICTY to 'rules of international humanitarian law which are *beyond any doubt* part of customary law'.[149] The latter, on the other hand, reflects the stricter principle that crimes must be interpreted strictly, not by analogy, and in favour of the defendant.[150] The principle of legality at the time of the ad hoc tribunals was clearly understood in the former sense.[151] This was reflected in the practice of the tribunals, which took 'a relatively relaxed approach, much in the spirit of their predecessors at Nuremberg'.[152]

To conclude, the principle of legality has been viewed as a malleable principle that has changed shape with the development of the legal regime. As noted above, 'much like the beginning of criminal law jurisprudence in common law jurisdictions, legality was originally

---

Criminal Law (OUP 2003) 72; Jain, 'Judicial Lawmaking and General Principles of Law', 144. Cf T. Meron, *War Crimes Law Comes of Age: Essays* (OUP 1999) 244.

[148] L. van den Herik, 'Interpretation in International Law: The Object, the Players, the Rules and the Strategies', in J. G. Drienyovszki & M. Clark (eds), *Event Report: Temple Garden Seminar Series in International Adjudication* (London: British Institute of International and Comparative Law, 2015), online: www.biicl.org/documents/715_report_tgc_inter pretation_in_international_law_140515.pdf. Van den Herik draws the law ascertainment/content determination distinction from Jean d'Aspremont. See J. d'Aspremont, 'The Multidimensional Process of Interpretation: Content-Determination and Law-Ascertainment Distinguished' in A. Bianchi et al. (eds), *Interpretation in International Law* (OUP 2015) 111.

[149] Report of the Secretary-General pursuant to Paragraph 2 of Security Council Resolution 808, UNSC, 48th Session, UN Doc S/25704, (1993), para 34 (emphasis added).

[150] Rome Statute, Article 22(2).

[151] See e.g., *Prosecutor v. Hadzihasanovic*, IT-01-47-AR72, Decision on Interlocutory Appeal Challenging Jurisdiction with respect to Command Responsibility (16 July 2003), para 34 (International Criminal Tribunal for the former Yugoslavia, Appeals Chamber) (recognising that the accused must have understood 'that the conduct is criminal in the sense generally understood, without reference to any specific provision'); *Prosecutor v. Delalic and Others*, IT-96-21-T, Judgment (16 November 1998), para 403 (International Criminal Tribunal for the former Yugoslavia, Trial Chamber). See also, *Prosecutor v. Karemera and Others*, ICTR-98-44-T, Decision on the Preliminary Motions by the Defense of Joseph Nzirorera, Édouard Karemera André Rwamakuba and Mathieu Ngirumpatse Challenging Jurisdiction in Relation to Joint Criminal Enterprise (11 May 2004) at para 43 (International Criminal Tribunal for Rwanda, Trial Chamber). See also, Meron, 'Remarks', 108.

[152] Schabas, *The UN ICTs*, 63.

conceived of as a flexible concept to allow for critical legal developments, even if they occurred retroactively'.[153] Whilst one might claim that a strict conception of the principle has reached the status of custom in contemporary international criminal law,[154] to claim that was the case for the ad hoc tribunals is a different – and quite unsustainable – proposition.[155]

Strict adherence to the principle of legality has not, then, been mandated as a rule of international law, nor did it feature in the practice of the ad hoc tribunals. One could nevertheless maintain that the tribunals should have narrowly interpreted the crimes within their subject-matter jurisdiction. However, to do so would be an avowedly normative argument. Such an argument would be based on the idea that the value of a strict interpretation of the principle of legality is in itself sufficiently important to override countervailing considerations of substantive justice, condemnation and deterrence, amongst others. It would have to counter the claim that 'by subordinating the principle of [*nullum crimen sine lege*] to a vision of substantive justice, tribunals have determined that the former injustice is less problematic than the other'.[156]

What values does the principle of legality uphold that might override considerations of 'substantive justice'? On the domestic plane, four purposes of the principle have been identified: the protection of human rights of the would-be accused, increased legitimacy of the criminal system, respect for the separation of powers between the legislature and judiciary and effective pursuance of the purposes of criminalisation.[157] However, none of these purposes inherently outweigh the countervailing considerations: breaching the human rights of the accused is not inherently worse than letting a breach of the victim's human rights go

---

[153] Grover, *Interpreting Crimes in the Rome Statute*, 188. See also, Van Schaack, 'The Principle of Legality & International Criminal Law', 102; Gallant, *The Principle of Legality*, 405.

[154] Gallant, *The Principle of Legality*, 352–404.

[155] For an interesting view on legality, tracing the differences in conceptions of the principle back to the division between international lawyers and criminal lawyers, see D. Jacobs, 'International Criminal Law' in J. Kammerhofer & J. d'Aspremont (eds), *International Legal Positivism in a Post-Modern World* (CUP 2014) 451, 471–3.

[156] B. Van Schaack, '*Crimen Sine Lege*: Judicial Lawmaking at the Intersection of Law and Morals', (2008) 97 Georgetown Law Journal 119, 140. See also, Grover, *Interpreting Crimes in the Rome Statute*, 152–4. See also, *Furundžija* (Trial Chamber Judgment), para 184.

[157] Gallant, *The Principle of Legality*, 20–30. See also, Grover, *Interpreting Crimes in the Rome Statute*, 137–51. Cf Jain, 'Judicial Lawmaking and General Principles of Law', 115–16; Jeffries, 'Penal Statutes', 201 et seq.

unpunished, nor is it clear that the legitimacy of the international criminal system would be augmented by adherence to the principle of legality instead of advancing the battle against impunity. The separation of powers argument posits that it is for the legislature as the democratically elected lawmaker to determine criminal conduct in a society, not the judiciary. However, on the international plane, the concept of the separation of powers is notably different to that within domestic law. Indeed, it could even be argued that the Security Council in effect delegated the task of defining certain crimes to the ICTY by including those crimes within its subject-matter jurisdiction.[158] With regard to the final justification of the principle of legality, the purposes of criminalising conduct are myriad, including considerations of accountability, restorative justice and reconciliation. Each of these purposes, it might be argued, could be fulfilled not by adherence to a strict principle of legality, but rather by judicial flexibility that permitted the extension of crimes to acts that were known to be wrong (*malum in se*)[159] or to which the accused was put on notice regarding potential future criminalisation.[160]

To conclude, the argument that the use of domestic law breached the principle of legality holds no weight with regard to the classification of oral sex as rape by the Trial Chamber in *Furundžija*. In relation to the extension of the crime by the Trial Chamber in *Kunarac,* one cannot make the argument that the use of domestic law violated the principle of legality insofar as it existed as a rule of international law at the time, nor was the reasoning of the Chamber incongruent with the general approach to legality taken by the ad hoc tribunals. To critique the use of domestic law would have to be based on an argument of moral values, not law, the strength of which is unclear at best.

7.6   Methodological Failings and the Specificity of International Criminal Law

Another strand of criticism that has been levelled at the Tribunal is based on purported methodological flaws in the reasoning of chambers. These critiques can be gathered in two broad categories: those that criticise the breadth and depth of the Tribunal's comparative survey and those that

---

[158] For a similar argument, see T. Ginsburg, 'International Judicial Lawmaking', (2005) University of Illinois College of Law Working Paper No. LE05-006 13–14.
[159] Gallant, *The Principle of Legality,* 41.
[160] Van Schaack, '*Crimen Sine Lege*', 167.

take issue with using domestic law on the international plane more generally.

The first criticism echoes a sentiment that has been expressed in relation to other courts and tribunals' use of comparative law. It argues that the Tribunal should have surveyed the law of more countries and taken account of contextual differences that might affect the operation of the law in practice. Jaye Ellis, for example, argues that the *Furundžija* Trial Chamber 'took a far too narrow approach, paying no attention to questions of culture, legal or otherwise', as well as criticising the Tribunal for not conducting a sufficiently extensive comparative survey.[161] However, others, such as Fabian Raimondo, have defended the reasoning of the Tribunal, claiming that '[t]he choice of legal systems it made was appropriate for demonstrating the universality of the general principle of law thus found, as they were representative of the different legal families and regions of the world'.[162]

This methodological critique holds little weight, although not for the reasons Raimondo claims. The argument presupposes a certain vision of the appropriate method transposed from the scholarly realm, in which it is the job of comparative law to present a representative, comprehensive, contextualised survey of the legal approaches taken in different systems.[163] Methodological concerns certainly have a place in an examination of the judicial use of extra-systemic law, but these concerns must be tailored to the justification for recourse to that law advanced (or presupposed) by the court. Ellis' critique, for example, is based on the assumption that the Tribunal attempted to induce a general principle of law from its comparative surveys, which would be applicable by virtue of Article 31(3)(c) of the Vienna Convention on the Law of Treaties.[164] However, none of the chambers examined in this chapter justified their recourse to comparative law on the basis that it allowed them to induce general principles of law that were applicable by virtue of Article 31(3)(c).

---

[161] J. Ellis, 'General Principles and Comparative Law', (2011) 22 EJIL 949, 968; Cf B. Markesinis, 'National Self-Sufficiency or Intellectual Arrogance? The Current Attitude of American Courts towards Foreign Law', (2006) 65 Cambridge Law Journal 301 at 306 (arguing that 'it is thus one of the primary functions of the comparatist to warn national lawyers against the danger of thinking that they can understand foreign law simply because they have mastered a foreign language. The exegesis of foreign law is an art that has to be learned . . . ').

[162] Raimondo, *General Principles of Law in the Decisions of International Criminal Courts and Tribunals,* 114.

[163] See Chapter 5, Section 5.4.2.

[164] Vienna Convention on the Law of Treaties, 23 May 1969, UN Doc A/Conf 39/27.

To hold the Tribunal to the methodological yardstick of a general principle of law presupposes too much.

The second strand of criticism is based on the purported impropriety
of transposing domestic law concepts to the international level. Within
public international law, this idea is often illustrated by reference to Lord
McNair's admonition that domestic law concepts cannot be transposed
'lock, stock and barrel'[165] to the international sphere but instead must be
tailored to the peculiarities of international law.

Within the ICTY, this argument has been most forcefully put in
some of the opinions and judgments of the Tribunal itself.[166] In the
appeals phase of the *Erdemović* case, Judge Cassese, in a section of his
separate and dissenting opinion entitled 'The Notion of a Guilty Plea
(or: The Extent to which an International Criminal Court can rely
upon National Law for the Interpretation of International
Provisions)', argued that domestic law could only be drawn upon in
limited circumstances. In particular, he thought that such recourse
was permissible if the international instrument expressly provided so,
or if reference to domestic laws was necessarily implied by the 'very
nature and content of the concept', such as determination of nationality for the purposes of diplomatic protection.[167] Underlying
Cassese's argument was the idea that *prima facie* similar concepts in
international criminal law were hardly ever identical to those in
domestic criminal law: international criminal law had a different
focus and applicability, was a fusion of civil and common law systems,
and faced challenges and issues specific to a supra-national criminal
tribunal.[168] Those that used domestic laws to interpret the provisions
of the Statute of the ICTY or RPE too readily, he argued, were not
cognizant of these potential incongruities.[169]

---

[165] *International Status of South-West Africa*, Advisory Opinion, [1950] ICJ Rep 28, 148
(separate opinion of Sir Arnold McNair).

[166] See also, F. Mégret, 'Beyond "Fairness": Understanding the Determinants of
International Criminal Procedure', (2009) 14 UCLA Journal of International Law and
Foreign Affairs 37.

[167] *Prosecutor v. Erdemović*, IT-96-22-A, Separate and Dissenting Opinion of Judge Cassese
(7 October 1997), para 3 (International Criminal Tribunal for the former Yugoslavia,
Appeals Chamber).

[168] ibid., paras 3-5.

[169] For a defence of this view, see H. G. van der Wilt, 'Commentary' in A. Klip & G. Sluiter
(eds), *Annotated Leading Cases of International Criminal Tribunals* (Hart Publishing
1999) vol 1, 654.

Similarly, in *Blaškić*, the Appeals Chamber, which was presided by Judge Cassese, reprimanded the Trial Chamber for the use of 'domestic analogy':

> [t]he Appeals Chamber wishes to emphasise at the outset that the Prosecutor's reasoning, adopted by the Trial Chamber in its Subpoena Decision, is clearly based on what could be called 'the domestic analogy' ... The setting is totally different in the international community ... the transposition onto the international community of legal institutions, constructs or approaches prevailing in national law may be a source of great confusion and misapprehension. In addition to causing opposition among States, it could end up blurring the distinctive features of international courts.[170]

There is, however, reason to think that the distinction between domestic and international law is to some extent overstated. This is aptly demonstrated by reference to the Appeal Chamber Judgement in *Erdemović*, in which the majority, having surveyed the domestic law of Canada, the United States, Malaysia and England and Wales, concluded that a valid guilty plea must meet three criteria: it must be voluntary, informed and unequivocal.[171] As noted in Section 7.4, these domestic laws were relevant because the concept of a guilty plea had been imported into international criminal procedure from common law systems. In contrast to the majority, Cassese considered that interpretation must be based on the object and purpose that the provision served within the context of international criminal law.[172] However, having reflected on the object and purpose of the guilty plea, he was of the view that the same three criteria identified by the majority in *Erdemović* were applicable:

> by virtue of a contemplation of the unique object and purpose of an international criminal court and the constraints to which such a court is subject [namely, to respect the rights of the accused under Article 21 of the Statute], rather than by reference to national criminal courts and their case law.[173]

---

[170] *Prosecutor v. Blaškić*, IT-95-14, Judgement on the Request of the Republic of Croatia for Review of the Decision of Trial Chamber II of 18 July 1996 (29 October 1997), para 40 (International Criminal Tribunal for the former Yugoslavia, Appeals Chamber).

[171] *Prosecutor v. Erdemović*, IT-96-22-A, Joint Separate Opinion of Judge McDonald and Judge Vohrah (7 October 1997), paras 6–8 (International Criminal Tribunal for the former Yugoslavia, Appeals Chamber).

[172] *Erdemović* – Judge Cassese, para 8; *Blaškić* Appeals Chamber, para 47.

[173] *Erdemović* – Judge Cassese, para 10.

In this case, at least, the specificity of international criminal law did not call for a different solution than that adopted by domestic systems. The claim of 'exceptionalism' of the ICTY therefore seems somewhat overstated.[174]

In relation to rape, one could argue that the definition of the crime in domestic law embodies the values of a certain society that cannot simply be transposed to international law. Indeed, the difficulties that states parties to the Rome Statute encountered when trying to settle upon a statutory definition of rape certainly gives weight to this idea. However, this does not suggest that, as a matter of principle, domestic laws cannot be used to inform the Tribunal's definition of the crime of rape, but rather that domestic law should be drawn on by the Court when it accords with the values that underpin international criminal law. Indeed, such a limitation was acknowledged by Judges McDonald and Vohrah, who, when drawing on domestic law, emphasised that:

> We would stress again that no credence may be given to such national law authorities if they do not comport with the spirit, object and purpose of the Statute and the Rules.[175]

The judgments of the Trial and Appeals Chambers in *Furundžija* and *Kunarac* could certainly have made the link between the values under-pinning the definition of rape in domestic jurisdictions and international criminal law more explicit. If they did so, it would be significantly harder to argue that it was inappropriate to draw on domestic law concepts to inform their understanding of international criminal law.

7.7   Contextualising the Tribunal's Reasoning

The methodology of the ICTY may be criticised for its incompleteness, brevity or acontextuality.[176] However, the reasoning of the Tribunal must be viewed in context. As a nascent tribunal that was initially underfunded and understaffed, the inability of the bench to carry out exhaustive comparative research is unsurprising. More extensive, representative

---

[174] Cf *International Status of South-West Africa*, Advisory Opinion, [1950] ICJ Rep 28, 148 (separate opinion of Sir Arnold McNair) ('the true view of the duty of international tribunals in this matter is to regard any features or terminology which are reminiscent of the rules or principles of private law as an indication of policy and principles rather than as directly importing these legal institutions').

[175] *Erdemović* – Judges McDonald and Vohrah, para 5.

[176] See Ellis, 'General Principles of Law', 968.

and thorough comparative surveys of domestic law would have been ideal. However, this does not fatally undermine the Tribunal's reasoning. Instead, the flaws must be balanced against the values that the use of domestic law furthered and the legacy left by the judgments examined in this chapter.

How, then, are we to judge the ICTY's use of domestic law? The Tribunal's use of domestic law should be seen as a way to reconcile competing values that were at tension in the early days of its operation. On the one hand, there was the clear desire amongst members of the international community to punish those that had committed war crimes in the former Yugoslavia. On the other hand, there was recognition that this should be achieved via legal, not political, means. Several statements made before the UN Security Council in the debates leading up to the creation of the ICTY give voice perfectly to these competing values. In the lead up to the adoption of Security Council Resolution 808 (1993), for example, the Spanish representative to the Security Council stated that:

> the establishment of an international criminal tribunal . . . fulfils its dual objective of meting out justice and discouraging such grave violations in the future, we believe that this undertaking is so important and so sensitive that it is necessary to ensure the maximum respect for legal rigour in its functioning.[177]

The desire for 'legal rigour', in the words of the Spanish Representative, was, however, quite impossible considering the nascent state of international criminal law in 1993. As noted in Section 7.2, not only was the Statute of the ICTY laconic, but it also had little to draw on in terms of precedent from its predecessors, notably the international military tribunals in Nuremberg and Tokyo. Once these competing values are acknowledged, the use of domestic law is comprehensible. Faced with an insufficiently defined rule, but still required to mete out justice as a court of law, the ICTY used the only external material that was available to it which was relevant to the provisions being interpreted: domestic law. This allowed the judges to ground their reasoning in an external source, demonstrating that the interpretation was not a simple transposition of

---

[177] UNSC, 48th year, 3175th Mtg, UN Doc S/PV.3175 (1993) [provisional], reprinted in V. Morris & M. P. Scharf, *Insider's Guide to the ICTY*, vol 1, 173. See also, the statements of the representative of the USA, the UK and New Zealand. See also, the statements by the representatives of Japan, Morocco, New Zealand and Russia in the debates leading up to the adoption of Resolution 827 (1993), UNSCOR 3217th Mtg, 179.

their own moral values.[178] Domestic laws were used as a tool of last resort that allowed the tribunal to thread a *via media* between indeterminacy and the radical subjectivity that loomed without recourse to external material.[179]

Whilst the judges at the ICTY and ICTR were faced with vague provisions and scant precedent upon which to draw, judges at the ICC have the benefit of a more elaborate definition of the applicable law, which is – as noted above – partly thanks to the pioneering and innovative interpretations made by the ad hoc tribunals. However, certain areas of international criminal law, such as modes of responsibility, command responsibility and defences, remain underdeveloped.[180] As such, the ICC may find it necessary to have recourse to domestic law to fill these gaps. In contrast to the Statutes of the ICTY and ICTR, however, Article 21(1) of the Rome Statute explicitly permits judges to have recourse to 'general principles of law derived by the Court from national laws of legal systems of the world' in the absence of other applicable law.[181] Although the ICC has already addressed arguments based on domestic law in certain cases, it remains to be seen whether it will continue to utilise this source in the same manner as the ad hoc tribunals.[182]

---

[178] Cf Van Schaak, '*Crimen Sine Lege*', 167 (arguing that the ICTY considered domestic law as 'sufficiently robust to provide notice to the defendant of a novel construction of ICL').
[179] This is supported by the justification given for the use of domestic law by the majority of the Appeals Chamber in *Erdemović* – Judges McDonald and Vohrah, para 3.
[180] Jain, 'Judicial Lawmaking and General Principles of Law', 129.
[181] Article 21(1) of the Rome Statute provides:
   'The Court shall apply:

   (a) In the first place, this Statute, Elements of Crimes and Its Rules of Procedure and Evidence;
   (b) In the second place, where appropriate, applicable treaties and the principles and rules of international law, including the established principles of the international law of armed conflict;
   (c) Failing that, general principles of law derived by the Court from national laws of legal systems of the world including, as appropriate, the national laws of States that would normally exercise jurisdiction over the crime, provided that those principles are not inconsistent with this Statute and with international law and internationally recognized norms and standards.'

[182] See for example, Situation in the Democratic Republic of Congo, ICC-01/04–168, Judgment on the Prosecutor's Application for Extraordinary Review of the Pre-Trial Chamber I's 31 March 2006 Decision Denying Leave to Appeal (ICC Appeals Chamber) (13 July 2006), paras 21–32; *Prosecutor v. Lubanga,* ICC-01/04–01/06, Decision Regarding the Practices Used to Prepare and Familiarise Witnesses for Giving Testimony at Trial (ICC Trial Chamber I) (30 November 2007), paras 39–42.

7.8   Domestic Law and the Development of International Criminal Law

This chapter has demonstrated that the use of domestic law as an interpretative aid has had an indelible impact on the jurisprudence of the ICTY and on international criminal law more generally. Against the backdrop of scant precedent and a laconic Statute, domestic law proved to be an invaluable tool for the Tribunal in order to fulfil its judicial function. This chapter has examined the use of domestic law to interpret the crime of rape and legal institutions that were imported into the Statute from common law jurisdictions. The judgments examined raise issues regarding adherence to the principle of legality, methodology and the *sui generis* nature of the international criminal regime.

The Tribunal's use of domestic law raises numerous questions of interest for scholars of international law, including broader questions regarding interpretation that are recurrent throughout this book. Some of these themes will be revisited in the conclusion.

8

Conclusion

The preceding chapters demonstrate that domestic law has been used by international courts and tribunals in a variety of different ways to interpret international legal rules or instruments. Each instance of comparative reasoning is inextricably linked to the legal and historical context in which it occurs and in which the court or tribunal operates. The novelty of the specific legal regime, the presumed knowledge of other states parties or the presence of nebulous treaty standards are all factors that have led to the use of domestic law as a means of interpretation. As such, drawing general conclusions from a study such as this is difficult.

As a preliminary point, the case studies examined in this book show that the use of domestic law is only infrequently justified in relation to Articles 31 and 32 of the Vienna Convention. As Chapter 2 demonstrated, the drafters of the Vienna Convention did not have one preconceived notion of what was a 'correct' interpretative method, but instead recognised that interpretation was inevitably a context-dependent process that largely rested on the judgment of the interpreter. The chapters that followed demonstrated that the use of domestic law is often motivated by – and is only comprehensible in relation to – certain factors that are extrinsic to the VCLT provisions, such as the presence of lacunae in the relevant legal regime or the character of the norm being interpreted. To rally the practice of international courts and tribunals under the rubric of the Vienna Convention provisions would only therefore tell half the story.

Whilst one of the principal arguments of this book is that the practice of each court or tribunal cannot be divorced from the context in which it occurs, certain cross-cutting themes arise in relation to several of the jurisdictions examined. The purpose of this conclusion is to draw together these threads, recapitulate the lessons learned in the relevant chapters and suggest areas for further enquiry. Four issues will be addressed: first, the use of domestic law as evidence of the intention of states; second, the use of domestic law as a means of interpreting treaty standards; third, the use of domestic law as an auxiliary or subsidiary means of interpretation; and, lastly, the question of methodology of comparative reasoning.

8.1 The Use of Domestic Law as an Indication of the Intention of a State

Although widely recognised as capable of reflecting the *opinio juris* of a state for the purposes of customary international law formation, or of constituting subsequent practice that is relevant under Article 31(3)(b) of the Vienna Convention, the practice of international courts and tribunals – and particularly those that adjudicate upon inter-state disputes – demonstrates that domestic law has also been used to elucidate the intention of a state. However, it is only when one considers the language of the international instrument and the domestic law, the context in which they were concluded and the circumstances in which they were drafted and approved, that one could give an informed response regarding whether the domestic law might be relevant to determine the intention of the state.

The practice of the ICJ and WTO panels and AB, examined in Chapters 3 and 4, demonstrate that those jurisdictions have found domestic law to be particularly probative evidence of intention in relation to certain kinds of legal instruments; namely, Optional Clause declarations, reservations to multilateral treaties and WTO schedules of commitments. The unilateral origins of these instruments, it was suggested, justified reference to the intention of the state whose declaration, reservation or schedule was at issue.

In determining whether a domestic law might be probative evidence of the intention of a state, context is everything. In this respect, the relevance of a domestic law could be viewed on a spectrum. On the one hand, there are reasonably clear instances when domestic law may elucidate the intention of the state. The *Anglo-Iranian Oil* judgment before the ICJ provides such an example. Recall that, in that case, the Court found that an Iranian domestic law ratifying Iran's Optional Clause declaration clarified the latter, as it described the temporal reservation in slightly different, clearer language.[1] Plainly, in this context, the domestic law related to the

---

[1] See Chapter 3, section 3.2.1.

international legal obligations that the state intended to undertake. In a similar vein, in *Fisheries Jurisdiction (Spain v. Canada)*, the fact that the reservation to Canada's Optional Clause declaration explicitly related to the same subject-matter as the Canadian domestic legislation, and that both were submitted to the Secretary-General of the UN and the Canadian Parliament on the same day, created a straightforward presumption that Canada intended to exclude the subject-matter of the legislation from the scope of its Declaration.[2]

At the other end of the spectrum, however, are invocations of domestic law that seem to bear little or no relation to the international instrument at issue. The Award in *Saar Papier v. Poland* illustrates the point.[3] In that case, the Tribunal considered the domestic administrative law of the states parties to be relevant to its interpretation of Article 4 of the Germany–Poland BIT, which prohibited 'measures equivalent to expropriation'. The fact that the Tribunal referred primarily to the domestic laws of states parties shows that the assumption underlying the Tribunal's reasoning was that such laws were relevant to discern the intention of those states as regards Article 4. It is not clear, however, how or why German and Polish administrative law related to the BIT provision, and the Tribunal did not attempt to explain its reasoning in this regard.

Whilst necessarily dependent on the facts of the case at hand, certain factors may be useful to determine whether a domestic law is indicative of the intention of a state. These include: whether the domestic law explicitly relates to the international legal instrument, or *vice versa*; whether the domestic law was passed at or around the same time as the state undertook its international legal obligation; and whether the instrument resulted from the will of one state, or was the outcome of a process of negotiation that embodied the common intention of multiple states.

A related question is whether domestic law should be used as evidence of the intention of the state, or whether other states should be 'entitled to accept that document at face value; they are not required to go back to the municipal law of that State for explanations of the meaning or significance of the international instrument'.[4] In relation to this issue, the manner by which the instrument has legal effect is relevant. Whilst reservations to multilateral treaties and WTO schedules of commitments depend on the acceptance of other states to take effect, Optional Clause

---

[2] See Chapter 3, section 3.2.3.

[3] See Chapter 5, section 5.4.2.

[4] *Anglo-Iranian Oil,* Dissenting Opinion of Judge Hackworth, 137. See also Chapter 4, section 4.3.2.

declarations rely on a pre-existing conventional framework to have legal validity, but are ultimately put into force, modified and revoked at the behest of one state. Reference to domestic law to interpret a reservation or schedule of commitments hence presupposes that other states parties have examined, or at least have had the opportunity to examine, the relevant domestic law, and thus that their acceptance of the reservation or schedule is based on knowledge, whether actual or constructive, of the relevant domestic law. As such, international courts and tribunals should be more cautious when invoking domestic law to interpret these instruments. In this context, it was suggested that the factors of relevance expounded by the AB in *Chicken Cuts* provide a useful framework within which to consider whether states might reasonably be expected to have relied on domestic law in a given context.[5]

8.2 The Use of Domestic Law to Substantiate Conventional Standards

The preceding chapters also demonstrated that domestic law has been used to interpret treaty standards, particularly by international investment tribunals and the European Court of Human Rights (ECtHR). Unlike rules, standards are vague legal norms that 'collapse decisionmaking back in to the direct application of the background principle or policy to a fact situation'.[6] In doing so, they provide the interpreter with significant discretion to determine the meaning of the treaty provision. Domestic law acts as both a tool to structure the wide discretion afforded to interpreters, and a link between the values upheld by the international and domestic spheres.

Chapter 5 examined arbitral awards in which domestic law was adduced to interpret terms such as 'fair and equitable', 'arbitrary' or 'discriminatory', whilst Chapter 6 demonstrated that 73.3 per cent of the judgments in which the ECtHR drew on comparative law over a 10-year period (2005–15) related to standards enshrined in the Convention, such as what is considered to be 'necessary', 'fair' or duly diligent. This practice leads to the broader question of why standards on the international level should be understood in relation to domestic law, and what function this reasoning serves.

---

[5] See Chapter 4, section 4.3.2.
[6] K. M. Sullivan, 'The Supreme Court 1991 Term, Foreword: The Justices of Rules and Standards', (1992) 106 Harvard LR 22, 58.

From a theoretical point of view, it was suggested that reference to domestic law for the purposes of interpreting treaty standards necessarily presupposes that the cited domestic laws embody the values that should be reflected and protected by the international legal regime.[7] Put another way, the selection of particular domestic jurisdictions is in effect a tacit approval of the values underpinning that system; it is a choice of the interpreter that is based on a (potentially subconscious) assessment of, and decision regarding, political values. It is on this basis that the consensus doctrine of the ECtHR and the use of comparative public law by international investment tribunals should be understood and evaluated.

The use of comparative law to interpret standards also responds to what some have called the 'tyranny of choice'.[8] Faced with vague, unsubstantiated standards, interpreters draw on domestic law as a guideline or benchmark that structures the otherwise broad discretion afforded to them. By referring to comparative law, as well as to arbitral decisions, treaties and case law of other international courts and tribunals, decision-makers are able to construct some benchmark of, for example, 'fairness' and 'equitableness' to which they can adhere, structuring their reasoning and absolving them of the responsibility and burden of substantiating the standard from scratch. The use of domestic law is particularly pertinent in legal regimes that are relatively novel, such as the international investment regime, as interpreters have little or no relevant international precedent upon which to draw.[9]

In relation to the interpretation of standards, further research could usefully focus on an examination of the values that the cited domestic law implicitly approves and the consonance of these with the values that the international regime professes to – or should – uphold, as well as a study into the other interpretative materials that are commonly used to interpret standards.

8.3 The Use of Domestic Law as an Auxiliary Means of Interpretation

Throughout this book, one recurrent theme is that domestic law is used as a subsidiary or auxiliary means of interpretation. The practice surveyed in the preceding chapters shows that domestic law is rarely

---

[7] See Chapter 5, section 5.4.2 and Chapter 6, section 6.5.2.
[8] See Chapter 5, section 5.4.1.
[9] Cf. M. Bobek, *Comparative Reasoning in European Supreme Courts* (OUP 2013) 254–6.

determinative of a particular interpretation, but instead often plays a role to confirm or embellish an interpretative argument that has been made on other grounds. Indeed, when domestic law does play a more influential role, it is primarily due to the paucity of other interpretative sources.

In this context, contrasting the approaches of the ICJ and certain investment tribunals, on the one hand, and the ICTY, on the other, is instructive. In *Anglo-Iranian Oil, Aegean Sea Continental Shelf* and *Fisheries Jurisdiction (Spain* v. *Canada),* the ICJ used domestic law as confirmation of an interpretation that was determined by another means of interpretation, primarily textual or circumstantial.[10] It did not alter or dictate the interpretation of the Court; rather, it provided an embellishment to a conclusion already reached. Similarly, the awards of the Tribunals in *Noble, Plama* and *Lemire,* examined in Chapter 5, used domestic law simply as means of confirmation of a conclusion reached on other grounds.[11] This is to be contrasted to the influential role that domestic law played in certain judgments of the ICTY, and in particular in the *Furundžija* and *Kunarac* cases. Chapter 7 argued that the Tribunal's reasoning must be viewed in light of the international criminal regime at the time of those judgments, and, in particular, the unclear definition of the crime of rape as incorporated in the Statute of the ICTY and the absence of relevant international precedent.[12]

Whilst one cannot say *a priori* whether particular courts or tribunals will use domestic law as a primary means of interpretation or in a subsidiary manner, the practice analysed in this book demonstrates that a number of factors influence the reasoning of the interpreters. These include, most importantly, the relative precision of the provision being interpreted and the existence of analogous case law or other international instruments on which to draw.

The auxiliary use of domestic law also raises the question why interpreters consider it persuasive to support their interpretation in such a manner. Chapter 5 drew on the work of John Wisdom and Neil MacCormick to suggest that the process of interpreting treaty standards could not be captured by reference to deductive reasoning (as legal reasoning is often characterised), and that it was this peculiar 'horizontally-extensive' form of reasoning that resulted in reference to domestic law.[13] This also seems to capture, to a certain extent, the use of domestic law as a subsidiary means of

[10] Chapter 3, section 3.2.
[11] Chapter 5, section 5.3.2.
[12] Chapter 7, section 7.3.2.
[13] Chapter 5, section 5.4.1.

interpretation. Further work could build on this theoretical base in order to explore this question.

8.4   The Comparative Method and the Question of the Appropriate Methodology

Throughout the book, methodological criticisms made in relation to the judgments of particular courts and tribunals were identified and addressed. One recurrent criticism is that the comparative surveys carried out by courts and tribunals are not sufficiently representative, detailed, or do not give enough importance to the context in which the domestic law operates.[14] As a result, some commentators argue that judges and arbitrators are able to obfuscate their subjective preferences and biases with 'careless comparativism'.[15]

Although this criticism may have purchase in particular contexts, it rests on the assumption that in order to be successful the comparative survey of domestic law must be exhaustive, or at least representative, to meet the requisite methodological standard. This approach would indeed be desirable if courts and tribunals justified their recourse to domestic law on the basis that it evidenced a general principle of law, within the meaning of Article 38(1)(c) of the Statute of the ICJ. Yet there is nothing to say that this standard is valid and applicable to all uses of domestic law, and the preceding chapters have demonstrated that domestic law is frequently referred to outside the context of Article 38(1)(c).

The appropriate methodology very much depends on the justification advanced or presupposed for the use of domestic law. For example, if domestic law is used to elucidate the intention of a state in relation to a reservation to its Optional Clause declaration, there is no reason why the court should cite any domestic law other than that of the declarant state.[16] Similarly, in order to understand how imported legal institutions operate, the court or tribunal need only refer to the domestic systems from which those institutions were imported.[17] In the latter case, the court or tribunal should of course be cognisant of any change intended to the institution for its operation in the international sphere, but that does not rule out the potential utility of domestic law as a matter of principle.

---

[14] See Chapter 5, section 5.4.2 and Chapter 6, section 6.4.1.
[15] J. E. Alvarez, 'Is Investor–State Arbitration "Public"?', (2016) 7 JIDS 534, 569.
[16] See Chapter 3, section 3.3.
[17] See Chapter 7, section 7.4.

The standard methodological criticisms fail to take into account the diverse manners and contexts in which domestic law is used. But they also fail to take into account the practical realities faced by most international courts and tribunals. Whilst a full, comprehensive, contextualised comparative survey would certainly help to demonstrate that the identification of a general principle of law is not based on the judges' whim, it would also be impossible in practice for a court or tribunal to carry out such work given time and budgetary constraints.[18] In this context, the improvements to the comparative surveys conducted by the ECtHR as a result of the creation of a dedicated Research Division are notable, but perhaps also demonstrate the limits to the comparative work possible by a full-time court or tribunal.[19]

*

This book demonstrated that domestic law is used in the interpretation of international law. Whilst this phenomenon has been explored in a limited number of sub-fields, the literature to date lacked a multi-jurisdictional analysis that attempts to address why domestic laws are used to interpret international law and why such use is accepted in certain situations. In the course of this enquiry, more fundamental issues were raised regarding the centrality of the Vienna Convention provisions to the interpretative process, and the irreducibly context-dependent nature of the interpretative process.

In the 1918 case of *Towne* v. *Eisner*, Oliver Wendall Holmes loquaciously stated that 'A word is not a crystal, transparent and unchanged, it is the skin of a living thought and may vary greatly in color and content according to the circumstances and the time in which it is used.'[20] In international law, just as in domestic law, it is only when we acknowledge this mutability that we are able to start to understand the complexity and contextuality that interpretation inevitably entails.

---

[18] See Chapter 6, section 6.4.1.
[19] See Chapter 6, section 6.4.1.
[20] *Towne* v. *Eisner*, 245 US 418 (1918) (Holmes J, for the Court).

BIBLIOGRAPHY

Articles and Books

Abi-Saab, G., 'The Appellate Body and Treaty Interpretation', in Sacerdoti, G. et al. (eds), *The WTO at Ten: The Contribution of the Dispute Settlement System* (CUP 2006).

Abrahamson, S. S. & Fischer, M. J., 'All the World's a Courtroom: Judging in the New Millennium', (1997) 26 Hofstra LR 273.

Affolder, N. A., 'Tadic, the Anonymous Witness and the Sources of International Procedural Law', (1998) 2 Michigan Journal of International Law 445.

Alexandrov, S. A., 'Accepting the Compulsory Jurisdiction of the International Court of Justice with Reservations: An Overview of Practice with a Focus on Recent Trends and Cases', (2001) 14 LJIL 89.

Alford, R. P., 'In Search of a Theory for Constitutional Comparativism', (2005) 52 UCLA LR 639.

Alland, D., 'L'interprétation du droit international public', (2012) 362 Recueil des cours 47.

Allott, P., 'Interpretation – An Exact Act', in Bianchi, A., Peat, D. & Windsor, M. (eds), *Interpretation in International Law* (OUP 2015).

Alvarez, J. E., '"Beware: Boundary Crossings" – A Critical Appraisal of Public Law Approaches to International Investment Law', (2016) 17 JWIT 171.

'Is Investor–State Arbitration "Public"?', (2016) 7 JIDS 534.

'The Public International Law Regime Governing International Investment', (2009) 344 Recueil des cours 193.

An-Na'im, A. A., 'Islam and Human Rights: Beyond the Universality Debate', (2000) 94 ASIL Proceedings 95.

Anand, R. P., *Compulsory Jurisdiction of the International Court of Justice* (Asia Publishing House 1961).

Arai-Takahashi, Y., *The Margin of Appreciation Doctrine and the Principle of Proportionality in the Jurisprudence of the ECHR* (Intersentia 2002).

Arato, J., 'Accounting for Difference in Treaty Interpretation over Time', in Bianchi, A. et al. (eds), *Interpretation in International Law* (OUP 2015).

'The Margin of Appreciation in International Investment Law', (2014) 54 Virginia JIL 545.

'Subsequent Practice and Evolutive Interpretation: Techniques of Treaty Interpretation over Time and their Diverse Consequences', (2010) 9 Law & Practice of International Courts and Tribunals 443.

Arsanjani, M. H. & Reisman, W. M., 'Interpreting Treaties for the Benefit of Third Parties: The "Salvors' Doctrine" and the Use of Legislative History in Investment Treaties', (2010) 104 AJIL 597.

Aust, A., *Modern Treaty Law and Practice* (3rd edn, CUP 2014).

Aust, H. P. & Nolte, G. (eds), *The Interpretation of International Law by Domestic Courts: Uniformity, Diversity, Convergence* (OUP 2016).

Bacchus, J., 'WTO Appellate Body Roundtable', (2005) 99 ASIL Proceedings 175.

Bader Ginsburg, R., '"Decent Respect for the Opinions of [Human]kind": The Value of a Comparative Perspective in Constitutional Adjudication', (2005) 64 CLJ 575.

'Looking Beyond our Borders: The Value of a Comparative Perspective in Constitutional Adjudication', (2003) 40 Idaho LR 1.

Bankowski, Z. et al., 'On Method and Methodology', in Summers, R. S. & MacCormick, D. N. (eds), *Interpreting Statutes* (Dartmouth Publishing 1991).

Bantekas, I., 'Reflections on Some Sources and Methods of International Criminal and Humanitarian Law', (2006) 6 International Criminal LR 121.

Bassiouni, M. C., *The Legislative History of the International Criminal Court: An Article-by-Article Evolution of the Statute* (Transnational Publishers, 2005).

The Law of the International Criminal Tribunal for the former Yugoslavia (Transnational Publishers 1996).

Bates, E., *The Evolution of the European Convention of Human Rights: From its Inception to the Creation of a Permanent Court of Human Rights* (OUP 2010).

Beckett, E., 'Comments by Sir Eric Beckett', (1950) 43[I] Annuaire de l'Institut de Droit international 435.

'De l'interprétation des traites', (1950) 43[1] Annuaire de l'Institut de Droit international 440.

Bederman, D. J., *Classical Canons: Rhetoric, Classicism and Treaty Interpretation* (Ashgate 2001).

Bell, J., 'Researching Globalisation: Lessons from Judicial Citations', (2014) 3 CJICL 961.

'The Argumentative Status of Foreign Legal Arguments', (2012) 8 Utrecht LR 8.

Bentele, U., 'Mining for Gold: The Constitutional Court of South Africa's Experience with Comparative Constitutional Law', (2009) 37 Georgia Journal of International and Comparative Law 219.

Benvenisti, E., 'The Margin of Appreciation, Subsidiarity and Global Challenges to Democracy', (2018) 9 JIDS 240.

'Margin of Appreciation, Consensus, and Universal Standards', (1999) 31 NYU JILP 843.

Berman, F., 'Why do we Need a Law of Treaties?', (2016) 385 Recueil des cours 9.

Bernhardt, R., 'Comparative Law in the Interpretation and Application of the European Convention on Human Rights', in Busuttil, S. (ed), *Mainly Human Rights: Studies in Honour of JJ Cremona* (Fondation Internationale Malte, 1999).

Bianchi, A., 'Textual Interpretation and (International) Law Reading: The Myth of (In)determinacy and the Genealogy of Meaning' in Bekker, P. et al. (eds), *Making Transnational Law Work in the Global Economy: Essays in Honour of Detlev Vagts* (CUP 2010).

Bjorge, E., 'Comparative Law and the Method of Law: Ascertainment of the International Court of Justice', in Andenas, M. & Fairgrieve, D. (eds), *Courts and Comparative Law* (OUP 2015).

'The Vienna Rules, Evolutionary Interpretation, and the Intention of the Parties', in Bianchi, A. et al., *Interpretation in International Law* (OUP 2015).

Domestic Application of the ECHR: Courts as Faithful Trustees (OUP 2015).

The Evolutionary Interpretation of Treaties (OUP 2014).

Björgvinsson, D. T., *The Intersection of International Law and Domestic Law: A Theoretical and Practical Analysis* (Edward Elgar 2015).

Bjorklund, A. K. & Nappert, S., 'Beyond Fragmentation', in Weiler, T. & Baetens, F. (eds), *New Directions in International Economic Law: In Memoriam Thomas Wälde* (Brill 2011).

Black, R. C. et al., 'Upending a Global Debate: An Empirical Analysis of the US Supreme Court's Use of Transitional Law to Interpret Domestic Doctrine', (2014) 103 Georgetown LJ 1.

Boas, G. et al., *International Criminal Law Practitioner Library, Volume III: International Criminal Procedure* (CUP 2011).

Bobek, M., *Comparative Reasoning in European Supreme Courts* (OUP 2013).

Bogdan, M., 'General Principles and the Problem of Lacunae in the Law of Nations', (1977) 46 Nordic JIL 37.

Boon, K., 'Rape and Forced Pregnancy under the ICC Statute: Human Dignity, Autonomy, and Consent', (2001) 32 Columbia Human Rights LR 625.

Bradford, W., 'International Legal Compliance: Surveying the Field', (2005) 36 Georgetown Journal of International Law 495.

Brauch, J. A., 'The Dangerous Search for an Elusive Consensus: What the Supreme Court Should Learn from the European Court of Human Rights', (2009) 52 Howard LJ 277.

Brierly, J. L., 'The Codification of International Law', (1948) 47 Michigan LR 2.

Briggs, H. W., 'Book Review of "The Interpretation of Agreements and World Public Order – Principles of Content and Procedure"', (1968) 53[3] Cornell LR 543.

Brower, C., 'W(h)ither International Commercial Arbitration', (2008) 24 Arbitration International 181.

Brown, C., *A Common Law of International Adjudication* (OUP 2007).

'The Protection of Legitimate Expectations as a "General Principle of Law": Some Preliminary Thoughts', (2009) 1 Transnational Dispute Management.

Brownlie, I., *Principles of Public International Law* (6th edn, OUP 2003).

Brunnée, J. & Toope, S., *Legitimacy and Legality in International Law: An Interactional Account* (OUP 2010).

Brunet, P., 'Aspects théoriques et philosophiques de l'interprétation normative', (2011) 115 RGDIP 311.

Burke-White, W. W. & von Staden, A., 'Private Litigation in a Public Sphere: The Standard of Review in Investor–State Arbitrations', (2010) 35 Yale JIL 283.

Cabrillac, R. (ed), *Dictionnaire du vocabulaire juridique* 2014 (5th edn, LexisNexis 2013).

Calabresi, S. & Zimdahl, S., 'The Supreme Court and Foreign Sources of Law: Two Hundred Years of Practice and The Juvenile Death Penalty Decision', (2005) 47 William & Mary LR 743.

Caron, D., 'The Interpretation of National Foreign Investment Law as Unilateral Acts under International Law', in Arsanjani, M. H. et al. (eds), *Looking to the Future: Essays on International Law in Honor of W. Michael Reisman* (Martinus Nijhoff 2010).

Carozza, P. G., '"My Friend is a Stranger": The Death Penalty and the Global *Ius Commune* of Human Rights', (2003) 81 Texas LR 1031.

'Subsidiarity as a Structural Principle of International Human Rights Law', (2003) 97 AJIL 38.

'Uses and Misuses of Comparative Law in International Human Rights: Some Reflections on the Jurisprudence of the European Court of Human Rights', (1998) 73 Notre Dame Law Review 1217.

Cassese, A., 'The Legitimacy of International Criminal Tribunals', (2012) 25 LJIL 491.

International Law (2nd edn, OUP 2005).

International Criminal Law (OUP 2003).

Cassese, A. et al., *Cassese's International Criminal Law* (3rd edn, OUP 2013).

Chang, Y. -T., *The Interpretation of Treaties by Judicial Tribunals* (Columbia UP 1933).

Charlesworth, H. et al., 'International Law and National Law: Fluid States', in Charlesworth, H. et al. (eds), *The Fluid State: International Law and National Legal Systems* (The Federation Press 2005).

Chinkin, C., 'Due Process and Witness Anonymity', (1997) 99 AJIL 75.

'International Tribunal for the former Yugoslavia: Amicus Curiae Brief on Protective Measures for Victims and Witnesses, Submitted by Dean and Professor of Law Christine Chinkin', (1996) 7 Criminal Law Forum 179.

Chow, P. Y. S., 'Reservations as Unilateral Acts? Examining the ILC's Approach to Reservations', (2017) 66 ICLQ 335.

Chung, O., 'The Lopsided International Investment Law Regime and Its Effect on the Future of Investor–State Arbitration', (2007) 47 Virginia JIL 953.

Churchill, R., 'Fisheries Jurisdiction Case (Spain v. Canada)', (1999) 12 LJIL 597.

Clark, I., *Legitimacy in International Society* (OUP 2005).

Clayton, R. & Tomlinson, H., *The Law of Human Rights* (OUP 2000).

Cohen, H. G. 'Theorizing Precedent in International Law', in Bianchi, A., Peat, D. & Windsor, M. (eds), Interpretation in International Law (OUP 2015).

Conforti, B., 'Cours général de droit international public', (1988) 212 Recueil des cours 9.

Cook, G., *A Digest of WTO Jurisprudence on Public International Law Concepts and Principles* (CUP 2015).

Corten, O., 'Motif légitime et lien de causalité suffisant: un modèle d'interprétation rationnel du "raisonnable"', (1998) Annuaire français de droit international 187.

Corten, O. & Klein, P. (eds), *The Vienna Convention on the Law of Treaties: A Commentary* (OUP 2011).

Cot, J. P., 'La conduite subséquente des parties à un traité', (1966) 70 RGDIP 633.

Cram, I., 'Resort to Foreign Constitutional Norms in Domestic Human Rights Jurisprudence with Reference to Terrorism Cases', (2009) 68 CLJ 118.

Crawford, J., 'A Consensualist Interpretation of Article 31(3) of the Vienna Convention', in Nolte, G. (ed), *Treaties and Subsequent Practice* (OUP 2013).

Brownlie's Principles of Public International Law (8th edn, OUP 2012).

Crema, L., 'Subsequent Agreements and Subsequent Practice Within and Outside the Vienna Convention', in Nolte, G. (ed), *Treaties and Subsequent Practice* (OUP 2013).

D'Amato, A., 'Can Legislatures Constrain Judicial Interpretation of Statutes?', (1989) 75 Virginia L Rev 561.

d'Aspremont, J., 'The Multidimensional Process of Interpretation: Content-Determination and Law-Ascertainment Distinguished', in Bianchi, A., Peat, D. & Windsor, M. (eds), *Interpretation in International Law* (OUP 2015).

Darcy, S., 'The Principle of Legality at the Crossroads of Human Rights and International Criminal Law', in deGuzman, M. M. & Amann, D. M. (eds), *Arcs of Global Justice: Essays in Honour of William A. Schabas* (OUP 2018).

David, R., Jauffret-Spinosi, C. & Goré, M. *Les grands systèmes de droit contemporains* (12th edn, Dalloz 2016).

de Aréchaga, J., 'International Law in the Past Third of a Century', (1978) 159 Recueil des cours 1.

de Londras, F. & Dzehtsiarou, K., 'Managing Judicial Innovation in the European Court of Human Rights', (2015) 15 Human Rights Law Review 523.

De Ly, F. et al., 'Who Wins and Who Loses in Investment Arbitration? Are Investors and Host States on a Level Playing Field? The Lauder/Czech Republic Legacy', (2005) 6 JWIT 59.

Desierto, D., *Necessity and National Emergency Clauses: Sovereignty in Modern Treaty Interpretation* (Martinus Nijhoff 2012).

Djeffal, C., *Static and Evolutive Interpretation: A Functional Reconstruction* (CUP 2015).

Donnelly, J., 'The Relative Universality of Human Rights', (2007) 29 Human Rights Quarterly 281.

Dörr, O. & Schmalenbach, K. (eds), *Vienna Convention on the Law of Treaties: A Commentary* (Springer 2012).

Dorsen, N., 'The Relevance of Foreign Legal Materials in US Constitutional Cases: A Conversation between Justice Antonin Scalia and Justice Stephen Breyer', (2005) 3 International Journal of Constitutional Law 519.

Douglas, Z., 'The Hybrid Foundations of Investment Treaty Arbitration', (2003) 54 BYIL 151.

Dowds, E., 'Conceptualizing the Role of Consent in the Definition of Rape at the International Criminal Court: A Norm Transfer Perspective', (2018) International Feminist Journal of Politics 1.

Dupuy, P. -M., 'The Constitutional Dimension of the Charter of the United Nations Revisited', (1997) 1 Max Planck YB UN Law 1.

La responsabilité internationale des états pour les dommages d'origines technologique et industrielle (Pedone 1976).

Dzehtsiarou, K., *European Consensus and the Legitimacy of the European Court of Human Rights* (CUP 2015).

'Does Consensus Matter? Legitimacy of European Consensus in the Case Law of the European Court of Human Rights', (2011) Public Law 534.

'Consensus from within the Palace Walls', UCD Working Papers in Law, Criminology & Socio-Legal Studies, Research Paper No. 40/2010.

Easterbrook, F., 'Abstraction and Authority', (1992) 59 University of Chicago LR 349.

Easterbrook, F. H., 'Foreign Sources and the American Constitution', (2006) 30 Harvard Journal of Law and Public Policy 223.

Eckhart, C., *Promises of States Under International Law* (Hart 2012).

Ehrlich, L., 'L'interprétation des traités', (1928) 24 Recueil des cours 5.

Ellis, J., 'General Principles and Comparative Law', (2011) 22 EJIL 949.

Elkins, Z. et al., 'Competing for Capital: The Diffusion of Bilateral Investment Treaties, 1960–2000', (2006) 60 International Organization 811.

Elsig, M., 'The World Trade Organization's Legitimacy Crisis: What Does the Beast Look Like?', (2007) 41 Journal of World Trade 75.

Eriksson, M., *Defining Rape: Emerging Obligations for States under International Law* (Martinus Nijhoff 2011).

European Court of Human Rights, ECHR: Overview 1959–2017 (Council of Europe 2017).

ECHR, 'References to the Inter-American Court of Human Rights in the Case-law of the European Court of Human Rights: Research Report', (Council of Europe 2012).

Falk, R., 'On Treaty Interpretation and the New Haven Approach: Achievements and Prospects', (1967–8) 8 Virginia JIL 323.

Fartache, M., 'De la competence de la cour international de justice dans l'affaire de l'Anglo-Iranien Oil Co.', (1953) 57 RGDIP 584.

Fatima, S., *Using International Law in Domestic Courts* (Hart 2005).

Fauchald, O. K. & Nollkaemper, A., 'Introduction', in Fauchald, O. K. & Nollkaemper, A. (eds), *The Practice of International and National Courts and the (De-)Fragmentation of International Law* (Hart 2012).

Feliciano, F. P., 'The Anglo-Iranian Oil Dispute', (1951) 26 Philippine LJ 55.

Fiori, M., 'The Foca "Rape Camps": A Dark Page Read through the ICTY's Jurisprudence', (2007) 2[3] Hague Justice Journal 9, www.haguejusticeportal .net/Docs/HJJ-JJH/Vol_2%283%29/The%20Foca_Fiori_EN.pdf. Archived at www.webcitation.org/6SQvJhsUY.

Fish, S., 'Intention Is All There Is: A Critical Analysis of Aharon Barak's Purposive Interpretation in Law', (2008) 29(3) Cardozo L Rev 1109.

'Fish v. Fiss', (1984) 36 Stanford LR 1325.

Is There a Text in This Class? (Harvard UP 1980).

Fiss, O., 'Objectivity and Interpretation', (1982) 34 Stanford LR 739.

Fitzmaurice, G., '*Vae Victis* or Woe to the Negotiators! Your Treaty or Our "Interpretation" of It?', (1971) 65 AJIL 358.

'The Law and Procedure of the International Court of Justice 1951–4: Questions of Jurisdiction, Competence and Procedure', (1958) 34 BYIL 1.

'The General Principles of International Law Considered from the Standpoint of the Rule of Law', (1957) 92 Recueil des cours 1.

'The Law and Procedure of the International Court of Justice 1951–4: Treaty Interpretation and Other Treaty Points', (1957) 33 BYIL 203.

'De l'interprétation des traités', (1956) 46 Annuaire de l'Institut de Droit international 317.

'Délibérations: interprétation des traites', (1952) 44[2] Annuaire de l'Institut de Droit international 372.

'The Law and Procedure of the International Court of Justice: Treaty Interpretation and Certain Other Treaty Points', (1951) 28 BYIL 1.

Fitzmaurice, G. & Vallat, F. A., 'Sir (William) Eric Beckett, KCMG, QC (1896–1966): An Appreciation', (1968) 17 ICLQ 267.

Fitzmaurice, M., 'The Optional Clause System and the Law of Treaties', (1999) 20 Australian YBIL 127.

Fitzmaurice, M. & Flinterman, C. (eds), *Interactions between International and Municipal Law: A Comparative Law Case Study* (TMC Asser 1993).

Fitzmaurice, M. et al. (eds), *Treaty Interpretation and the Vienna Convention on the Law of Treaties: 30 Years On* (Martinus Nijhoff 2010).

Flanagan, B. & Ahern, S., 'Judicial Decision-Making and Transnational Law: A Survey of Common Law Supreme Court Judges', (2011) 60 ICLQ 1.

Franck, T. M., 'Is the UN Charter a Constitution?' in Frowein, J. A. et al., *Verhandeln für den Frienden/Negotiating for Peace* (Springer 2003).

'Word Made Law: The Decision of the International Court of Justice in the Nuclear Test Cases', (1975) 69 AJIL 612.

Friedmann, W., 'The Use of "General Principles" in the Development of International Law', (1963) 57 AJIL 279.

Fuller L. L., *The Morality of Law* (Revised edn, Yale UP 1969).

'Positivism and Fidelity to Law: A Reply to Professor Hart', (1958) 71 Harvard LR 630.

Gaja, G., 'Loi (national): un simple fait', in Ascencio, H. et al. (eds), *Dictionnaire des idées reçues en droit international* (Pedone 2017).

Gallant, K. S., *The Principle of Legality in International and Comparative Law* (CUP 2009).

Galmot, Y., 'Réflexions sur le recours au droit comparé par la Cour de justice des Communautés européennes', (1990) 6 Revue française de droit administratif 255.

Gardiner, R., *Treaty Interpretation* (2nd edn, OUP 2015).

Gelter, M. & Siems, M., 'Citations to Foreign Courts – Illegitimate and Superfluous, or Unavoidable? Evidence from Europe', (2014) 62 American Journal of Comparative Law 35.

'Language, Legal Origins, and Culture before the Courts: Cross-Citations Between Supreme Courts in Europe', (2013) 21 Supreme Court Economic Review 215.

'Networks, Dialogue or One-Way Traffic? An Empirical Analysis of Cross-Citations between Ten of Europe's Highest Courts', (2012) 8 Utrecht LR 88.

Gentili, A., *De Jure Belli Libri Tres* (Trans J. C. Rolfe, OUP 1933).

Gény, F., *Méthode d'interprétation et sources en droit privé positif* (2nd edn, LGDJ 1919).

Ginsburg, T., 'International Judicial Lawmaking', University of Illinois College of Law, Illinois Law and Economics Working Paper Series Working Paper No. LE05-006.

Goldsmith, J. L. & Posner, E. A., *The Limits of International Law* (OUP 2005).

Goodman, R. & Jinks, D., 'How to Influence States: Socialization and International Human Rights Law', (2004) 54 Duke LJ 621.

Gottlieb, G., 'The Conceptual World of the Yale School of International Law', (1968) 21 World Politics 108.

Grotius, H., *De iure Belli ac Pacis Libri Tres* (trans A. C. Campbell, Batoche 2001).

Grover, L., *Interpreting Crimes in the Rome Statute of the International Criminal Court* (CUP 2014).

Guerra-Pujol, F. E., 'Probabilistic Reasoning', (2016) 38 University of La Verne LR 102.

Guinchard, S. (ed), *Lexique des termes juridiques* (20th edn, Dalloz 2012).

Hackworth, G. H., *Digest of International Law* (US Government Printing Office 1943).

Halpin, A., *Reasoning With Law* (Hart 2001).

Harbour, G., 'International Concern Regarding Conflict-Related Sexual Violence in the Lead-up to the ICTY's Establishment', in Brammertz, S. & Jarvis, M. (eds), *Prosecuting Conflict-Related Sexual Violence at the ICTY* (OUP 2016).

Hart, H. L. A., *The Concept of Law* (3rd edn, OUP 2012).
  Essays in Jurisprudence and Philosophy (Clarendon Press 1983).
  'Positivism and the Separation of Law and Morals', (1958) 71 Harvard LR 593.

Hart, H. M. & Sacks, A., *The Legal Process: Basic Problems in the Making and Application of Law* (Foundation Press 1994).

Harvard Research in International Law, 'Harvard Draft Convention on the Law of Treaties', (1935) 29 AJIL Supp 653.

Hathaway, O. A. & Lavinbuk, A. N., 'Rationalism and Revisionism in International Law', (2006) 119 Harvard LR 1404.

Hayes, N., 'Creating a Definition of Rape in International Law: The Contribution of the International Criminal Tribunals' in Darcy, S. & Powderly, J. (eds), *Judicial Creativity at the International Criminal Tribunal* (OUP 2010).

Helfer, L. R., 'Redesigning the European Court of Human Rights: Embeddedness as a Deep Structural Principle of the European Human Rights Regime', (2008) 19 EJIL 125.

Helfer, L. R. & Voeten, E., 'International Courts as Agents of Legal Change: Evidence from LGBT Rights in Europe', (2014) 68 International Organization 77.

Henkin, L., 'The Universality of the Concept of Human Rights', (1989) 506 Annals of the American Academy of Political and Social Science 10.

Henrard, K. & Mak, E., 'The Use of Consensus Arguments in Transnational Decision-Making: Confirming or Jeopardizing Human Rights', http://papers.ssrn.com/sol3/papers.cfm?abstract_id=2444682.

Hernández, G., 'Interpretation' in Kammerhofer, J. & d'Aspremont, J. (eds), *International Legal Positivism in a Post-Modern World* (CUP 2014).

'Interpretative Authority and the International Judiciary', in Bianchi, A. et al. (eds), *Interpretation in International Law* (OUP 2015).

Higgins, R., *Problems and Process: International Law and How We Use It* (Clarendon Press 1994).

Hoda, A., *Tariff Negotiations and Renegotiations Under the GATT and the WTO: Procedures and Practices* (CUP 2001).

Hoekman, B. M. & Kostecki, M. M., *The Political Economy of the World Trading System: The WTO and Beyond* (OUP 2009).

Hollis, D., 'The Existential Function of Interpretation in International Law', in Bianchi, A. et al. (eds), *Interpretation in International Law* (OUP 2015).

Horn, H. & Howse, R., 'European Communities – Customs Classification of Frozen Boneless Chicken Cuts' in Horn, H. & Mavroidis, P. (eds), *The WTO Case Law of 2004–2005* (CUP 2008).

Howse, R., 'Adjudicative Legitimacy and Treaty Interpretation in International Trade Law: The Early Years of WTO Jurisprudence' in Weiler, J. H. H. (ed), *The EU, the WTO and NAFTA: Towards a Common Law of International Trade?* (OUP 2001).

Hudson, M. O., *The Permanent Court of International Justice* (Macmillan 1934).

Independent International Commission on Kosovo, *The Kosovo Report: Conflict, International Response, Lessons Learned* (OUP 2000).

Institut de Droit international, 'De l'interprétation des traités', (1956) 46 Annuaire de l'Institut de Droit international 349.

Jackson, V., 'Constitutional Law and Transnational Comparisons: The Youngstown Decision and American Exceptionalism', (2006) 30 Harvard Journal of Law and Public Policy 191.

'Constitutional Comparisons: Convergence, Resistance, Engagement', (2005) 119 Harvard LR 109.

Jacobs, D., 'International Criminal Law', in Kammerhofer, J. & D'Aspremont, J. (eds), *International Legal Positivism in a Post-Modern World* (CUP 2014).

Jacobs, F. G., 'Varieties of Approach to Treaty Interpretation', (1969) 18 ICLQ 318.

Jain, N., 'Judicial Lawmaking and General Principles of Law in International Criminal Law', (2016) 57 Harvard Intl L J 111.

'Comparative International Law at the ICTY: The General Principles Experiment', (2015) 109 AJIL 486.

Jeffries, J. C., 'Legality, Vagueness, and the Construction of Penal Statutes', (1985) 71 Virginia LR 189.

Jennings, R. & Watts, A., Oppenheim's International Law, vol 1 (9th edn, OUP 2008).

Jessup, J., 'Observations of Judge Philip Jessup', (1985) 61 [I] Annuaire de l'Institut de Droit international 252.

Johnstone, I., 'Treaty Interpretation: The Authority of Interpretive Communities', (1990) 12 Michigan Journal of International Law 371.

Jones, J. R. W. D. & Powles, S., *International Criminal Practice* (3rd edn, OUP 2003).

Kakouris, C. K., 'Use of the Comparative Method by the Court of Justice of the European Communities', (1994) Pace International Law Review 282.

Kammerhofer, J., 'Taking the Rules of Interpretation Seriously, but Not Literally? A Theoretical Reconstruction of Orthodox Dogma', (2017) 86 Nordic JIL 125.

'Review of Alexander Orakhelashvili, *The Interpretation of Acts and Rules in Public International Law*', (2009) 20 EJIL 1282.

Kelsen, H., *Pure Theory of Law* (2nd edn, University of California Press 1967).

General Theory of Law and State (Russell & Russell 1961).

The Law of the United Nations: A Critical Analysis of its Fundamental Problems (Stevens & Sons 1950).

Law and Peace in International Relations (Harvard UP 1942).

Kennedy, D., 'Form and Substance in Private Law Adjudication', (1976) 89 Harvard LR 1685.

Ketcheson, J., *The Application of Domestic Law by International Tribunals* (PhD Thesis, University of Cambridge 2013).

Khan, K. A. A. et al., *Principles of Evidence in International Criminal Justice* (OUP 2010).

Kiikeri, M., *Comparative Legal Reasoning and European Law* (Springer 2001).

Killander, M., 'African Human Rights Law in Theory and Practice', in Joseph, S. & McBeth, A. (eds), *Research Handbook on International Human Rights Law* (Edward Elgar 2010).

Kingsbury, B., Krisch, N. & Stewart, R. B., 'The Emergence of Global Administrative Law', (2005) 68 Law & Contemporary Problems 15.

Klabbers, J., *International Law* (CUP 2013).

'Virtuous Interpretation', in Fitzmaurice, M., Elias, O. & Merkouris, P. (eds), *Treaty Interpretation and the Vienna Convention on the Law of Treaties: 30 Years On* (Martinus Nijhoff 2010).

'On Rationalism in Politics: Interpretation of Treaties and the World Trade Organization', (2005) 74 Nordic Journal of International Law 405.

'International Legal Histories: The Declining Importance of the Travaux Préparatoires in Treaty Interpretation?', (2003) 50 NILR 267.

Klabbers, J. et al., *The Constitutionalization of International Law* (OUP 2009).

Kläger, R., *'Fair and Equitable Treatment' in International Investment Law* (CUP 2011).

'Fair and Equitable Treatment: A Look at the Theoretical Underpinnings of Legitimacy and Fairness', (2010) 11 JWIT 435.

Klamberg, M., *Evidence in International Criminal Trials: Confronting Gaps and Reconstruction of Disputed Events* (Martinus Nijhoff 2013).

Knop, K., 'Here and There: International Law in Domestic Courts', (2000) NYU JILP 501.

Koh, H. H., 'The 1998 Frankel Lecture: Bringing International Law Home', (1998) 35 Houston International Law Journal 623.

'Why do Nations Obey International Law? Review of *The New Sovereignty: Compliance with International Regulatory Agreements* by A. Chayes and A. Handler Chayes, and of *Fairness in International Law and Institutions* by T. M. Franck', (1997) 106 Yale LJ 2599.

'"Transnational Legal Process" – The 1994 Roscoe Pound Lecture', (1996) 75 Nebraska LR 181.

Kolb, R., *The International Court of Justice* (Hart 2013).

Interprétation et création du droit international (Bruylant 2006).

La bonne foi (Presses Universitaires de France 2000).

Korhonen, O., 'New International Law: Silence, Defence or Deliverance', (1996) 7 EJIL 1.

Korobkin, R. B., 'Behavioral Analysis and Legal Form: Rules vs. Standards Revisited', (2000) 79 Oregon L Rev 23.

Koskenniemi, M., *From Apology to Utopia: The Structure of International Legal Argument* (Reissue with New Epilogue, CUP 2005).

'The Case for Comparative International Law', (2009) 20 Finnish YBIL 1.

Kraus, H., 'Réponse de H. Kraus', (1950) 43[I] Annuaire de l'Institut de Droit international 446.

Krisch, N., 'The Decay of Consent: International Law in an Age of Global Public Goods', (2014) 108 AJIL 1.

'Review of Jutta Brunnée and Stephen Toope, *Legality and Legitimacy in International Law: An Interactional Account*', (2012) 106 AJIL 203.

Beyond Constitutionalism: The Pluralist Structure of Postnational Law (OUP 2010).

Kwiatkowska, B., 'Fisheries Jurisdiction (Spain *v.* Canada*)*', (1999) 93 AJIL 502.

Lamm, V., *Compulsory Jurisdiction in International Law* (Edward Elgar 2014).

Lauterpacht, E., *The Life of Hersch Lauterpacht* (CUP 2010).

Lauterpacht, H., 'De l'interprétation des traités', (1954) 45[1] Annuaire de l'Institut de Droit international 225.

'Observations complémentaires et projet définitif de Résolutions', (1952) 44[I] Annuaire de l'Institut de Droit international 197.

'De l'interprétation des traites', (1950) 43[1] Annuaire de l'Institut de Droit international 367.

'Remarques complémentaires du rapporteur, M. Lauterpacht', (1950) 43[I] Annuaire de l'Institut de Droit international 457.

'Restrictive Interpretation and the Principle of Effectiveness in the Interpretation of Treaties', (1949) 26 BYIL 48.

'Some Observations on Preparatory Work in Treaty Interpretation', (1935) 48 Harvard LR 549.

Private Law Sources and Analogies of International Law (With Special Reference to International Arbitration) (Longmans, Green & Co. 1927).

Private Law Analogies in International Law with Special Reference to International Arbitration (LLD London School of Economics 1926).

le Bouthillier, Y., 'Article 32', in Corten, O. & Klein, P. (eds), *The Vienna Conventions on the Law of Treaties: A Commentary* (OUP 2011).

Legrand, P., 'What "Legal Transplants?"' in Nelken, D. & Feest, J. (eds), *Adapting Legal Culture* (Hart 2001).

Leigh, M., 'Witness Anonymity Is Inconsistent with Due Process', (1997) 99 AJIL 80.

Lenaerts, K., 'Interlocking Legal Orders or the European Union Variant of E Pluribus Unum' in Canivet, G. et al. (eds), *Comparative Law Before the Courts* (BIICL 2005).

Lenaerts, K. & Gutman, K., 'The Comparative Law Method and the Court of Justice of the European Union: Interlocking Legal Orders Revisited', in Andenas, M. & Fairgrieve, D. (eds), *Courts and Comparative Law* (OUP 2015).

Letsas, G. 'Intentionalism and the Interpretation of the ECHR', in Fitzmaurice, M. et al., *Treaty Interpretation and the Vienna Convention on the Law of Treaties: 30 Years On* (Brill 2010).

'Strasbourg's Interpretative Ethic: Lessons for the International Lawyer', (2010) 21 EJIL 509.

A Theory of Interpretation of the European Convention on Human Rights (OUP 2007).

Lefebvre, A., 'Hart, Wittgenstein, Jurisprudence', (2011) 154 Telos 99.

Linderfalk, U., 'Is Treaty Interpretation an Art or a Science', (2015) 26[1] EJIL 169.

On the Interpretation of Treaties: The Modern International Law as Expressed in the 1969 Vienna Convention on the Law of Treaties (Springer 2007).

Linos, K., *The Democratic Foundations of Policy Diffusion: How Health, Family, and Employment Laws Spread Across Countries* (OUP 2013).

Lowe, V., 'The Politics of Law-Making: Are the Method and Character of Norm Creation Changing?', in Byers, M. (ed), *The Role of Law in International Politics: Essays in International Relations and International Law* (OUP 2001).

MacCormick, D. N. & Summers, R. S., 'Interpretation and Justification', in MacCormick, D. N. & Summers, R. S. (eds), *Interpreting Statutes* (Dartmouth Publishing 1991).

MacCormick, N., *Rhetoric and the Rule of Law* (OUP 2005).

Mahoney, P., 'The Relationship between the Strasbourg Court and the National Courts', (2014) 130 LQR 568.

'The Comparative Method in Judgments of the European Court of Human Rights: Reference Back to National Law', in Canivet, G. et al. (eds), *Comparative Law before the Courts* (BIICL 2005).

'Universality versus Subsidiarity in the Strasbourg Case Law on Free Speech: Explaining Some Recent Judgments', (1997) 4 European Human Rights Law Review 364.

Mahoney, P. & Kondak, R., 'Common Ground: A Starting Point or Destination for Comparative-Law Analysis by the European Court of Human Rights', in Andenas, M. & Fairgrieve, D. (eds), *Courts and Comparative Law* (OUP 2015).

Mak, E., *Judicial Decision-Making in a Globalised World* (Hart 2013).

Markesinis, B., 'National Self-Sufficiency or Intellectual Arrogance? The Current Attitude of American Courts towards Foreign Law', (2006) 65 CLJ 301.

Markesinis, B. & Fedtke, J., *Judicial Recourse to Foreign Law: A New Source of Inspiration?* (UCL Press 2006).

Marmor, A., *Social Conventions: From Language to Law* (Princeton UP 2014).
   The Philosophy of Law (Princeton UP 2011).
   Interpretation and Legal Theory (2nd edn, Hart 2005).

Martens, P., 'Perplexity of the National Judge Faced with Vagaries of European Consensus', in European Court of Human Rights, *Dialogue between judges* (Council of Europe 2008).

Mattli, W., 'Private Justice in a Global Economy: From Litigation to Arbitration', (2001) 55 International Organization 919.

Maupin, J., 'Public and Private in International Investment Law: An Integrated Systems Approach', (2014) 54 VJIL 367.

Mavronicola, N., 'What is an Absolute Right? Deciphering the Absoluteness in the Context of Article 3 of the European Convention on Human Rights', (2012) 12[4] Human Rights Law Review 723.

McCrudden, C., 'CEDAW in National Courts: A Case Study in Operationalizing Comparative International Law Analysis in a Human Rights Context', in Roberts, A. et al. (eds), *Comparative International Law* (OUP 2018).

McDonald, G. K., 'Problems, Obstacles and Achievements of the ICTY', (2004) 2 JICJ 558.

McDougal, M. S. et al., *The Interpretation of International Agreements and World Public Order: Principles of Content and Procedure* (Yale UP 1967).

McDougal, M., 'The International Law Commission's Draft Articles upon Interpretation: Textuality *Redividus*', (1967) 61 AJIL 992.

McGrady, B., 'Fragmentation of International Law or "Systemic Integration" of Treaty Regimes: EC–Biotech Products and the Proper Interpretation of Article31 (3)(c) of the Vienna Convention on the Law of Treaties', (2008) 43 Journal of World Trade 589.

McLachlan, C., 'The Principle of Systemic Integration and Article 31(3)(c) of the Vienna Convention', (2005) 54 ICLQ 279.

McLachlan, C. et al., *International Investment Law: Substantive Principles* (2nd edn, OUP 2017).

McNair, A. D., 'Observations de Sir Arnold D. McNair', (1950) 43[I] Annuaire de l'Institut de Droit international 449.

Mégret, F., 'Beyond "Fairness": Understanding Determinants of International Criminal Procedure', (2009) 14 UCLA Journal of International Law and Foreign Affairs 37.

Mehrish, B. N., 'The Role of *Travaux Préparatoires* as an Element in the Interpretation of Treaties', (1970) 40 Yearbook of the Association of Attenders and Alumni of The Hague Academy of International Law 43.

Meron, T., 'Remarks on the Principle of Legality in International Criminal Law', (2009) ASIL Proc 107.

War Crimes Law Comes of Age (OUP 1999).

Henry's Wars and Shakespeare's Laws: Perspectives on the Law of War in the Later Middle Ages (OUP 1993).

'Rape as a Crime under International Humanitarian Law', (1993) 87 AJIL 424.

Merrills, J. G., 'Two Approaches to Treaty Interpretation', (1969) 4 Australian YBIL 55.

Mettraux, G., *International Crimes and the ad hoc Tribunals* (OUP 2005).

Mitchell, A. D., *Legal Principles in WTO Disputes* (CUP 2008).

Moglen, E. & Pierce, R., 'Sunstein's New Canons: Choosing the Fictions of Statutory Interpretation', (1990) 57 University of Chicago LR 1203.

Mokhtar, A., '*Nullum Crimen, Nulla Poena Sine Lege*: Aspects and Prospects', (2005) 26 Statute LR 41.

Montt, S., *State Liability in Investment Treaty Arbitration: Global Constitutional and Administrative Law in the BIT Generation* (Hart 2012).

Moremen, P. M., 'National Courts Decisions as State Practice: A Transjudicial Dialogue?', (2006) 32 North Carolina JIL 259.

Morris, V. & Scharf, M. P., *The International Criminal Tribunal for Rwanda* (Transnational Publishers 1998).

An Insider's Guide to the International Criminal Tribunal for the former Yugoslavia (Transnational Publishers 1995).

Mortenson, J. D., 'The *Travaux* of *Travaux*: Is the Vienna Convention Hostile to Drafting History?', (2013) 107[4] AJIL 780.

Mowbray, A., 'Subsidiarity and the European Convention on Human Rights', (2015) Human Rights LR 313.

Mumba, F., 'Ensuring a Fair Trial whilst Protecting Victims and Witnesses – Balancing of Interests?' in May, R. et al. (eds), *Essays on ICTY Procedure and Evidence: In Honour of Gabrielle Kirk McDonald* (Kluwer Law International 2001).

Murray, J. L., 'Consensus: Concordance, or Hegemony of the Majority?' in European Court of Human Rights, *Dialogue between judges* (Council of Europe 2008).

Neuman, G. L., 'The Uses of International Law in Constitutional Interpretation', (2004) 98 AJIL 82.

Neven, D. J. & Mavroidis, P. C., 'Mexico–Measures Affecting Telecommunications Services (WT/DS204/R: DSR 2004:IV, 1537): A Comment on "El mess in TELMEX"' in Horn, H. & Mavroidis, P. C. (eds), *The American Law Institute Reporters' Studies on WTO Case Law: Legal and Economic Analysis* (CUP 2007).

Nollkaemper, A., 'Conversations Amongst Courts: Domestic and International Adjudicators', in Romano, C. P. R. et al. (eds), *The Oxford Handbook of International Adjudication* (OUP 2013).

National Courts and the International Rule of Law (OUP 2011).

'The Independence of the Domestic Judiciary in International Law', (2006) 17 Finnish YBIL 261.

'The Role of Domestic Courts in the Case Law of the International Court of Justice', (2006) 5 Chinese JIL 301.

'Decisions of National Courts as Sources of International Law: An Analysis of the Practice of the ICTY', in Boas, G. & Schabas, W. (eds), *International Criminal Law Developments in the Case Law of the ICTY* (Martinus Nijhoff 2003).

Nollkaemper, A. & Fauchald, O. K. (eds), *The Practice of International and National Courts and the (De-)Fragmentation of International Law* (Hart 2012).

Nolte, G. (ed), *Treaties and Subsequent Practice* (OUP 2013).

Nordeide, R., '*Demir & Baykara* v. *Turkey*', (2009) 103 AJIL 567.

Oosterveld, V., 'Legal Traditions and International Criminal Gender Jurisprudence', (2013) 2[4] CJICL 825.

Orakhelashvili, A., *The Interpretation of Acts and Rules in Public International Law* (OUP 2008).

Ortino, F., 'Treaty Interpretation and the WTO Appellate Body Report in *US–Gambling*: A Critique', (2006) 9 JIEL 1.

Örücü, E., 'The Courts and the Legislator' in Örücü, E. & Nelken, D. (eds), *Comparative Law: A Handbook* (Hart 2007).

Pahuja, S. & Storr, C., 'Rethinking Iran and International Law: The Anglo-Iranian Oil Company Case Revisited', in Crawford, J. et al. (eds), *The International Legal Order: Current Needs and Possible Responses* (Brill 2017).

Paparinskis, M., 'Analogies and Other Regimes of International Law', in Douglas, Z. et al. (eds), *The Foundations of International Investment Law: Bringing Theory into Practice* (OUP 2014).

The International Minimum Standard and Fair and Equitable Treatment (OUP 2013).

Pargendler, M., 'The Rise and Decline of Legal Families', (2012) 60 American J Comp L 1043.

Parlett, K., *The Individual in the International Legal System* (CUP 2011).

Patterson, D., 'Interpretation in Law', (2005) 42 San Diego LR 685.

'Law's Pragmatism: Law as Practice and Narrative', (1990) 76 Virginia LR 937.

Pauwelyn, J., *Conflict of Norms in Public International Law* (CUP 2003).

Peat, D. & Windsor, M., 'Playing the Game of Interpretation: On Meaning and Metaphor in International Law', in Bianchi, A. et al. (eds), *Interpretation in International Law* (OUP 2015).

Pillay, N., 'Equal Justice for Women: A Personal Journey', (2008) 50 Arizona LR 657.

Posner, E. & Sunstein, C., 'The Law of Other States', (2006) 59 Stanford LR 131.

Posner, R., 'No Thanks, We Already Have Our Own Laws', (2004) Legal Affairs (July–August), www.legalaffairs.org/issues/July-August-2004/feature_pos ner_julaug04.msp.

Posner, R. A., 'The Supreme Court 2004 Term – Foreword: A Political Court', (2005) 119 Harvard LR 32.

Postema, G., 'Positivism and the Separation of Realists from Their Scepticism' in Cane, P. (ed), *The Hart–Fuller Debate in the Twenty-First Century* (Hart 2010).

'Conformity, Custom and Congruence' in Kramer, M. (ed), *The Legacy of H. L. A. Hart: Legal, Political, and Moral Philosophy* (OUP 2008).

'Implicit Law', (1994) 13 Law and Philosophy 361.

Pufendorf, S., Of the Law of Nature and Nations (trans B. Kennett, 1719).

Radi, Y., *La standardisation et le droit international: Contours d'une théorie dialectique de la formation du droit* (Bruylant 2013).

Raimondo, F. O., 'General Principles of Law, Judicial Creativity, and the Development of International Criminal Law', in Darcy, S. & Powderly, J. (eds), *Judicial Creativity at the International Criminal Tribunals* (OUP 2010).

General Principles of Law in the Decisions of International Criminal Courts and Tribunals (Martinus Nijhoff 2008).

Rainey, B. et al., *The European Convention on Human Rights* (6th edn, OUP 2014).

Ramsey, M. D., 'International Materials and Domestic Rights', (2004) 98 AJIL 69.

Raz, J., *The Morality of Freedom* (OUP 1988).

The Authority of Law: Essays on Law and Morality (OUP 1979).

Roberts, A., *Is International Law International?* (OUP 2017).

'Clash of Paradigms: Actors and Analogies Shaping the Investment Treaty System', (2013) 107 AJIL 45.

'Comparative International Law? The Role of National Courts in Creating and Enforcing International Law', (2011) 60 ICLQ 57.

Roberts, A. et al., 'Conceptualizing Comparative International Law', in Roberts, A. et al. (eds), *Comparative International Law* (OUP 2018).

Rosenne, S., 'Conceptualism as a Guide to Interpretation', in Rosenne, S., *An International Law Miscellany* (Martinus Nijhoff 1993).

'Interpretation of Treaties in the Restatement and the International Law Commission's Draft Articles: A Comparison', (1966) 5 Columbia J Transnational L 205.

Roy, B., 'An Empirical Survey of Foreign Jurisprudence and International Instruments in Charter Litigation', (2004) 62 University of Toronto Faculty Law Review 99.

Rubenfeld, J., 'Unilateralism and Constitutionalism', (2004) 79 NYU LR 1971.

Rubin, A. P., 'An International Criminal Tribunal for the former Yugoslavia?', (1994) 6 Pace International Law Review 7.

'The International Legal Effects of Unilateral Declarations', (1977) 71 AJIL 1.

Sathanapally, A., *Beyond Disagreement: Open Remedies in Human Rights Adjudication* (OUP 2012).

Scalia, A., *A Matter of Interpretation: Federal Courts and the Law* (Princeton UP 1998).

Schabas, W., *An Introduction to the International Criminal Court* (4th edn, CUP 2011).

The UN International Criminal Tribunals: The former Yugoslavia, Rwanda and Sierra Leone (CUP 2006).

'Interpreting the Statutes of the ad hoc Tribunals' in Vohrah, L. C. et al. (eds), *Man's Inhumanity to Man: Essays on International Law in Honour of Antonio Cassese* (Kluwer Law International 2003).

Schauer, F., 'The Tyranny of Choice and the Rulification of Standards', (2005) 14 Journal of Contemporary Legal Issues 803.

'The Convergence of Rules and Standards', (2003) NZLR 303.

'The Politics and Incentives of Legal Transplantation', Center for International Development at Harvard University Working Paper No. 44 (2000).

'Formalism', (1988) 97 Yale LJ 509.

Schermers, H., 'The Role of Domestic Courts in Effectuating International Law', (1990) 3 LJIL 77.

Schill, S. W., 'Sources of International Investment Law: Multilateralization, Arbitral Precedent, Comparativism, Soft Law', in Besson, S. & d'Aspremont, J. (eds), *The Oxford Handbook on the Sources of Law* (2017).

'Editorial: Towards a Normative Framework for Investment Law Reform', (2014) 15 JWIT 795.

'The Sixth Path: Reforming Investment Law from Within', (2014) 11 Transnational Dispute Management.

'Deference in Investment Treaty Arbitration: Reconceptualising the Standard of Review', (2012) 3 JIDS 577.

'International Investment Law and Comparative Public Law – An Introduction', in Schill, S. W. (ed), *International Investment Law and Comparative Public Law* (OUP 2010).

Schlag, P., 'No Vehicles in the Park', (1999) 23 Seattle University LR 381.

'Fish v. Zapp: The Case of the Relatively Autonomous Self', (1987) 76 Georgetown LJ 37.

'Rules and Standards', (1985) 22 UCLA LR 379.

Schneiderman, D., *Constitutionalizing Economic Globalization: Investment Rules and Democracy's Promise* (CUP 2008).

Schreuer, C., 'Fair and Equitable Treatment in Arbitral Practice', (2005) 6 Journal of World Trade 357.

Senden, H., *Interpretation of Fundamental Rights in a Multilevel Legal System: An Analysis of the European Court of Human Rights and the Court of Justice of the European Union* (Intersentia 2011).

Shahabuddeen, M., 'Municipal Law Reasoning in International Law', in Lowe, V. & Fitzmaurice, M. (eds), *Fifty Years of the International Court of Justice: Essays in Honour of Sir Robert Jennings* (CUP 1996).

Shaw, M., *Rosenne's Law and Practice of the International Court: 1920–2015* (5th edn, Brill 2016).

Siems, M., 'The Methods of Comparative Corporate Law', in Tomasic, R. (ed), *Routledge Handbook of Corporate Law* (Routledge 2016).

Comparative Law (CUP 2014).

Simmonds, N. E., 'Between Positivism and Idealism', (1991) 50 CLJ 308.

Sinclair, I., *The Vienna Convention on the Law of Treaties* (2nd edn, Manchester UP 1984).

Sitaraman, G., 'The Use and Abuse of Foreign Law in Constitutional Interpretation', (2009) 32 Harvard Journal of Law and Public Policy 653.

Slaughter, A. -M., *A New World Order* (Princeton UP 2004).

'A Global Community of Courts', (2003) 44 Harvard International Law Journal 191.

Sloss, D. (ed), *The Role of Domestic Courts in Treaty Enforcement: A Comparative Study* (CUP 2010).

Sluiter, G., 'Procedural Lawmaking at the International Criminal Tribunals' in Darcy, S. & Powderly, J. (eds), *Judicial Creativity at the International Criminal Tribunals* (OUP 2010).

Solum, L., 'The Unity of Interpretation', (2010) 90 Boston University LR 551.

Sorel, J. -M. & Boré Eveno, V., 'Article 31' in Corten, O. & Klein, P. (eds), *The Vienna Convention on the Law of Treaties: A Commentary* (OUP 2011).

Spano, R., 'Universality or Diversity of Human Rights?', (2014) 14 Human Rights Law Review 487.

St. John MacDonald, R., 'The Margin of Appreciation', St. John MacDonald, R. et al. (eds), *The European System for the Protection of Human Rights* (Martinus Nijhoff 1993).

Stone Sweet, A. & Keller, H., 'The Reception of the ECHR in National Legal Orders', in Stone-Sweet, A. & Keller, H. (eds), *A Europe System of Rights: The Impact of the ECHR on National Legal Systems* (OUP 2008).

Stone Sweet, A. & della Cananea, G., 'Proportionality, General Principles of Law, and Investor–State Arbitration: A Response to José Alvarez', (2014) 46 NYU J Intl L & Pol 911.

Stone, J., 'Fictional Elements in Treaty Interpretation – A Study in the International Judicial Process', (1955) 1[3] Sydney Law Review 344.

Sullivan, K. M., 'The Supreme Court 1991 Term, Foreword: The Justices of Rules and Standards', (1992) 106 Harvard LR 22.

Sutton, J. S., 'The Role of History in Judging Disputes about the Meaning of the Constitution', (2009) 41 Texas Tech LR 1173.

Suy, E., *Les actes juridiques unilatéraux en droit international public* (LGDJ 1962).
  'Unilateral Acts of States as a Source of International Law: Some New Thoughts and Frustrations', in Angelet, N. (ed), *Droit du pouvoir, pouvoir du droit: Mélanges offerts à Jean Salmon* (Bruylant 2007).

Swaak-Goldman, O. Q., 'The ICTY and the Right to a Fair Trial: A Critique of the Critics', (1997) 10 LJIL 215.

Swart, M., 'Judicial Lawmaking at the ad hoc Tribunals: The Creative Use of the Sources of International Law and "Adventurous Interpretation"', (2010) 70 ZaöRV 459.
  Judges and Lawmaking at the International Criminal Tribunals for the former Yugoslavia and Rwanda (PhD Thesis, Leiden University 2006), https://open access.leidenuniv.nl/bitstream/handle/1887/5434/Thesis.pdf?sequence=1. Archived at https://web.archive.org/web/20151017144933/

Thirlway, H., *The International Court of Justice* (OUP 2016).
  'The Sources of International Law', in Evans, M. D. (ed), *International Law* (4th edn, OUP 2014).
  The Sources of International Law (OUP 2014).
  'Concepts, Principles, Rules and Analogies: International and Municipal Legal Reasoning', (2002) 294 Recueil des cours 265.

Tomuschat, C., 'Article 36', in Zimmerman, A. et al. (eds), *The Statute of the International Court of Justice: A Commentary* (2nd edn, OUP 2012).

Törbar, G., *The Contractual Nature of the Optional Clause* (Hart 2015).

Tudor, I., *The Fair and Equitable Treatment Standard in the International Law of Foreign Investment* (OUP 2008).

Tutt, A., 'Interpretation Step Zero: A Limit on Methodology as "Law"', (2013) 122 Yale LJ 2055.

Twining, W. & Miers, D., *How to do Things with Rules* (5th edn, CUP 2010).

Twiss, T., *The Black Book of the Admiralty* (Longman 1871).

Ulfstein, G., 'Interpretation of the ECHR in light of other international instruments', Pluricourts Research Paper No. 15–05.

Vadi, V., *Analogies in International Investment Arbitration* (CUP 2016).

Vagts, D. F., 'Treaty Interpretation and the New American Ways of Law Reading', (1993) 4 EJIL 472.

Van Damme, I., 'The Interpretation of Schedules of Commitments', (2007) 41[1] Journal of World Trade 1.

     Treaty Interpretation by the WTO Appellate Body (OUP 2009).

van den Herik, L., Presentation at the British Institute of International and Comparative Law Seminar 'Interpretation in International Law', 14 May 2015, www.biicl.org/documents/715_report_tgc_interpretation_in_international_law_140515.pdf. Archived at https://web.archive.org/web/

van der Wilt, H., 'Commentary', in Klip, A. & Sluiter, G. (eds), *Annotated Leading Cases of International Criminal Tribunals* vol 1 (Hart 1999).

Van Harten, G., 'Arbitrator Behaviour in Asymmetical Adjudication (Part Two): An Examination of Hypotheses of Bias in Investment Treaty Arbitration', (2016) 53 Osgoode Hall LJ 540.

     Investment Treaty Arbitration and Public Law (CUP 2008).

Van Harten, G. & Loughlin, M., 'Investment Treaty Arbitration as a Species of Global Administrative Law', (2006) 17 EJIL 121.

Van Schaack, B., '*Crimen Sine Lege*: Judicial Lawmaking at the Intersection of Law and Morals', (2008) Georgetown LJ 119.

     'The Principle of Legality in International Criminal Law', (2009) 103 Proceedings of the ASIL Annual Meeting 101.

Vattel, E., *The Law of Nations* (trans anon., Liberty Fund 2008).

Venzke, I., *How Interpretation Makes International Law* (OUP 2012).

Verhoeven, J., *Droit International Public* (Larcier 2000).

Villiger, M., *Commentary on the 1969 Vienna Convention on the Law of Treaties* (Martinus Nijhoff 2009).

von Bogdandy, A. & Venzke, I. (eds), *In Whose Name?: A Public Law Theory of International Adjudication* (OUP 2014).

von Bogdandy, A. et al., 'From Public International to International Public Law: Translating World Public Opinion into International Public Authority', (2017) 28 EJIL 2017.

Wählisch, M., 'Cognitive Frames of Interpretation in International Law', in Bianchi, A. et al. (eds), *Interpretation in International Law* (OUP 2015).

Wälde, T. & Kolo, A., 'Environmental Regulation, Investment Protection and "Regulatory Taking" in International Law', (2001) 50 ICLQ 811.

Waibel, M., 'Interpretive Communities in International Law', in Bianchi, A. et al. (eds), *Interpretation in International Law* (OUP 2015).

'Demystifying the Art of Interpretation', (2011) 22 EJIL 571.

Waldron, J., *'Partly Laws Common to All Mankind': Foreign Law in American Courts* (Yale UP 2012).

'Foreign Law and the Modern *Ius Gentium*', (2005) 119 Harvard LR 129.

'The Rule of Law and the Importance of Procedure', NYU School of Law Public Law & Legal Theory Research Paper Series, Working Paper No. 10–73.

Waldock, H., 'Decline of the Optional Clause', (1955–6) 32 BYIL 244.

Weiler, J. H. H., 'The Geology of International Law – Governance, Democracy and Legitimacy', (2004) 64 ZaöRV 547.

Weiner, P., 'The Evolving Jurisprudence of the Crime of Rape in International Criminal Law', (2013) 54[3] Boston College LR 1207.

Wildhaber, L. et al., 'No Consensus on Consensus? The Practice of the European Court of Human Rights', (2013) 33 Human Rights LJ 248.

Wisdom, J., 'Gods', (1945) 45 Proceedings of the Aristotelian Society 185.

Wood, M., '"Constitutionalization" of International Law: A Sceptical Voice', in Kaikobad, K. H. & Bohlander, M. (eds), *International Law and Power: Perspectives on Legal Order and Justice* (Martinus Nijhoff 2009).

'The Interpretation of Security Council Resolutions', (1998) 2 Max Planck Yearbook of UN Law 73.

Wroblewski, J., 'Statutory Interpretation in Poland', in MacCormick, D. N. & Summers, R. S. (eds), *Interpreting Statutes* (Dartmouth Publishing 1991).

Wuerth, I. B., 'Sources of International Law in Domestic Law', in d'Aspremont, J. & Besson, S. (eds), *The Oxford Handbook of the Sources of International Law* (OUP 2017).

Yanovich, A. & Zdouc, W., 'Procedural and Evidentiary Issues', in Bethlehem, D. et al. (eds), *The Oxford Handbook of International Trade Law* (OUP 2009).

Young, E. A., 'Foreign Law and the Denominator Problem', (2005) 119 Harvard LR 148.

Yu, T. C., *The Interpretation of Treaties* (Columbia UP 1927).

Zakaria, F., 'The Rise of Illiberal Democracy', (1999) 76 Foreign Affairs 22.

Zarbiyev, F., 'A Genealogy of Textualism in Treaty Interpretation', in Bianchi, A., Peat, D. & Windsor, M. (eds), *Interpretation in International Law* (OUP 2015).

Le discours interprétatif en droit international contemporain (Bruylant 2015).

Zwart, T., 'More Human Rights than Court: Why the Legitimacy of the European Court of Human Rights Is in Need of Repair and How It Can Be Done' in Flogaitis, S. et al. (eds), *The European Court of Human Rights and Its Discontents* (Edward Elgar 2013).

Zweigert, K. & Kötz, H., *An Introduction to Comparative Law* (3rd edn, OUP 1998).

UN Documents

Final Report of the Commission of Experts Established Pursuant to Security Council Resolution 780 (1992), annexed to Letter Dated 24 May 1994 from the Secretary-General to the President of the Security Council, UN Doc S/1994/674 (27 May 1994).

Further Report of the Secretary-General pursuant to Security Council Resolution 749 (1992) S/23900 (12 May 1992).

ICTR, Rules of Procedure and Evidence 6 June 1997, www.unictr.org/Portals/0/English%5CLegal%5CEvidance%5CEnglish%5C970606e.pdf.

ICTR, Rules of Procedure and Evidence 8 June 1998, www.unictr.org/Portals/0/English%5CLegal%5CEvidance%5CEnglish%5C010698.pdf.

ICTY, Rules of Procedure and Evidence, 14th Plenary Session 20 October 1997 & 12 November 1997, UN Doc IT/32/Rev. 12.

ICTY, Rules of Procedure and Evidence, 19th Plenary Session 3 & 4 December 1998, UN Doc IT/32/Rev. 14.

ICTY, Rules of Procedure and Evidence, UN Doc IT/53/Rev. 9 (5 July 1996).

ICTY, Updated Statute of the International Criminal Tribunal for the former Yugoslavia September 2009 Article 24(1) www.icty.org/x/file/Legal%20Library/Statute/statute_sept09_en.pdf.

ILC, Articles on the Responsibility of States for Internationally Wrongful Acts, as annexed to the UN General Assembly Resolution of 12 December 2001, UN Doc A/RES/56/83 (12 December 2001).

ILC, Draft Articles of the Law of Treaties with commentaries [1966] II YBILC 177.

ILC, Draft Articles on Responsibility of States for Internationally Wrongful Acts, with commentaries, (2001) II [2] YBILC 31.

ILC, Fifth Report on Subsequent Agreements and Subsequent Practice in Relation to the Interpretation of Treaties, by Georg Nolte, Special Rapporteur, UN Doc A/CN.4/715 (28 February 2018).

ILC, First Report on Subsequent Agreements and Subsequent Practice in Relation to Treaty Interpretation, by Georg Nolte, Special Rapporteur, UN Doc A/CN.4/660 (19 March 2013).

ILC, First Report on the Law of Treaties, by Sir Humphrey Waldock, Special Rapporteur, (1956) II YBILC 105.

ILC, First Report on the Unilateral Acts of States, by Mr Víctor Rodríguez Cedeño, Special Rapporteur, (1998) II [2] YBILC 332.

ILC, Fourth Report on the Unilateral Acts of States, by Mr Víctor Rodríguez Cedeño, Special Rapporteur, [2001] II [1] YBILC 134.

ILC, Guide to Practice on Reservations to Treaties, in Report of the International Law Commission, Sixty-Third session (26 April–3 June and 4 July–12 August 2011), UN Doc A/66/10/Add. 1.

ILC, Guiding Principles application to unilateral declarations of States capable of creating legal obligations, with commentaries thereto, [2006] II [2] YBILC 377.

ILC, Identification of Customary International Law: Text of the draft conclusions, Report of the ILC on the work of its seventieth session, 30 April–1June and 2 July–10 August 2018, UN Doc A/73/10.

ILC, Law of Treaties: Comments by Governments on Parts I, II and III of the Draft Articles on the Law of Treaties drawn up by the Commission at its fourteenth, fifteenth and sixteenth sessions [1966] II YBILC 93.

ILC, Report of the ILC on the second part of its seventeenth session and on its eighteenth session [1966] II YBILC 221.

ILC, Report of the International Law Commission on its Work of its First Session, (1949) I YBILC 278.

ILC, Second Report of the Special Rapporteur on the legal regime for the allocation of loss in case of transboundary harm arising out of hazardous activities, UN Doc A/CN.4/540.

ILC, Second Report on Subsequent Agreements and Subsequent Practice in Relation to Treaty Interpretation, by Georg Nolte, Special Rapporteur, UN Doc A/CN.4/671 (26 March 2014).

ILC, Second Report on the Identification of Customary International Law, by Michael Wood, Special Rapporteur, UN Doc A/CN.4/672.

ILC, Sixth Report on the Law of Treaties, by Sir Humphrey Waldock, Special Rapporteur, [1966] YBILC, vol II, 94.

ILC, Summary Records of the Eighteenth Session, 4 May–19 July 1966, [1966] YBILC, vol I [II].

ILC, Summary Records of the Sixteenth Session, 11 May–24 July 1964, [1964] YBILC, vol I.

ILC, Third Report on reservations to treaties, by Mr Alain Pellet, Special Rapporteur, (1998) II [1] YBILC 245.

ILC, Third Report on the Law of Treaties, by Sir Humphrey Waldock, Special Rapporteur, [1964] YBILC, vol II.

Interim Report of the Commission of Experts Established Pursuant to Security Council Resolution 780 (1992) annexed to Letter Dated 9 February 1993 from the Secretary-General Addressed to the President of the Security Council, UN Doc S/25274 (10 February 1993).

Letter Dated 10 February 1993 from the Permanent Representative of France to the United Nations Addressed to the Secretary-General, UN Doc S/25266 (10 February 1993).

Letter Dated 13 April 1993 from the Permanent Representative of Canada to the United Nations Addressed to the Secretary-General, UN Doc S/25594 (14 April 1993).

Letter Dated 18 February 1993 from the Permanent Representative of Italy to the United Nations Addressed to the Secretary-General, UN Doc S/25300 (18 February 1993).

Official Records of the Assembly of States Parties to the Rome Statute of the International Criminal Court, First session, New York, 3–10 September 2002 (United Nations publication, Sales No. E.03.V.2 and corrigendum).

Provisional Verbatim Record of the Three Thousand One Hundred and Seventy-Fifth Meeting of the Security Council, UN Doc S/PV.3175 (22 February 1993).

Provisional Verbatim Record of the Three Thousand Two Hundred and Seventeenth Meeting of the Security Council, S/PV.3217 (25 May 1993).

Report of the Secretary-General on the Activities of the International Conference on the former Yugoslavia, UN Doc S/25221 (2 February 1993).

Report of the Secretary-General pursuant to Paragraph 2 of Security Council Resolution 808 (1993), UN Doc S/25704 (3 May 1993).

Report of the Secretary-General Pursuant to Paragraph 5 of Security Council Resolution 955 (1994), UN Doc S/1995/134 (13 February 1995).

Report of the UN Secretary-General, The Rule of Law and Transitional Justice in Conflict and Post-Conflict Societies, UN Doc S/2004/616 (3 August 2004).

Report on the situation of human rights in the territory of the former Yugoslavia prepared by Mr Tadeusz Mazowiecki, Special Rapporteur of the Commission on Human Rights, pursuant to paragraph 15 of the Commission Resolution 1992/S-1/1.

Statement by the President of the ICTY Made at a Briefing to Members of Diplomatic Missions, IT/29 (11 February 1994).

UN SC Res 780 (1992), UN Doc S/RES/780 (9 October 1992).

UN SC Res 827 (1993), UN Doc S/RES/827 (25 May 1993).

UN Conference on the Law of Treaties, First Session: 26 March–24 May 1968, Official Records: Summary Records of the Plenary Meetings and of the Meetings of the Committee of the Whole, UN Doc A/Conf.39/11.

UN Conference on the Law of Treaties, Second Session: 9 April–22 May 1969, Official Records: Summary records of plenary meetings and of the meetings of the Committee as a whole, UN Doc A/CONF.39/SR.13.

Miscellaneous

Conservative Party, 'Protecting Human Rights in the UK: The Conservatives' Proposals for Changing Britain's Human Rights Laws', http://web.archive.org/web/ and www.conservatives.com/~/media/files/downloadable%20Files/human_rights.pdf.

Constitution of South Africa, available at www.gov.za/DOCUMENTS/CONSTITUTION/CONSTITUTION-REPUBLIC-SOUTH-AFRICA-1996-1.

Council Control Law No. 10, Article 2(1)(c) (1946) 3 Official Gazette Control Council for Germany 50–55.

ECtHR Rules of Court; ECHR Registry of the Court, Rules of Court (1 June 2015).

Fried, J. T., '2013 in WTO Dispute Settlement: Reflections from the Chair of the Dispute Settlement Body', www.wto.org/english/tratop_e/dispu_e/jfried_13_e .htm. Archived at https://web.archive.org/web/.

General Orders No. 100: Instructions for the Government of Armies of the United States in the Field, prepared by Francis Lieber, LL.D. (Government Printing Office 1898), avalon.law.yale.edu/19th_century/lieber.asp#sec2.

High Level Conference on the Future of the European Court of Human Rights, Interlaken Declaration (2010), www.echr.coe.int/Documents/2010_ Interlaken_FinalDeclaration_ENG.pdf.

High Level Conference on the Future of the European Court of Human Rights, Izmir Declaration (2011), www.echr.coe.int/Documents/2011_Izmir_ FinalDeclaration_ENG.pdf.

High Level Conference on the Future of the European Court of Human Rights, Brighton Declaration (2012), www.echr.coe.int/Documents/2012_Brighton_ FinalDeclaration_ENG.pdf.

High Level Conference on the Implementation of the European Convention of Human Rights, Our Shared Responsibility, Brussels Declaration (2015), www .echr.coe.int/Documents/Brussels_Declaration_ENG.pdf.

Lamy, P., 'The AWCL at Ten – Looking Back, Looking Forward', (4 October 2011), www.wto.org/english/news_e/sppl_e/sppl207_e.htm. Archived at https://web .archive.org/web/.

McCain, J., Statement of Senator John McCain, Chairman of Senate Armed Services Committee, on Obama Administration's Response to Iran's Detainment of US Sailors, 13 January 2016, available at www.mccain.senate. gov/public/index.cfm/press-releases?ID=6c628211-5f08-4029-9a7e-51454e8cdcd3.

Orbán, V., Speech at the 25th Bálványos Summer Free University and Student Camp, 26 July 2014, available at www.kormany.hu/en/the-prime-minister/the-prime-min ister-s-speeches/prime-minister-viktor-orban-s-speech-at-the-25th-balvanyos-summer-free-university-and-student-camp.

Pan-American Draft Convention on Treaties, (1935) 29 AJIL Supp 1205.

Procès des Grands Criminels de Guerre Devant Le Tribunal Militaire International Tome 1: Documents Officiels (Secretariat of the International Military Tribunal 1947).

Procès-Verbaux of the Proceedings of the Committee of Jurists, June 16th–July 24th 1920 with Annexes.

Proposal Submitted by Costa Rica, Hungary and Switzerland on Certain Provisions of Article 8 para 2(b) of the Rome Statute of the International Criminal Court: (viii), (x), (xiii), (xiv), (xvi), (xxi), (xxii), (xxvi), Preparatory Commission for the International Criminal Court (19 July 1999) PCNICC/ 1999/WGEC/DP.8.

Seventh International Conference of American States, 'The Interpretation of Treaties', 1933, (1935) 29 AJIL Supp 1225.

Special Proclamation by the Supreme Commander for the Allied Powers at Tokyo, 19 January 1946, 4 Bevans 20.

Spielmann, D., 'Judgments of the European Court of Human Rights: Effects and Implementation', Speech at Georg-August-University, Göttingen (20 September 2013). http://web.archive.org/web/20150806194346/ and www .echr.coe.int/Documents/Speech_20130920_Spielmann_Gottingen_ENG.pdf.

The Tower, 'Defence Secretary Carter: Iran's Treatment of Sailors "Inconsistent with International Law"', The Tower, 18 March 2016, available at www.the tower.org/3112-defense-secretary-carter-irans-treatment-of-sailors-inconsis tent-with-international-law.

UK Gender Recognition Act 2004: Explanatory Notes (HMSO 2004), available at www.legislation.gov.uk/ukpga/2004/7/pdfs/ukpgaen_20040007_en.pdf.

UK Sexual Offences Act 2003, available at www.legislation.gov.uk/ukpga/2003/42/ contents.

US Chief of Naval Operations Admiral John Richardson, 'Riverine Command Boat Investigation Press Remarks', available at www.navy.mil/navydata/people/cno/ Richardson/Speech/RiverineCommandBoat_Investigation_PressConference_ CNORemarks.pdf.

US Senate Committee on the Judiciary, 'Confirmation Hearing on the Nomination of John G. Roberts, Jr to be Chief Justice of the United States, September 12–15, 2005', Serial No. J-109–37, 201.

Washington Post, 'Iran just made another claim about the Navy sailors it detained. Add it to the list.', The Washington Post, 15 March 2016, available at www.washington post.com/news/checkpoint/wp/2016/03/15/iran-just-made-another-claim-about-the-navy-sailors-it-detained-add-it-to-the-list/?utm_term=.6f702f348a80.

INDEX

CAMBRIDGE STUDIES IN INTERNATIONAL AND COMPARATIVE LAW

Books in the Series

For EU product safety concerns, contact us at Calle de José Abascal, 56–1°,
28003 Madrid, Spain or eugpsr@cambridge.org.

www.ingramcontent.com/pod-product-compliance
Ingram Content Group UK Ltd.
Pitfield, Milton Keynes, MK11 3LW, UK
UKHW020336140625
459647UK00018B/2178